BRITISH SOCIAL DEMOCRACY

British Social Democracy

A Study in Development and Decay

DAVID HOWELL

ST. MARTIN'S PRESS   NEW YORK

CONTENTS

PREFACE AND ACKNOWLEDGEMENTS

This book is, in part, a history of the Labour Party. The opening of the National Executive Committee's Minutes to researchers, subject to a fifteen-year rule, has provided new and sometimes very revealing information. While it is hoped that the study will have some value in this direction, it has been written primarily in an attempt to understand the present state of the party through an examination of its past record. My central contention is that an epoch of social democratic politics is drawing to a close in Britain.

I have incurred many debts in the preparation of this book. I am extremely grateful to the staffs of the City of Manchester Central Reference Library and the Labour Party Library, Transport House, for their unfailing efficiency and good humour. The responsibility for typing successive drafts has been widely shared. Miss Marilyn Dunn and Mrs Joyce Ingham of the Department of Government, University of Manchester, have dealt very effectively with all stages of the preparation. Miss Jill Owen, Miss E.M. Gillett and the staff of the Secretarial Reserve, Faculty of Economic and Social Studies, and Miss Olive Davies and Mrs Diane Cook of the Department of Government all played a part in the efficient production of the final draft.

My intellectual debts are shared amongst all those colleagues and students in the University of Manchester, and all those with an interest in Labour politics, who have discussed the issues with me. In particular, I must thank Anne Evans, Theresa Kerin and Roger Williams for their substantive and stylistic comments on sections of earlier drafts.

William McCluckie's help with the proofs was greatly appreciated. Lewis Minkin of the Department of Government has helped me in numerous ways. He has read successive drafts with a sharp eye for loose arguments, and ambiguous phraseology, while our lengthy discussions have clarified several crucial points for me.

My last debt — but far from the least — is to my wife. Her encouragement and patience have sustained me. I only hope that the result is some compensation for her hours as a library widow.

Naturally, I bear all the responsibility for inaccuracies and political judgements. For the former but not the latter I apologise in advance.

Manchester
April 1976

1 SCAFFOLDING

The year 1931 was the 'annus terribilis'. Hopes of resurrecting the pre-1914 society collapsed in the face of falling world trade, shrinking production and mounting unemployment. Orthodox economic doctrines seemed irrelevant. Optimism about the viability of the capitalist economic system dwindled, and leader writers indulged in apocalyptic prophecies. The increasing despair inevitably damaged the stability of governments, and sometimes of political institutions. The crisis helped to terminate the brief spring of German parliamentary democracy: Britain, too, had its political crisis — but it was pitched in a characteristically minor key.

Britain entered 1931 under its second Labour Government. Its existence was the culmination of a rapid rise to power. The world's first industrial working class had been slow to develop its own mass political organisation. Through the second half of the nineteenth century, most British labour leaders pursued a strategy of peaceful advance, usually through an alliance with the Liberal Party. This strategy could appear reasonably successful in the context of an expanding economy, and when a separate party was formed in 1900, the dominant weight of trade union opinion ensured that it was a willing heir to this tradition. The new party secured a place in the political sun only after 1918. It now had a formal commitment to 'socialism' and with the aid of an expanded electorate and Liberal disintegration its growth in the twenties was dramatic. Its commitment to moderation remained firm, despite demands for something stronger from radicals in both political and industrial sections. This caution was epitomised by the parliamentary leadership. Ramsay MacDonald, the party leader, was committed to the establishment of the party's credentials for responsibility and practicality. He seemed to have succeeded. A brief governmental interlude in 1924 was followed in May 1929 by Labour's emergence as the largest party in the Commons.

This meteoric rise had occurred however with little idea of what would be achieved in office. Party programmes had been produced in 1918 and in 1928. These suggested a vague commitment to socialism but afforded little indication of the immediate steps that a Labour Government would take. This deficiency was demonstrated painfully

after 1929. The Government endured the perplexing rigours of depression
for two years without suggesting any solutions. It was then confronted
in August 1931 by a combination of demands for major economies and
a financial crisis. Almost half of the Cabinet opposed attempts to balance
the budget by economies that included a cut in unemployment benefit.
The Government collapsed, but three of its major figures, MacDonald,
Phillip Snowden the Chancellor, and J.H. Thomas the railwaymen's
leader entered into a coalition with leaders of the Conservative and
Liberal Parties. This National Government introduced the economy
measures, opposed by the vast majority of Labour MPs. Within weeks an
election was called, and the National campaign attacked Labour for
financial irresponsibility: Labour spokesmen attacked their former
leaders with growing vehemence. The disorientated Labour Party was
almost destroyed.

The débâcle meant much more than the defeat of 230 Labour MPs.
The party's first generation of leaders had vanished: they never returned
to positions of influence. It was the end of an epoch in much more than
changes in personnel. The Government's barren record and
disintegration seemed to demonstrate the consequences of an imprecise
or vacuous programme. In the wilderness, Labour began to develop
a much clearer perception of the measures that it would introduce when
next elected to office. Most of the specific proposals were in the
economic and social fields. They could be justified as providing
specific and immediate improvements in the condition of Labour's
working-class supporters. They could be advocated also as the first
steps towards the qualitative transformation of society. So long as
Labour lacked the opportunity to implement its proposals, the
immediate and long-term justifications could coexist easily. The
perspective could offer a coherent basis for unity satisfactory to most
tendencies within the party. This social democratic perspective
developed during the thirties: it was implemented after 1945; it has
not been renewed since. This pattern of development, realisation and
decay is the central theme of the following chapters. In order to make
them intelligible the analysis of policy changes is related to the
changing distribution of power. The party's commitment to electoral
politics was a crucial influence on the evolution of the social
democratic perspective, and appropriate attention is paid to Labour's
electoral fortunes.

The developmental part of this process occurred in what was in many
respects a new world. Inside Britain, the crisis wrote the last of the old
Liberal Party's many obituaries. This political demise was yoked with a

major economic change. Britain's long adherence to free trade ended. This – and Britain's move off the gold standard – signified the end of attempts to resuscitate *laissez-faire* capitalism. The era of tariffs, managed currencies, increasing state intervention, and eventually Keynesian economics, was beginning. In Britain, the new managed capitalism limped in hesitantly, but in the end, irrevocably. Labour's attempts to clarify its economic and social policies took place in the context of a changing economic system whose innovations were frequently ignored. Equivalent lack of perception about the changing international scene was impossible. Hopes of disarmament and conciliation were killed by the economic blizzard, and replaced by the problem of containing aggression. Labour's international outlook reflected the old optimism, but it too required reappraisal. This protracted and painful process was superimposed upon, and sometimes dominated, the development of domestic policies.

The discontinuities were major, but they were not total. Labour's structure was relatively little affected by the events of 1931. Many party institutions and practices were unchanged. The bulk of the membership remained, although greatly shocked. Many had been enthusiastic supporters of MacDonald. Now they provided their own pale version of de-Stalinisation, but the political assumptions that had guided their behaviour in the past persisted, often unquestioned. Labour had evolved as a committed exponent of gradualist parliamentary socialism. The years before 1931 had witnessed the erection of Labour's structural and ideological scaffolding. Much of this was to remain, and to be employed in the construction of the social democratic perspective.

Structure

The evolving structure of the party reflected the influence of pre-existing trade union institutions. These provided the principal organisational experience for many participants and served as their guide. The party structure also demonstrated trade union leaders' determination to retain control over the new organisation. The foundation Conference created an Executive to run the party between conferences.[1] Committed socialists could take heart from their disproportionately large representation on this Executive and from its protection by sectional elections. But these features were marginal. The Executive was dominated by trade union representatives.

Although trade union preponderance on the Executive grew, the socialists retained the protection of sectional elections. However, in the

Table 1: Changes in the Composition of the Executive 1900—17[2]

Year	Trade Unions	Independent Labour Party	Social Democratic Federation	Fabian Society	Trades Councils (from 1901)
1900	7	2	2	1	—
1902	9	2	—	1	1
			Socialist Societies		Trade Councils & Local Lab. Parties
1908	11		3		1

(The Party Treasurer became an elected member of the Executive from 1912.)

controversies over the 1914-18 War, the January 1917 Conference
rebuffed the Executive and narrowly carried an amendment abolishing
the sectional principle.[3] This prepared the way for the new structure
of the 1918 Constitution.[4] The Executive now consisted of 22 members
plus the Treasurer. These were divided into: thirteen from affiliated
organisations (mostly trade unions); five from local Labour Parties; and
four women. All were to be elected by the whole Conference.
This was the crucial feature. So long as the large unions remained
in broad agreement about their priorities, they could dominate the
Executive.

Most of Labour's leading figures were on the Executive from the
early years. MacDonald was involved initially as Secretary and then as
Treasurer: Henderson moved from the trade union section to the
Secretaryship: Clynes was a perennial in the trade union section.
Sydney Webb entered the Executive as a Socialist Societies' representative
in 1916, and remained until 1924. Some trade union representatives
were influential on the Executive, but others served only briefly. Such
short tenures reflected the career patterns and changing factional
balances within their own organisations. The sectional elections had
allowed a few dissenters to participate, and they did not vanish in
1918. A handful of more critical members was elected in the twenties.
Lansbury was returned regularly in the local party section, Jowett of
the ILP spent several years as a member of the affiliated organisation

group; later, Sir Oswald Mosley joined the Executive. Their inevitable minority position resulted in their membership being largely decorative.

The predominantly moderate Executive found management of the Party Conference to be an increasingly easy matter. From the beginning, the bloc vote was normally employed in the Conference, again a reflection of trade union practice. During the early years, the lack of precedents and uncertainties about the identity and the future of the organisation made Conference behaviour rather unpredictable. Nevertheless, by 1914 it was clear that leading performers were developing Conference management into a fine art. The romantic idealism of MacDonald and Henderson's robust appeals to 'loyalty' and common sense' normally triumphed.[5] The passions of wartime made the relationship more problematic. The platform's control of Conference was weakened by divisions inside the leadership. The difficulties were encapsulated in the behaviour of Henderson, determined to maintain contact with the rank and file, but feeling a need to persuade delegates of the necessity for unpopular government measures. The events of 1917-18 re-forged the Labour consensus, and subsequently the leadership re-established its dominance.[6] Successive gatherings demonstrated Henderson's skill in providing a stage for MacDonald's beguiling talents.[7] Apart from their quiescence, the most striking feature of Party Conferences in the twenties is the triviality of much of their business. The interminable topic of relationships with the Communist Party occupied much time, and assisted the leadership's mobilisation of support. Until 1928 there was little discussion of central issues of policy and strategy. The cloudy rhetoric of MacDonald reigned supreme.

The formal view of party structures depicted the Conference as the 'Parliament of the Movement', the body with ultimate authority. The election in 1906 of a sizeable group of Labour MPs raised the thorny problem of the relationship between Conference and the party's MPs. Did the conception of Conference sovereignty undermine the traditional mores of British political practice, through the suggestion that MPs should be responsible to the Party Conference, rather than to the party in Parliament, or the electorate? This question received an airing at the 1907 Conference, when the Executive responded to demands that Labour MPs should be bound by Conference decisions. The Executive's resolution was shrouded in that ambiguity that was to mark successive declarations on the subject. The ambiguity came with the *caveat* that 'the time and method of giving effect to these instructions be left to the Party in the House in conjunction with the

National Executive.'[8] Nevertheless, the views of Conference were regarded as of major significance. Special conferences were called to give an authoritative verdict on urgent questions. Thus, in November 1918, most Labour Ministers accepted the Conference decision to sever all relations with the Lloyd George Coalition. Those who did not left the party.

The problem was given a sharper expression by the 1918 Constitution, and the accompanying programmatic commitment. Under the heading 'Party Programme', it was laid down that

> It shall be the duty of the Party Conference to decide, from time to time, what specific proposals of legislative, financial or administrative reform, shall receive the general support of the party, and be promoted, as occasion may present itself, by the National Executive and the Parliamentary Labour Party ...[9]

The 'as occasion' qualification introduced a crucial flexibility, while the probability of Conference policies being both authoritative and unwelcome to the leadership was reduced by a further qualification. 'No such proposal shall be made definitely part of the General programme of the Party, unless it has been adopted by the Conference by a majority of not less than two-thirds of the votes recorded on a card vote.'[10]

The question of Conference supremacy was almost irrelevant in the twenties, since there was little likelihood of a division between the Conference and the party leadership. The problem of leadership-rank and file relations was raised, however, by the record of the 1924 Government. The Government's policies produced demands that any future Labour Government must be based on a parliamentary majority, and an appropriate resolution was moved at the 1925 Conference.[11] The proposal was defeated with MacDonald arguing strongly against any attempt to control Labour Members of Parliament. Such controls could be presented persuasively as damaging to Labour's future prospects.

While it is relatively easy to establish the salient characteristics of Labour's development at the national level, it is much more difficult to chart the party's crucial growth at the grass roots. During the first decade local organisation developed in a haphazard fashion that reflected Labour's uncertain political status. In theory, there was no individual membership. All party members joined through an affiliated body, which could be, of course, the ILP or the Fabian Society. In practice, several local parties appear to have permitted individual membership. The local organisation was often a trades council, frequently under a different label. In some cities there were central Labour Parties, modelled on the national organisation. In some mining seats, nominally held by Labour, the local party was a myth. Former Liberal MPs forcibly transferred to Labour ranks as a consequence of union affiliation often made little effort to set up new political machinery.[12]

In principle, these local idiosyncrasies were swept away by the 1918 Constitution. The bid for major political status involved the idea of individual membership through local Labour Parties. In fact, the change was much less than it might appear.[13] The 'inauguration' of individual membership was a national acceptance of what was often a local fact. Many existing Trades Councils renamed themselves Divisional Labour Parties. These DLPs were often dominated by local union interests and genuine individual members were often sparse. Nevertheless, by the mid-twenties there was a Labour presence in practically every constituency, although effectiveness tended to be determined by local union strength. The growth of individual membership raised peculiar problems for the ILP. Before 1918, it had had a crucial status within the wider Labour Party as the 'socialist engine-room'. It was the means whereby many committed socialists entered the wider party, and tended to be the major focus of their loyalties. Now there was a danger of duplication. Since the whole party was committed to 'socialism', the ILP could appear redundant. Some ILP members came to see its future place as Labour's evangelical wing, but in the late twenties, the ILP leadership passed to a group who were ready to use the party as a means of advancing distinctive radical left-wing policies. Political differences apart, this produced a problem of dual authority. ILP spokesmen could cite their own Conference decisions as legitimising their opposition to the policies of the Labour Party.[14]

The growth of individual membership was overshadowed by the magnitude of trade union affiliation based on the payment of a political levy. The Taff Vale Judgment had jolted many unions into affiliating[15] and by 1906, the only significant exception was the Miners' Federation of Great Britain. The Miners' tardiness reflected the continuing close attachment of many miners to the Liberal Party. Eventually, the MFGB decided on affiliation in 1908, and brought a membership of 550,000 into the party.[16] This was by far the largest union bloc; otherwise only the Textile Workers boasted a six figure affiliation. At the time, many on the left of the party regarded the potential domination by Coal and Cotton with very mixed feelings. They saw it as a major obstacle to the development of radical policies. This certainly proved to be an accurate assessment of the Textile Workers, but after 1910, the Miners abandoned their Liberalism. The growth of party resources through union affiliation received a setback in 1909. The judgment of the Lords in the Osborne Case prevented the use of trade union funds for political purposes. The party did not obtain some legal redress from the Liberal Government until 1913. Subsequent union amalgamations and increased unionisation meant that by the mid-twenties, large bloc votes were not restricted to these two industries.

Table 2: 1926 Affiliations[17]

Miners' Federation of Great Britain	800,000
General & Municipal Workers	323,465
National Union of Railwaymen	317,538
Textile Workers	292,570
Transport & General Workers	250,000
Amalgamated Engineering Union	129,606

This was a peak for union affiliation. After the General Strike union membership generally fell, while the affiliation figures were cut, sometimes drastically, by the 1927 Trades Disputes Act. This required the consent of individual unionists to their payment of a political levy. Nevertheless, the contrast between affiliated and individual membership remained striking. The first individual membership figure was published for 1928: it was only 215,000.[18]

The potential domination of Labour Conferences by the large trade unions inevitably raised the question of how representative their political positions were of the bulk of their membership. Their internal decision-making procedures varied enormously; their political postures reflected a weight of industrial and political traditions — and also often the preferences of their leaders. In the twenties, for example, the Transport and General Workers and the Railwaymen tended to mirror the political positions of Bevin and Thomas.[19] The first was prickly and not always with the leadership; the second was much more committed to a loyalist position. The Textile Workers and the General and Municipal Workers competed for the mantle of most orthodox union. The Miners however were much less reliable. Their position as the shock troops of trade unionism had generated considerable radicalisation, and the federal structure covered very varied regional traditions. Overall, however, throughout the twenties,

the big battalions — and most of the medium-sized ones — could be
relied on to support the party leadership.

Party development also involved the expansion of the central
administration. In the first three decades, the Secretary, firstly
MacDonald and then Henderson, was a major power. His involvement
in administration led to considerable influence over the decisions
of the Executive. The party machine expanded significantly after 1917.
Growth was closely linked with attempts to develop closer links
between the party and the TUC. Henderson had attempted in 1917 to
create a Research Department that would include not just party and
TUC officials, but also the Fabian Research Department. Only a
party-Fabian link was achieved and the latter restructured their
organisation as the Labour Research Department. This included several
who were critical of prominent trade union leaders. When a party-union
concordat eventually emerged, the LRD was a not unwelcome casualty.[20]
The new scheme came into operation in January 1922. A National Joint
Council was created with very limited powers, and joint departments
were formed for Research, Publicity and International matters.
The departments only lasted until March 1926. TUC officials were
always unhappy about dual control, and were reluctant to develop too
close an identity with the party. This unhappiness was deepened by the
rather cool relations between the 1924 Government and the TUC.[21]
After the 1926 changes, only the NJC survived as a permanent joint
body, although its role was negligible. The TUC began to develop its
own sizeable administrative structures under its new General Secretary,
Citrine.[22] In contrast, the party's administration seemed impoverished.

The commitment to comprehensive policies led also to the
construction in 1918 of a complex of Advisory Committees. At first,
these were staffed wholly by sympathetic experts and generated a
forbidding quantity of reports. They were reorganised to incorporate
MPs and to bring them within the ambit of party-TUC co-operation.
They continued, throughout the twenties, to produce information
on a wide range of subjects although any pretensions to independent
influence were gradually curtailed.[23]

By the mid-twenties, Labour had evolved most of the characteristics
of a parliamentary party, and had added one peculiar to itself, the
organic connection with the unions. Labour was similar to its rivals,
even in ways that seemed at variance with its professed commitment
to social reconstruction. Possibly its conformity was demonstrated
most clearly by the gradual emergence of the Party Leader as a crucial
office. In the first decade, it had been meaningless to talk of a leader.

Keir Hardie was probably the most prominent parliamentarian, but the Chairmanship of the Parliamentary Party rotated. However, MacDonald succeeded to the post in 1911, and held it until the outbreak of war, despite considerable criticism of his leadership. The wartime disruption led to the nominal chairman Henderson being supplemented by deputies, while in the undistinguished post-1918 PLP the Chairmanship lay first with Adamson, and then with Clynes. It was only with MacDonald's narrow election to the post in November 1922 that it became possible to talk of a leader. Over the next nine years, despite repeated minority rumblings, MacDonald exercised an awesome domination over his party. No future leader has equalled his control, backed by the varied talents of Henderson, Clynes, Snowden[24] and Thomas.

These 'Big Five' were not personally close to one another, but they exercised a power and a patronage unmatched by their successors. They had all entered Parliament by 1910 and together they moulded the party. They had served varied political apprenticeships: Henderson, Clynes and Thomas in the unions: MacDonald and Snowden in the ILP and associated radical groups. Most were active in late Victorian politics, when radicalism was normally equated with radical Liberalism. It would be difficult to state clearly what socialism meant for any of them. At best, it was a broad human fellowship: at worst, an easy rhetorical device for silencing critics. Their routes to the leadership blended commitment and expediency. MacDonald and Henderson, in many ways so different, shared an early attachment to Liberalism, and rejection by its local leaders.

While the 'Big Five' had a distinctiveness because of their formative role, neither this nor the eventual breach between three of them and the party should be allowed to hide the elements of continuity. Although aspects of the Big Five's leadership inevitably reflected their specific formative position, they helped to etch out roles in the developing organisation that have persisted through subsequent generations of leaders. MacDonald's elastic symbolism, his willingness to talk in Utopian terms, while acting with resolute orthodoxy, his desire to socialise Labour into the acceptance of existing institutional norms: none of these traits ended with him. Similarly Henderson, the robust, sometimes devious, man of common sense, and Clynes, the eloquent unobtrusive moderate; both were to be replicated amongst successive generations of trade union leaders. Thomas, the skilled negotiator with a taste for 'Society', 'Sir Stuffed Shirt', did not quit the Labour Party in 1931. And then there was Snowden, the old ILP evangelist, linked with the paragon of financial orthodoxy. How many of his successors have evoked radical imagery, but in their actions clung tenaciously to the accepted wisdom? Equally, roles developed within the rank and file. The critics epitomised by the gaunt Maxton upholding socialist virtues in the face of leaders' apostasy, the serried ranks of trade union loyalists using their bloc votes against all deviants, the few sympathisers with the Communist Party readily utilised to smear all opposition — all these developed during the twenties. Roles were forged along with structure. They were given a particular quality by the personnel and issues of the twenties, but when these passed away, they remained.

Electoral Progress — and Disaster

In May 1929 Labour became the largest party in the Commons for the first time. Its expansion from a parliamentary presence of two in 1900 to 287 in 1929 was a dramatic consequence of a multitude of factors. Initially, Labour faced an electoral system that discriminated severely against third parties, and a limited male franchise. In September 1900, the Labour Representation Committee contested 15 seats with two successes. Both involved the capture of one seat in a two-member borough. Hardie at Merthyr demonstrated the socialist face of the Labour alliance, but Richard Bell's Derby victory was a herald of future problems. Bell, General Secretary of the Amalgamated Society of Railway Servants was a committed Liberal who fought on the Labour platform only because of his union's decision. Once in Parliament, he became indistinguishable from the old trade union Liberal members.[25]

The new party's uncertain identity and prospects, and the historic Liberal affiliation of much of organised labour, produced a danger that Labour might become no more than an appendage of the Liberal Party. The LRC's by-election gains in the 1900 Parliament underlined this problem. Two — Clitheroe and Woolwich — did not involve Liberal opposition, and the new Labour members Shackleton and Crookes enjoyed much local Liberal support.[26] Arthur Henderson's Barnard Castle victory was the first against both major parties. But Henderson had been Liberal Agent in the constituency, and enjoyed considerable backing from local Liberals.[27]

The development in 1903 of a secret Liberal-Labour pact is hardly surprising. This was intended to provide a limited number of Labour-Conservative straight fights, and a restriction of Liberal candidacies to one in some two-member seats. The accommodation was at the national level, between MacDonald and Herbert Gladstone, and

was mirrored imperfectly in local arrangements.[28] Nevertheless, it
functioned impressively in the Liberal landslide of January 1906.
Labour's parliamentary strength increased to 29 (30 from the meeting
of Parliament). The contribution of the pact is obvious, Labour ran
45 candidates — 15 of them had Liberal opposition and only five of
these were successful. The parliamentary bridgehead produced by this
arrangement provided no guide to any specifically Labour strength.
Thirteen of the Labour seats were in the north-west where Liberalism
had lost ground over the last few elections, although much was
regained in 1906. Here local Liberals had been ready to make
concessions, but elsewhere they were much less accommodating.[29]

Many of the Labour victors of 1906 were indistinguishable in their
views from the Liberals. Labour's election platform contained nothing
that could offend orthodox Liberals. Candidates were typically
zealous defenders of free trade, and their views on unemployment and
social problems were distinguished by their prominence rather than
their content. Despite the similarity of views and the success of the
unpublished pact, strong pressures developed for Labour to assert
its individuality by contesting by-elections in Liberal seats. Such
pressures obviously presented Labour leaders with a dilemma since
repeated candidacies could only destroy the pact, and thereby
much of the party's existing representation. Yet scrupulous
observance of a truce with Liberals would lead to Labour independence
becoming no more than a fiction. In the 1906 Parliament, Labour
gained two seats from the Liberals at Jarrow and Sheffield Attercliffe.
In the Colne Valley, Victor Grayson, refused endorsement as an
official Labour candidate, achieved a sensational victory.[30] However,
the most significant development served to blur the Liberal-Labour
distinction still further. When the MFGB finally affiliated to the
Labour Party, it brought 13 MPs over from the Liberal to the Labour
ranks. Many of these remained Liberals in all but their title. They did
not change their views, nor sometimes the structure of their local
organisation.[31]

In January 1910 Labour ran 78 candidates with the following
consequences:

Table 3: January 1910 Election Results (Labour)

1906 Successes	By-Election Gains	Miners' Seats	New Gains[32]
Held 24	Held 1	Held 12	3
Lost 6	Lost 1	Lost 1	—

No victory involved the defeat of a Liberal. This moderate performance helped lead to a reduction in candidacies in December 1910. Only 56 were run with five gains and three losses.

These performances showed how the alliance with the Liberals might be disadvantageous in the long run. Apart from the mining seats, Labour remained confined to the bridgehead established in 1906. Liberal spokesmen emphasised that any major Labour attempt to expand would meet with retaliation. The dominance of the two 1910 elections by the House of Lords question meant that pressures for a Progressive understanding remained strong. Committed socialists chafed at the prominence of what they saw as a marginal issue, but for Labour leaders with their Liberal backgrounds, co-operation in such circumstances was a natural response.

The status of Labour's mining seats remained unclear after 1910. Were they to be regarded as exempt from Liberal attack, or as normally Liberal seats, temporarily transferred to Labour by a trade union decision? By 1914, after some confused by-elections, there was a much wider acceptance within the MFGB of the political consequences of affiliation to the Labour Party. Eventually such an acceptance implied a powerful attack on Liberalism in some of that party's traditional strongholds. Such an attack backed with the miner's customary solidarity would produce a group of safe, specifically Labour, seats.

Retrospective wisdom can uncover subtle ways in which the Labour-Liberal understanding was being undermined by the industrial happenings of the immediate pre-war years. The growth of industrial conflict, the Government's partisanship in this field, the emergence of class-based politics: all these now seem part of a coherent, inevitable progression accelerated but not initiated by wartime developments. Certainly in some regions — notably South Wales — pre-war conflicts meant that new class-based divisions were likely to supplant the old Liberal hegemony based on shared cultural sentiments. Even here, the transition was slow. Any traditional change brought about by industrial struggles percolated through only slowly into mass voting behaviour.[33] Between 1910 and 1914, the party's broad electoral strategy was obscure. National leaders continued to be cautious, but Labour broke new ground in seven by-elections. Although no seats were gained, the vote was often encouraging, and it seems clear that Labour would have fought the next general election on a much broader front. No doubt the consequences would have been unspectacular, but there was some hope of a more durable basis than those secured in 1906 and 1910.[34]

Labour's electoral prospects were clearly improved by two wartime developments, the major extension of the franchise,[35] and the rift, still confused in 1918, between the Liberal supporters of Asquith and of Lloyd George. In its early pro-war mood Labour had been ready to support an electoral truce, but the shifting attitudes that helped produce a new party constitution also produced a change here. In May 1918, the party abandoned the electoral truce. The immediate cause was a decision by the miners to contest a vacancy at Morpeth created by the death of one of the last Liberal trade unionists. This decision was underlined six months later when the party decided to withdraw totally from the Lloyd George Coalition and fight the forthcoming election as an independent force.

In the short term, this bid for major party status was submerged in khakhi euphoria. Labour produced 361 candidates but only 57 were successful, often by small margins. The limited improvement on December 1910 obscured major changes. All the Labour leaders who had condemned the war or who had been strongly for political independence failed. MacDonald, Snowden, Jowett and even Henderson lost their seats. Those who had stayed in the Government until instructed to leave were successful. Often this was because they lacked significant opposition. Clynes was returned unopposed: Hodge had to face an Independent Conservative and the Socialist Labour Party: Walsh was challenged only by the SLP. Sometimes their attitude to the remodelled party was unclear, and they frequently spoke bitterly of forces to their left.[36] The new PLP was dominated by unadventurous patriotic trade unionists. Only eight MPs were sponsored by local parties or the ILP while the MFGB was responsible for 25. Yet this small group whose parliamentary performance was to be notable for its mediocrity was larger than the devastated Independent Liberals. Labour had secured almost 2,400,000 votes: in many unsuccessful contests its poll was respectable. It looked beyond its meagre parliamentary representation with optimism.[37]

Such optimism seemed justified by Labour's by-election performance in the 1918 Parliament.[38] Fourteen gains were made and the party came close to victory in some very unlikely places.[39] Nevertheless, Labour advance must be viewed in the context of the period's extremely confused politics. In retrospect this immediate post-war period can be viewed as a crucial phase in Labour's replacement of the Liberals, but at the time the options seemed open. Sometimes Labour and Independent Liberal candidates competed for the anti-government vote; on some occasions Labour gained from a

split Liberal vote, on others, attempts were made to unite behind
one candidate. Liberalism's internal divisions tended to deepen, but
Labour's expansion was rather uneven. The party achieved most in
1919, but then tended to stagnate.[40]

This picture of uneven growth was reflected in Labour's performance
in the confused November 1922 election.[41] While various brands of
Liberal and Conservative mixed collusion and fratricidal strife, Labour's
representation grew to 142 seats, and its total vote rose to almost
4¼ million. The party was beginning to establish an industrial base.
Sizeable gains were made in mining areas, and in some large cities, most
notably Glasgow, but Labour failed totally in some other urban centres
such as Birmingham and Liverpool. Success and failure seemed to be
influenced both by recent industrial experiences and tenacious
traditional values. Most miners had been weaned away from Liberalism
through industrial conflict, but Labour made little headway against
the dominance of the Chamberlains or the Orange Lodges. Labour's
advance had two crucial features. Eighty-nine of its victories involved
an absolute majority of the votes cast. The party was beginning to
establish a core of safe seats. In addition, the PLP's composition was
now much broader. The old middle-class leadership who had lost
in 1918 returned, and were joined by the beginnings of a younger,
white-collar generation.

In November 1922, the growth in the party's parliamentary
representation reflected a significant expansion of the party's support.
Labour's success in the next election in December 1923 was very
different. Although its total vote increased by less than 200,000, its
representation expanded to 191. This involved the gain of 65 seats,
and the loss of 18. The apparent Liberal reunion and the centrality
of the free trade issue produced many genuinely three-cornered contests,
with complicated transfers of votes. In many seats, Labour prospects
were improved by Liberal intervention or by Liberals forfeiting the
Tory support that they had enjoyed thirteen months earlier. Similarly
complex factors produced the Labour losses. Often, local Liberals
and Conservatives combined, despite the national campaign, to defeat
the sitting Labour member. Over all, the contest reaffirmed Labour's
arrival as a permanent electoral force. Although the issues were
peculiarly favourable to the Liberals, Labour kept 33 seats ahead.
Yet Labour's advance remained very uneven. Several industrial seats
were won by the Liberals, while the party's rural performance was
pathetic. In nearly all the rural seats, the battle remained one between
the two older parties, and Labour candidates often failed to save their

deposits.

While the 1923 election confirmed the permanent status of Labour, the October 1924 contest produced a further move towards a Conservative-Labour dominated system.[42] Liberal hopes of office were effectively extinguished. Although Labour lost 40 seats, compared with December 1923, it gained over 1¼ million votes. The alternatives were beginning to clarify. Anti-Labour ranks were congregating under the Conservative banner: industrial workers who had formerly voted Liberal were tending to switch to Labour. The fact of a Labour Government, and the tone of the Conservative campaign with its Bolshevik scares ensured that Labour and its policies were more to the forefront than ever before. Although this simplification of alternatives was the central feature, the anatomy of Labour's defeat was extremely complicated. Labour lost 63 seats. Only ten of these had a straight Labour-Conservative fight in 1923 and 1924. In these constituencies, there was a sizeable swing to the right. The other 53 cases were characterised by many Liberal withdrawals, a few Conservative withdrawals, or the collapse of the Liberal vote. Similar variations are present in Labour's 23 gains. Sixteen of these were gains from the Liberals, the visible signs of Labour's slowly developing control over industrial Britain. The growing evidence of this control could give Labour encouragement. The increased concentration of opposing forces within the Conservative Party foreshadowed major problems.

These crucial developments tended to be overshadowed over the next four years by speculation about a Liberal revival. But while the Liberals made some well-publicised by-election gains, Labour made steady progress. In the 1924 Parliament 11 seats were gained from the Conservatives, two from the Liberals – and just one lost.[43] Labour organisers complained often about electoral apathy. The party's mood was certainly very different from the optimism of the immediate post-war years. Success in 1923 had come as a surprise, but in the event, Labour's progress proved rather more significant than Liberal dreams. In May 1929, Labour's total vote rose to almost 8,400,000 and the vagaries of the electoral system reflected this in a parliamentary representation of 287 seats. Labour broke much new ground. Most dramatically, six seats were captured in Birmingham, while more generally the party held the vast majority of industrial constituencies. Rural representation remained minimal. The 1929 election demonstrated that Labour had made a major advance in most of urban Britain, but it exaggerated the strength of that hold. Only just over half of Labour's seats were held with an absolute majority of all votes cast.

The electoral promise of the twenties was misleading. There were of course factors strengthening Labour's position. The expansion of the franchise should not be underestimated, while the industrial experiences of some groups of workers, most notably the miners, guaranteed an irreducible minimum of support. But the three-party politics of the twenties produced an exaggeration of Labour's real strength. Crucial realignments were taking place, but the translation into seats was premature. In May 1929, Labour supporters admired their party's rapid growth — but its position was like a house of cards on a concrete base. The spadework was being done, but the representative success was a very fragile thing.

This fragility was soon demonstrated. After a promising start, the by-election record of the 1929 Government deteriorated. Even normally secure seats showed heavy swings to the Conservatives. By the summer of 1931, it was clear that any early election would produce a Government defeat. This unpropitious outlook was obviously worsened by the circumstances of the 1931 election. The exit of three prominent leaders into the National Government created confusion and was underlined by public bitterness between former colleagues. More crucially it was the first contest in which the issue was clearly Labour versus the rest. The virtual absorption of the Liberals into the National ranks produced many pacts, and ended most Labour hopes of victories on a minority vote.

These circumstances, plus the strident appeals for a vote in the 'national interest' clearly indicated a Labour defeat. However, few expected the devastation that occurred. Labour held only 46 seats plus 5 more retained by the now semi-independent ILP. Of these, 32 had a sizeable mining vote[44] and in some of these Labour was almost as secure as in 1929. Labour failed in the coal-fields only in Durham and in Scotland. The general solidarity of the miners was unique. Labour representation in the great cities was decimated. The only partial exceptions were nine successes in East London and five in Glasgow — three of the latter were by ILP members. Elsewhere Labour held one Liverpool seat on religious loyalties, one in Leeds and one in Bristol. In many industrial areas there was a total failure. No members were returned from the West Midlands, from the cotton towns, nor from Tyneside. The catastrophe was also significant in terms of individual leaders. Only Lansbury remained from the 1929 Cabinet. In effect, this marked the passing of Labour's first generation. The younger coming men fared just as badly.

Attlee and Cripps both scraped in: Morrison, Dalton and Arthur Greenwood all lost. One major consolation emerged from the wreckage. The disaster was one of representation rather than electoral support. In this unique contest, Labour lost just over 1,700,000 votes compared with 1929, but its total, almost 6,650,000, was much higher than in any earlier election. The house of cards had collapsed, but the base remained largely intact.

Towards a Programme

'This Conference is in favour of establishing a distinct Labour Group in Parliament who shall have their own Whips and agree upon their policy, which must embrace a readiness to co-operate with any party which for the time being may be engaged in promoting legislation in the direct interest of Labour.'[45]

'The Labour Interest'

The creation of the Labour Representation Committee in February 1900 was a compromise. The new organisation united committed socialists with trade unionists who had come to accept the necessity of independent Labour representation often without abandoning their Liberalism. Since 1874, there had always been a few trade union MPs. They functioned as a minor element in the Liberal alliance, but their number remained small since most Liberal Associations were unwilling to adopt working-class candidates. During the 1890s this approach had come under pressure. Socialists were becoming influential in some unions, but more significantly, a series of legal decisions went against trade unions. The need for parliamentary influence became more acute and the idea of independent representation grew more attractive. Inevitably at the birth of the new organisation, many union spokesmen were unsure about its scope, and suspected the motives of the socialists. They were prepared to support an organisation for the furtherance of trade union claims, but were unwilling to see it employed as a Trojan Horse for the advocacy of socialism.[46]

The Socialists were divided fundamentally about strategy. The Social Democratic Federation, the nearest to a Marxist group within the British left, made an unsuccessful attempt to commit the LRC to a militant socialist position, 'based on the recognition of the class war, and having for its ultimate object, the socialisation of the means of production, distribution and exchange.' The SDF soon withdrew from the new organisation.[47] The small Fabian Society was a sharp contrast. It played only a marginal role in the foundation of the LRC but in the long run, its impact was to be very significant. This was a consequence of key individuals, most notably Sidney Webb, occupying major positions at crucial times. Fabian beliefs provided major motifs in the party's development: the commitment to gradualism, the denial of inevitably opposed class interests, the faith in the neutrality of the existing state. These were central Fabian tenets and were to be basic beliefs of successive generations of Labour leaders. The Fabian doctrines provided an intellectual rationale for the instinctive attitudes of leaders.[48] Faith in gradualism, class co-operation and the neutrality of the state came readily to many working-class spokesmen. The parliamentary system was well established, working-class movements had no recent history of suppression and illegality: economic difficulties were only just becoming apparent. But Fabianism, however well it fitted with the predilections of working-class leaders, was not a doctrine for mass consumption. It could provide a rationale for a party but not the necessary attraction. This was given by the Independent Labour Party. Its umbrella covered a wide range of opinions, but all could subscribe to its evangelical, Utopian vision. The ILP was strong on idealism and emotional appeals, but weak on practical proposals and strategic considerations. While its other-worldly vision provided a qualitative alternative to existing society, this was reserved for the distant future. Much of the ILP's vision and rhetoric had affinities with religious nonconformity, and with the more radical varieties of Liberalism. ILP propagandists might claim to offer a distinctive solution — socialism, but on many immediate · issues their positions showed a similarity with those of the more advanced Liberals. From the beginning a major strain in Labour's socialism was in sympathy with the existing order.[49]

The nature of this Labour coalition meant that the development of any programme would be difficult. Many leaders had neither an understanding of socialist theory, nor a sympathy for it.[50] Their support of the organisation was esentially tactical; their aims were restricted largely to lobbying for legislation on specific trade union matters. The tentative nature of the ILP's commitment to socialism also worked against the construction of a programme. It was therefore prepared to avoid commitments in the interests of maintaining unity. Furthermore, after 1906, there were increasing pressures within the Liberal Party for a greater commitment to social reform. Many advocates of this 'Social Liberalism' dreamt of a new 'Progressive' synthesis that would incorporate both Labour and

Liberal reformers. Arguably the emergence of such an understanding can be seen in some regions prior to 1914, but equally there were forces tending to drive the two parties further apart. The divisive factors clearly increased the pressures for a distinctive party programme.[51]

During the 1906 Parliament, the performance of Labour MPs had produced growing rank and file criticism.[52] The small Labour group's inability to secure legislation, and its members' readiness to conform to all parliamentary mores outraged the more militant sections of the ILP.[53] Party Conferences witnessed a series of confrontations between the critics and both moderate trade unionists, and compromisers who were committed to the defence of the 'Labour Alliance'. So long as the trade union presence within the party remained suspicious of any overt 'socialism' then nothing could change.[54] But after 1910, their complacency and moderation came under pressure. British industry was convulsed by a series of disputes, most notably in the coal-fields, in the docks and on the railways.[55] The widespread use of troops and the consequential violence drew a taut line between sections of organised labour and the Liberal Government. Labour's parliamentarians responded to the outbreaks with a mixture of caution and confusion. An observer noted 'the almost complete collapse of the Labour Party in the House as an effective influence in labour disputes.'[56] Such marginality is hardly surprising. Labour members could hardly align themselves with the Government against trade unionists, but militant industrial action involved a challenge to their own position. The sometimes spectacular advances achieved by strikers contrasted with the plodding anonymity of Labour's parliamentarians.[57]

Such reservations were increased by the emergence of syndicalist ideas within some sections of the trade unions. These attacked the moderate gradualism of Labour leaders at its base. Parliamentarianism and reformism were seen as damaging illusions. Working-class interests must be furthered by industrial action aimed at the seizure of political power. Existing political institutions could not be used. Such challenges were obviously anathema to Labour's moderate leadership. Most strikes during these years were not attributable, of course, to the impact of syndicalist doctrines upon masses of workers. There were abundant grounds for industrial action in the long-term fall in real wages. Nevertheless a new generation of union leaders emerged, their outlook greatly influenced by 'direct action'. This inevitably affected strategic discussions within the party. For the first time, the assumptions of the Fabians, the moderate MPs and union leaders were laid bare, and debated intensively. The pragmatic promotion of the 'Labour interest' was becoming difficult to sustain.

These early years were not wholly devoid of programmatic commitments, sometimes capable of a socialist interpretation. Gradually the Party Conference began to pass policy resolutions. Often these dealt with questions of a trade union or a welfare variety, but by 1914, the party had declared itself in favour of the nationalisation of mines, railways and canals. Indeed, in 1908, it had passed narrowly a resolution declaring that the party's 'definite object' should be 'the socialisation of the means of production, distribution, and exchange.'[58] The specific proposals for nationalisation did not signify any clear commitment to socialism. They could be viewed as attempts to deal with problem industries, and could be supported by Liberal critics of inefficiency and monopoly. The general statement was purely rhetorical, but even then, many objected. Labour had taken only minimal steps away from its original distaste for programmes. The trade union world was changing rapidly after 1910; debates about socialist strategy multiplied. Inevitably, those involved discussed the role of the Labour Party — but within the party, the controversies provoked little response.

The Impact of War

Prior to August 1914, Labour politicians had spent little time debating international issues. Officially the party shared the vague hope that war could be prevented by international working-class co-operation, but characteristically, opposition to war owed much to traditional liberal criticisms of power politics and secret diplomacy. Most Labour politicians abandoned any internationalist pretensions as soon as war started. Some adopted a crudely patriotic position, but most stolidly placed national interests first.[59] The critical minority were centred around the ILP. A few condemned the war as an imperialist conflict, but many more did so on the basis of a humane, principled liberalism. This tendency was strengthened by a small group of radicals who entered the Labour Movement on account of their disillusion with the Government's foreign policy. The liberal inspiration of much of the criticism was important. It resulted in the critics restricting their opposition to matters of high principle. Such people as Snowden and the ambiguous MacDonald were unlikely to connect their concern about the war to specifically working-class discontents.[60]

The divisions inevitably produced recriminations: tensions between middle-class ILP critics and patriotic trade unionists sometimes became acute. But unlike major social democratic parties elsewhere in Europe, the war did not produce a major schism. Possibly Labour's lack of ideological self-consciousness helped in this, while the party's diverse elements found a common focus for their work on the War Emergency Workers' National Committee.[61] This large body was designed as the counterbalance to Labour's general support for the national effort. Initially it was viewed as the instrument protecting the wage-earner against the ravages of war.

The general Labour support for the war inevitably resulted in the party being drawn into the making and enforcement of Government decisions. Such political responsibilities were preceded by major industrial concessions. By the Treasury Agreement of March 1915 most unions agreed to abandon strikes, suspend many workshop practices and accept Government arbitration.[62] Two months later the Liberal Government was replaced by a coalition. After some disagreement between the PLP and the National Executive, Henderson accepted the Presidency of the Board of Education.[63] From the start of his ministerial career, Henderson was involved in the mitigation of the consequences of unofficial industrial stoppages. Although such a role produced inevitable strains within the labour movement, the party remained resolutely pro-war. Labour's involvement in government was increased when Lloyd George became Prime Minister in December 1916. Henderson joined the small War Cabinet, and the chauvinistic Hodge became the first Minister of Labour. By then, the controls over organised labour had been extended greatly; military conscription had been accepted. Subjugation seemed complete.

This marked the zenith of Labour's support for the Government.[64] In 1917 and 1918, the party moved, in a typically ambiguous fashion, to a more independent political position. It would be mistaken to see this as an unequivocal shift to the left, although it was made as a response to left-wing pressures. The patriotism of most trade union leaders meant that the articulation of rank and file grievances passed to unofficial leaders. Stoppages grew, particularly in the engineering industries, and raised a potential threat to the authority of established leaders.[65]

Increasing war weariness provided the backcloth to Labour's change in direction. The immediate catalysts were the two Russian revolutions of 1917. The first revolution produced widespread enthusiasm from British Labour. It offered encouragement to radicals everywhere, and also the hope that the military stalemate might end. Even Labour moderates

responded with visions of major changes. This was not their response
to the October Revolution. Most sections of the party shared a distaste
for Bolshevik doctrines and methods. Now Labour leaders responded
to a challenge from their left. Henderson, MacDonald and Webb all
felt the need to develop a social democratic alternative to the
revolutionary threat that would channel the enthusiasm of the rank
and file into constitutional paths.[66]

Labour's move away from involvement in the Lloyd George
Coalition was epitomised by Henderson. In the summer of 1917, he
visited Russia as a Government representative. Doubts had arisen
about the strength of Russian commitment to the war, especially in
the context of Dutch-sponsored proposals for a meeting of all
European socialist parties in Stockholm. Henderson's Russian
experiences led to a change of his attitude on this. He returned as
a supporter of Stockholm since he now believed that only an
attempt to secure an early peace could prevent a Bolshevik take-over.
This new position produced his resignation from the Government in
August 1917. His subsequent attempt to reconstruct the party was
influenced by his Russian experiences. The fragility of the
Provisional Government's position impressed him. A British alternative
to the lure of revolutionary socialism could be founded
on the newly expanded trade unions but while Henderson's reforms
were inevitably centred on problems of structure, the attempt to
develop Labour as a major party obviously raised the question of a
programme.[67]

The initial exercise in programme construction occurred within the
WENC. In 1916 and 1917, there developed, largely through Webb's
influence, a demand for the conscription of riches. This was completely
compatible with support for the war, and could be justified as an
efficient means of pursuing victory. It had the Fabian characteristic
of claiming to advance towards socialism through technical responses
to immediate difficulties.[68] A similar tone is apparent in the policy
debates at the 1917 Conference,[69] but policy preparation became more
significant after Henderson's departure from office. Webb's contribution
was crucial in both international and domestic fields. He blended
together liberal and socialist sentiments in a Statement on War Aims.
Peace should be protected by thorough democratisation, and the
creation of a supra-national authority.[70] The developments in the
domestic field were even more significant. The party's 1918
Constitution contained a significant fomula. It would be a future
occasion for controversy, but in 1918 it was a means of maximising

agreement.

> To secure for the producers by hand or by brain the full fruits of
> their industry and the most equitable distribution thereof that may be
> possible, upon the basis of the Common Ownership of the
> Means of Production and the best obtainable system of popular
> administration and control of each industry and service.[71]

The statement can be viewed as committing the party in some way
to socialism. Such a commitment could have little relevance for the
immediate future; but it differentiated the party, and provided some
token reassurance for committed socialists.[72] A similar maximisation
of agreement was achieved by Webb's draft — 'Labour and the New
Social Order' — the first detailed statements of Labour's home
policy. This reflected many of Webb's preoccupations. Proposals were
seen as natural consequences of recent developments. Reconstruction
should be based on the lessons of four years of war. There were
prescriptions for reducing the dislocations of the immediate post-war
period, and hopes for long term qualitative change: 'a genuinely
scientific reorganisation of the nation's industry ... on the basis of
the Common Ownership of the Means of Production.'[73] Specific
proposals for public ownership covered mining, electricity,
railways, canals, roads, shipping and harbours, industrial insurance
and brewing. The private sector was to have a much closer
relationship with the state. The party committed itself to full
employment, progressive taxation and a minimum standard of
subsistence.

This was a significant milestone in the development of a Labour
programme — but it was an extremely uncertain one. How deep was
the commitment to socialism? It was a major change for the party
to profess any commitment, but was the programme — rhetoric apart —
anything more than an attempt to rationalise and humanise
existing society? Doubts are only underlined by the policy debates
at the June 1918 Conference. A resolution on 'The Control of
Capitalist Industry' envisaged the control of profits through an
armoury of controls.[74] There was no suggestion that the programme
aimed to redistribute power between classes. Indeed, there seemed
no suspicion that socialist policies might meet with firm resistance.
The proposals were presented as in the interests of all reasonable
people, capable of implementation through discussion and the use
of existing administrative machinery.[75] The continuities with pre-war

attitudes were thus well marked. The programme, along with the new structure, exemplified the post-war Labour consensus. It could stretch from extremely moderate trade union leaders to the left-wing of the ILP. Each tendency could take reassurance and hope from the remodelled party. It only excluded the revolutionary left, and a few ultra-Patriots who took the socialist claims too seriously. The great bulk of the British labour movement were now committed, at least formally, to parliamentarianism through an independent party, and to a socialist objective.

The Failure of an Alternative

Labour's development after 1918 appears as a slow, dogged progress towards office, abetted by the extended franchise and Liberal disagreements. Labour politicians became engrossed with the minutiae of electoral success. Yet although parliamentary expansion was the central feature, this involved the defeat of alternative strategies for the labour movement. The principal challenge came from the proponents of direct action. The crucial year was 1919.[76] Several union leaders, pessimistic about Labour's parliamentary prospects, advocated industrial action for political purposes. Such a strategy was supported by most leaders in the Triple Alliance of Railwaymen, Miners and Transport Workers.[77] It did not involve a conscious commitment to revolutionary politics; industrial action was seen as a means of achieving limited objectives. Yet this advocacy took place in an extremely uncertain situation. Major political changes in Europe were paralleled by widespread unrest in Britain. The tactic was advocated particularly over the public ownership of the mines and the abandonment of British intervention in Russia. In the first case, the Government successfully played for time: in the second, it withdrew its forces. Given the attitudes of some larger unions, it is not surprising that the 1919 Conference backed direct action,[78] although Henderson and Clynes expressed their fundamental commitment to parliamentarianism. The Conference decision meant little. Verbal posturing was one thing: significant action was another. Admittedly, the doctrine had a brief renaissance when all sections combined to oppose further British involvement in the Polish-Russian war. The opposition was probably mere rhetoric, since the Government had set its face against further involvement. It was an exceptional case capable of appealing not just to the committed socialist, but also to a widespread fear of a new war.[79] This brief interlude was overshadowed by the fiasco of April 1921.[80] The

Government's decision to relinquish their wartime control of the mines led to the coal-owners proposing sizeable wage reductions. In response the MFGB stood firm and called, rather belatedly, on support from its partners in the Triple Alliance. Support seemed likely, but some confused comments by Frank Hodges, the Miners' General Secretary, led to the collapse of the Alliance. The Miners fought on alone to defeat. After this 'Black Friday', the alternative of direct action receded. In part this reflected organisational deficiencies, but there were also changing priorities. Growing unemployment influenced the retreat from the forward policy of 1919.

There was a tragic postscript to the direct action controversy. After 'Black Friday', the parliamentarians recovered the initiative, until the loss of office by the first Labour Government. Its unspectacular career helped to produce a shift to the left within the TUC, assisted by the emergence of a sizeable left-wing group on the General Council. This was demonstrated in the mood of the 1925 TUC. Self-confidence had been increased by a successful attempt to halt a cut in miners' wages through the threat of united trade union action. The resulting willingness of the Government to subsidise the industry until May 1926 was greeted euphorically by the supporters of direct action, but with regret by Labour's parliamentary moderates.[81] During the period of the subsidy, union leaders did little to prepare for its termination. When the negotiations between miners and mine-owners, Government and TUC broke down, direct action had its last fling. The General Strike lasted only nine days.[82] The doubts of many union leaders and the distaste of many Labour parliamentarians contrasted with the enthusiasm shown in many local committees. Despite subsequent folklore, the stoppage was not the cosy tea party painted by advocates of 'The British Way of Life'. It was a potential threat, not just to the claims of capital but also to the consensual spirit of Labour leaders and to their control over their organisations. The logic of the strike violated those political mores that they subscribed to so fervently. It is hardly surprising therefore that the General Council terminated the stoppage at the earliest opportunity, leaving the miners, the 'kamikaze' of the labour movement, to fight on to defeat.

Confrontation was forgotten. Under the emerging leadership of Bevin and Citrine, the TUC came to seek accommodation with employers for mutual advantages. Such a shift was based on a broad acceptance of the existing economic system and an optimism about its potential for reform. Such acceptance by the majority of unions was a crucial feature of Labour's economic and industrial debates over the next forty years.[83]

While direct action was the major challenge to the party, it was hardly debated inside the party after 1919. Here the controversy over strategy assumed a different and artificial form. This resulted from the formation in 1920 of the Communist Party, its repeated attempts to affiliate to the Labour Party, and its repeated failures. The question of strategy became coloured by the strident formalism of many Communist spokesmen, and allowed Labour's leaders to secure easy conference victories. There were many within the party who had severe reservations about Labour's policies, but who rejected the dogmatic application of Russian methods to Britain. The casting of the alternatives in this form meant that many party discussions were of little value.[84]

The defeat of direct action and the perennial Communist question both furthered the role of Labour's moderates. Electoral successes deepened leaders' moderation, and increased rank and file loyalty. This dedicated pursuit of moderation was blemished somewhat in 1922 by the arrival of a small vociferous group of Scottish ILP MPs.[85] To the disquiet of MacDonald and his supporters, they tended to capture the headlines with their calculated distaste for parliamentary customs. Such irritations did not deflect the first Labour Government from a resolute attempt to establish its orthodoxy. The minutiae of constitutional and social conventions were adhered to religiously; although some reforms were enacted, most actions were calculated not to disturb the *status quo*.[86] Such conservatism had considerable party support. It was gratifying for Labour activists to see their leaders conducting the affairs of state. The essay in Labour constitutionalism was only a qualified success. There were inevitable criticisms from the left and also from some trade unionists resentful of the Government's attitude towards industrial stoppages.[87] Doubts were increased by the defeat of the Government, but although MacDonald's hold over the party was shaken, it was restored rapidly. The experience of office was held to have demonstrated Labour's lack of preparation. The 1918 document seemed inadequate and there was increasing awareness of a need for a more precise programme.

The False Start

The attempt to develop a party programme after 1924 became largely a controversy between MacDonald and the prudent moderates — including the bulk of trade union leaders — and the ILP, identified more and more with the Clydesiders, especially Maxton and Wheatley.

Debate settled around two problems. If protestations of socialist faith were to be more than rhetoric, then there must be a lucid strategy for transformation. Here both sides of the argument tended towards imprecision. The critics demanded socialist (typically public ownership) measures immediately. The moderate position was even less coherent: the gap between practice and Utopia was often blatant. The vague link provided by MacDonald's organic metaphors only increased confusion.

More immediately, the party had to produce an unemployment policy. From 1921 unemployment stayed above a million, concentrated in the traditional industries that were bastions of trade unionism. The official Labour response was implacably orthodox. This reflected, in part, the intellectual dominance of Snowden, but it also showed Labour's general acceptance of conventional attitudes. Unemployment could be removed only through the revival of affected industries. Any attempts to provide assistance must be financially sound.[88]

On the left, it was persuasively argued that little could be achieved under capitalism, and all palliatives were a vicious deception. Gradually some alternatives did emerge. By 1926 an ILP Study Group had produced a detailed statement, 'The Living Wage'. This diagnosed the central problem as one of inadequate purchasing power, and proposed to correct this by the principle of a minimum income. This would involve the introduction of a system of family allowances, and also specifically socialist measures such as the public ownership of the Bank of England, and of industries reluctant to pay the minimum wage.[89] The policy was sidetracked at the 1926 Conference when the ILP agreed to a joint Party-TUC Inquiry. This moved very slowly and trade union divisions over family allowances prevented any firm declarations.[90]

This response did not end the debate over policy. During the following year, ILP spokesmen prepared detailed documents. Again at the 1927 Conference, substantive discussion was avoided. MacDonald moved a resolution instructing the Executive to produce a programme,[91] and the NEC then formed a Sub-Committee to produce the document. The Sub-Committee continued a moderate majority. MacDonald and Henderson were backed by Cramp of the NUR, Roberts of the Typographical Association, and the rising Londoner, Herbert Morrison. Lansbury, despite his radical enthusiasms, was likely to act as a conciliator. The opposition would come from only three members — the ex-Conservative Mosley, the ex-Liberal Trevelyan, and the ex-Communist Ellen Wilkinson.[92] From the beginning there was disagreement over the type of document. Mosley and Wilkinson wanted a short statement, but

MacDonald presented a lengthy draft which was adopted as a basis.[93] This was later redrafted by Tawney,[94] but when the document went to the full Executive the minority continued to demand a short statement 'presenting in unmistakable terms the actual measures on which a Labour Government would at once embark.'

This did not happen. 'Labour and the Nation'[95] was a lengthy amalgam of broad principles and moderate proposals.[96] It began with the inevitable protestation of a socialist commitment, but diluted political differences by arguing that all parties were beginning to adopt socialist policies. This clearly equated socialism with government intervention in the economy. More specifically there were proposals for the public ownership of land, coal, power, transport and industrial insurance. Sizeable increases in welfare benefits were envisaged. The section on international policy was inevitably vague, placing major emphases on conciliation, arbitration, disarmament and the League. These protestations blended well with the international atmosphere of the late twenties, and the party's liberal inspirations. They produced minimal criticism, and were not to be discredited by the experience of office.

In contrast, the domestic proposals provoked the anger of the ILP radicals, but the 1928 Conference was the last total triumph of the Old Régime.[97] The NEC decided that draft amendments to the document would not be allowed, but sections could be referred back for rewriting. Suspicions about the absence of firm commitments could only be deepened by MacDonald's initial remarks. The document was 'not merely something for May 1929 ... full not only of one programme, but pregnant with programme after programme after programme.'[98] His predilection for organic metaphors and the relegation of socialism to the distant future was more apparent than usual, but they satisfied the bulk of the Conference. Maxton might speak of the need for a clear programme of immediate measures;[99] Wheatley might argue that the proposals would produce a rationalised capitalism.[100] But they were minority voices swamped by rhetoric, appeals to loyalty and personal attacks. The critics had virtually no influence in the unions:[101] their attempts to change the document were an almost total failure. The 1929 Manifesto echoed the mood of 'Labour and the Nation'. It provided 'the only alternative to Reaction and Revolution'[102] and reflected the fervent moderation of the bulk of the parliamentarians and trade union leaders.

Götterdämmerung

The performance of the 1929 Labour Government is overshadowed by
its melodramatic collapse, but the record over the previous two years is
more significant. Everything was dominated by the world recession.
The number of unemployed in Britain rose from 1,164,000 in May
1929 to 2,800,000 in July 1931. These figures were a major disaster
for a party that claimed a special tenderness towards working-class
interests,[103] but which remained rigidly attached to orthodox economic
policies.

The failure became associated closely with those who were to leave
the party. MacDonald's rhetoric grew increasingly obscure as he
endured the present and contemplated the beauties of the distant
socialist paradise. He was matched by the performance of Thomas
as the Minister responsible for unemployment. His *bonhomie* and
negotiating talents were of little value. He produced no solutions and
gladly left for the safety of the Dominions Office. Above all, it was
Snowden who emerged as the strict adherent of economic orthodoxy.
He gave unquestioning loyalty to the doctrines of free trade and the
balanced budget, and his established position as the party's financial
expert meant that few questioned his judgment.

The orthodoxy of Labour leadership produced little criticism
from the rank and file. In part, this was due to the leadership's
continuing use of socialist rhetoric. The crisis was, after all a crisis
of capitalism: socialists could not cope with the consequences, unless
the economic system was changed fundamentally. For this, Labour
needed a parliamentary majority. This was the great alibi used
repeatedly to calm the doubts of the faithful. Not that much
reassurance was needed. Most Labour back-benchers remained
instinctively loyal to their leaders, a crucial obstacle to any critical
challenge.[104]

The great alibi begged two basic questions. Would Labour, even with
a majority, have the knowledge and the will to introduce major changes?
'Labour and the Nation' gave little evidence of any clear strategy for
social transformation, while the arguments of Loyalists hardly suggested
an appetite for adventurous policies. More immediately, was the choice
portrayed correctly as being between orthodoxy and socialism? There
were some indications of an alternative approach. While most economists
remained fixed in their orthodoxy, Keynes was working towards his
major revolution in economic thought. He had acquired an appreciation
of the multiplier effect of public works programmes, and by early 1931
was calling for an abandonment of free trade.[105] Such dangerous

heresies left Snowden unmoved, but inevitably influenced some within the labour movement. Most colourfully, they attracted Mosley, one of Thomas's assistants. His proposals covered protection, industrial rationalisation, increasing purchasing power and the control of credit. These were described by Lloyd George as an injudicious mixture of Karl Marx and Lord Rothermere. It was not a brew likely to appeal to Labour's leaders. Mosley resigned and subsequently left the party. His subsequent career for several years distracted attention from the content of his proposals.[106]

Dissenting voices were ineffective. Mosley, tlte aristocrat, was viewed with suspicion by many trade union leaders who were unhappy about deflationary policies. The continuing criticisms of Maxton and his allies were dismissed easily as the self-indulgence of perennial malcontents. Ministerial lethargy was protected by the inevitable tendency to give the Government the benefit of the doubt.[107]

Failure was not restricted to the level of unemployment. The party might accept its inability to reform the economic system that produced unemployment, but at least it expressed a commitment to help those who were that system's victims. However, government initiatives on the level and terms of unemployment benefit demonstrated again its acceptance of financial orthodoxy.[108] The crucial response was not the attacks of the few ILP critics, but the much more discreet opposition of many trade union representatives. This was constrained to some extent by underlying loyalty and distaste for 'histrionics'. Moreover, Labour attitudes to unemployment relief were not wholly favourable. A puritanical strand in party culture encouraged attacks on so-called 'abuses': Labour spokesmen for retrenchment claimed to express the views of the decent working class.[109]

The painful implications of the commitment to orthodoxy were becoming increasingly obvious early in 1931. The growing cost of unemployment benefits conflicted with the dedication to the principle of a balanced budget. The obvious orthodox remedy was to cut public expenditure and Snowden duly appointed the May Committee to investigate possible economies. The Report recommended cuts of £97 million and the Cabinet formed an Economy Committee to consider the problem. The Government was faced with the stark warning that despite their scrupulous orthodoxy 'the trouble lay in the complete want of confidence in H.M.G. existing among foreigners.' There seemed no alternative to compliance. All five members of the Economy Committee[110] accepted the need for a balanced budget that must involve welfare cuts of some kind, while MacDonald and Snowden ascertained what level of economies would gain the support of other parties and the Bank of England.

These deliberations took place in an atmosphere of growing financial panic, and pessimism about the survival of the economic system. Labour Ministers had no alternative strategy and succumbed to orthodox demands. Opposition to cuts was expressed however by the General Council. This was the turning point in the crisis. Although one Minister might condemn members of the General Council as 'pigs',[111] their opposition strengthened the doubts of several within the Cabinet. Their dissent was not based on any attachment to radical solutions, but on an instinctive, rarely articulated but extremely powerful sense of class. The proposed economies were not the kind of imposition that a Labour Government could enforce on its own people. Nevertheless, it is significant that a bare majority of the Cabinet were still prepared to support a programme of economies that included a 10 per cent cut in unemployment benefit. This majority included not just MacDonald and Snowden and Thomas – but also Webb and Morrison. The sizeable minority reflected the trade union element and included Henderson, Clynes and Lansbury. This was not in any sense a split between right and left, but rather between those ready to take a national view as prescribed by the orthodoxy of the time, and those who were concerned to protect working-class interests.

This Cabinet division was the prelude to the formation of a National Government. The 'betrayal' was a godsend to Labour's moderate leaders.[112] Their responsibility for the Government's failures could be forgotten. All could be explained by the inadequacies of the 'traitors'. Initial Labour responses to the Government's collapse were generally restrained. A meeting of the NEC and the PLP and – significantly – the General Council rapidly produced a joint manifesto.[113] Although this expressed total opposition to the new Government, the tone was moderate. There was little immediate condemnation of MacDonald and his colleagues. Henderson, now leader, accepted that their defection was 'a direct loss to the labour movement'.[114] More significantly, the 1931 TUC showed a continuing scepticism about radical policies. Although there was blanket opposition to the Government, there was no readiness to reverse the recent drive for industrial conciliation.[115]

Bitterness within the party increased as the full extent of the Government's measures became apparent. When the Party Conference met early in October, there were indications of an increasing awareness that Labour's problems had not begun with the publication of the May Report. Many references to socialism were mere rhetoric, but advocacy of public ownership was more apparent than for several years. In particular there was a growing concern about the power of finance. It was generally argued that Labour had been toppled by the machinations of bankers.[116] The Conference showed little willingness to echo the earlier view that the MacDonald Government had made 'a most gallant effort to achieve a measure of Socialist transformation'.[117]

The Party Manifesto for the October election reflected an inevitable schizophrenia. It referred to the breakdown of capitalism and emphasised the need for public ownership and planning.[118] But there was a reaffirmation of faith in 'Labour and the Nation', and an expression of pride in the efforts of the minority Labour Government. How could it be otherwise? Henderson and his colleagues had worked assiduously to sell 'Labour and the Nation'. Any major shift would involve a rejection of their political strategy since 1918.

The extent of Labour's election defeat sharpened the break with the past. The old leadership was destroyed, and criticism of the 1929 Government's record appeared more permissible. In particular there could be a rejection of the woolly ambiguities epitomised by MacDonald. Such reactions could mean much or very little. They could indicate just a distaste for the earlier style of leadership — or they could involve a claim that previous policies had been inadequate and required replacement. Such changes would be compatible with the broad parliamentary perspective that had been established since 1918. A much more radical rejection of these fundamental assumptions would meet with many more obstacles. The younger parliamentarians were generally as committed to parliamentary methods as their predecessors. The collapse was a great shock, but commitment to existing institutions ran deep. Moreover, the continuation of such a commitment would be strengthened by the determination of trade union leaders to have a more central role in the party. This reaction to the crisis meant the continued involvement of a group who had deliberately rejected extra-parliamentary methods in favour of operating through existing institutions. They wanted a break with the past — but they wanted it within the broad framework of gradualism and accommodation.

Notes

1. *Report of Conference on Labour Representation*, pp.13-14.
2. *Report of Conference of Labour Representation Committee 1902*, p.20. *Labour Party Conference Report 1908*, pp.13 and 60. *LPCR 1912*, p.86.
3. *LPCR 1917*, pp.137-8. Also Ross McKibbin, *The Evolution of the Labour Party 1910-24* (Oxford University Press, London, 1974), pp.190-224.

4. For 1918 Constitution see ibid., pp.91-106, and also *LPCR January 1918,* pp.98-104.
5. For these, see G. Elton, *Life of James Ramsay MacDonald* (Collins, London, 1939), M.A. Hamilton, *J. Ramsay MacDonald* (London, Cape, 1929); also C.L. Mowat, 'Ramsay MacDonald and The Labour Party' in A. Briggs and J. Saville (eds.), *Essays in Labour History 2* (Macmillan, London, 1971), pp.129-51. M. Hamilton, *Arthur Henderson* (Heinemann, London, 1938).
6. See ibid, chs. 7 and 8 and also J. Winter, *Socialism and The Challenge of War* (Routledge, London, 1974), ch. 8.
7. See for example Hamilton, op. cit., pp.259-60 on the 1925 Conference.
8. *LPCR 1907,* pp.49-50.
9. *LPCR January 1918,* Appendix I, p.141.
10. Ibid.
11. By Ernest Bevin on behalf of the Transport Workers; see *LPCR 1925,* pp.244-52. The vote was 2,587,000 to 512,000.
12. See McKibbin, op. cit., ch. 1, sec. 3, also ch. 2.
13. See ibid., ch. 7. Also Michael Kinnear, *The British Voter* (Batsford, London, 1968), pp. 108-11.
14. For the ILP see R.E. Dowse, *Left in the Centre: The Independent Labour Party 1893-1940* (Longmans, London, 1966).
15. On the background to Taff Vale see John Saville, 'Trade Unions and Free Labour: The Background to the Taff Vale Decision' in A. Briggs and J. Saville (eds.), *Essays In Labour History* (Macmillan, London, 1960), pp.317-50. For the complex relationship between unions and party in the first decade see H.A. Clegg, Alan Fox and A.F. Thompson, *A History of British Trade Unions Since 1889, Vol. I, 1889-1910* (Clarendon Press, Oxford, 1964), chs. 7 and 10.
16. See Roy Gregory, *The Miners and British Politics 1906-14* (Oxford University Press, London, 1968).
17. *LPCR 1926,* pp.100-27.
18. *LPCR 1928,* p.58.
19. See Alan Bullock, *The Life and Times of Ernest Bevin, Vol. 1, 1881-1940* (Heinemann, London, 1960), and G. Blaxland, *J.H. Thomas: A Life for Unity* (Muller, London, 1964).
20. McKibbin, op. cit., ch. 9, sec. 1.
21. V.L. Allen, 'The Reorganisation of the T.U.C. 1918-27', *British Journal of Sociology,* 11, 1960, pp.24-43.
22. V.L. Allen, *Men and Work* (Hutchinson, London, 1964).
23. McKibbin, op. cit., ch. 9, sec. 2.
24. See his autobiography (Nicholson and Watson, London, 1934).
25. See *Report of Conference of LRC 1901,* pp.32-4.
26. See Frank Bealey and Henry Pelling, *Labour and Politics 1900-6* (Macmillan, London, 1958), ch. 5.
27. Ibid., pp.152-4
28. Ibid., ch. 6.
29. See ibid., chs. 10, 11 and Appendix C. Also Phillip Poirier, *The Advent of the Labour Party* (Allen and Unwin, London, 1958), chs. 14 and 15.
30. See Henry Pelling, 'Two By-Elections, Jarrow and Colne Valley 1907,' in his *Popular Politics and Society in Late Victorian Britain* (Macmillan, London, 1968). For Attercliffe see the entry on Joseph Pointer in Joyce Bellamy and John Saville, *Dictionary of Labour Biography Vol. II* (Macmillan, London, 1974), pp.300-3.
31. See McKibbin, op. cit., ch. 2, sec. 1.
32. Ibid., ch. 1, sec. 3. Also Neil Blewett, *The Peers, The Parties and The People: The General Elections of 1910* (Macmillan, London, 1972), ch. 12.

33. See K. Morgan, *Wales in British Politics 1868-1922* (University of Wales Press, Cardiff, 1970), pp.240-55.
34. See McKibbin, op. cit., ch. 3, sec. 4, and ch. 4.
35. On the limitations of the old franchise see Neil Blewett, 'The Franchise in the United Kingdom 1885-1914', *Past and Present*, 32, 1965.
36. Walsh even toyed with the idea of joining the new Government. See *Minutes of the Lancashire and Cheshire Miners' Federation*, January 1919.
37. See Kinnear, op. cit., pp.38-40.
38. See C. Cook and J. Ramsden (eds.), *By-Elections in British Politics* (Macmillan, London, 1973), pp.17-21.
39. In December 1919, Labour was near to victory in Bromley and in St Albans.
40. On relations with Liberals see McKibbin, op. cit., ch. 6.
41. See Kinnear, op. cit., for this and other elections in the twenties – also C. Cook, *The Age of Alignment: Electoral Politics in Britain 1922-9* (Macmillan, London, 1975).
42. See C. Cook, 'By-Elections of the First Labour Government' in Cook and Ramsden, op. cit.
43. Here at Southwark North, the sitting Labour member fought as an Independent Constitutionalist. See *LPCR 1927*, pp.11-12.
44. See Kinnear, op. cit., pp. 116-18.
45. Resolution moved by Keir Hardie, *Report of Conference on Labour Representation*, p.12.
46. Henry Pelling, *The Origins of the Labour Party 1880-1900* (Clarendon Press, Oxford, 1965, 2nd edition).
47. C. Tsuziki, *H.M. Hyndman and British Socialism* (Oxford University Press, London, 1961). Also Henry Collins, 'The Marxism of the Social Democratic Federation' in Briggs and Saville, *Essays in Labour History 2*, pp.47-69.
48. A.M. McBriar, *Fabian Socialism and English Politics 1884-1918* (University Press, Cambridge, 1962).
49. See Dowse, op. cit.
50. W.T. Stead, 'The Labour Party and the Books that Helped to Make It', *Review of Reviews 33*, (June, 1906). It is symptomatic of Labour's lack of distinctiveness that some MPs covered were not members of the separate Labour group.
51. See P.F. Clarke, *Lancashire and The New Liberalism* (University Press, Cambridge, 1971), especially ch. 15.
52. For a detailed account of the pre-war parliamentary party see J.H.S. Reid, *The Origins of the British Labour Party* (University of Minnesota Press, 1955), chs. 10 and 11.
53. See particularly the 'Green Manifesto' – *Let Us Reform the Labour Party*, 1909.
54. The tensions were also evident within the ILP. See particularly the *1909 ILP Conference Report*.
55. For one interpretation see H. Pelling, 'The Labour Unrest 1911-1914' in his *Popular Politics and Society*. For opposing contemporary positions see Unofficial Reform Committee, South Wales Miners' Federation, *The Miner's Next Step* (1912) and J.R. MacDonald, *Syndicalism: A Critical Examination* (Constable, London, 1912).
56. Sidney Buxton cited in Winter, op. cit., p.25.
57. For the problems of Labour MPs see *LPCR 1914*, pp.73-85.
58. *LPCR 1908*, pp.76-7.
59. On the super-patriots see R. Douglas, 'The National Democratic Party and the British Workers' League', *Historical Journal*, September 1972, pp.533-52, and J.O. Stubbs, 'Lord Milner and Patriotic Labour 1914-18', *English Historical Review*, October 1972, pp.717-54. Amongst these were John Hodge,

Will Thorne, G.H. Roberts.
60. See A.F. Brockway, *Inside the Left* (Allen and Unwin, London, 1941);
M. Gilbert, *Plough My Own Furrow: the Story of Lord Allen of Hurtwood
as Told Through his Writings and Correspondence* (Longmans, London, 1965).
Elton, op. cit. Snowden, op. cit.
61. See Royden Harrison, 'The War Emergency Workers National Committee'
in Briggs and Saville, *Essays in Labour History,* 2, pp.211-59, and Winter,
op. cit., ch. 7.
62. Ralph Miliband, *Parliamentary Socialism* (Allen and Unwin, London, 1961),
pp.47-58.
63. See *LPCR 1916,* pp.5-9, pp.124-5. Participation in government was approved
by 1,674,000 to 269,000.
64. *LPCR 1917,* pp.3-4 and pp.86-98. The vote here was 1,849,000 to 307,000.
65. See James Hinton, *The First Shop Stewards Movement* (Allen and Unwin,
London, 1973), also his 'The Clyde Workers' Committee and the Dilution
Struggle' in Briggs and Saville, *Essays in Labour History 2,* pp.152-84.
66. See Winter, op. cit., ch. 8.
67. See ibid. and McKibbin, op. cit., pp.91-2. For reactions to the Russian
developments, see Miliband, op. cit., p.54 and S.R. Graubard, *British Labour
and the Russian Revolution 1917-24* (Harvard University Press, Cambridge,
Mass., 1956). Also *LPCR January 1918,* pp.3-12.
68. See Winter, op. cit., pp.207-23.
69. See *LPCR 1917,* pp.101-5, 112-29, 134-6, 141-8.
70. This was approved at a Special Conference of the Labour Party and the TUC
on 28 December 1917. See also *LPCR June 1918,* pp.7-11. Winter, op. cit.,
p.262.
71. See *LPCR January 1918,* p.140.
72. For discussion of background see McKibbin, op. cit., pp.96-7.
73. *Labour and the New Social Order.*
74. *LPCR June 1918,* p.78.
75. See McKibbin, op. cit., p.97, for concern to attract middle class.
76. See *LPCR 1919,* p.27 (NEC statement): also the Chairman's Address by
John McGurk of the Lancashire Miners.
77. By 1,893,000 to 935,000.
78. See Bullock, *Vol. 1,* pp.133-40.
79. R. Page Arnot, *The Miners: Years of Struggle* (Allen and Unwin, London,
1953); for the other unions' viewpoints see Bullock, *Vol. 1,* pp.165-79, and
P.S. Bagwell, *The Railwaymen* (Allen and Unwin, London, 1963), pp.453-65.
80. See *TUC Report,* 1925, esp. Purcell's Address, p.77. For a portrait of one of
this group, see 'A.A. Purcell' in *Dictionary of Labour Biography,* Vol. I,
pp.275-9. See also R. Martin, *Communism and the British Trade Union
Movement: a Study of the National Minority Movement* (Clarendon Press,
Oxford, 1969).
81. For J.H. Thomas's views see W. Crook, *The General Strike* (Chapel Hill, New
York, 1931), p.296.
82. See Page Arnot, *The Miners,* Crook, op. cit., P. Renshaw, *The General Strike*
(Eyre Methuen, London, 1975), Bullock, *Vol. 1,* chs. 11-12.
83. See *Report of Conference of Trade Union Executives,* January 1927, and
the controversy over the Mond-Turner talks. Miliband, op. cit., ch. 15.
84. See L.J. Macfarlane, *The British Communist Party* (MacGibbon, London,
1966), and McKibbin, op. cit., pp.191-204.
85. K. Middlemass, *The Clydesiders* (Hutchinson, London, 1965).
86. See R. Lyman, *The First Labour Government 1924* (Chapman and Hall,
London, 1957), and *Beatrice Webb's Diaries 1924-32,* pp.1-54. Margaret
Cole (ed.), (Longmans, London, 1956).

87. See Bullock, *Vol. 1*, pp.236-43.
88. See R. Skidelsky, *Politicians and The Slump: the Labour Government of 1929-31* (Macmillan, London, 1967), ch. 2.
89. See Middlemass, op. cit., pp.182-4.
90. See *LPCR 1926*, pp.259-61. There had also been some consideration of future policy the previous year, see *LPCR 1925*, pp.218-24. For later developments see *LPCR 1927*, pp.51-2, pp.216-21, *1928*, pp.55-6, *1930*, pp.51-2, pp.169-70 and pp.303-7.
91. *LPCR 1927*, pp.181-90.
92. *NEC Minutes*, 26 December 1927.
93. Ibid., 29 February 1928.
94. Ibid., 28 March 1928. Further work on the draft was done by Greenwood, Henderson, and MacDonald. There were also consultations with the General Council, ILP, Miners' Federation, the transport unions and the Co-operative Union.
95. For further stages in its genesis see ibid., 2 May, 23 May, 26 May, and 27 June 1928. There is also a short account in *LPCR 1928*, p.4. See also R. Skidelsky, *Oswald Mosley* (Macmillan, London, 1975), p.169.
96. See *Labour and the Nation* (Labour Party, 1928).
97. For general debate, see *LPCR 1928*, pp.196-219.
98. Ibid., p.197.
99. Ibid., pp.200-3.
100. Ibid., pp.212-5.
101. In the summer of 1928, ILP leaders had been associated with Arthur Cook of the Miners in an unsuccessful campaign against the new TUC industrial policy. See Middlemas, op. cit., pp.213-21.
102. See *Labour's Appeal to the Nation*, 1929.
103. See Skidelsky, *Politicians and the Slump*, for a detailed account dominated by adherence to Keynesianism and aversion to socialism. Also Miliband, op. cit., ch. 6 and Ross McKibbin, 'The Economic Policy of the Second Labour Government' in *Past and Present*, August 1975, pp.95-123.
104. For a classic example of leaders' persuasion of the rank and file see MacDonald's speech to the 1930 Conference, *LPCR 1930*, pp.179-85. For the issues see ibid., pp.186-204.
105. See Skidelsky, *Politicians and the Slump*, pp.203-15.
106. See Skidelsky, *Oswald Mosley*, chs. 9-12.
107. For other critical figures see Middlemass, op. cit., pp.236-58. M. Foot, *Aneurin Bevan, Vol. I, 1897-1945* (MacGibbon, London, 1962), and Jennie Lee, *Tomorrow is a New Day* (MacGibbon and Kee, London, 1963), with her comment that Labour back-benchers reacted 'like a load of wet cement'. For a very different approach, Bullock, op. cit., chs. 16-17.
108. See Skidelsky, *Politicians and the Slump, passim*. Also entry on Margaret Bondfield in *Dictionary of Labour Biography*, 2, pp.39-45.
109. See for example the debates on the Anomalies Bill, July 1931, as cited in Skidelsky, op. cit., pp.319-21.
110. MacDonald, Snowden, Thomas, Henderson, Graham. For the most detailed examination see R. Bassett, *1931: Political Crisis* (Macmillan, London, 1958), a militantly pro-MacDonald analysis, also Bullock, *Vol. 1*, ch. 18.
111. Lord Passfield (Sidney Webb): see Beatrice Webb, *Diaries*, p.281.
112. Biographies of labour leaders have little to say on individual reactions to the drift of government policy from 1929 to 1931. They either ignore the question or explain that their subject was preoccupied with other matters!
113. For the 'official' account of the crisis see *LPCR 1931*, pp.3-6 with the manifesto on pp.5-6.
114. In the Commons on 8 September 1931.

115. *TUC Report*, 1931. See the debate on economic policy, pp.406-26.
116. See in particular the debate on Monetary and Banking Policy,
    LPCR 1931, pp.187-95.
117. Mary Agnes Hamilton in the *New Statesman*, 15 September 1931.
118. See *Labour's Call to Action: the Nation's Opportunity*.

2 TOWARDS A PROGRAMME 1931-1935

Labour's convalescence after 1931 was slow and uncertain. The optimism of the twenties was severely shaken. The experience of office had demonstrated that vague generalities furnished an inadequate programme and that the hostility of Labour's opponents was matched apparently by their capacity to frustrate any reforms. Furthermore, the party had presided over, and was identified with, a deteriorating economy. It had failed to protect its 'own people' from the rigours of depression. All this generated abundant debate within the party and raised doubts that could not be stilled by the convenient 'treachery' of MacDonald and his followers.

The débâcle gave the party a chance to rethink its strategy. The solutions developed provided Labour with a programme – and, in the long run, problems. A social democratic perspective emerged. Although not uncontroversial, it reflected a broad area of agreement between political and trade union leaders. The perspective was, in many ways, a response to the 1931 collapse, but two crucial developments also influenced the response to the party.

Although it appeared to many that the old economic order was collapsing, the economy slowly revived, in Britain and elsewhere. Unemployment reached a peak of 23 per cent of the insured population in August 1932, and then drifted downwards until 1938. Two aspects of this recovery are of particular importance. First, it was uneven. In areas dominated by traditional industries, recovery was tardy. In Scotland, South Wales, the North-East, Cumberland and Lancashire unemployment remained high. But in the Midlands and the South-East there was a contrasting industrial expansion. This had a significant effect on the politics of the labour movement. The trade unions representing the older depressed and heavily unionised industries – the Miners, the Railwaymen, the Cotton Workers – lost members and industrial power. The general unions – the Transport Workers, the Municipal Workers and the Distributive Workers – expanded amongst the new industries. The second feature of Britain's economic recovery was that it was unspectacular. It was presided over by a Government that professed its adherence to the purest economic orthodoxy, although there were new departures in several directions. The Government's style was epitomised by the austere

Chancellorship of Neville Chamberlain, and contrasted with the American New Deal, or even the approach of Swedish social democracy. Yet this caution reflected attitudes far beyond the Government. The response of the Labour Party to economic crisis was hardly iconoclastic.

Although its 1931 experiences led Labour to reconsider its domestic strategy, there was little criticism of the 1929 Government's record on international affairs. In this sphere a critical review was provoked by the events of the thirties. As the world economy gradually showed signs of revival, the international outlook darkened. The Sino-Japanese conflict, the inauguration of the Third Reich and the Italian attack on Abyssinia all compelled Labour to reconsider its international policies. Woven in with these crises, there was the perennially delicate question of the Labour attitude towards the Soviet Union, and by implication towards Communism. These issues preoccupied the party more and more; the resulting divisions were more fundamental and more passionate than those over domestic policy.

Although Labour in the years after 1931 seemed remote from office, the responses of the party to long-term strategic problems and to immediate crises set the direction of the party for a generation. The debates were often fierce: the flow of events was kaleidoscopic, but beneath the drama and the oratory, one fact was crucial. Labour's internal distribution of power had changed. This was the greatest single influence on the party's direction.

Whose Party? Labour and the Unions

The most immediate and obvious impact of the 1931 'events' was on the Parliamentary Party. Its reduction to 46 members meant that it occupied an atypically marginal place within the party for the next four years. Moreover, the parliamentary leadership underwent a generational change. Of the Big Five, MacDonald, Snowden and Thomas were now classed as renegades, while Clynes and Henderson both lost their seats in 1931. Both of these returned to Parliament, Henderson in a 1933 by-election and Clynes at the 1935 general election — but neither occupied a central place in the party. From 1931 to 1935, the PLP was led by a triumvirate, Lansbury (the only Cabinet Minister to survive the election), Attlee and Cripps.[1] The septuagenarian Lansbury was an inspirational rather than a practical leader, although he was endowed with considerable tactical and administrative skill. Attlee had made little impact in the 1929 Parliament but after 1931 he took a major share of the parliamentary

burden, and deputised for Lansbury while the latter was ill. Cripps was
a recent entrant to Labour politics. He had reacted to the 1931 collapse
by adopting a fervent and sometimes simplistic radicalism. This
impeccably upper-class lawyer spoke constantly of the need for
class-based action against capitalism. Yet the common portrait of Cripps
as a histrionic extremist is misleading. He sought answers to the basic
questions faced by the party, and in day-to-day parliamentary
exchanges his debating skills were formidable. The parliamentary
leadership was strengthened by the return of Greenwood at a 1932
by-election, but nothing could disguise the weakness of the PLP.
Many of its back-benchers were politically inexperienced trade unionists
who required guidance in debates. No less than 26 of them were
members of the Miners' Federation; most of them were stalwart loyalists
who had followed MacDonald almost to the end. They had underwritten
his condemnations of left-wing critics, but had drawn the line at his
desertion of the labour movement. Certainly the back-benchers
contained a few articulate members, but these tended to be rebels,
most notably Aneurin Bevan.[2] Overall, the temper of the PLP
was set by the articulate minority who held the dominant positions
because of their parliamentary gifts, but who did not always represent
accurately the conformity of many back-benchers. Younger figures
defeated in 1931 tended to look askance at the triumvirate's
leadership. The PLP was seen as 'a poor little affair'[3] dominated by
unreliable elements.

One problem emerging from 1931 was that the normal overlap
between the party's parliamentary and extra-parliamentary bodies was
greatly reduced. At one time, Lansbury was the only MP on the
National Executive. This body was a crucial forum for the
re-examination of Labour strategy and policy. Its most obvious
characteristic was the considerable continuity of membership. Both
the trade union and the women's sections were largely unaltered,
and were pillars of loyalty and orthodoxy. The constituency section,
although its composition could be dominated in the same way by the
large unions, was more varied. Two of the younger defeated Ministers,
Dalton and Morrison,[4] were always returned to this section, and thereby
retained a central position in the party's counsels. Both of them could
be seen as moderates who were ready to throw their weight against
what they saw as the wilder reactions to 1931. However, trade union
leaders sometimes seemed prepared to use the constituency places as
a means of involving (and compromising) their critics. Thus, Cripps
was elected to the Executive in 1934 in place of another critic,

Trevelyan. Basically, however, the Executive remained dominated by moderate trade unionists and their allies who mobilised support for policy initiatives frequently inspired by Dalton and Morrison.

One consequence of the 1931 experience was a rationalisation of the Executive's sub-committee structure. On 16 December 1931, the NEC decided to create a Policy Committee. This contained initially eight members — four from the trade union section, one Co-operator, plus Dalton, Morrison and Lansbury.[5] This became the forum where policy documents were examined in detail before presentation to the full Executive. Its membership symbolised the emerging concordat between trade unionists and the coming generation of moderate Labour politicians. The Policy Committee subsequently spawned four sub-committees: Finance and Trade; Reorganisation of Industry; Local Government and Social Services; and Constitutional. These sub-committees, a blend of Executive members and co-opted 'specialists', produced the documentary reactions to 1931.

The domination of the Executive by a normally unshakeable moderate majority meant that policy documents rarely received substantial critical amendment. Similarly, Executive proposals to the Party Conference were prima facie, unlikely to cause concern within the delegations of the large unions, since the process of policy formulation had been dominated by people who shared largely the same aspirations. In the fragmented and depressed union world of the early thirties only five unions could boast affiliated memberships of more than 100,000,[6] and these five unions could dominate the Party Conference if they cared to.[7]

Table 1: Unions over 100,000 (1931)

Miners	400,000
Transport Workers	254,096
Railwaymen	253,442
Municipal Workers	250,000
Textile Workers	188,875

It is true that in the early thirties, only the Textile Workers showed an unblemished loyalty to the Executive, but the deviations of the other four were only on specific issues. In general, the leaderships of these unions were only too willing to support the pronouncements of the Executive, both by card votes and by vigorous speeches. The more

critical trade union delegations controlled fewer votes: the Distributive
Workers with just over 90,000 votes in 1932 was the most consistently
critical sizeable union throughout the decade.

Within the purely party structures, there was good reason to believe
that trade unionists could influence considerably the development of
policy, or if they chose a more passive role, they could protect the
initiatives of moderates such as Dalton and Morrison. Such influence
was weakest inside the PLP, since the back-bench stalwarts tended to be
overshadowed by their leaders. How far this potential for union
dominance led to particular policies being adopted is something that
will be analysed later, but clearly there existed the potential for a
significant degree of control.

Such potential had always been there; but during the twenties, the
appeal of direct action and the dominance of MacDonald had prevented
its realisation. Now these inhibitions had gone. Trade union suspicions
of Labour politicians and 'intellectuals' had been inflamed by the collapse,
and concerted attempts were made to harmonise the relationship
between the political and industrial wings of the labour movement.
Such attempts centred around the need to ensure that party and TUC
pronouncements on the same issue were in agreement, although
obviously the influence of trade unionists within the purely party
organisations reduced the scope for conflict. Nevertheless after 1931
trade union leaders of the highest rank devoted themselves almost
totally to the TUC: only at the Party Conference did they appear to
chastise their critics. Their acolytes usually carried out their wishes on
the Executive and in the PLP, although after 1931 some large unions
had no parliamentary representation.

This division of labour intensified the need to harmonise the
party-TUC relationship at the apex. This involved the reinvigoration
of the largely moribund National Joint Council (National Council of
Labour from 1934). It was significant that the initiative came from the
General Council. A memorandum from the TUC's General Secretary,
Citrine, provided a basis for discussion in January 1932. The General
Council's desire for a reconstructed Joint Council showed that they
considered one cause of the previous year's disaster to lie in the
separation of the Labour Movement's two wings. Now it was claimed
that

> the General Council should be regarded as having an integral
> right to initiate and participate in any political matter which
> it deems to be of direct concern to its constituents.[8]

Citrine's proposals were generally accepted by both the Executive and the Parliamentary Party.[9] The Council's membership was revised to cover the Chairman and six members of the General Council; the Chairman and two members of the National Executive; and the Chairman and two members of the Parliamentary Party.[10] The strength of the TUC contingent is notable, and the Executive group normally included at least one trade unionist. The Council now met monthly instead of quarterly, on the day before the Executive convened.

It is clear that on some issues the Council (or an expanded variant, consisting of the full General Council, NEC and the Parliamentary Committee) played more than its formal harmonising role. Especially in the crucial areas of foreign policy, defence and relations with Communists, the pronouncements of the Council were crucial. Obviously such pronouncements were the outcome of sometimes prolonged discussions, but the membership ensured that the end product would not be distasteful to the General Council. Equally, although Council pronouncements could be contradicted by the TUC and the Party Conference, the likelihood of this was remote.

The importance of the Council was demonstrated by the role envisaged for it when the formation of a future Labour Government was under discussion. One understandable reaction to 1931 was a reluctance to grant much freedom to parliamentary leaders. The reaction to the spells cast by MacDonald had been to pass the problem over to the new Constitutional Committee. Its meetings were attended by two TUC representatives, and the Joint Council was kept informed of its discussions. When a report, 'Labour and Government', was published in 1933, it contained few novelties. But it did note that the NJC, 'the most representative body in the Labour Movement ... should meet and record its opinion as to the advisability or otherwise of the Labour Party taking office.'[11]

Although in 1945 there was no suggestion that this procedure should be followed, the suggestion is indicative in two ways. One is clearly the extent to which TUC supervision of party behaviour was accepted in the years after 1931; the other is the clear suggestion that what mattered was the labour *movement* rather than the party. The party should be seen as one hopefully integrated element in this larger body.

Collaboration was not only pursued through the machinery of the NJC. The party and the TUC exchanged representatives on significant committees. The most important case was the development of a dual exchange between the NEC Policy Committee and the TUC Economic Committee.[12] It was also significant that the two party representatives

on the latter body were Dalton and Morrison. Sometimes the two
committees met together in an attempt to solve seemingly intractable
problems — for example, the production of an agreed statement on
worker representation in publicly-owned industries. A further
integrating development began in the autumn of 1932 with a decision
that the development of an agreed industrial policy should be assisted
by a division of labour.[13] Initially, it was decided that the party
should deal with schemes for coal and power; and the TUC with iron
and steel. Thus, the plan for the public ownership of iron and steel
was developed largely on the industrial side of the movement, in
close consultation with the Steelworker's union. The party's role was
comparatively small.

The new party-union relationship, in which the TUC was both
more distinctive and yet more involved, was associated with two men.
Bevin, the Transport Workers' leader, and Citrine, the TUC General
Secretary, were temperamentally poles apart. The forceful, ostentatiously
proletarian 'Dockers' KC' contrasted with the precise, lucid Citrine.
Yet on the central policy issues they agreed. On international affairs,
Communism and the economy, the Bevin-Citrine axis dominated
the General Council and the TUC, and accordingly, the TUC side
of any joint discussions.

Labour, after 1931, was not a trade union-dominated party. Certainly
it was most unlikely to conflict radically with TUC interests, but
there were tensions as the TUC sought, usually with success, to secure
a larger and more regularised share in party counsels. The TUC leaders
and the moderate politicians could normally work closely but inevitably
there were occasions when industrial and political interests conflicted.
Even trade union MPs tended to react to problems in a political or
parliamentary fashion rather than in an industrial or union one. Such
misunderstandings were at their greatest when policy differences were
added to different priorities. Inevitably, therefore, the attitude of Bevin
and his colleagues towards Lansbury and Cripps was often critical.
Basically the growth of trade union influence led not to a meddlesome
interference with the minutiae of party policy, but to a broad
paternalistic supervision of a potentially unruly infant who had been
inclined to stray in the past and might do so again. Such a tendency
to stray was increased for some by the experiences of 1931 and
the accompanying depression. The party might be linked more closely
to the trade unions, but the political and economic situation arguably
included factors likely to produce a radicalisation.

Reactions to Disaster: Labour Opinion in the Early Thirties

The collapse of the second Labour Government and the subsequent electoral disaster led to prolonged debate over the causes of the débâcle. The depth of the discussion was unique in party history and produced several analyses of the strengths and weaknesses inherent in Labour's commitment to parliamentary gradualism.

The most superficial answers emphasised contingent factors. The 1929 Government had been dependent on Liberal votes and therefore could not produce any radical policies. This argument conveniently ignored the fact that some Liberals were ready to promote more radical responses to economic crisis than most Labour Ministers. A second argument of this type emphasised the personal failings of MacDonald and his immediate circle. Now that the party had been purged, the problems were removed. Once again the argument evaded crucial factors. It was convenient for those Ministers who had supported MacDonald and Snowden in Cabinet to shift all the opprobrium on to the defectors. The same applied to the ranks of parliamentary loyalists who had provided MacDonald with unquestioning support, and had systematically crucified any dissenters. Why had Labour in office appeared at best sterile and unimaginative and at worst ready to consider penalising those whom it claimed to represent? In the immediate aftermath of defeat, in an environment of deepening economic crisis, the debate widened to produce a critical analysis of Labour's basic strategy.

Most participants in the debate who were prepared to extend their examination beyond the failings of MacDonald and his friends were ready to agree on some points. They could unite in their opposition to what they now viewed as the vague commitments of 'Labour and the Nation'. What was needed in future programmes was a set of practical, well-researched proposals, backed by a thorough, informed and tenacious commitment.[14] Such a reaction was central to the early decision to establish a Policy Committee. For the first time, most Labour politicians began to face the problem of how to realise the party's ideals through a series of specific proposals.

Equally there was a general reaction against what was viewed as an inappropriate obsession with ceremonial trappings. The superficially comical concern of Labour leaders with the social niceties of their positions produced scathing denunciations: 'Who will believe that the Labour Party means business so long as some of its stalwarts sit up and beg for sugar plums like poodles in a drawing room?'[15] This was underlain by a broad agreement that Labour in office had strayed from

its roots, a diagnosis interpreted by some as necessitating a rediscovery
and revision of basic principles, and by others as requiring a tightening
and strengthening of links with the unions.

Agreement on the need for clarity, a firm political will, and the
need for Labour to rediscover its lost soul, left all the options open. The
substantive response to 1931 had to involve clarity about *specific*
proposals, and commitment to whatever methods appeared necessary
to implement them. This is where the disagreements developed. They
centred around the question of how far the 1931 experience had
undermined the traditional Labour belief in the effectiveness of the
parliamentary road, and in the neutrality of existing administrative
institutions. A significant rift developed between those who claimed
that these two pillars of Labour orthodoxy should be at least inspected,
and those who continued to believe that existing political institutions
and processes would work satisfactorily, given clear proposals and a
firm commitment.

The most articulate exponents of the more radical thesis were
Harold Laski and Stafford Cripps.[16] In each case, this commitment
involved a development of their thought as a response to 1931. Laski
came to graft a broadly Marxist view of the possibility of a gradualist
transformation on to his radical liberalism. Cripps switched rapidly
from a position of orthodox moderation to an uncritical and often
superficial recital of Marxist terminology that sometimes hid his
continuing commitment to Anglicanism. The strengths and ambiguities
of this position can be seen clearly in Laski's immediate reaction to the
collapse of the Labour Government. Having attributed the disaster to
the machinations of financial interests, Laski drew the moral that:

> the road to power is far harder than Labour has so far been led to
> imagine. If it retains its faith in Socialism, it will meet a challenge
> that does not passively accept its right to govern in a Socialistic
> way ...[17]

What did this involve? For Laski, it would lead to 'drastic emergency
measures', whose consequences could not be foreseen. He was still
ready to accept the possibility that, unlike 1789, 1848 or 1917, the
powerful vested interests of Great Britain may concur in the erosion of
their authority,[18] but if not, then the prospect was uncertain. Two
related points arise from this argument, and also from the similar
analyses of Cripps. The scenario developed by the critics was within
the parliamentary tradition. The party should secure a parliamentary

majority and then put the matter to the test. Appropriate changes should be made to parliamentary practice in order to implement government policies. Emergency powers could be taken, the Lords swamped with sympathetic new peers — but these changes were essentially moves within the parliamentary arena. There was no suggestion that Labour's strength might be increased by a concurrent mobilisation of industrial power. The radical critics were thus encased for the most part within Labour's parliamentary tradition. Their proposals tended to concentrate on how far such institutions could be turned to Labour's benefit, instead of acting as obstacles.

Although these apparently radical critiques of parliamentarianism were not dismissals of Labour's basic position, this did not prevent them being attacked as undemocratic by many moderates who feared the ease with which Labour could become identified with opposition to 'democracy'. It also reflected a specifically trade union reaction to 1931, a deepened distrust of 'unreliable intellectuals'. This was epitomised by Bevin's onslaughts on Cripps and his sympathisers.[19] The flirtation of 'intellectuals' with new ideas was irresponsible. To several trade union leaders it made for instability, it jeopardised the future of the labour movement, and above all, whatever price would be paid as the result of radical gestures would fall with greatest impact on the already hard-pressed ranks of organised labour. Although the critical analysis of parliamentarianism that developed after 1931 is unique in party history, it was limited by two factors. The critics remained imprisoned within the broad parliamentary framework; they did not envisage any way in which this might be replaced. More important, the analysis received an unsympathetic hearing inside the party. Cripps's statements were seen as electorally embarrassing, and the whole issue seemed of limited importance to politicians and above all trade union leaders preoccupied with ameliorating the worst effects of the depression.

A more profound radical response to 1931 could be found by focusing on another issue — what did the experience of office show about the durability of Labour's socialist commitment? Tawney argued that durability could be increased by focusing upon specifically socialist proposals. This was really a variant of the agreed need for clarity and tenacity, although Tawney suggested that a firm commitment to socialism would produce considerable stress. The party:

> must create in advance a temper and a mentality of a kind to carry
> it through not one crisis, but a series of crises ... Onions can be

eaten leaf by leaf, but you cannot skin a live tiger paw by paw; vivisection is its trade, and it does the skinning first.[20]

Other critics of moderation suggested that the problems were more deep-rooted and could not be met by determination alone. A more pessimistic view was taken by Bevan in a private statement, written after 1931. The party's problem was seen as political schizophrenia, its class base meant that it climbed to power 'by articulating the demands of the dispossessed ... although all the time, its heart is tender with the promise of peaceful gradualism.'[21] Bevan highlighted strategic dilemmas that were perceived only dimly even in the aftermath of 1931. Was Labour to depend on a class base or a national one? How could it deal with centres of private power in the short run, while seeking to eliminate them over the long term? Could any gradualist position be reconciled with a meaningful socialist commitment? What, if anything, was the alternative to gradualism? These were — and are — the basic dilemmas of social democracy. They were not really discussed after 1931: a solution, as we shall see, emerged, not as the result of a theoretical disputation, but as the outcome of a lengthy convoluted debate about specific policies.

Many of the pessimistic claims about the irreconcilability of socialism and gradualism were based on an often unarticulated economic premise. Only by a thorough social transformation was there any possibility of satisfying the demands of the working class. The accompanying stark dichotomy between increasing misery and equity, chaos and rational planning was particularly plausible, as unemployment continued to increase. In contrast, 'there was no unemployment in the Soviet Union. That was the biggest claim of all that Russian planners could make in the early thirties.'[22] The contrast with the apparently collapsing 'Capitalist West' led to a strengthening of the identification of the Soviet Union with socialism. In some cases — for example the Webbs — the identification was almost uncritical;[23] in many others, it was more mixed but still significant. Before the 1931 disaster, Labour thinking on economic questions had been a blend of vague Utopianism, and rigid outdated orthodoxy, one for the distant future and one for the present. After the collapse, specifically socialist analyses of the economic crisis became far more central to party thinking. Basically, it was agreed that only socialism could end large-scale unemployment. For many this became an article of faith: in so far as an explanation was provided, it was usually in terms of increased mechanisation, leading to redundancies, depressed wages, stagnant consumption and a crisis of overproduction. This 'inevitable' process could be counteracted only by a rationalisation of the economic system through public ownership and socialist planning.

There is no doubt that this was the primary Labour reaction to depression. Socialism was the only answer; until then, all that could be done was to make the position of the 'inevitably' unemployed as tolerable as possible. Yet during the early thirties, a new economic perspective, Keynesianism, began to acquire its first adherents. Its eventual acceptance by the wartime Government was to circumscribe debates on socialist strategy for the next thirty years. Indeed by suggesting the feasibility of a fully employed largely private economy, it could be said to have consigned many interpretations of socialism into an ideological museum.

During the early thirties Keynesian elements appeared in some policy documents; there were references to the need for the Government to make good the failure of industrialists to invest, and to the multiplier effect of such government spending. Nevertheless these were small elements when viewed alongside the central belief that socialism was the only answer, and also the apparent continuing commitment to a balanced budget. The limited impact of Keynesianism on Labour thinking was attributable perhaps to a revulsion against 'mere tinkering'.[24] The orthodoxy of Snowden had been replaced largely by the new orthodoxy of public ownership and socialist planning. There were influential Labour spokesmen — especially in the trade unions — for whom Keynesianism could be extremely attractive. It promised them most of what they wanted without a major social upheaval: in the long run, it was this strand in the thinking of the thirties that was to have most influence on the policies of the party.

It had a strong affinity with the characteristic pattern of trade union leadership that developed during the thirties. Such leaders were influenced not just by Labour's political collapse, but also by the failure of the General Strike and the rigours of the depression. In contrast to the twenties, the thirties were a decade of industrial quiescence. Only in the cotton industry in 1932 and amongst London busmen in 1937 was there widespread and official industrial action. The TUC had moved away from its flirtation with direct action. Instead, it collaborated with employers to reorganise industries. This shift had been symbolised by the abortive Mond-Turner talks in 1928, but in the partial recovery after 1932 it produced some results. Trade unions, especially the two larger general ones, established close relationships with some major employers. Although the approach was symbolised by

Bevin, Citrine and later by Dukes of the GMW, it enjoyed wider
support. The unions in the traditional and contracting industries simply
did not feel strong enough to confront the employers with strike action.
This strategy of seeking a consensus with employers' organisations was
obviously of great significance. It led not only to the acceptance in
practice of the broad contours of the economic system, but also to a
degree of collaboration with the National Government. The creeping
interventionism of that Government's economic policies meant that
part of the TUC strategy was a search for membership of government
committees.[25] This enjoyed a limited success in the thirties as a prelude
to the massive wartime incorporation of trade unionists into the
Whitehall machinery. The opposition within the trade union movement
to this strategy of collaboration was always weak. It was difficult after
the 1926 collapse to argue that confrontation could be successful, and
the critical position was complicated and compromised by becoming
intertwined with the emotive question of Communist 'subversion'
within the trade union movement.

The behaviour of most trade union leaders during the thirties
allied to the early exercises in government control, were amongst
the first signs of an 'agreed' position on economic affairs, that would
eventually produce severe difficulties for the Labour Party. A more
obvious development of this kind was the growth of cross-party or
non-party groupings on economic and social matters. In part, this
reflected the collapse of the Liberals as a significant political force.
Refugees from the Liberal Party were ready to use other vehicles to
develop and expound their ideas. The production of 'agreed solutions'
under the aegis of such bodies as the Council of Action and the Next
Five Years Group showed how far politicians of all parties, trade union
leaders and liberal academics could unite on a programme that
involved some economic planning and reasonable standards of welfare.
The thirties are often remembered as the decade when orthodox
Marxism secured a place in intellectual life, but beneath the rhetoric,
the embryo of the mixed economy was already being formed.[26]

Labour reactions to 1931 were normally from within the confines
of established British political practice. Some articulate individuals
questioned the effectiveness of Labour's parliamentary strategy, but
they did so from within shared assumptions about the centrality of
parliamentary politics. It did become an accepted tenet of party
policy to recommend socialism as the only answer to unemployment.
Here the experience of depression perhaps could be said to have
radicalised the party's outlook. But, although Keynesianism had little

direct influence, the distinctiveness of Labour's prescriptions was diluted by the increasing readiness of some Liberals and Conservatives to accept government intervention in the economy. It is schematic but useful to see the fight for Labour's soul in the early thirties as a contest between Marx and Keynes. Superficially the former made some striking conversions — but while they were endowed with literary and rhetorical skills, they did not command the allegiance of the 'big battalions'. In their strategy, most trade union leaders sought not to change the system radically, but to make incremental improvements. They subscribed to Keynes's dictum that 'in the long run we are all dead'.

Inside and Outside Lefts

The Labour left's criticisms of the 1929 Government were always treated with contempt by the party leadership and its back-bench supporters. The critics were portrayed as a strident ill-disciplined minority who failed to appreciate the responsibilities of office. The opposition had centred around the small ILP group identified in particular with Maxton and the other Clydesiders. Now their criticism could be said to be vindicated by the Government's collapse, yet there remained an abyss between the style of the critics and that of the 'responsible' trade union leaders. The problem of influence still remained.

The position of the party's left-wing critics was weakened further during the early thirties by two developments. The Independent Labour Party disaffiliated from the Labour Party in July 1932. This destroyed the critics' established organisation within the wider Labour Party.[27] Secondly, the Communist Party, having condemned Labour politicians as 'Social Fascists' since the initiation of their 'new line', began in 1933 to advocate united working-class action against the menace of Fascism.[28] This change was crippling to the Labour left, as all the latter's criticisms could be labelled once again as Communist-inspired.

The eventual exit of the ILP was superficially over the question of party discipline. The problem had been a peculiar one since the ILP had its own Conference whose decisions often conflicted with the decisions of wider Labour Party bodies. It might be thought that the friction would have lessened after October 1931 since the reaction to MacDonald within the party as a whole reduced the occasions for conflict. Nevertheless the dispute continued. Underneath the disciplinary question, it is clear that the spokesmen of the ILP held fundamentally distinct views on policy. They considered that the

problems of the Labour Party had not been settled by the exit of
MacDonald and his friends. The *whole* strategy had been mistaken
because of the unquestioning reliance on Parliament. ILP
pronouncements began to shift away from criticisms of the tenacity of
Labour leaders to claims that only a revolutionary policy, not a
reformist one, would suffice. 'The duty of the ILP was to prepare the
workers for the struggle for power and for maintenance of that power
during the introduction of Socialism.'[29] This was an intelligible reaction
to the experiences of 1929-31, although what it entailed in positive
terms was never spelt out. Eventually in July 1932 an ILP Conference
voted to disaffiliate by 241 votes to 142. The majority included several
of the ILP's leading figures, especially Maxton, but their individual
prominence did not prevent the weakened party from becoming little
more than a very small parliamentary group. The predictions of a broad
radical upsurge that would lead to the ILP replacing the Labour Party
proved to be grotesquely unrealistic.[30]

The large minority vote against disaffiliation showed that many who
were critical of the direction of Labour policy were nevertheless anxious
to maintain a connection with the larger organisation. These
'affiliationists', led by E.F. Wise, clearly needed to develop a new
organisational base. It was this need that led in October 1932 to the
formation of the Socialist League.[31] The ILP exiles were not the only
element that contributed to the new body. A smaller influx came from
the absorption of the Society for Socialist Inquiry and Propaganda
(SSIP), founded by Cole in June 1931. The officers of this organisation
represented a wide range of Labour opinion. Bevin was Chairman while
Vice-Chairmen ranged from the Sovietphile D.N. Pritt, to the extremely
moderate Steel Workers' leader, Arthur Pugh. The marriage of the
ex-ILP members and this propagandist and research group was not an
easy one. Several of those involved had doubts about the exercise.
They feared that any attacks on Labour policy would only replicate the
ILP situation. This doubt was enough to inhibit Bevin from any
involvement in the new organisation, and Cole, Pugh and Attlee soon
ceased to take much part in the League's affairs.

With this departure of the more moderate elements, the League
became dominated by representatives of the left. Cripps, Mellor, Wise
(until his death), Horrabin and J.T. Murphy were all articulate critics of
Labour policy. The League became affiliated to the party, in spite of
reservations by some Executive members. It was governed by a National
Council and held annual conferences, at which policy resolutions were
debated. Thus, there was always scope for divergence between League

and Labour Party policies.

The spokesmen of the League were overwhelmingly from the professions and included Etonians, Harrovians and Wykehamists. At first, the organisation received a sympathetic hearing amongst the PLP leadership. Cripps was close to both Lansbury and Attlee and four other articulate parliamentarians were also involved. Such support was relatively unimportant, given the distribution of power within the labour movement. The League had minimal support amongst trade union leaders. Bevin took an extremely hostile view although the T & GW Assistant General Secretary, Clay, remained a League member. He was almost unique. The disinterest or hostility of other trade unionists doomed the League as an aspirant for influence from the very start.

After a diplomatic beginning, League spokesmen began to oppose official policy. The research component of the League's work was forgotten as League policies began to be rejected by an NEC filled with moderate politicians and trade unionists. Inevitably this process of differentiation in policy reinforced a separateness originating in the League's development of its own organisation. By the 1933 Conference, the League was the principal — and ineffective — opposition to the NEC. It had been earmarked by some as an undisciplined threat to the hopes of electoral victory. Its 'Programme of Action' focused on two areas. Both were highly sensitive. Socialist legislation should be introduced with the help of Emergency Powers, and the public ownership of industry should be extended more rapidly and more widely than official policy suggested.

The final failure of the League to change party policy at the 1934 Conference emphasised the difficulties faced by a Labour left, unlikely to secure any worth-while trade union support. Its opposition to party policy was both outspoken and vague. The melodramatic phrases in which Executive views were attacked were paralleled by uncertainties about the left's alternative prescriptions. The melodrama heightened moderate opposition, while the vagueness made collapse in the face of moderate onslaughts more likely. It is difficult to escape the conclusion that for many of the League's supporters, rhetoric was almost everything. Objections to official policy were portrayed in lurid terms, but that was all. The League was frequently referred to as 'intellectual'. This is misleading in that its spokesmen were strong on rhetoric and weak on doctrine. They spoke of 'a will to power' in order to achieve 'real socialism'; but they did not clarify what this involved. In this as in their ambivalent relationship with the party, they typified successive generations of the Labour left. Above all, the League was a paper tiger: although full of sound and fury, its formal membership never rose above 3,000 and its spokesmen occupied roles which gave them much more publicity than influence. The League was important as a specific manifestation of the frustrations of the Labour left, but that was all.

The early thirties demonstrated the problems faced by the Labour left in another direction, that of its relationship with the Communist Party. Within this controversy, there were several interrelated debates. Prior to 1931, both the party and the TUC had made their attitudes clear. In a series of decisions in the mid-twenties, the Labour Party had severed all connections with the Communists, while the TUC, in the aftermath of the General Strike, had taken a firm line against Communist 'disruption'. These positions generated little criticism so long as the Communist Party stood in not very splendid isolation, but its proposal for united action against Fascism in February 1933 reactivated a debate that was to occupy the party for more than six years.

During these years, the basic arguments remained constant. They are important as indicators of basic disputes about the nature of Labour's commitment to socialism and to parliamentary democracy. Those who advocated no dealings at all with the Communists based many of their arguments on the threat that would be posed by any such alliance to the integrity and success of the Labour Party. At its most reasonable, the integrity argument was based on suspicion of Communist motives, but it often included a proprietorial attitude towards all left-wing political activity. Perhaps the most powerful objection to any united activity was that it would be electorally disastrous. Besides these short-term arguments, there were objections to Communist strategy. As in the ILP case, these turned on the question of parliamentarianism, typically linked by the Labour leadership with 'democracy': 'The Communist Party does not believe in Parliamentary Democracy. Communist Parties are allowed by the Third International to enter Parliament in order to destroy it "from within".'[32]

Apart from differences over political strategy in Britain, opponents of united action sometimes introduced the issue of the lack of democracy inside the Soviet Union. Sometimes, this was spelt out in sharp terms: in 1933, a General Council Report unambiguously labelled the Soviet system as a dictatorship, comparable with those of Germany and Italy.[33] More often, it was simply argued that the Soviet experience was an unreliable guide in British conditions.

These organisational, electoral and doctrinal arguments against united action were countered above all by claims that working-class and socialist unity must be the first priority. This was backed frequently by the argument that the differences between Communists and social democrats must be bridged in order to deal with the continuing crisis of capitalism. It was difficult for supporters of this position to argue that united action would greatly increase the strength of the left. By 1933, the Communist Party was in an extremely parlous state, with a membership of only 6,000, and would bring little weight to any joint effort. A more powerful argument concerned the lack of enterprise shown by official Labour leaders in the face of economic and international crises. Their commitment to the painstaking restatement of policy, and their suspicion of any extra-parliamentary agitation led to Labour protests against unemployment and the rise of Hitler having a staid ultra-respectable tone. The weighty measured pronouncements of the National Joint Council were of little appeal when contrasted with the heady enthusiasms of the National Unemployed Workers' Movement. This body, labelled by Citrine as 'a subsidiary of the Communist Party',[34] dominated the organisation of the unemployed.[35] United action did make an appeal to some activists on these grounds: it offered a vague hope of achieving something in a period of economic despair, when official Labour seemed remote from office, and concerned with the minutiae of policies.

Advocates of the United Front never had a hope of capturing the party. Professional politicians and trade unionists combined to forestall any such move. Above all, as with the Socialist League, the cause made very little headway within the unions. Amongst those with sizeable votes only the Distributive Workers, and on one occasion the Miners, showed much enthusiasm. At the 1933 Conference, the issue was easily disposed of, but it proved difficult to 'control' all activists.[36] Eventually in May 1934, the Executive decreed that any united action with the Communist Party or its subsidiaries was incompatible with Labour Party membership.[37] This widening of the restriction to cover association marked the first instalment in a vigorous campaign by the Executive. It produced a vehement clash at the 1934 Conference between Bevan and Bevin; it also produced an overwhelming victory for the Executive.

There is no doubt that the United Front agitation further weakened a Labour left that was already weak in resources. Throughout the decade it was an unhappy minority in a party that it had no hope of conquering. To the trade union leaders and the professional moderate politicians, the critics were misguided, unrepresentative and dangerous.

In turn, the critics reacted against what they viewed as the lack of enterprise characteristic of the party leadership. Yet the critics failed to present any alternative. They never resolved whether it was better to remain an impotent minority within the party, or to become impotent and isolated outside. Their energies were captured and dissipated by the tortuous United Front question. They chafed at the constraints imposed by the parliamentary strategy, but they never began to elaborate a clear alternative.

The Formulation of Home Policy 1931-5

'One of the causes of our fiasco in 1931 was the complete lack of a policy on the more important domestic questions.'[38] This diagnosis inspired much of Labour's policy-making in the early thirties. Labour's economic and social policies under MacDonald had combined Utopian aspirations with conventional specific proposals. Now, an attempt was made to provide detailed policy statements on central problems. These were coupled with a suggestion that the solutions could be seen as steps towards a qualitative social change. The results of this exercise were crucial in that they provided the core of Labour's domestic policy for the next twenty years.

Preparation of policy statements for presentation to the 1932 Conference was centred around two of the new Policy Committee's sub-committees. The Finance and Trade one began work in February 1932 under the chairmanship of Dalton.[39] Its membership of five included the co-opted expert Pethick-Lawrence. At the first meeting, it was decided that Dalton, along with Greenwood, the Head of the Research Department, and Middleton, the Sub-Committee's Secretary, should discuss key problems with the 'City Group', a new unofficial group of City experts who were sympathetic to Labour. The basic question faced by the Sub-Committee was the extent of public ownership of the banking system. All could agree on the public ownership of the Bank of England but there was debate over whether this should be extended to include the joint-stock banks. Such an extension had been accepted in rather ambiguous terms by the Executive at the 1931 Conference.

The two leading figures on the Sub-Committee prepared memoranda; Pethick-Lawrence on 'Currency and Banking Organisation', and Dalton on 'The National Investment Board'. The latter was envisaged as a means of controlling credit creation and investment. These proposals were discussed by the Sub-Committee early in May 1932, and then were examined by a larger group. This contained not only members of the City Group, but also Ernest Bevin. His interest in these questions had grown following his appointment to the MacMillan Committee on Finance and Industry in 1930. The larger meeting examined a wide range of related issues including the desirability of taking the joint-stock banks into public ownership. Eventually the full Executive approved a report on currency, banking and finance.[40] This was basically written by Dalton and Pethick-Lawrence and was presented to the 1932 Conference, along with a summarising resolution. Inevitably, the dominance of the experts meant that their view tended to prevail. On the contentious question of the joint-stock banks, there was no reference to public ownership.

This retreat from the vague promise of 1931 provoked criticism. For the moderate Dalton, the 1932 Conference was characterised by the 'irritability'[41] of the delegates. Certainly attempts by Executive spokesmen to expand moderate arguments often met with a hostile reception. Basically, this was the first occasion that the mass party had debated its future policy after the election defeat, and the backlash against any hint of MacDonald's influence remained strong. On the level of broad principle, a resolution was carried without a vote calling on the next Labour Government to stand or fall by its socialist principles.[42] The lack of positive proposals on the joint-stock banks also produced opposition, and eventually a resolution was carried to include them – and other financial institutions – within the party's public ownership proposals.[43] The margin was just over 150,000 votes, and the critics succeeded with the assistance of at least two large unions – the Railwaymen and the Miners. As a result of this, the Conference verdict was accepted. Public ownership of the joint-stock banks became formally part of party policy. It enjoyed the support of three leading parliamentarians, Attlee, Cripps and Lansbury, but it was never accepted readily by many moderates on the Executive. Gradually it was to disappear from party documents, until the pre-1932 position was restored.

The Sub-Committee on the Reorganisation of Industry was also deeply involved in the preparation of declarations for the 1932 Conference. Here the dominant figure was Herbert Morrison who, as Minister of Transport in the 1929 Government, had introduced legislation for the public ownership of London's transport system.[44] The broad question of industrial policy was also being considered by the TUC. This inevitably had implications for the scope and the content of the Sub-Committee's work.[45] At its first meeting, it was decided to concentrate on the production of statements on the power and transport industries. By the end of April 1932, Morrison had produced a memorandum on transport, which was then considered along with a variety of other relevant documents. The concern of particular unions with the future of these industries led to the conclusions being circulated to interested unions. This produced varying responses.[46] The Railwaymen's interest in detailed plans for public ownership had been stimulated by their recent experience of wage cuts, and they expressed general approval. However, the Transport Workers were more critical, and their opposition led to a lengthy and indeterminate controversy which was of great importance for Labour's commitment to public ownership.

As so often with Labour's internal controversies, a major issue became encapsulated within a superficially minor difference of opinion. Morrison's approach was basically a rendition on a national scale of his London proposals. Existing transport (and electrical) undertakings were to be brought under the control of National Transport and National Electricity Boards. The problems arose over the place of trade unions within these public corporations. Morrison's position had always been that the members of the boards should be selected solely on account of their competence but some trade unions, including the Transport Workers, demanded a more guaranteed role for the unions.[47] In spite of Bevin placing his weight behind the critics, the statements on transport and electricity went forward to the Party Conference as examples of the Morrisonian position. Once again Executive statements had been heavily influenced by a committed enthusiast.

The question of 'Workers' Representation' on the boards of publicly-owned industry was debated extensively at the 1932 TUC.[48] Opposition to the 'competence only' position was sufficient to secure the promise of further discussion. The concern of some of the large unions, especially the Transport Workers, produced a similar promise of reconsideration at the Party Conference. The Conference debate showed the basic issues raised by this apparently fine point.[49] Although the critics were only recommending that board members should be appointed after consultation with interested unions, the questions raised covered the fundamental objectives of public ownership. 'Worker participation' was needed in order to redistribute power within industry. Morrison's proposals would leave the existing power structures unchanged and would lead to irresponsible bureaucracy. Obviously the position of most of the critics was remote from any suggestion of syndicalism, but it did raise the vital question of how a programme of public ownership would change the position of the workers within the industries concerned. It also by implication raised the question of whether Morrison and his supporters saw this as a central aim of a public ownership programme.

Opposition to the public corporation did not come only from some trade unions. After the 1932 Conference, Lansbury expressed his dissatisfaction,[50] but it was in negotiations with the TUC that the matter was most thoroughly explored. The General Council consulted individual unions on the question, while the Party's Policy Committee initially reaffirmed its support for Morrison's position. Early in 1933, two joint meetings of the Policy Committee and the TUC Economic Committee were held in an attempt to produce an agreed solution. The party position was expressed by Clynes, an 'elder statesman' with an established reputation on both sides of the movement.[51] However it was clear that a majority of trade unions favoured some form of direct representation, and when a compromise statement was eventually issued, this involved a superficial concession to the critics. It accepted organised labour's claim that 'it shall have its place in the control and direction of publicly-owned industries.'[52] The nature of the place was left obscure: it was a classic Labour compromise. Trade unions were to have the right to nominate people for the Boards, but in the final analysis, the Minister concerned could ignore their claims.

The compromise was ratified by the General Council and the National Executive. Bevin and the Transport Workers were prepared to give support, and it passed the 1933 TUC by a majority of 383,000.[53] However, the compromise failed to carry the Party Conference; instead, the Conference accepted by a margin of 140,000 a resolution moved by Charles Dukes of the Municipal Workers.[54] This asked that the representation of the workers in the industry should be a statutory right. The division of opinion on this issue was a singular one and was not classifiable in terms of the normal left-right divisions. In spite of this further rebuff, there was no immediate sequel to the 1933 debate. The compromise had passed the TUC, but the critics had triumphed at the Party Conference by just a narrow majority. Furthermore, any suggestion of workers' control was viewed unsympathetically by most parliamentarians. In such a context, the verdict of the 1933 Conference was decently buried, and the 1945 Government implemented its public ownership proposals in the best Morrisonian tradition. Yet the controversy was a harbinger of the disillusion that was to follow this implementation. It showed how far political leaders saw public ownership as a means of achieving industrial efficiency, and how little they thought about any change in the power relationships within those industries.

If Labour spokesmen were divided about the purposes of public ownership, they remained generally agreed on its scope. Apart from the joint-stock banks case, there was little debate about this. The public ownership of the transport and power sectors was universally accepted and the list was subsequently extended. In both cases, the bulk of the work was done by the TUC Economic Committee under the agreed division of labour. The 1931 TUC had considered a proposal for the public ownership of the iron and steel industry, brought forward by the union most involved, the Iron and Steel Trades Confederation.[55] The Party's Reorganisation of Industry group had paid some attention to this industry at its very first meeting, but most of the preparatory work was done on the TUC side. However, liaison with the party was facilitated not only by the continuing attendance of Dalton and Morrison at meetings of the Economic Committee but also by the emergence of Walker, the Steelmen's representative on the NEC, as one of its most involved trade union members. The TUC Report on the industry proposed public ownership by public corporation, with no mention made of any statutory right of worker representation. After a unanimous acceptance at the 1934 TUC, the scheme was discussed briefly by the Party Conference. The role of the specifically party bodies was marginal, and the policy document on the industry was regarded as a TUC statement.[56]

A similar procedure was followed over the next year with the cotton industry. A statement recommending its socialisation was accepted by the 1935 TUC, and then by the Party Conference.[57] Once again debate was brisk and uncontroversial. These cases were notable for two reasons apart from the marginal involvement of the party. In both cases, the proposal was supported very strongly by the union concerned. These unions were recognised as amongst the most moderate in the party — yet in the context of economic depression, they were led to advocate detailed proposals for public ownership. Second, there was a sense in which both proposals were not wholly assured of their inclusion in all Labour Party programmes. They lacked the pedigree that came from long-standing acceptance within the party. Thus steel was to become a matter of great controversy after 1945, while cotton was to disappear from Labour's public ownership proposals.

The development of a list of public ownership proposals was the central feature of Labour's post 1931 re-examination of policy. Some candidates were clearly more firmly accepted than others, and individuals' expectations of such a programme varied, but in most cases there was a clear consensus. Yet the production of such a list was obviously not enough. The events of 1931 had produced fears that any attempt to introduce radical reforms would founder. The broad theoretical contours of this debate have already been explored. The concern of the Labour left was expressed at length at the 1933 Conference. Cripps initiated a debate that reflected the left's doubts about the compatability of socialist reforms and existing constitutional practices, and also moderate trade union leaders' commitment to existing political institutions. At the end of the debate the Executive agreed to consider the problem, and to report to the next Conference.[58] The question was discussed at length by the Constitutional Committee. Its deliberations were given added bite by the horror of some Labour leaders at Cripps' public pronouncements on the matter. Eventually the emotive question of emergency powers was dissolved in a language so vague that the issue was lost. Repeated discussions in the party's committees, the clear moderate majority and the passage of time all helped to neutralise the issue.[59] Beneath the vagueness, Labour's commitment to existing parliamentary forms remained unbroken.[60]

Although it was the public ownership proposals that gave Labour's developing programme its distinctiveness, policies were developed in other directions. The vagueness of Labour's economic policy has been noted. Keynesianism made only a limited impact: in most respects the new economic proposals were unremarkable. However, the party advocated a wide range of social improvements. Some, for example educational reform, were backed by few solid proposals, but others — most notably unemployment maintenance and welfare services — involved specific commitments. This was important, indicating as it did a bifurcation in Labour's policies. Whereas the public ownership proposals were seen as a means of effecting fundamental changes, the welfare pledges involved a commitment to amelioration within the existing system. This was the central dualism of Labour's emerging domestic perspective. It was a combination of proposals for transforming the system, and proposals for improving it. A successful pursuit of palliatives would carry implications for the attractiveness of apparently fundamental change. The position would be complicated still further if the impact of the supposedly radical measures proved to be ambiguous. In the early thirties these problems lay in the future, but were foreshadowed by the clashes between trade union moderates and their left-wing critics.

One result of this detailed examination of policy was that the party's overall position became a veritable mosaic. Detailed policy documents, compromise statements and Conference decisions combined to produce uncertainty about Labour's overall position. There was an obvious need for a general declaration of policy. An early attempt was made in 1933 when a brief statement, 'Socialism and the Condition of the People', was presented to the Conference.[61] This showed an absorption of the critical reception given to Executive proposals at the previous year's Conference. The statement proclaimed that socialism was the only way of solving economic and social problems. It included few positive proposals, although it did include the amended policy on banking.

The preparation of a general policy statement for the 1934 Conference was a much more significant process. The idea appears to have originated with Henderson. He suggested to the Executive in January 1934 that that year's Conference might take as its agenda a provisional election manifesto. Shortly afterwards, the Policy Committee authorised him to secure a first draft of a general policy statement. This was apparently written by Tawney and was envisaged as equivalent in status to 'Labour and the New Social Order', and 'Labour and the Nation'. This was discussed in June by the Policy Committee who instructed party officials to prepare a more concise version.[62] This emerged as the still rather lengthy document 'For Socialism and Peace', and was approved by the full Executive. As its title implied, the document covered both home and international affairs. Its general tone was more radical than its predecessors or successors. Certainly many of the proposals could be seen as measures of social improvement or industrial rationalisation, but the statement also bluntly proclaimed that: 'what the nation now requires is not mere social reform, but socialism.'[63]

Cynics could no doubt argue that this was not so different from the Utopian platitudes of the MacDonald era, but as a result of the current re-examination of policy, specific measures were now proposed as means of realising this goal:

> banking and credit, transport, electricity, water, iron and steel, coal, gas, agriculture, textiles, shipping, ship-building, engineering – in all these, the time has come for drastic reorganisation, and for the most part, nothing short of public ownership and control will be effective.[64]

The ambiguity is important. The list of candidates for public ownership is wider than the subjects of the detailed policy statements: but in no case is public ownership specified as the appropriate policy.

The solution to the vexed question of the compatability of socialism and constitutional methods reflected the dominance of the moderates. Although attention was paid to possible reforms of parliamentary procedure, there was an unequivocal expression of Labour's commitment to parliamentary democracy. The domestic sections of the document were a clear expression of Labour's reaction to 1931. There had been a radicalisation, in so far as the party's commitment to social transformation was more explicit and related to specific proposals. However, Labour's position regarding any transfer of power inside industry remained vague, and its belief in the possibility of gradual change through existing institutions remained basically unshaken.

It is not surprising that the document provoked opposition from the Socialist League and its sympathisers. The League tabled 75 amendments in preparation for the 1934 Conference. Even after these had been substantially reduced, the attack was mounted on a variety of fronts — the document's lack of precision regarding Labour's aims, public ownership and compensation, and workers' control in the iron and steel industry. Attempts to amend the document in a radical direction were defeated overwhelmingly. The largest vote for a critical amendment was only 206,000. The Distributive Workers were the only large union to show any enthusiasm for the critics' case.[65]

Despite the unhappiness of this minority, it is clear that something approaching a consensus was emerging on Labour's domestic programme. This was based on the concordat between political moderates and their trade union counterparts. Apocalyptic reactions to the 1931 collapse and to the economic depression had been rejected. Instead there was a continuing acceptance of existing political institutions and procedures. Within this, proposals covered a combination of palliatives and apparently radical proposals. The latter centred around a generally agreed programme of publicly-owned industries. This was normally taken as the most distinctive ingredient in the party's programme, although it was clear that beneath the consensus there lurked disagreements about its purpose. Was it to be an instrument of socialist transformation that would produce a significant redistribution of power, or was it really just a technique for modernising and rationalising an antiquated economy? This divergence was not really explored in the debates of the early thirties. For the moment an agreed programme and the vague hope of a better world were enough.

Pacifists, Socialists and Realists — The Debate Over Foreign Policy

The collapse of 1931 did not carry any significant implications for Labour's attitude to foreign affairs. It was widely agreed within the party that the Ministers involved, Henderson and Dalton, had done their best to implement Labour's proclaimed policy. There was broad agreement on the principal tenets of the Labour approach to international questions. Conflicts were understood as the products of capitalism with its balance of power politics, escalating armaments and secret diplomacy. The long-term solution was the establishment of socialism; the short-term one was to work for pacification through the League of Nations and for general disarmament. This broad position under which almost all the diverse tendencies within the party could gather was symbolised by Henderson's last years, spent in an unsuccessful pursuit of disarmament at Geneva. So long as the international scene was free of major problems, this policy united the party. It left unclear such sensitive questions as its attitude towards armaments, and whether support of the League might involve, in the final analysis, military as well as economic sanctions.[66]

The first major challenge to the party's position was the Japanese invasion of Manchuria in the autumn of 1931. This generated little discussion in the labour movement and at the 1932 Conference international affairs received only a perfunctory debate. It was the collapse of the Weimar Republic and the emergence of the Third Reich that brought international questions to the centre of party debates.

It is crucial to emphasise the role of the trade union section, especially Bevin and Citrine,[67] in developing Labour's attitudes to a worsening international situation. This was the policy area above all others that was the subject of joint consultations between the political and industrial wings and where the pronouncements of the National Council achieved most prominence. The reaction of most trade union leaders to the advance of Nazism was unequivocal: the suppression of German trade unions produced a thorough condemnation. Although the initial response of the TUC was concerned with the domestic consequences of Nazism, this clear condemnation had implications for trade union reactions to any attempts to expand German power.

Emotions within the party were much more complex. A central feature of Labour's international pronouncements since Versailles had concerned the harshness of the terms meted out to Germany. The view persisted that sweet reasonableness would satisfy German demands. At the 1933 Conference, the rise of Hitler received very little attention. The standard Labour position on universal disarmament was reiterated, but more important was the first dispute between trade union leaders and the Labour left in the international field. This originated in a lengthy resolution moved by Trevelyan. It expressed a general distaste for war, and called on all sections of the labour movement to consider various anti-war proposals including a general strike in the event of war. Such sentiments tapped very deeply rooted emotions within the labour movement: they harked back to the aspirations of the Second International. It was accepted by Dalton on behalf of the Executive in order to avoid a wrangle.[68] This meant superficially that the party was committed to a strategy of direct action in order to prevent war.

This suggestion appalled the moderate trade union leaders. Bevin reflected: 'Who and what is there to strike? Trade Unionism has been destroyed in Italy and Germany.'[69] Eventually the 'Three Executives' discussed the problem on 28 February 1934, and it was agreed eventually that a Committee draw up a statement for submission separately to each Executive and then to another joint meeting. The question provoked further debate at the following National Executive meeting. Henderson, clearly unhappy about the direct action proposals, emphasised that they did not distinguish between aggressive wars, and obligations resulting from membership of the League of Nations. The resulting memorandum 'War and Peace' came before a further joint meeting on 28 June. It was introduced by Henderson as the result of an amalgam of the views of the party and the TUC. It was an amalgam that removed the contentious element in the previous year's resolution.[70] The insistence on collective security was backed by a rejection of the general strike. One consideration advanced was the lack of significant trade union movements in several countries, while it was also argued that 'the responsibility for stopping war ought not to be placed on the trade union movement alone.'[71] Moreover the report noted that there might be situations where Britain might have to use force to restrain an aggressor. This was a significant development which was to have crucial consequences for the party. The document had an easy passage through the 1934 TUC. In so far as there was a division it was not based on the pacifist issue, but on a question much more central to the ideological difficulties of the British labour movement. What should be the attitude of socialists towards the defence of a Britain ruled by a despised National Government? The majority of the Congress echoed the view that: 'We have to deal with the world as it is. We cannot wait for the remodelling of the whole social structure.'[72] It was predictable that the minority position would receive a more vigorous airing at the Party Conference with the Socialist League in the forefront of the

critics. They based their position on the belief that 'the workers of
one country have no quarrel with the workers of any other country'.[73]
Seeing the League of Nations as the product of a capitalist system, they
condemned this central feature of Labour policy as impotent. Rather
they advocated an alliance with other socialist countries. This was
obviously a long-term proposal: in so far as the present British
Government was concerned, the critics opposed any war:

> for under the capitalist system, it is impossible to allocate the blame
> for War, which is inherent in the system, springs from contradictions
> and brings to the workers added misery and exploitation.[74]

This was an intelligible position with a long ancestry. Its attraction in
the context of economic depression is readily understandable. Yet at
the 1934 Conference, it attracted only a handful of votes; as always in
the thirties, the development of Labour policy was dominated by the
moderate alliance between the industrial and political wings.
Nevertheless, the uncertain hold that the latest policy had on sections
of the Labour Party was demonstrated by the vote on the 'War and
Peace' declaration. The critics managed to secure the relatively high
vote of 619,000, a figure bolstered by the contributions of the Miners
and the Distributive Workers.

The attachment of the party to the 'War and Peace' position was to
be tested sharply within a year. Mussolini's attack on Abyssinia meant
that the party now had to consider how far it should advocate resistance
to an aggressor in the name of collective security. Difficulties were
anticipated from three directions. Cripps, now on the National
Executive, adhered to the Socialist League position as rejected in 1934.
Distinct from this, there were the pure pacifists. These were few in
number, but they included Lansbury. For several months he had hidden
this personal position, and acted as spokesman for a party policy
which he could not accept.[75] As the Abyssinian crisis intensified and
the need for a Labour pronouncement grew, so the tensions increased.
Apart from these clearly defined minority positions, the party was
inevitably influenced by an anti-war sentiment that affected many in all
parties. Such vague concern was more of an obstacle to the acceptance
of the implications of 'War and Peace' than either the pure pacifist or
the anti-imperialist positions, exacerbated as it was by distaste for the
National Government.

Prior to the 1935 Trades Union Congress the three Executives met
to consider the position, and decided on a policy statement supporting

'any action consistent with the principles and status of the League'. This was sufficient to produce Cripps' resignation from the NEC, but the statement passed the TUC very comfortably with a minority vote of only 170,000.[76]

This was a watershed in the development of the party's international policy. It was no longer possible for the umbrella of collective security to cover the whole spectrum of party opinion. What would have been a deep crisis over the content of Labour's international policy was compounded by the personal position of its parliamentary leader. Lansbury began to criticise publicly the joint policy statement, and advocates of military sanctions began to accuse him of abandoning a position he had accepted prior to the Trades Union Congress. Conversely, Lansbury believed that his position had been systematically misrepresented by Citrine and that only a personal dissociation could correct the record.[77]

Thus, the clash at the 1935 Conference was not just between different doctrines — the 'tough realism' of Bevin and Dalton, the 'no war under capitalism' stance of Cripps, the pure pacifism of Lansbury, and the uncertainties of the genuinely confused.[78] It was also a conflict between two conceptions of loyalty: Bevin's dedication to the rule of majority decisions, and Lansbury's commitment to the rule of individual conscience. The confrontation between these two epitomised the division. Lansbury with his evocation of the early Christian martyrs was answered by Bevin recommending the virtues of loyalty and responsibility. Certainly the large unions held together on the issue; only 102,000 votes were cast against the policy statement.

The destruction of Lansbury symbolised the development of the party since 1931. There was no likelihood that the leader's speech could have affected the result of the debate. This was shown by the earlier decisive vote of the TUC. Bevin's response ensured the eviction from the party leadership of the last vestige of what the trade union leaders regarded as unreliable emotionalism. Labour's international policy now reflected clearly the views of the dominant moderate group within the industrial and the political wings. Controversy would continue but the basic arguments were settled.

The Blue Thirties: Labour and the Electorate

The short-term significance of the 1931 election lay in the catastrophic Labour defeat, but in a longer perspective, the contest can be seen as ushering in a new period of party politics. The three-party competition of the twenties was dead. Now it was to be Labour against the rest. Up to 1929, Labour's parliamentary successes had been aided by the presence of genuinely three-party contests in many constituencies. The Labour defeat in 1931 had been transformed into a rout by the mobilisation of almost all non-Labour voters behind the 'National' appeal. The post-1931 electoral situation offered the party both problems and hope. The simplification of electoral choice made whatever seats Labour gained much more secure than in the twenties. The converse of this was, of course, that Labour faced a much harder task in registering gains, although it was widely believed that the National majority was inherently unstable because of the peculiar circumstances in which it had been obtained. One complicating factor was obviously the allegiance of former Liberal voters who had gone 'National' but had retained a basically Liberal identity and now often lacked the opportunity to vote for a Liberal candidate. Obviously their behaviour would be influenced by the allegiance of local Liberal leaders and by the brand of Liberalism — anti-Tory or anti-Socialist — that was traditional in a particular area.

During the 1931-5 Parliament Labour gained ten seats,[79] nine from the Government, and one, Lambeth North, from the anti-Government Liberals. Of the nine taken from the Government, one, Liverpool Wavertree, need not be considered since its capture was attributable to a split Conservative vote. All but one of the remaining eight had been held by Labour prior to 1931 and six of them were retained by the party in the 1935 election. These gains can be seen as a recouping by Labour of what might be regarded as its normal territory, although in some cases the margin of victory was small. The most spectacular of these recaptures was that of Rotherham in February 1933 where in a contest dominated by the means test and the general economic situation, a National majority of 762 was turned into a Labour one of 15,874.

The slowness of the recovery from economic crisis coupled with the peculiar circumstances of the 1931 election made such Labour gains predictable. The best period for the party covered the autumn of 1933 and much of 1934, when spectacular Labour advances were made in seats which the party had failed to capture even in 1929. These included one gain at East Fulham in October 1933. This success achieved considerable notoriety. The claim that the conversion of a National majority of 14,521 into a Labour one of 4,840 was attributable to Labour's use of pacifist propaganda is one that has been assiduously investigated by researchers who have produced very different answers.[80] Given the evidence available, no conclusive assessment is possible. What is certain is that the East Fulham gain was followed by a series of close contests in hopeless seats. It seems likely that in some of these cases concern with the Government's record was not the only factor. Labour generally made a greater advance in those seats as Rutland and Stamford and Manchester Rusholme where the Liberals had polled in strength in 1929, but had now collapsed. In places, where an anti-Government Liberal organisation still retained some vitality, the Labour advance was much less marked.

Labour's performance in by-elections was satisfactory in so far as it was reclaiming its own. Only one seat went Labour in 1929, but was not regained at a by-election in the 1931 Parliament. There was little evidence, East Fulham apart, that Labour was capturing new ground. Two aspects of the situation caused particular concern to Labour strategists. One concerned the apathy of the electorate. Turnouts were frequently low: the celebrated capture of East Fulham was achieved on a poll of under 60 per cent while in May 1934 Labour captured West Ham Upton with almost half the electorate not bothering to vote. Many of the lowest polls were in the poorer areas of large cities.[81] The party had spent much energy denouncing the iniquities of the National Government, but often this did not result in a mobilisation of what many party members regarded as their natural supporters.

The pronouncements of spokesmen of the Socialist League, especially Cripps, also produced concern. This was particularly so over the question of Labour's attitude towards emergency powers, a question that was given particular prominence by Government spokesmen following the East Fulham disaster. This led to the NEC issuing a statement emphasising the party's unequivocal commitment to parliamentary democracy,[82] but fears about the electoral unpopularity of radical proposals and slogans continued to haunt Labour's moderate leaders. Opposition to the proposal to nationalise the joint-stock banks was fuelled by such doubts, and was expressed forcibly by members of the General Council.[83]

When a general election was announced by Baldwin in October 1935, Labour's divisions over the sanctions question were still apparent. Lansbury had only just resigned as leader, and the party went into the contest under the former Deputy Leader in the Commons, Attlee. The production of an election manifesto out of the plethora of documents was left initially to the NEC's Election Sub-Committee, who decided in favour of a short statement rather than the lengthy arguments that avoided the lists of specific proposals characteristic of earlier manifestoes.[84] The production of a draft was left to Greenwood as Head of the Research Department, and this was presented to the full Executive, together with a list of policy items from which a selection might be made. This draft was then passed over to a Sub-Committee — Attlee, Morrison, Dalton and Greenwood, plus Mrs Adamson the Executive Chairman — prior to approval by the Executive. Thus, after the prolonged policy debates of the previous four years, the production of the final manifesto lay with the four most prominent members of the party.

The resulting document — 'The Labour Party's Call to Power' — was succinct. Its international section emphasised the commitment to collective security, and was unspecific on how far the League should go over the Abyssinian crisis. The domestic policy restatement was reflected in the list of proposals for public ownership: 'banking, coal and its products, transport, electricity, iron and steel and cotton.' This was a list unequalled in its specificity and length. The party's position on unemployment policy was vague. There was nothing other than the promise of 'special steps' to deal with the problems of the distressed areas, together with references to 'national planning' and 'far-reaching schemes of national development'. Finally, the party protested its adherence to 'constitutional and democratic means'.[85]

Equipped with this summary of its work since 1931 and headed by an apparently interim leader, Labour fought the campaign in a context of international crisis, and against a National combination led by a Baldwin, then probably near the height of his prestige. The result reflected the by-election record of the previous four years. Labour regained most of the votes that it had lost in 1931, although its total support was still 50,000 less than in 1929. Moreover, under the new rules of 'Labour versus the Rest' its parliamentary representation of 154 was 133 less than in 1929. Compared with the situation at the dissolution of Parliament, Labour had lost three of its by-election gains, and had captured 97 new seats.

The distribution of these gains shows the limited nature of Labour's appeal. The party was emphatically a party of the older industrial areas, plus the poorer parts of London.[86] Twenty-two gains were registered in London and the surrounding districts. Elsewhere Labour gains were almost absent in the south, apart from a Bristol seat and the coal-dominated Forest of Dean. Otherwise, Labour advance was almost wholly north of the Trent. The 1931 Durham disaster was reversed and Labour took all the county divisions. Scotland provided 18 gains including the unexpected Western Isles. Most of the northern cities provided Labour gains: four in Sheffield, three each in Manchester and Stoke, two in Hull and one each in Liverpool, Leeds and Bradford.

There were several other gains in the West Riding, the Black Country and Derbyshire. Yet even in these areas of traditional depressed industry there were inconsistencies. Labour achieved just one gain in Northumberland and none in Newcastle. In spite of the parlous state of the cotton industry, Labour took only four of the seats that were dominated by the industry. Salford, whose poverty two years earlier had inspired the writing of 'Love on the Dole' returned three Government members.

Thus, even in economically deprived areas, Labour did not always reap the benefit. Within the areas of Labour strength, the party's performance varied between regions and industries. Yet with this qualification, the north-south contrast remained marked. London and South Wales apart, the outposts of Labour were Nottingham, Nuneaton and West Bromwich. Further south only three Labour seats disturbed a Government monopoly. Birmingham remained a desert for Labour, an example followed by those other urban centres further south that had shown some Labour leanings in 1929. Above all the party had failed to make inroads into the areas of new industry and expanding population. These were also frequently areas of weak unionisation and lacked the sense of working-class community that was found in the older industrial areas. Twenty-five years later Labour strategists were to debate the problems posed for the party by an increasingly affluent working class. Yet in the 'two nations' of 1935, a similar problem was posed. For a majority, Labour had to make inroads into the New England of:

> arterial and by-pass roads, of filling stations and factories that look like exhibition buildings, of giant cinemas and dance halls and cafes, bungalows with tiny garages, cocktail bars, Woolworths, motor coaches, wireless, hiking, factory girls looking like actresses, greyhound racing and dirt tracks, swimming pools, and everything given away for cigarette coupons.[87]

The party might have seen itself as the party of tomorrow, but its appeal was still strongest in the industrial graveyards. It might have seen itself as the party of the working class, but many of its supposedly natural supporters still preferred government by their 'betters'.

This four-year period was crucial for Labour's development. Laski, the Webbs and other Labour intellectuals all drew radical conclusions from the 1931 experience. Such reactions were important in that they helped to foster the myth of the 'Red Thirties' in which the alternatives were clear. Yet the manoeuvres of the Socialist League and the agitations for a United Front occupied the attention of the committed few. Power within the labour movement lay conclusively with men who shared very different aspirations. The future lay not with the critical intellectuals, nor with the saintly Lansbury. Rather it rested with the assiduous moderation of Dalton and Morrison, the robust empiricism of Bevin, the tidy administration of Citrine, and the flexible leadership of Attlee. They were the principal authors of the social democratic perspective that was to dominate Labour politics.

The alarums and excursions of the early thirties fall into perspective when placed alongside one small but illuminating incident. In 1935 three prominent Labour figures, Citrine, Pugh and the Labour Chief Whip, Charles Edwards, were offered knighthoods in the Silver Jubilee Honours List. They accepted them. Despite all the polemic against the National Government and Towney's references to 'poodles' and 'sugar plums', it was obvious that some influential Labour leaders accepted not just the constraints of the existing political and economic system but also its symbolic rewards. Although the emerging social democratic perspective contained a rhetorical rejection of existing society, it was fashioned principally by men who sought not to replace it, but to have it recognise their claims. So long as office remained a distant prospect, the two elements, the consensual and the critical, remained in reasonable harmony: short-term programmatic agreement and potential for discord were the major legacies of those years.

Notes

1. For the leaders see Raymond Postgate, *The Life of George Lansbury* (Longmans, London, 1951); Roy Jenkins, *Mr. Attlee: An Interim Biography* (Heineman, London, 1948); Colin Cooke, *The Life of Sir Richard Stafford Cripps* (Hodder and Stoughton, London, 1957).
2. See Michael Foot, *Aneurin Bevan Vol. I 1897-1945.*
3. Hugh Dalton, *Memoirs Volume 2: The Fateful Years* (Muller, London, 1957), p. 3.
4. See B. Donoughue and G. Jones, *Herbert Morrison: Portrait of a Politician* (Weidenfeld, London, 1973).
5. *NEC Minutes,* 16 December 1931; *LPCR 1932*, pp. 49-51. The other members were George Lathan (Railway Clerks), Stanley Hirst (TGW), J.R. Clynes (GMW), Joe Compton (Vehicle Builders), and T.E. Williams (Royal Arsenal Co-operative Society).
6. For union attitudes see R. Page Arnot, *The Miners in Crisis and in War* (Allen & Unwin, London, 1960); P.S. Bagwell, op. cit.; A. Bullock, *Vol. 2* (Heinemann, London, 1960).
7. For 1931, individual membership was given as 297,003. *LPCR 1932*, p. 58.
8. Citrine Memorandum cited in Henry Pelling, *A History of British Trade*

Unionism, Second Edition (Macmillan, London, 1972), p. 199.
9. For discussions see *NEC Minutes*, 16 December 1931 and 27 January 1932: *National Joint Council Minutes,* 26 January 1932; *Minutes of PLP Executive*, 27 January 1932.
10. For revised NJC Constitution see *LPCR 1932*, p. 67.
11. *LPCR 1933*, p. 8.
12. See *Policy Committee Minutes*, 21 April 1932.
13. *NEC Minutes*, 26 October 1932.
14. Dalton, *Vol. 2*, pp. 58-9. See also the writings of Morrison, especially his *Socialisation and Transport* (Constable, London, 1933).
15. R.H. Tawney, 'The Choice Before The Labour Party', *Political Quarterly*, July-September 1932.
16. Harold Laski, *The Crisis and The Constitution* (Hogarth Press, London, 1932); Sir Stafford Cripps, *Can Socialism Come By Constitutional Means?* (Socialist League, London, n.d.).
17. Laski, op. cit., p. 53.
18. Ibid., p. 56.
19. See Bullock, *Vol. 2*.
20. Tawney, op. cit., p. 341.
21. Cited in Foot, *Vol. I*, pp. 151-2.
22. Dalton, *Vol. 2*, p. 28.
23. Sidney and Beatrice Webb, *Soviet Communism: A New Civilisation*, Second Edition (Gollancz, London, 1937); also the concluding pages of M. Cole (ed.), op. cit.
24. See Robert Skidelsky, *The British Labour Party: Sources of Resistance to Keynesianism* (Paper presented to the Society For the Study of Labour History, November 1974).
25. V.L. Allen, *Trade Unions and the Government* (Longmans, London, 1960), pp. 32-3.
26. Arthur Marwick, *Britain in the Century of Total War* (Bodley Head, London, 1968), pp. 239-47; *The Next Five Years: An Essay in Political Agreement* (Macmillan, London, 1935).
27. For ILP see Dowse, op. cit.; F. Brockway, op. cit. – and also his *Socialism Over Sixty Years: The Life of Jowett of Bradford* (Allen and Unwin, London, 1946).
28. For Communist Party see Neil Wood, *Communism and British Intellectuals* (Gollancz, London, 1959). Martin, op. cit.; Hugh Thomas, *John Strachey* (Eyre Methuen, London, 1973).
29. Brockway, *Inside the Left*, p. 240.
30. ILP membership fell from 16,773 in 1932 to 4,392 in 1935.
31. See Ben Pimlott, 'The Socialist League: Intellectuals and The Labour Left in the 1930s', *Journal of Contemporary History*, Vol. 6, No. 3, 1971.
32. Henderson, Letter to Communist Party Secretariat, cited *LPCR 1934*, p. 11.
33. 'Dictatorship and the Trade Union Movement', *TUC Report 1933*, pp. 425-35. For the left's reaction see Foot, *Vol. I*, pp. 217-9; for typical confrontations *TUC Report 1933*, pp. 318-40; *LPCR 1934*, pp. 138-42.
34. Citrine in *TUC Report 1932*, p. 302.
35. See W. Hannington, *Unemployed Struggles 1919-36* (Reprint of 1936 edition, EP Publishing, Wakefield, 1973).
36. *LPCR 1933*, pp. 200-1.
37. *NEC Minutes*, 16 May 1934.
38. Dalton, *Vol. 2*, p. 22.
39. *Finance and Trade Group Minutes*, 26 February 1932.
40. The developments can be traced in *Finance and Trade Group Minutes*, 29 April, 3 May, 12 May (the larger meeting), 18 May and 7 June 1932.

Policy Committee Minutes, 19 May 1932; *NEC Minutes*, 22 June 1932.
41. Dalton, *Vol. 2*, p. 30.
42. Moved by Sir Charles Trevelyan. See *LPCR 1932*, p. 204.
43. Ibid., pp. 182-94.
44. Donoughue and Jones, op. cit., pp. 182-8.
45. *Reorganisation of Industry Committee Minutes*, 3 March, 28 April and 12 May 1932.
46. Ibid., 6 June 1932.
47. For background see Geoffrey Ostergaard, 'Labour and the Development of the Public Corporation', *Manchester School*, 1954.
48. *TUC Report 1932*, pp. 389-97.
49. *LPCR 1932*, pp. 211-25.
50. *NEC Minutes*, 26 October 1932.
51. See *Minutes of Joint Meeting of Policy Committee and Reorganisation of Industry Committee*, 9 February 1933; *Minutes of Joint Meetings of Policy Committee and TUC Economic Committee*, 15 February and 8 March 1933.
52. *LPCR 1933*, p. 14.
53. *TUC Report 1933*, pp. 369-79.
54. *LPCR 1933*, pp. 204-10.
55. *TUC Report 1931*, pp. 445-54.
56. *TUC Report 1934*, pp. 189-205 (Statement); pp. 359-66 (Debate). *LPCR 1934*, pp. 201-3.
57. *TUC Report 1935*, pp. 202-6 (Report); *LPCR 1935*, pp. 230-6.
58. Ibid., *1933*, pp. 159-66.
59. See *Constitutional Committee Minutes*, 30 November 1933; 16 and 18 January 1934. *NEC Minutes*, 20 and 24 January 1934. Also the memoranda by Citrine (No. 170) and Laski (No. 172).
60. See Appendix to *LPCR 1934*, pp. 261-3, 'Parliamentary Procedures and Problems'.
61. *LPCR 1933*, pp. 156-82.
62. For the statement's genesis see *NEC Minutes*, 24 January 1934; *Policy Committee Minutes*, 7 February and 14 June 1934.
63. *For Socialism and Peace*.
64. Ibid., p. 15.
65. *LPCR 1934, passim*.
66. For a general survey see J.F. Naylor, *Labour's International Policy* (Wiedenfeld, London, 1969).
67. For Bevin's reactions, see Bullock, *Vol. 2*, chs. 19 and 20.
68. *LPCR 1933*, pp. 185-8; Dalton, *Vol. 2*, p. 45.
69. General Secretary's Quarterly Report to the TGW Executive, cited in Bullock, *Vol. 2*, p. 550.
70. The process can be traced in *NEC Minutes*, 27 February and 1 March 1934; *Minutes of Meetings of the Three Executives*, 28 February and 28 June 1934.
71. 'War and Peace', in *TUC Report 1934*, p. 160.
72. Ibid., p. 325 (Clynes).
73. *LPCR 1934*, p. 175.
74. Ibid., p. 176. For the debate see pp. 152-8, and pp. 166-78.
75. For Lansbury's reservations see *NEC Minutes*, 19 September 1935.
76. See *TUC Report 1935*, pp. 346-71.
77. For diverging accounts see Postgate, op. cit., pp. 297-305. Bullock, *Vol. 2*, pp. 562-71; Foot, *Vol. I*, pp. 210-14.
78. *LPCR 1935*, pp. 153-93.
79. For the party's by-election record, see Cook and Ramsden, op. cit., pp. 108-15.
80. See M. Ceadel, 'Interpreting East Fulham', ibid., and also the appended

references at p. 139.

81. See the Memorandum on the West Toxteth By-Election attached to *NEC Minutes*, 26 June 1935.

82. *NEC Minutes*, 24 January 1934: *LPCR 1934*, p. 9.

83. *Minutes of the Joint Meeting of the NEC and the General Council*, 27 February 1935.

84. *Election Sub-Committee Minutes*, 16 October 1935.

85. *The Labour Party's Call To Power, passim.*

86. See M. Kinnear, op. cit., pp. 52-4.

87. J.B. Priestley, *English Journey* (Heinemann in association with Gollancz, London, 1934), p. 401.

3 THE MODERATES TRIUMPHANT 1935-1940

Labour's development after its 1935 defeat was essentially a tracing of the implications of earlier crucial decisions. There were no revolutionary departures in policy and no dramatic changes in the party's mode of operation. Such changes as there were involved a further rejection of the radical vistas that had been conjured up by the 1931 crisis. Labour's position in 1939 was generally more moderate than it had been in 1935. This change occurred by stealth: the major policy debates that had marked the previous four years were much less frequent. The consensus on policy was much more firmly established, with wide agreement about the central features of the social democratic perspective.

The worsening international situation inspired what dramas there were within the party. The need to respond to successive crises produced a final onslaught by the 'realists' on the defenders of pacifist and class-based international policies, while the Spanish Civil War provided a further dimension to the controversy. The commitment of the Labour left to the Spanish Republic complicated the party debate. This could not be analysed as a dispute between realism and idealism, since in the Spanish case, the agonising reality and the ideals of the Labour left seemed to fit. The kaleidoscope of international events provided a dramatic backdrop to the politics of Labour. It was also a revealing contrast. While the Left Book Club expanded and some British intellectuals became passionately committed to left-wing causes,[1] the party leadership remained on its sober moderate course.

This moderation was yoked with a fierce determination to protect the party's independence, and to avoid entanglements with other parties. In part, this was an instinctive reaction to 1931, but it also indicated a basic optimism that Labour could achieve office alone without making alliances with other progressive groups, and without compromising basic values. For these optimists, the way forward was by patient propaganda, rejecting the blandishments of the Communists and the more radical Liberals. This prescription provoked fierce criticism from those who condemned its inadequacy at a time of international crisis. Yet the optimists retained undisputed control until the military disasters of April 1940. Then they surrendered Labour's independence 'for the duration'. They entered a coalition much more broadly based than anything suggested by their impatient critics. It was a paradoxical but significant conclusion to the patient construction of a social democratic perspective.

Attlee's Arrival

Relationships between different sections of the party were inevitably altered by the strengthening of the Parliamentary Party. This did not just involve a trebling of the number of Labour MPs. It also included a significant shift in the balance within the PLP. The younger ex-Ministers who had lost their seats in 1931 now returned: Dalton, Morrison, Alexander and Shinwell were all destined to play significant roles in future Labour administrations. These, together with Attlee and Greenwood, formed the core of Labour's parliamentary leadership. Only Clynes of the pre-1931 leaders had returned and he was content to play the role of elder statesman.

The first significant task of the new PLP was to choose a leader. It had been widely accepted that Attlee's succession to Lansbury was only a transitional arrangement, and with a greatly expanded parliamentary party, a new election was only natural. Morrison was seen widely as the 'coming man', and in the event he was the only re-entrant to stand for the leadership. Attlee was also opposed by Greenwood, but in the build-up to the vote, many leading figures seemed ready to support Morrison. He enjoyed wide support amongst the 'ideas men' of both left and right, and also had strong backing amongst the London MPs. Greenwood's strengths lay in his links with the party machine, his close connections with the trade unions, and his provincial base. In contrast, it was difficult to see where Attlee's strengths lay. But he already held the post and had acted as leader for a considerable part of the previous Parliament. His support on the first ballot, 58 votes, almost mirrored the size of the old parliamentary party. This placed him ahead of Morrison's 44 votes and Greenwood's 33. On the second ballot, Greenwood's support shifted almost totally to Attlee, and he was returned as leader by 88 votes to 48.[2]

This surprising result, at first viewed by many MPs as tentative, gave Labour its leader for the next twenty years. In retrospect Morrison's defeat was understandable. He had limited parliamentary experience, his attitude in August 1931 had been ambivalent, he was too closely identified with London. Perhaps most important of all, the ratification of Attlee's leadership can be seen as part of the reaction against MacDonald. There was concern lest Morrison as leader would become too dominant: this was hardly likely with Attlee. A disappointed Dalton might reflect ruefully that 'a little mouse shall lead them'.[3] But it was not to be like that. During the frustrations of the next five years there were vague expressions of concern with Attlee's leadership but these always petered out. Morrison as heir apparent lacked, as he always would, support in crucial sections of the party. Bevin's intense dislike for him reflected a much wider trade union suspicion.

Although Attlee was leader of a much strengthened parliamentary party, his style of leadership gave considerable scope to other major figures. The PLP was his principal bastion, and as yet he had not acquired an equivalent dominance within the extra-parliamentary sections. The most significant extra-parliamentary development during this period concerned the reform in 1937 of the National Executive Committee. For several years, there had been dissatisfaction about the representation of the constituency parties. The grievances concerned both the number of representatives and the method of election. The practice of electing these representatives through the vote of the whole Conference meant that constituency preferences could be swamped by the votes of the large unions.

The question was not merely one of representation: the debate became entwined with political differences. The increased union influence within the party after 1931 was seen by critics as establishing a false near-unanimity in the party's decision-making bodies, while many trade union leaders saw proposals for separate election of the constituency section as a means of introducing carping criticism and unreliability into the party's discussions. Originally, the question was to have been discussed at the 1936 Conference, but because of lengthy debates over Spain, the matter was not reached. Prior to the Conference the NEC had considered a proposal to alter the basis of the Executive elections, and had decided by fifteen votes to five not to go forward with it.[4] Criticism of the existing arrangements was growing, however, and following the 1936 Conference Dalton, the new Party Chairman, expressed a need to raise morale inside the party.[5] It became clear that the desire for independent constituency representation was widely felt by local parties, and eventually the reform was approved narrowly by the Executive.[6] The question of Conference approval remained. Some of the large unions — the GMW, the Railwaymen and the Textile Workers — were opposed to changes. During his year of office, Dalton had worked closely with Bevin, then Chairman of the General Council, and during the debate the Transport Workers agreed to support the main constitutional reforms. The Conference vote for the increase of constituency representation was very close, 1,408,000 to 1,134,000, but on the separate elections question, the margin was much greater.[7]

The new system was put into operation immediately. Of the seven constituency representatives, Morrison, Dalton and Dallas continued through from the old system, while one newcomer, Noel Baker, was certainly not identified with the Labour left. However Cripps, Laski and Pritt, all advocates of the united front, were returned. This produced a small left-wing nucleus on the Executive, that was strengthened further by the election of Ellen Wilkinson to the Women's Section. Yet obviously these successes gave no cause for concern to the moderate trade union and parliamentary leaders. The remaining members remained implacably opposed to the proposals of the new arrivals, while the left-wing representatives failed to remain united. Laski and Wilkinson both diluted their views when necessary but as demonstrated below, Cripps and Pritt both failed to survive within the party. The unanimity of the moderate majority was not total. There was a significant divergence in the approach to dissent. The bulk of the moderates preferred to take an implacable line — these were largely but not wholly the trade union representatives — while a few others, including on occasions Attlee and Morrison, were ready to take a more conciliatory position. Over all, though, the reforms of 1937 were merely a cosmetic; they made the moderate domination of the Executive marginally more palatable to the more critical constituency parties.

The domination on the Executive was reflected in the Party Conference. Changing patterns of employment had produced some shifts in the strengths of the largest unions. The Textile Workers continued their steady decline: by 1939, their affiliated membership was down to 124,000. In contrast, the growth of new service industries had produced a major expansion of the general unions. That of the GMW was not yet reflected in the affiliation figure which remained at 242,000, but by the outbreak of war, the Transport Workers had reached 380,000 and the Distributive Workers 160,000. Apart from the divisions over the constitution, the loyalty of the large unions was even more predictable than in the early thirties. The Transport Workers and the GMW were consistently loyal: so too were the Railwaymen. The Miners and the Engineers were slightly less predictable; the lure of the united front had its attractions there. But only the Distributive Workers offered a fairly consistent challenge to the Executive covering Spain, the united front, the expulsion of Cripps and defence policy. Some smaller unions — most notably the Locomotive men, were often critical of the platform, and it is clear that during these years the division of opinion with the Conference was not simply between unions and local parties. Often a large proportion of the usually small critical vote came from the Distributive Workers and other trade unions. Overall the Conference's behaviour was predictable: there might be oratorical highlights on the part of critics, but the difficulties faced by the Executive in the early thirties were now much reduced. In so far as the crucial Conference operation was the securing of pro-Executive votes, there were few problems, although on sensitive issues such as Spain and rearmament, the mobilisation of support necessitated calculatedly ambiguous declarations.

Trade union influence also continued to be exerted through the mechanisms developed after 1931. The NEC Policy Committee and the TUC Economic Committee continued to operate a division of labour, while if anything, the National Council's importance increased with the need to respond to successive international crises. The issuing of NCL statements generated a suspicion that the power of purely party bodies was being usurped, and led to a critical resolution being debated at the 1939 Conference.[8] This was easily defeated, but it is clear that concern was not restricted to constituency activists. Thus, in September 1937, Morrison had queried the Council's publication of the pamphlet 'International Policy and Defence', which subsequently provided the Executive's position at the 1937 Conference.[9] Defenders of the NCL always emphasised the consultative aspect of its work, but obviously the outcome of consultations reflects the varying tenacity of those involved. It seems clear that on international matters the Council's pronouncements frequently reflected the Bevin-Citrine viewpoint, to a greater extent than any purely Executive statement would have done.

By the end of the decade, the evolving pattern of party relationships had become much clearer. The strengthening of the PLP and the reversal of the post-1931 drift to the left highlighted the emergence of a moderate coalition, moderate politicians and trade union leaders dominated all party bodies. Obviously there were tensions occasioned by the different priorities of the two sections, and by stylistic and personality factors, but at all levels, the rule of the moderates was secure.

The Destruction of the Left

The agitation over the Spanish Civil War, the campaigns for United and Popular Fronts, the Left Book Club with its 60,000 members, all help to bolster the image of the thirties as a golden age for the Labour left. There is, of course, an element of truth in this. The enthusiasm of

British intellectuals for progressive politics, was stronger than ever before. Yet the moderates' domination of the Labour Party remained unbroken. In the end, all the enthusiasm shattered against the unwillingness of Labour leaders to support any radical agitation outside the institutions of the party.

The Labour left's predicament after the 1935 election was unenviable. Its assessment of the National Government's capacity for reaction was much more pessimistic than that of the labour leadership. The party seemed far from the attainment of power. What possible responses were there? The left's criticisms of the Leadership's strategy in the final analysis became encapsulated in one demand, for a United or Popular Front of all progressive forces against reaction. This encapsulation was in the end a weakness, as it proved impossible to win the Labour Party for such a strategy. In every forum of the party, demands for united fronts were resoundingly defeated.

The pattern of debate on these issues was demonstrated clearly at the 1936 Conference. A resolution favouring Communist affiliation received 592,000 votes, a figure swollen by the Miners' vote of 400,000 while an Engineers' plea for united front activities collected 435,000.[10] In spite of these rebuffs, the campaign developed in response to the Spanish Civil War, and was influenced also by the election of a Popular Front Government in France. In January 1937, the Socialist League backed now by a new weekly *Tribune*, decided to launch a unity campaign, along with the Communists and the ILP. The delegates at the League's special conferences were not unanimously in favour of this. There were good grounds for such reservations. Already in December 1936, the NEC's Organisation Sub-Committee had decided to recommend the convening of a special Executive meeting to deal with Communist activities in local parties.[11] The Executive subsequently published, with four dissentients, an appeal to party loyalty,[12] and once the League had openly adopted a united front policy, it moved swiftly into action. On 27 January, the Executive decided to disaffiliate the League.[13] This draconian action was taken after an initial attempt to delay had been lost by fourteen votes to nine. A similar split between hard-line disciplinarians and compromisers appeared two months later. By then it was abundantly clear that the League had no intention of ending the campaign and the Executive's hard-liners now decided to proscribe the League. This was resisted by, amongst others, Morrison and Attlee. They wanted to delay and to allow League representatives to express their views at the 1937 Conference. The suggestion of the party leader was defeated on the Executive by fourteen votes to six.[14] The representatives of the trade unions were unwilling to play for compromise.

The reaction of the League was to dissolve itself at its Whitsun Conference. Thus, in less than five years, the Socialist League fell foul of the same difficulties as the ILP. This was a major landmark in the campaign against the united front. The rebels had been forced to dismantle their organisation. They declared their intention of continuing with United Front propaganda as individuals, but even this was subsequently opposed by the Executive.[15] Debate on these questions was truncated at the 1937 Conference. Although 43 resolutions had been tabled on the United Front, the Executive ruled all of them out of order under the three-year rule. Instead, battle was joined on the section of the Executive's Report dealing with the events of the spring. The minority secured only 331,000 votes, of which a high proportion came from trade unions including the Distributive Workers and the Shop Assistants.[16] All that the unity campaigners could take comfort from was the election of three of their spokesmen to the reconstituted constituency section of the NEC.

The weakness of these representatives was exposed in May 1938, when the Executive met to consider a memorandum, 'The International Situation', produced by the three, plus Ellen Wilkinson. This proposed not just a United Front with other socialist groupings, but a wider Popular Front also covering anti-Government Liberals. Within the Executive the only support came from the four compilers of the memorandum.[17] The deteriorating situation both in Spain and elsewhere had also produced demands for a Special Conference. There was concern amongst the Executive majority lest this be used for Popular Front agitation. Such demands were resisted throughout the summer of 1938, although on occasions the majority was small. The interest of the Executive in all manifestations of Popular Front activity remained intense. A detailed investigation was conducted into the Left Book Club,[18] and there were recriminations over local Labour support for the popular front candidates in the Oxford and Bridgewater by-elections.[19] Executive members were pressurised by trade union leaders. Bevin wrote to the Executive, emphasising that: 'the liberty taken by a section of the Party to depart from Party policy makes it impossible for the NEC to ask the Trade Unions to remain loyal.'[20]

In this context, it is clear that any further initiatives for a Popular Front campaign would meet with a very negative response from the party leadership. Nevertheless, in January 1939 Cripps circulated a memorandum to the Executive reiterating the case made eight months earlier, in much more detail. He now included a twelve-point programme that could serve as a platform for a Popular Front Government. This proposal was predictably defeated in the Executive by seventeen votes to three,[21] but Cripps now appealed to the party rank and file. He circularised them with copies of his memorandum. The Executive majority reacted sharply, and expelled him from the party by eighteen votes to one.[22] Other expulsions followed including two MPs, Bevan and Strauss.

The whole agitation[23] was buried at the 1939 Conference. Although Cripps was given permission to address the Conference, his narrow legalistic appeal was an anti-climax. His expulsion was ratified by the overwhelming margin of 2,100,000 to 402,000. The Distributive Workers' 150,000 votes helped to bolster the minority as did the 60,000 to 70,000 votes accruing from other smaller unions. On this basis, it is clear that Cripps enjoyed the support of less than half of the constituency parties.[24] The popular front position received a still more humiliating rebuff. The Distributive Workers again contributed their 150,000 votes, this time to a total of 248,000. Support from the constituency parties was clearly limited.[25] After the Conference, only the debris remained. Strauss and Bevan re-entered the party within a few months, but Cripps chose to retain his independence until 1945. Support for Popular Front activities declined rapidly with the signing of the Soviet-German Pact and the outbreak of war. Some local parties continued to express sympathy with the Communist position on the war, and were rapidly 'reorganised' by the Executive. Pritt wrote long defences of the Soviet invasion of Finland and was expelled from the party.[26] A whole epoch of Labour left agitation was over.

These conflicts were fought on ground that was extremely disadvantageous for the left. Any suggestion of co-operation with Communists produced the predictable reactions from Labour moderates. Why then did the left persist in the series of campaigns? Partly responsible was the distance of Labour from power, combined with increasing pessimism about the international situation, which created longing for some sort of activity that appeared more rewarding than patient preparation for the next election. No doubt, involvement in the various agitations gave a sense of purpose in what appeared otherwise to be a hopeless situation. Yet it would be facile to set the whole of the explanation in these terms. The question of left-wing unity raised basic and sensitive issues for all members of the Labour Party. To what was the primary commitment of the party? Was it to liberal democracy or to socialism? Some advocates of the United Front visualised the problems in still starker terms. For them, the National Government was pro-Fascist, and given this, the appropriate response was to advocate a union of anti-Fascists. Underlying all this advocacy and categorisation, there was a positive and simplistic assessment of the Soviet Union. Stalinist purges notwithstanding, the régime was a socialist one and should be treated as such.

Each of these bases for action was mute as to the appropriate strategy. But supposing a Popular Front had been formed, what was it to do? There were frequent references to some sort of extra-parliamentary agitation that would eventually weaken the Government. But there was little said regarding the content of such agitation. There was no suggestion that industrial action might be used to produce desired changes, and obviously the hope of such action was vain given the attitudes of almost all the large unions.

Perhaps the strongest point in the Popular Front case concerned the unreality of Labour's hopes for office after the next election. This required the capture of 150 extra seats compared with 1935. Labour's by-election record between 1935 and the outbreak of war hardly supported such hopes. The party captured thirteen seats: ironically the most spectacular victory was at Ipswich with a candidate who was hardly a model of party orthodoxy. Some of Labour's failures were striking. Thus the party failed early in 1937 to overturn the handful of votes needed to capture St Pancras North. In some cases Labour lost ground even compared with 1935. Party organisers continually reported apathy and lack of enthusiasm.[27] On this narrow question of electoral advantage, is there any evidence that some kind of progressive arrangement could have worked?

It is difficult to accept that a pooling arrangement with the Communists would have been electorally advantageous. Although the CPGB had developed local strongholds, it seems clear that such an arrangement would have had net disadvantages for Labour. An alliance with the Liberals offered perhaps a more promising outlook. Although Liberal parliamentary representation was meagre, it was believed by some strategists that an anti-Government alliance might be created if Labour did not oppose non-socialist progressives in rural and suburban areas. Some credence was given to this by the success of such a candidate in the Bridgewater by-election in November 1938.

It is doubtful whether this kind of exercise would have worked on a national basis, but Labour's leaders did not begin to discuss the problem. They merely reiterated their demand for all progressives to come into the Labour Party, a plea decorated by cautionary tales about Liberal-Labour relationships during the two minority governments. The question of electoral strategy was the one point in the Popular Front position that carried weight within the perspective of the moderate leadership. Otherwise, it was easy to mobilise trade union and moderate political support behind the official line.[28] Apart from the basic suspicion of 'disruptive Communists' and 'middle-class Liberals', there were sharp inconsistencies in the critics' position. Thus, Cripps in the United Front phase had pursued a rigidly class-conscious line, but later, in the memorandum he emphasised 'the difficulty of winning over large numbers of the middle class ...'[29] Furthermore in his 1939 proposals Cripps advocated a programme that appeared in many respects more moderate than official policy. This attempt to capture Liberal sympathies, most notably by advocating control rather than ownership of basic industries, provoked righteous indignation from official quarters.[30]

Labour had 'arrived' as a major party by the late thirties. Many of the rank and file could respond to the blandishments of popular front campaigns by protesting *their* loyalty to *their* party. More important, both sides of the moderates' alliance had good reason to repel any attempt to compromise Labour's independence. The career prospects of Labour leaders were bound up with the survival of the party as an independent organisation. They had doggedly reconstructed the party after 1931. Why now should they dissipate their investment for some dubious short-term advantage? Equally, the dominant trade union leaders were determined to protect the party against the brief, brittle enthusiasms of intellectuals and the subversion of Communists. Frequently in analyses of Labour in the thirties, the left hold the centre of the stage. Theirs is the drama and the excitement. But they were a stage army betrayed by their lack of strategy, and crushed by the entrenched majority.

The Domestic Consensus

The 1935 election was succeeded by a period of relative quiescence on the home policy front. There were no longer any debates about the possibility of implementing socialist reforms through the parliamentary system; nor were there major controversies over individual details such as the joint-stock banks, or the position of workers in publicly-owned industries. Yet there was, during these years, a significant refining of the policy positions reached prior to the 1935 election. Labour's home policy in 1939 was subtly different from four years earlier, and significantly more moderate than had appeared likely in 1932 and 1933.[31]

This refining process turned around the production of a short policy statement, 'Labour's Immediate Programme', early in 1937. At the previous year's Conference, a resolution had been remitted to the Executive asking for a brief statement of Labour's short-term policy. The Policy Committee considered this in the last two months of 1936,[32] and early in the following year they discussed a number of memoranda, including one from Dalton.[33] He has claimed that this formed the basis of the Committee's subsequent work,[34] but it should also be emphasised that Attlee was asked to submit a statement indicating some guiding principles. When the Policy Committee set up a drafting committee to produce a programme for submission to the Executive, it had before it a statement by Attlee plus amendments by Dalton.[35] It is apparent that they were principally responsible for the document, along with Greenwood as head of the Research Department.

After being discussed by the full Executive,[36] the 'Immediate Programme' was published in March 1937.[37] The contents of the statement were placed in the context of immediate needs. This was important: on this occasion, as so often in the future, the acceptance of this apparently uncontroversial principle could produce a purging of the more controversial elements from the programme. Thus on public ownership the 'Immediate Programme' mentioned transport, coal, electricity, gas and the Bank of England. It did not include iron and steel, cotton and the joint-stock banks. It is clear that the last, at least, was a deliberate omission: certainly, Dalton had always regarded it as unnecessary and electorally harmful. Beyond these proposals and omissions, the statement centred around suggestions for ameliorating conditions in the depressed areas, and for increasing general standards of welfare. The 'Immediate Programme' was an unequivocally Fabian document, a final testimony to the way in which the debates of the early thirties had been resolved. It symbolised the emerging social democratic consensus as supported by the moderate alliance. Several of the measures within the 'Immediate Programme' could be presented plausibly, as first steps in a socialist transformation, and yet the total set of proposals could be seen as a blueprint for increasing the efficiency and reducing the acerbities of the existing society. Certainly there was no indication of any desire to produce a significant shift in the distribution of power between classes, and no suggestion that the proposed changes would produce bitter resistance. Labour's programme was presented as the reasonable citizen's response to crisis.

This subtle but significant shift did not produce any notable opposition within the party. This can be explained in part merely by remembering the domination of the party by moderate groups: but it also reflects the ambiguities and doubts of potential critics. As we have seen, they never formulated a coherent alternative, and their tacit acceptance of the 'Immediate Programme' showed their theoretical poverty. The acceptance of the programme was also aided by its ambiguous status. The idea of a short statement of immediate measures could be seen as still leaving such items as the joint-stock banks within the party programme. In some senses, 'For Socialism and Peace' could still be regarded as the most authoritative statement of Labour policy. Yet the 'Immediate Programme', at the least, established an order of priorities and in time acquired standing as an authoritative statement. The manner of the document's publication also inhibited criticism. In an attempt to increase activists' enthusiasm, and to reduce the attraction of popular front agitations, the Party launched a nation-wide campaign. The 'Immediate Programme' was used as a central feature of this and achieved high sales before it had been approved by a Party Conference.[38] Thus, by the time of the 1937 Conference, the programme was firmly established at the centre of party propaganda, and received only a perfunctory debate.[39] Indeed, on occasions, the programme was presented as little more than a piece of propaganda, but the selection of policy items and any rewriting of existing policy statements carried implications for the party's view of what was entailed by its policy commitments.

One aspect of the development of home policy was certainly the production of this broad image of Labour's commitments, but it was also envisaged that detailed preparations would be made in opposition to enable the party to implement its policies efficiently, once office had been obtained. The contribution of the TUC's Research Department to this exercise has already been noted. It produced a further detailed statement in 1936, covering the socialisation of the coal industry. One reason for this joint research work was obviously the meagre resources of the party's Research Department. Its limited contribution generated widespread concern which led, in October 1937, to the formation of a committee under Dalton to consider possible reforms. The results of its enquiry were considered by the full Executive in June 1938.[40] The report was scathing about the state of the department: 'it is not either administratively or psychologically in a happy condition.'[41] Greenwood was considered to be overburdened, and therefore incapable of providing the necessary detailed guidance of the department's work. Although he remained titular head, he was relieved of the day-to-day operation. The department was also related much more closely to the Policy Committee. The hope was that a reinvigorated department would serve as the equivalent of the Civil Service. This remained a dream. Any hope of producing a much more efficient department was bedevilled by the characteristic Labour insistence on restricted expenditure. Although Labour's broad domestic strategy was clear by the late thirties, the anticipated wealth of detailed blueprints never materialised. Such statements as did appear soon became dated. By the outbreak of war, the party had plans for transport and electricity drawn up in 1933; a statement on coal from 1936, and statements on iron and steel and cotton from 1934 and 1935.[42] The gas industry had always featured in Labour's plans for public ownership, but no detailed statement had been prepared.

Labour in the thirties went through a lengthy restatement of home policy and emerged with a relatively clear programme. Yet underneath this clarity there were two problems, both of which were to have long-term importance. There was an ambiguity over the status of some of the proposals. In retrospect, it is useful to see the 'Immediate Programme' as an important milestone in the evolution of a perspective centred around the improvement, not the replacement of existing society. Yet the idea that Labour had a distinctively socialist commitment remained vital. It is this ambiguity, then largely concealed, that is at the heart of the social democratic perspective. There was also a problem over the content of the specific proposals. Most of these had become uncontroversial features of all Labour policy statements. Their content was taken as read, yet in many cases it had been barely explored. By 1939, Labour was prepared for office in that it had a programme that was accepted throughout the party. But it was unprepared in its failure to work out detailed proposals, and in its failure to consider whether its proposals were relevant to its commitment to socialism.

Arms for Britain and Arms for Spain

It was inevitable that Labour's domestic preoccupation during these years should pale into insignificance at the side of the deepening international crisis. The Brighton debate had appeared to leave the

initiative with Bevin, Dalton and Citrine, but the Hoare-Laval pact
appeared to confirm the worst fears of the Labour left. Surely it was
obvious now that the National Government was no more than an
accomplice of Fascism? Suspicion of the Government's motives
remained deeply rooted for many who did not accept the Labour left's
analysis of international affairs. Thus, it was not surprising that
controversy about the attitude of the party towards British rearmament
continued for two more years. There was much more at stake here
than the party's policy towards armaments. The basic question was the
perennial one of party identity. How far should the national interest
be considered? What should the party's attitude be towards liberal
democratic institutions? Could such considerations ever lead to support
for the National Government? For some, these questions had been
resolved, but for many within the party, the diverse sources of Labour's
international attitude continued to generate confusions and hesitations.

The extent of the doubts and the divisions, even at the leadership
level, was demonstrated in March 1936 when several meetings of the
National Council, the three Executives and all the separate decision-
making bodies were held, in order to decide the Labour attitude towards
the new Government White Paper on Defence.[43] Dalton apart, the
politicians appear to have urged opposition. Trade union spokesmen
were less inclined towards this position. It is clear from the records
that Citrine was unwilling to gloss over the discrepancies. At this stage,
the politicians' pleas seem to have carried the day; Labour MPs still
opposed government defence policies in the division lobbies. The claim
that this was because of opposition to the Government's
international policy, not to the principle of national defence, was
becoming less persuasive as the crisis intensified.

In July 1936, Dalton attempted to organise within the PLP in
order to prevent opposition being expressed in this way, but he failed.
Even on the Parliamentary Executive, only three people supported him,
and only 38 in the PLP.[44] The lack of agreement between moderate
politicians aware of the problems of party management and
trade union spokesmen was strikingly demonstrated at that year's
Conference. Unusually, there had been no prior international debate
at the TUC and the party debated international policy on a
resolution which was ambiguous, even by the standards of Labour
Party declarations.[45] After accepting the need to retain enough arms
to carry out League of Nations obligations, the resolution contrasted
this with the 'competitive' policy of the Government. The speeches of
the party's principal spokesmen served to increase the obscurity. Dalton

unequivocally claimed that a Labour Government would have to increase armaments; Morrison stressed the party's criticisms of the existing Government; Attlee did the same. In contrast to the subtleties of the platform speakers, Cripps and Bevin combined from very different positions to condemn the obscurities of the official statement. The debates at Edinburgh indicated that the maintenance of unity through calculated ambiguity could not survive much longer.[46]

Within the next twelve months, much of the uncertainty vanished. There were two aspects of this: the practice of opposing the Defence Estimates ceased, and a new clearer international policy statement was produced. The first purely parliamentary matter was the result of manoeuvres by Dalton and other sympathetic MPs. These began on the Parliamentary Executive, but here Dalton found only two supporters. Within the PLP, however, a majority for a change was found by 45 votes to 39, thereby overthrowing the Executive's decision. In this significant shift, it appears that considerable pressure was exerted by the TUC, although several trade union MPs supported the traditional position. The total vote at the meeting seems low: this possibly reflects the confused position of several back-benchers.[47]

Although this symbolic shift was important, the production of a new policy statement was a more significant move towards the exorcism of Labour's traditional views. The basis for the statement had been a memorandum prepared by Gillies, head of the party's International Department, and a strong advocate of rearmament. During the discussions at the National Council of Labour a major part was played in the redrafting by Dalton.[48] The final statement was not wholly clear: it was certainly apparent that a Labour Government, given the present crisis, would rearm, although it was argued that Labour's prescriptions should eventually make rearmament on this scale unnecessary. But on the delicate question of rearmament under the existing Government there was silence. The document received an easy passage at the TUC. Only 224,000 votes were cast against it but even in this comparatively apolitical forum, the basic problems raised for the party by the rearmament issue were clear.[49] Although the document was vague on Labour's attitude towards current rearmament, Citrine in his concluding speech asserted strongly that 'rearmament cannot await the advent of a Labour Government'. For the leading spokesmen of the TUC, acceptance of the document meant that Labour in opposition supported rearmament. Inevitably the debate at the Party Conference was contested more fiercely. The pacifists were now marginal to the debate and the real battle lay for the last time in the thirties between the moderate leadership and those who would support rearmament only when this was clearly linked to a socialist foreign policy.[50] This confrontation clearly highlighted the incoherencies at the heart of Labour's position. Critics of the policy document rested their case on the assumption that the principal target must be British capitalism. The most militant supporters of rearmament presented their position in unashamedly nationalist terms emphasising that: 'Britain, the Mother of Democracy has always stood for democratic liberty.'[51] Most defenders of the document were not so explicit: the whole tortured debate over rearmament indicates the duality of Labour's position, its schizophrenic commitment to both nation and class. Although the debate contained a vigorous presentation of the socialist viewpoint, the result was never in doubt. The large unions were overwhelmingly behind the leadership, and the minority position secured only 228,000 votes.

It is tempting but misleading to see the international debates cf 1936 and 1937 merely as footnotes to the decision of 1935. On this interpretation, the process was one of exploring the implications of an earlier decision within a deteriorating situation. From this perspective, the leadership's critics can be presented readily as impractical doctrinaires who failed to appreciate the gravity of the situation. Such an interpretation is inadequate on two counts. Firstly, it ignores the very sound domestic reasons for the Labour left's distrust of the National Government; but more significantly, within the context of 1936 and 1937, it omits the powerful impetus given to the Labour left's position by the outbreak of the Spanish Civil War. This strengthened the Labour left's belief in its own interpretation of international events, and deepened its suspicions of Labour's leadership.

The Spanish question was the most celebrated left-wing cause of the thirties. For once everything fell into place. Without too much artificiality the conflict could be defined as between progress and reaction, and between socialism and Fascism. Support for the Spanish Government could be justified on unambiguously doctrinal grounds. Although the Labour left reacted fiercely, the leaderships of the party and the TUC were diffident. Certainly a declaration was passed supporting the Spanish Republicans, but then the leadership entered a maze over the question of arms for Spain. Eventually the General Council, the NEC and the PLP met and decided to support the non-intervention policy advocated by the British Government. One reason for the relative ease with which the decision went through was that it enjoyed the support of the French Popular Front Government. From the beginning, Labour support for non-intervention was disputed. Certainly there were leading figures such as Dalton who had little sympathy with the Republicans, but there were many others who felt that the policy must discriminate against the Republicans, already opposed by the bulk of the Spanish Army.[52] Nevertheless, non-intervention was easily accepted by the 1936 TUC. Only 51,000 votes were cast against it.[53] In the weeks between the TUC and the Party Conference doubts about the policy increased. On the eve of the Conference the Executive discussed whether the breaking of the non-intervention agreement by the Italians justified any reconsideration. This tentative proposal was defeated by eleven votes to eight, and the existing position confirmed by fourteen votes to seven.[54] Beneath the Executive's façade of unity, there was a division, not reducible to conventional left-right terms. Morrison was one of the most forceful advocates of 'Arms for Spain'.

Despite this internal division, the Executive faced the Conference, as the advocate of non-intervention. Although this position was inevitably approved following the overwhelming TUC verdict, the minority vote was now 519,000.[55] Furthermore, the Executive's defence had been hesitant and apologetic. Critical speeches had come from beyond the normal critics on the left. The Executive's victory was undermined not by the critics within the party so much as by two oratorical triumphs by Spanish visitors.[56] By the end of the Conference, a series of joint meetings had produced a significant shift in Labour policy. Now at least the leaders took the claimed breaches to non-intervention seriously. This shift[57] does not appear to have been welcomed by at least one central figure, Dalton. He was dismayed by what he regarded as the 'sheer emotion ...'[58] of many delegates. Nevertheless in the month after the Conference, the party shifted to a policy of 'Arms for Spain'. For the next two and a half years Labour agitated consistently but unsuccessfully for a lifting of the embargo.

This shift should not be taken as indicated a healing of the breach between left and right. For the left, Spain was central to the whole international drama. The British Government's support for a non-intervention policy, that now appeared so flagrantly unfair, helped to preserve left-wing suspicions. The grudging response of Labour leaders also served to reinforce suspicions, this time of the priorities of the party moderates. They did not appear as a potentially radical Government but as a 'slouching leadership' with a 'parasitic attitude towards the Government of the other class'.[59] But for Bevin, Dalton and their sympathisers, Spain served to underline their suspicions of

the left. They translated commitment and passion as unreliable
emotionalism: they felt that the left's sympathy for the Republicans
was a minority viewpoint: they contrasted the left's advocacy of
'Arms for Spain' with its opposition to 'Arms for Britain' under the
National Government. Although all sections of the party came
together under the broad umbrella of 'Arms for Spain', the issue
showed how far different elements in the party inhabited different
political universes.

The discords remained largely below the surface. After the verdict
of the 1937 Conference, the party attacked government policy on
Spain, and then the collapse over Czechoslovakia. Only over the
introduction of conscription in the spring of 1939 did Labour's
traditional attitudes surface again. On this question, both political
and industrial wings seemed opposed to the Government, although
in retrospect some of the party's leaders expressed doubts about their
opposition. This however was only a brief interlude. Throughout
the 1939 summer Labour's official position remained strongly
opposed to any further German expansion.

It would be easy but mistaken to interpret the development of
Labour's international policy as the development of political
realism and the exorcism of emotional and misleading precepts.
It was much more complicated. The position epitomised by Bevin
and Dalton challenged a well-established consensus on international
affairs that in more stable times had maintained a united party.
The new perspective carried far-reaching implications for Labour's
sense of identity. Its complete emphasis on national interests was
an implicit denial of many left-wing criticisms of British society,
and a rejection of the idea that there could be a distinctively socialist
foreign policy. Any idea that this new 'realistic' position had
conquered the party was premature. The upholders of the
traditional viewpoint were temporarily silenced by the pace of
international developments, but the basic rift over international
affairs remained to dominate party controversies frequently in
the post-war period.

'My Country Right or Left'

The attitude of the party in September 1939 was in marked contrast
to the agonised debates of August 1914. Now there was little
internal opposition to the party's support for the war effort. Only the
Communist Party, after an early embarrassing somersault, and a few
pacifists opposed the war.[60]   Indeed many leading Labour spokesmen

argued that the Chamberlain Government was too lethargic. The first eight months of the war were a strange limbo for the party. It refused any role in the Government, but agreed to an electoral truce. Its official criticisms were generally muted, but behind the façade there were tensions.

The party's internal difficulties were largely legacies from the pre-war controversies. There was some strain in the relationship between Labour's industrial and political wings. Although there was basic agreement between the leaderships over the support for the war, and although trade union leaders were suspicious of the Government's labour policy, there seems to have been a desire on the part of trade union leaders for political activities to be kept in a low key. In the first months of the war, there were demands from some NEC members for a joint declaration on a peace settlement, but this was opposed by the industrial side of the National Council.[61] This had been preceded by anxiety about the Council's role in wartime. The old spectre of the Council's powers had re-emerged, but in spite of reservations it had been formally resolved that the 'National Council of Labour be the authority for the Labour Movement ...'[62]

These tensions stemming essentially from the distinctive functions of the political and industrial wings were complicated only marginally by political differences. The TUC backed the General Council almost unanimously. Within the party there were a few difficulties as a result of Communist opposition to the war. Some local parties were 'reorganised', and in March 1940 Pritt was expelled from the party because of his support for the Soviet invasion of Finland. These difficulties were unimportant, however. The Communist volte-face on the war lost it much of the support that it had slowly amassed since 1933, while within the party it strengthened the moderates and disorientated the left. For the first time for several years, controversy on traditional left-right lines almost ceased. Nevertheless one issue continued to generate disquiet. The electoral truce was discussed by the Executive in December 1939, and its maintenance was supported by seventeen votes to five.[63] This minority vote was significant in the circumstances. It was the first indication of what was to become a perennial controversy.

After its failure to persuade the National Council to produce a policy statement, the Executive developed statements on international and home policy.[64] Although these were couched in general terms, they marked the beginning of a lengthy wartime process of policy production. The combination behind the statements was also suggestive. The

practical men, Dalton and Morrison, contrasted with Laski, the critic
who was always willing to pool his ideas. This blend of practicality and
idealism was to be the hallmark of Labour's wartime policy statements.

During the first eight months of the war Labour remained on the
sidelines preparing its policies for the 1940 Conference, purging
Communist sympathisers and pinpricking the Government. Then in
May 1940, the party moved out of the comparative obscurity that had
enveloped it for nine years. The fiasco of the Norwegian campaign
produced revolt amongst a section of Conservative back-benchers. In a
debate on the conduct of the war the Chamberlain Government was
destroyed in just three parliamentary days. Tory critics and Labour
members united in opposition. The Government's majority sank from
around 240 to 81.

The resulting political crisis was complicated by the imminence
of the Party Conference. The Executive in its pre-Conference
meeting agreed, with one dissentient, to enter a Government
under a new Prime Minister.[65] This appears to have been the final
ingredient in Chamberlain's fall. With Churchill's acceptance of
the premiership, the concern of the Executive switched to Labour's
share in the new Government. There seems to have been
some debate over this, but eventually the Executive underwrote
the offer made by Churchill. The party was to have two men
(Attlee and Greenwood) in a War Cabinet of five; one Service
Department (Alexander) and various other offices. This solution was
then endorsed by the National Council. There remained the Conference.
All of the crucial decisions had been taken during the weekend before
the Conference met. There was little difficulty. A resolution moved by
Attlee and supporting the Executive's decision was overwhelmingly
supported. Critical remnants — pacifists and opponents of an 'imperialist
war' — were swept aside.[66] They were dismissed privately by one
leading figure as 'freaks talking pathetic rubbish'.[67]

May 1940 marked another crucial stage in the strengthening of
Labour's position. The plausibility of its social democratic perspective
and the penchant of its leaders for a 'realistic' international policy
were both to be enhanced by experience of office. Yet this crucial
strengthening had occurred in a singular fashion. Throughout the
thirties Labour's leaders had argued that the party's road to power must
lie through the creation of a self-sufficient parliamentary majority,
based on the party's own unambiguous electoral platform. Now Labour
had achieved a share in the Government through a parliamentary *coup*
and private negotiations. Moreover it was as part of an alliance much

wider than anything envisaged by the advocates of a Popular Front.

Notes

1. John Lewis, *The Left Book Club: a Historical Record* (Gollancz, London, 1970); also Hugh Thomas, op. cit., chs. 8-12.
2. See Dalton, *Vol. 2*, pp. 79-84, and Donoughue and Jones, op. cit., ch. 17.
3. Dalton, *Vol. 2*, p. 82.
4. *NEC Minutes*, 5 September 1936.
5. Dalton, *Vol. 2*, pp. 116-18.
6. *Organisation Sub-Committee Minutes*, 3 June 1937; *NEC Minutes*, 23 June and 4 October 1937.
7. *LPCR 1937*, pp. 140-55.
8. *LPCR 1939*, pp. 224-6.
9. *NEC Minutes*, 6 September 1937.
10. *LPCR 1936*, pp. 207-11, 250-7.
11. *Organisation Sub-Committee Minutes*, 22 December 1936.
12. *NEC Minutes*, 4 January 1937.
13. Ibid., 27 January 1937.
14. *Organisation Sub-Committee Minutes*, 17 March 1937; *NEC Minutes*, 24 March 1937.
15. Ibid., 28 July 1937.
16. *LPCR 1937*, pp. 25-8 and 268-70, for texts of NEC statements on the issue and pp. 156-64 for debate.
17. *NEC Minutes*, 5 May 1938.
18. *Memorandum on Left Book Club*, November 1938.
19. Ian McLean, 'Oxford and Bridgewater' in Cook and Ramsden, op. cit. pp. 140-64.
20. See *NEC Minutes*, 16 December 1938.
21. *NEC Minutes*, 13 January 1939.
22. Ibid., 18 January 1939. For documentation see *LPCR 1939*, pp. 44-53.
23. Described in Foot, *Vol. I*, pp. 296-8.
24. *LPCR 1939*, pp. 220 and 226-36. Also Dalton, *Vol. 2*, pp. 218-21. Cripps had been given permission to appeal to Conference by 1,227,000 to 1,083,000.
25. *LPCR 1939*, pp. 291-9.
26. *NEC Minutes*, 26 March 1940; *LPCR 1940*, pp. 161-6.
27. Expressed in *NEC Minutes*, 27 May 1936 (Peckham), 5 September 1936 (Balham); 24 February 1937 (St Pancras North and Gorton).
28. For an account of the debates see Miliband, op. cit.
29. Cripps Memorandum. Copy in *NEC Minutes*.
30. See, for a characteristically dubious argument, Greenwood's response to Cripps' 1939 proposals. The proposal for a Lib-Lab pact is denounced with a quotation from Asquith in 1924! This response is also in the *NEC Minutes*.
31. For an evocation of this mood see C.A.R. Attlee, *The Labour Party In Perspective* (Gollancz, London, 1937).
32. *Policy Committee Minutes*, 17 November and 15 December 1936.
33. Ibid., 20 January 1937.
34. Dalton, *Vol. 2*, pp. 124-8.
35. *Policy Committee Minutes*, 4 February 1937.
36. *NEC Minutes*, 24 February 1937.
37. For text see *LPCR 1937*, pp. 277-9.
38. See the complaint by George Strauss, *NEC Minutes*, 26 May 1937.

39. *LPCR 1937*, pp. 181-6.
40. *NEC Minutes*, 27 October 1937; 22 June 1938.
41. Report of Sub-Committee.
42. For an inventory see *Memorandum LG.149*, presented to Policy Committee 8 February 1940.
43. *NEC Minutes*, 4 March 1936; *Minutes of Joint Meeting of the Three Executives*, 4 March 1936; also Dalton, *Vol. 2*, pp. 87-8.
44. Dalton, *Vol. 2*, p. 132.
45. On background see *NEC Minutes*, 28 August, 18 September, 1 and 2 October 1936; *Minutes of Joint Meeting*, General Council and NEC, 4 September 1936.
46. *LPCR 1936*, pp. 181-207.
47. For divergent assessments see Dalton, *Vol. 2*, pp. 132-9, and Foot, *Vol. I*, pp. 265-6.
48. *NEC Minutes*, 26 May and 28 July 1937.
49. *TUC Report 1937*, pp. 402-26.
50. *LPCR 1937*, pp. 195-212.
51. Ibid., p. 211 (James Walker of the Steel Workers, and Executive spokesman).
52. See *NEC Minutes*, 4 and 9 September 1937: *Minutes of Joint Meeting of Three Executives*, same dates.
53. *TUC Report 1936*, pp. 359-90.
54. *NEC Minutes*, 4 October 1936. The motion to change the policy was moved by Joseph Henderson of the NUR, and seconded by Barbara Ayrton Gould.
55. *LPCR 1936*, pp. 169-81.
56. Ibid., pp. 212-5.
57. See *NEC Minutes*, 7 October 1936; *Minutes of Joint Meeting of NEC and General Council*, 8 October 1936; *Minutes of Joint Meeting of NEC, PLP Executive (with General Council joining later)*, 9 October 1936; also *LPCR 1936*, pp. 258-62.
58. Dalton, *Vol. 2*, p. 100.
59. H.N. Brailsford – cited in Allen Hutt, *The Post War History of The British Working Class* (Gollancz, London, 1937), p. 301.
60. For the Communist Party, see V. Gollancz (ed.), *The Betrayal of the Left* (Gollancz, London, 1941); for a balanced, retrospective view see Angus Calder, *The People's War* (Cape, London, 1969), pp. 243-7.
61. The opposition is reported in *NEC Minutes*, 25 October 1939; it had been expressed at the NCL five days earlier.
62. See *Minutes of Joint Meeting of the Three Executives*, 25 August 1939.
63. *NEC Minutes*, 20 December 1939.
64. *NEC Minutes*, 22 January and 6 February 1940; *Policy Committee Minutes*, 14 March 1940.
65. *NEC Minutes*, 10 May 1940. On these events see P. Addison, *The Road to 1945* (Cape, London, 1975), ch. 3.
66. *LPCR 1940*, pp. 123-34.
67. Dalton, *Vol. 2*, p. 316.

4 LABOUR AND THE WAR 1940-1945

Labour acquired office in May 1940, not as the result of an electoral victory, but as the consequence of a parliamentary *coup*, not as a party unencumbered with alliances, but as a partner in a coalition including some of the party's long-standing enemies. May 1940 was in some ways more crucial for the party than July 1945. It was after all on the fall of Chamberlain that Labour politicians regained office. Initially, Attlee and Greenwood entered the small War Cabinet, but the Labour figures who secured most public attention were Bevin, Morrison and Cripps. Bevin entered Parliament for the first time, and went immediately to the Ministry of Labour where he remained throughout the coalition; Morrison, after a brief period at Supply, spent much of the war at the Home Office, while Cripps, although occupying less senior posts, attracted extensive public attention. It was characteristic that Attlee did not achieve the same prominence.

Inevitably participation in a coalition generated tensions. Labour Ministers claimed that their participation was crucial if Labour was to acquire credibility as a governing party, and that their co-operation in the war effort could result in measures furthering Labour causes. However, the ghosts of 1918 and 1931 were never far from the thoughts of many Labour partisans. Twice in the past, some Labour leaders had foresaken the party, attracted by the lure of 'national co-operation' and in spite of continual reassurances by Attlee and Morrison, the suspicion lingered.

These tensions proved in the event to be productive. The party gained both from the radical expectations raised by wartime social changes, and from the aura of responsibility and competence acquired by Labour Ministers. Yet during the war years this optimal solution often seemed very remote. The conflicting images of party strategy and purpose that had dominated debates in the thirties still preoccupied all the different elements in the party.

Power in the Wartime Party

The entry into coalition inevitably affected the party's internal relationships but the moderate domination established during the thirties was unshaken. The inclusion of the most prominent Labour parliamentarians in the coalition necessitated changes in PLP organisation. The difficulties were noted ruefully in the Parliamentary Party's Report to the 1941 Conference:

> The role of the Parliamentary Party in these days of War is not an easy one. It is to keep a balance between the presentation of Labour policy in all its aspects and the maintenance of the unity essential towards the winning of the war.[1]

The Administrative Committee was composed of a mixture of *ex officio* Ministers and elected back-benchers, with a senior back-bencher as Acting Chairman. This post was occupied by Lees-Smith until his death in December 1941, and then by W. Pethick-Lawrence. Shortly afterwards, Greenwood left the Government, and resumed his role as Deputy Leader. Although, formally, Labour back-benchers had their own organisation, this was geared to the generation of support for the coalition. Party Whips mobilised Labour members in support of government policies, and rarely had to admit failure. Throughout the coalition period, the vast majority of Labour back-benchers firmly supported the Government. To a large extent, this can be explained by the dominant loyalty of many Labour MPs. They supported the Government out of respect for their leaders, an emotion that was increased by pride in their performance in office. This fundamental loyalty was strengthened by a further factor – the composition of the PLP. It was an ageing body of men. Labour back-benchers tended to be stolid, reliable, unimaginative trade unionists. They had preserved the Parliamentary Party after 1931, but as they grew older they looked less and less like the agents of radical change. Moreover, wartime vacancies in Labour seats were filled by similar figures who were often the only ones available. Certainly the dominance of such loyalists eased the difficulties of leader-back-bencher relationships, but there were occasions when even these stalwarts expressed disapproval. The most significant rupture in Minister-back-bencher relationships was the Beveridge debate, when revolt had the authoritative backing of a formal PLP decision. The discrepancy between ministerial and back-bench positions was resolved by ignoring it.[2]

This solution was possible precisely because such a mass revolt was so singular. Throughout most of the coalition period, Labour dissent remained the prerogative of a small group of individualistic back-benchers who criticised the Government over a wide range of issues.[3] In the early years, the central disputes concerned the conduct of the war, and culminated in July 1942 in a censure motion backed by a small but varied collection of Conservative and Labour critics. This occasion was notable only for a speech by Bevan, the most impressive of the Labour critics. His repeated brushes with the party leadership led eventually to serious trouble. His critical remarks about trade union officials in a Commons debate of 28 April 1944 provoked a violent response from many trade union leaders: the Administrative Committee attempted to isolate Bevan as a habitual offender and to expel him.[4] This draconian response split the PLP into almost equal sections, and subsequently was abandoned. In spite of the failure, it is clear that in the vast majority of cases, Labour's parliamentary rebels were a small predictable group. The antagonisms revealed in these wartime arguments showed a strong continuity with the Labour battles of 1931-40. Often the immediate slogans had changed, but at root, it was the perennial conflict between principles and pragmatism, individualists and conformists. The rebels were vigorous libertarians, gadflies keeping alive the idea of opposition in a coalition Parliament.

Although loyalty to their leaders was a central factor in maintaining satisfactory Ministerial-back-bench relationships, some leaders spent little time soothing the feelings of those who felt that Ministers were becoming too coalition-oriented. Bevin, after the Beveridge imbroglio, played little part in party affairs for over a year, while Attlee's unwillingness to take overtly Labour positions resurrected doubts about his leadership. Only Morrison spent much time in partisan speech-making, and the impact of this was balanced to some extent by the tendency for him to be used in Commons debates as a troubleshooter, cajoling critical Labour back-benchers into accepting compromise policies.

If there were always tensions between party leaders and back-benchers these did not lead normally to fragmentation. The same is true of the relationship between party leaders and the Conference, with only three defeats for the platform between 1940 and 1945. However, this record includes some substantial minority votes on contentious issues, so that problems of Conference management were significant for party leaders. The controversial issues at wartime Conferences were of three kinds. There was a series of broad policy statements on both domestic and international issues. Here the minority vote was usually small, although the case of the 1944 Reading resolution (see p. 125) counts as a major exception. Secondly, there was a range of substantive issues such as family allowances, often without the ideological overtones of the broader statements. Finally, there was a set of tactical issues — the electoral truce, relationships between the party and other left-wing organisations, most notably the Communist Party – that provoked considerable passion. At the pre-election Conference in 1945, the NEC removed all resolutions on progressive unity from the agenda, defended this by referring to the three-year rule, withstood concerted pre-Conference pressures from several trade unions, and narrowly survived an attempt from the Conference floor to move the reference back on this subject. Obviously this firm stand was generated by a desire to avoid electoral embarrassment, reinforced by a belief that the vote for progressive unity would be high.[5]

The primary determinant of Conference decisions was obviously the dispositions of the large trade unions. During the war years, individual party membership fell substantially, leaving the unions in a more dominant position than ever. Although it would be mistaken to suggest that all large unions formed a bulwark against criticism, it is clear that the party leaders could normally rely on a clear majority:

Table 1: Trade Union Attitudes to Party Policy: Votes in Conference

Habitually Loyal		Uncertain-Tending to Critical Position	
T & GW	400,000	AEU	135,875
GMW	242,000	NUR	227,834
Miners*	416,729	NUDAW	200,000
Textile Workers	100,041		
	1,158,770		563,709

*The Miners' Federation of Great Britain was transformed into the National Union of Mineworkers (NUM) as from 1 January 1945.

Source: Conference Report, 1945.

While specific votes showed some defections from the loyalist ranks (e.g. Miners on Communist affiliation at the 1943 Conference), the critics were much less predictable. Furthermore, several of the medium-sized unions, such as the Railway Clerks and the Steel Workers remained completely loyal. Thus, the 'loyalist pivot' was normally able to guarantee a result acceptable to the NEC. This control over Conference was ensured further by the procedure on policy issues, typical of wartime Conferences. This usually involved the moving of a broad unexceptional resolution, or document, by an NEC spokesman; this prevented most challenges from the floor over specific details. The most divisive debates occurred over issues such as the electoral truce, where broad ambiguous propositions were not feasible.

The NEC mirrored both PLP and Conference in that it contained a moderate majority, although usually only three Ministers of importance, Attlee, Dalton and Morrison. These were balanced by critics of the coalition's effect on the party, Laski, Shinwell and from 1944, Bevan. It was the silent majority of trade unionists and women's representatives who provided the crucial support for the party leaders. Such members as Clay of the TGW, Walker of the Steel Workers and Williamson of the GMW might have contributed little to Executive debates but their backing was always available for any 'moderate and responsible' course of action.

There were however issues on which divisions of opinion within the Executive became apparent, most significantly problems affecting the future independence of the party. Inevitably the tensions produced by Labour participation in the coalition were reflected in periodic NEC debates about the treatment of dissenters, but perhaps the most significant series of debates involved the implications of the electoral truce. Here the moderate majority barely held. When independent electoral opposition became serious in September 1941, Attlee raised the question of support for government candidates, and was authorised 'in appropriate instances' to issue statements of support jointly with Conservative and Liberal leaders in favour of the coalition candidate. However, such public backing for Conservative candidates only passed the Executive by thirteen votes to ten.[6] Subsequently, in April 1942, as the Coalition began to lose seats Attlee took the step of mobilising support for government candidates by soliciting Labour speakers. He claimed that this action was an inexorable consequence of the initial decision to form a coalition, and the Executive approved his action retrospectively by twelve votes to three.[7] If this issue with its implications for Labour independence produced divided counsels in the NEC, this was a fair reflection of opinion in the wider movement. Following these internal differences and the taking of a decision in favour of general public co-operation with the other coalition parties, the Executive avoided defeat at the 1942 Conference only by 66,000 votes.[8]

In contrast to this divisive question, the issues of Communist affiliation and progressive unity created few problems for the moderate Executive majority. A small group of Executive members — Laski, Shinwell, Collick of the Locomen, and Watson of the Miners, when that union was backing affiliation — were ready to support time for discussion, but on this issue the Loyalists remained solid.[9] This was the typical pattern — the only departures were when party leaders pursued the implications of the decision to form a coalition and appeared to be threatening the future of the party as a separate body.

During the coalition period, there were occasions when feelings were expressed that the different sections of the labour movement were getting out of step. The National Council of Labour ceased to occupy its dominant role of the thirties.[10] Friction between the General Council and the Parliamentary Party reached its peak at the time of Bevan's 1944 attack on trade union leaders. In another direction, tensions between the NEC and the PLP sometimes developed, with Executive loyalists, chastising parliamentary rebels for their disloyalty, and Ministers delivering homilies on the need to accept majority decisions.

In spite of the tensions invariably arising out of the existence of a coalition, it is clear that the party continued to be dominated by the traditional alliance of moderate politicians and trade unionists, symbolised by the close relationship of Attlee and Bevin. This was threatened only on those rare occasions when the actions of the political leadership appeared likely to undermine the power balance that had emerged out of the 1931 disaster.

The Integrationist Strategy

The coalition period represents a paradigm case of one classic Labour strategy, that of integrationism, the employment of existing administrative institutions as a means of securing benefits for those whom Labour claimed to represent. Labour Ministers frequently justified their participation in the coalition as a means whereby they could procure substantive concessions to the Labour viewpoint in the fields of economic and social welfare. These could be secured by means of an exchange relationship, with a benefit gained, as a reward for trade unionists' acquiesence in proposals to suspend traditional industrial practices.

Such a strategy had been foreshadowed in the early permeation theories of the Webbs, but a more important precursor had been the trade union shift away from direct action following the General Strike. Certainly, the arrival, in 1940, of organised labour, symbolised by Bevin's appointment to the Ministry of Labour contrasted sharply with the catastrophism and the cynicism about the neutrality of administrative institutions which had marked the pre-war pronouncements of many on the Labour left. This integration of trade union officials into the administrative machine produces problems of interpretation. Should it be regarded as a vital shift in the distribution of social power in favour of the organised working class, or as a conservative development insulating trade union leaders from the demands of the rank and file?

Apart from the brute fact of national emergency, which made inevitable a vast extension of economic intervention, the prospects for a successful pursuit of the strategy were enhanced by the loss of confidence suffered by many of those who had dominated the National Government. Dunkirk appeared as the epitaph on a decade of wasted opportunities; the classic polemic 'Guilty Men' focused the attack on the 'régime of little men' who had excluded from office those with challenging ideas.[11] For a time, the 'little men' and the interests that they represented seemed to accept that the inequalities and inefficiencies that had disfigured pre-war Britain must be reduced. When the threat of military disaster receded, this new flexibility declined. In tracing the successes and the failures of integrationism, it must be emphasised that the composition of the Commons still reflected the Conservative dominance of 1935, and that most of that majority had supported Chamberlain in the critical vote of May 1940. Any decline in flexibility on the part of entrenched groups would doubtless be reflected in the behaviour of a majority in the Commons.

It was Bevin, above all, who pursued the integrationist strategy. In part this reflected his departmental concerns, but also his own commitments. In many ways, he did not see himself as a party figure, but rather as a representative of organised labour. Above all, he gloried in the use of power, initially within his own union, then inside the wider labour movement, and from 1940 onwards, on the still broader canvas of national, and subsequently international affairs. He aimed to use his acquired power, not to overturn existing society, but to gain concessions for those whom he claimed to represent. In his first twelve months in office he profited from the favourable climate of opinion. While securing a significant shift in the distribution of manpower, largely on the basis of consent, he also helped to secure the redress of a long-standing Labour grievance through the introduction of legislation abolishing the household means test.[12] Yet the fact that the abolition was not quite total was enough to produce criticism within the party. A concession to the Labour viewpoint had been secured, but its incompleteness was seen by some as indicating a lack of resolve on the part of Labour Ministers. Even in this honeymoon period, requests for some concessions met with a strong response. Attempts by Bevin and others to secure the repeal of the 1927 Trade Disputes and Trade

Union Act 'as a gesture of national unity' met with no accommodation from Churchill. Indeed, even the flexible Citrine became impatient with the lack of progress and accused Labour Ministers of a lack of effort.[13]

This failure suggested that integrationism faced difficulties when the desired concession concerned an issue that had been a major symbol of party conflict. These difficulties were compounded when the issue was politically sensitive, crucial to the war effort, and when defenders of the old order were recovering their self-confidence. It was perhaps fitting that the first major crisis concerned the future of the coal industry, the state of which had come to symbolise Labour criticism of existing society. The industry could not cope with the demands of a war economy. Years of neglect and of acrimony had produced a cynical ageing work force, a lack of mechanisation and employers who rivalled the Bourbons in their ability to remember everything and learn nothing. The classic Labour prescription for the industry was, of course, public ownership, but there were many in the coalition and on the Conservative back-benches who would not accept this, even as a means to military victory. Equally, there were influential civil servants with painful memories of Whitehall's involvement in the industry after 1918.[14]

In the spring of 1942, the mining issue erupted into a party battle on two fronts. Initially the production problems of the industry led to a Labour President of the Board of Trade, Dalton, making plans to ration fuel. The prospect of this aroused strong opposition from Conservative MPs and from sympathetic sections of the Press; it was seen as a Trojan horse that would let in government control and then public ownership. This was the first stand by Conservative back-benchers against what they were coming to see as the domination of domestic policy-making by Labour spokesmen. It was successful; the rationing proposal was dropped in all but name, and attention switched to the reorganisation of the industry.

These Labour Ministers involved, Bevin and Dalton, accepted that coal nationalisation was not a practical option, but advocated requisition, apparently in the belief that this would preclude any subsequent return to private ownership.[15] This compromise was accepted by the miners' leaders, and unanimously accepted by the Party Conference in May 1942.[16] However it failed to gain the approval of the Cabinet which decided instead on a cumbersome arrangement of 'dual control' with reorganisation under the existing Defence Regulations, and through a new Ministry of Fuel and Power. This conveniently shelved the ownership question, but proved to be less effective in helping coal production. Opposition in the Miners' Federation and in the Parliamentary Party was considerable. There were strikes in the coal-fields, three heated party meetings, and accusations that Labour Ministers had not fought strongly enough. Discontent amongst the miners was reduced however by the next wages settlement; an independent board of enquiry granted an extra 2s.6d. a shift, and accepted the miners' long-standing case for a national minimum wage. Over all the miners leapt from fifty-fourth to twenty-third in the table of industrial earnings. Nothing could illustrate more sharply the limitations of integrationism. It could secure substantial gains where these raised no issues of political principle, but where they did, then the strategy failed.

A further example of the type of issue where the strategy could succeed came at the beginning of 1943. Within the regulated wartime economy, the catering industry remained notable for its low wages and working conditions free from collective agreement or statutory regulations. At the end of 1942, Bevin secured the support of both the Lord President's Committee – the body responsible for home policies – and the War Cabinet for legislation in this field. Despite vocal opposition from the industry and from a sizeable number of Conservative MPs, Bevin kept the support of the Cabinet, and piloted the legislation through the Commons.[17]

This concession was overshadowed, however, by the Labour Party's dissatisfaction with the Government's handling of the Beveridge Report on Social Insurance. This appeared in December 1942, and elaborated a thorough scheme for social insurance against illness, poverty and unemployment, plus proposals for a national health service, family allowances and the maintenance of full employment. Retrospectively, the Report appears not as a break with the past, but as an expression of that consensus on planning and welfare that had emerged in the thirties. Beveridge looked forward not to socialism, but to the brand of welfare capitalism that emerged after 1945. However, the Report was welcomed by all those elements in Britain that had seen 1940 as the collapse of the old order: the National Council of Labour backed the Report, although some within the party were concerned lest Beveridge appropriate their progressive credentials.[18]

Such reservations were trifling however compared with the problems facing Labour Ministers. These arose out of the concern of Churchill and some other Conservatives about the Report and the effect that it could have on the stability of the coalition. Inevitably Labour Ministers found themselves cross-pressured between the demands of their party and their belief that the coalition must be maintained. Attempts to push for a positive declaration within the Cabinet failed to secure any principled commitment to the proposals and when a three-day Commons debate began on 16 February 1943, the opening Government speaker, Sir John Anderson, showed little enthusiasm for the proposals. The result was a Labour crisis: support for a critical Labour amendment increased and Attlee, Morrison and Bevin tried to contain the revolt at private PLP meetings. Bevin's blunt appeals to loyalty and discipline served only to cement support for the amendment which became official PLP policy. In spite of a reconciliatory last-ditch Commons performance by Morrison, 97 Labour MPs backed the PLP amendment and only one Labour back-bencher supported the Government.[19] This was the cleavage dreaded within the party ever since the coalition had been formed. Ministers and the party had divided over a crucial issue yet the division did Labour no long-term harm. While Labour Ministers continued to acquire credibility through their participation in government, the party could use its quasi-independent position to demonstrate on issues of popular concern that it would go further than the coalition.

After Beveridge, reconstruction was never far from the surface of political debate; it was embodied in a series of White Papers bearing the compromise imprint of their coalition origin. The shape of post-war society was perceived as a question for partisan disagreements, and accordingly, in most policy areas reconstruction was only taken as far as the publication of a White Paper. By the later stages of the war, the content of wartime economic and industrial policy was largely determined, and therefore the scope for gaining further benefits was reduced.

The concluding stages of the war did witness, however, the emergence of a dispute implicit in the adoption of the integrationist strategy. Once again the arena of conflict was the coal industry. Discontent over wages and conditions led in March 1944 to stoppages in Scotland and South Wales — and most significantly one of almost a month in Yorkshire. Bevin utilised the machinery of the TUC to condemn the stoppages, and after the dispute had been settled, amended the Defence Regulations, strengthening the penalties for initiating strikes in essential services. This new Regulation, IAA, led to a bitter Commons confrontation between Bevin and Bevan.[20] The latter mocked the conspiratorial view of the stoppages, and condemned the introduction of the Regulation without a parliamentary debate. Beneath these points however, there lay an indictment of where, in Bevan's view, the integrationist strategy had led the labour movement. It had produced not a strengthening of working-class power but the separation of trade union officials from their followers and their utilisation as agents of government policy. The picture of 'the Trade Union official who has arterio-sclerosis and who cannot readjust himself to his membership', the contrast between 'the robust dignified normal worker' and 'the jaded cynical irresponsible Trade Union Official'[21] led to Bevan being pilloried as an opponent of the principle of trade unionism. Yet this is obviously a misconception: his concern was with a consequence of the integrationist strategy. Trade union leaders were absorbed into governmental processes and lost contact with their followers. They believed that they acquired new powers and yet they acted largely as executors of decisions arrived at elsewhere.

On the level of specific concessions, the integrationist strategy secured some significant gains for the Labour viewpoint, but it was inhibited by the increasing assertiveness of the Conservative parliamentary majority, and by the unwillingness of Conservative Ministers to offend their supporters. A distinction should also be made between the success of the strategy in securing benefits through piecemeal changes, and its failure whenever any suggestion arose that could have radical implications. Basically however it is the absorption aspect of the strategy that is of most importance: trade union leaders had acquired a new status. However this is interpreted, there can be no doubt that it had a major effect on the formulation of party policy.

Socialism in Wartime

During the thirties, Labour had attempted to elaborate detailed policies for achieving its socialist goals, and by 1937 'Labour's Immediate Programme' showed the results of this exercise. When Labour entered the coalition, it was as a programmatic party, committed to the achievement of a socialist commonwealth, and with a clear idea of what it wanted to do when it achieved a parliamentary majority. Inevitably, wartime experiences led to changes not in the party programme but in emphasis and interpretation. Attlee, reflecting on his experience in the wartime coalition has recalled that:

> We applied ourselves to winning the war. When one came to work out solutions they were often socialist ones because one had to have organisation and planning, and disregard private interests.[22]

This equation of socialism with, on one level, planning and controls, and on another, the public interest, came to dominate Labour discussions during the forties. It was an interpretation based on the Fabian emphasis on rational and efficient organisation. Significantly, this tended to gloss over the question of ownership of the means of production. The coalition measures labelled by Attlee as socialist involved the control of private industry by government agencies, and not the take-over of industries by the state. Certainly the coalition exercised an unprecedented degree of control over industry to an extent never envisaged by the party in its pre-war proposals. If such a relationship between government and industry showed an ability to achieve the economic goals traditionally sought by Labour, then this obviously had implications for the commitment to public ownership.

The party's interpretation of its socialist commitment was influenced also by its adherence to an integrationist strategy. The party had always been disposed to work through existing institutions, trusting in the rationality and acceptance of consensual values of those with whom it had to bargain. Integrationism was a meaningful strategy for politicians who accepted the fundamental values enmeshed within a culture shared with their opponents, seeing differences as negotiable and honouring the rules of the game. The strategy implied that Labour sought to improve the existing social order, not to change it. However much the party might remain symbolically committed to the achievement of a socialist commonwealth, its behaviour in the coalition was suggestive of a commitment to amelioration, not to radical transformation.

Labour leaders' views of their socialist goals were affected in other ways by their experience of office. Many of them had held moderate views on policy before 1940, but these were strengthened through socialisation into a cautious administrative perspective, and also by closer acquaintance with Conservative ministerial colleagues. Labour's predilection towards incremental change was certainly buttressed at the leadership level by the formation of some close personal ties across conventional party lines, and by the fact that the very existence of a coalition demonstrated that there were some goals that men of all parties could share. These factors were reflected in party debates: Ministers rejected the current left-wing view that Labour Ministers could use their indispensability to force through socialist measures now, on the grounds that the military victory must come first, and that the coalition was vital to its achievement.

What Ministers did not go on to say, perhaps to avoid difficulties but also possibly because they were unaware of it, was that there were other more fundamental problems. The moderation induced by participation in a coalition could be counteracted in principle within the party's traditional framework, but a more intractable challenge arose if central features of the framework appeared problematic. During the coalition period, Keynesian economic techniques became officially accepted, and culminated in May 1944 in the publication of a White Paper, 'Employment Policy'. This received little attention but obviously the acceptance of a doctrine holding that full employment and existing economic structures were not incompatible was of major significance for a socialist party. If the doctrine were found to be correct, then a major part of the socialist case for public ownership — at least as developed in Britain — collapsed. When the White Paper was debated in the Commons, most Labour speakers showed only a token awareness that the development of Keynesian theory undermined the old simplistic division into uncontrolled and socialist economies. It was Bevan who stated trenchantly the problem raised for the party by the advent of Keynesianism:

> The subjects dealt with ... represent all the matters which distinguish that side of the House from this ... If the implications of the White Paper are sound, there is no longer any justification for this party existing at all.[23]

This development was particularly significant for the party since its socialist commitment had been expressed typically in terms of economic improvements. The poverty of the party's policies in other domestic fields was shown on one of the few occasions when coalition reform went further than a White Paper. The 1944 Butler Education Act went through the Commons in a cloud of democratic rhetoric yet the Act produced an educational system that did little to remedy the imbalance in educational opportunities between classes. Labour failed to articulate an alternative viewpoint essentially because little thought had been given to the role that educational reform might play in the promotion of wider social changes. As with other aspects of Labour policy, the party's position on the education issue suggested that its socialism involved not a fundamental change in social patterns, but a larger stake in the existing order for those whom Labour claimed to represent.[24]

The coalition experience produced similar difficulties in the field of foreign policy. The experience of coalition led many Labour Ministers to deviate from traditional expectations, preparing the way for a basic continuity of international policy, irrespective of the party in power. Obviously the overwhelming decision in favour of the war had dismayed Labour's small, pure, pacifist element, but a more difficult problem emerged subsequently concerning the significance of the conflict for socialists. Although the position of support for the war could be backed by claiming that it was a defence of democracy against Fascism, this left open two major questions. What would be the nature of the post-war settlement; would this involve a re-establishment of pre-war régimes, or a major shift towards social revolution? Secondly, what should be the role of the Soviet Union in such changes? The party's official pronouncements continued to suggest through their rhetoric that its leaders were committed to a coherent socialist approach to international problems. The rank and file were informed that:

... War is inherent in the nature of a capitalist society. Capitalism means everywhere the protection of the privileges of the few by the sacrifice of the well-being of the many; and in the relations between States capitalism means a power-politics which is even more ugly and brutal.[25]

There were many within the party who welcomed the expected post-war changes, accepting that:

If the Labour Movement in Europe finds it necessary to introduce a greater degree of police supervision and more immediate and drastic punishment for their opponents than we in this country would be prepared to tolerate, we must be prepared to understand their point of view.[26]

In contrast, Labour Ministers — most notably Attlee — were suspicious of Russian motives and were ready to desert the idea of a socialist foreign policy for one centred around the promotion of national interests.

The far reaching post-war dispute over the relevance and content of a socialist foreign policy was foreshadowed in December 1944, when Labour back-benchers strongly condemned government involvement in the suppression of Communist-dominated resistance groups in Athens.[27] It was an intimation of the future that Bevin was prepared to face a Party Conference to defend Government policy, but it was equally significant that while union votes were cast in support of Bevin's position, the centre of gravity of opinion both in the PLP and in the

Party Conference appeared, at the very least, to be suspicious of government policy.[28]

A variety of factors served therefore to dilute or undermine the party's socialist commitment. Some were situational; as Labour leaders grew accustomed to office, they found the edges of their doctrinal distinctiveness blurring and softening. Other factors represented a weakening of central features within the party's conception of socialism. There were two dominant ones – the Stalinist revolution which was beginning to unfold in Eastern Europe, subverting dreams of British-Soviet co-operation, and the Keynesian revolution which was beginning to exercise a dominant influence on the minds of politicians and administrators, subverting part of Labour's socialist case.

An analysis of these factors, whose impact was restricted largely to party leaders, must be counterbalanced by an examination of the factors in wartime Britain favouring radicalisation. The alliances with the Soviet Union and with Roosevelt's America aided attempts to portray the war as a radical crusade, while the expansion of economic benefits suggested that governments could avoid the problems that had dominated the inter-war years. More basic social factors must be noted also. The high mobility of population and the dilution of class differences occasioned by wartime exigencies acted as a solvent upon pre-war society, increasing the expectations of the disadvantaged, and perhaps in some cases chastening the consciences of the privileged. In this context, a vague popular radicalism developed; it was not for the most part explicitly socialist, but it centred around an instinctive rejection of the old order.

The scope in wartime for the expression of such radical sentiments was restricted. The maintenance of the electoral truce meant that such sympathies could be expressed only through independent candidates, while the increasing obsolescence of an electoral register drawn up in 1939 meant that by-elections were inadequate indicators of public opinion.[29] Nevertheless, from the autumn of 1941 it was apparent that a sizeable proportion of electors were ready to support Independents against official Conservative candidates. In 1942 four Independents were victorious, all against Conservative nominees. The first three cases, Grantham, Rugby and Wallasey, were examples of individualists successfully canalising widespread discontent with the progress of the war. None stood on a socialist platform, although all had been at some stage party members – one indeed had been a Labour MP in the 1929-31 Parliament. Subsequently, in June 1942, a self-confessed socialist, Driberg, scored an overwhelming victory at Maldon in the immediate aftermath of the fall of Tobruk. These successes caused dismay in established Labour circles. Party officials had only mixed success in their attempts to dissuade local parties from supporting such Independents. Labour had fought long and hard for an undisputed position as a major party, and now as its leaders were demonstrating their devotion to the national interest, a threat appeared based on the iconoclasm of a few opportunistic radical upstarts.[30]

The challenge of the radical Independents soon became centred around two distinct organisations that eventually reached an accommodation after a clash at the Newark by-election in June, 1943. There was a motley grouping centred around Kendall and Brown, the victors of Grantham and Rugby. However the more significant grouping developed around the previously Liberal and now Independent MP Sir Richard Acland, and the writer and broadcaster J.B. Priestley. This grouping crystallised, in July 1942, into the Common Wealth Party, proclaiming that the war effort required more socialism and that socialism was ethically correct anyway. The conception of socialism proclaimed by Common Wealth was one perhaps with a special appeal to the professional middle class. It emphasised not class interests, but the ideal of service to the community. It was the earnest Acland who came to personify Common Wealth. His principal significance was his success in persuading a section of the middle class that socialism was worth a try. Common Wealth, which had acquired 321 branches, over 12,000 members and a highly organised machine by September 1944, was essentially a middle-class movement. It was strong in suburbia, weak amongst manual workers and regarded with suspicion or even hostility by the spokesmen of organised Labour, who stigmatised it as 'a rich man's party'.[31] This sneer did contain an important kernel of truth. In 1943 Common Wealth had a total income of £20,000, of which Acland and just one other supporter donated almost £17,000. Common Wealth's publicity might have been based on the wealth of the few rather than the contributions of the many, but it brought young middle-class idealists into contact with socialist ideas and political activity, and influenced a section of the electorate where Labour's attempts had been notable for their failure. While Acland spoke in Utopian terms, other leading figures had a less elevated view of Common Wealth's role. They saw it not as a vanguard movement for a new society, but as a substitute for a Labour Party, manacled by the electoral truce, or at most an insurance policy in case Labour leaders remained in the coalition after military victory.

The Common Wealth machine acquired prestige through its successes in three by-elections, Eddisbury, Skipton and Chelmsford, although in retrospect it is clear that a significant portion of this success was attributable to the general growth in radical sentiments. The Common Wealth machine was also placed at the service of other radical Independents. In some cases, these were prospective Labour candidates who dropped their official label to contest a vacancy. Such developments highlighted the anomalous position of the Labour central organisation. Support for the coalition forced it to disavow local activists when they abrogated the truce. This dilemma was demonstrated at Peterborough in October 1943, and more dramatically early in 1944, in the Conservative citadel of West Derbyshire. Here, the former Labour candidate captured the seat as an Independent, backed by the full range of radical dissent. In contrast, official Labour spokesmen came and spoke for the Conservative candidate. The spectacle of Labour MPs supporting the heir to Chatsworth against their former standard-bearer is a striking illustration of the Labour dilemma.[32] Continuing support for the coalition could mean that Labour might be dismissed as just another part of the political Establishment. The bifurcation in wartime socialism between the moderate views of the leadership and this diffuse, iconoclastic upsurge posed both a problem and a promise for the party. While there was a risk of falling between two stools, the way lay open for the development of policies that were a subtle blend of practicality and idealism.

Policy-making in Wartime

Party policy-making in wartime fulfilled two major purposes — it was an attempt to ensure that party proposals had taken proper account of wartime requirements and changes, and it was also a possible mechanism whereby a sense of party identity could be maintained. Inevitably party activities diminished greatly, but the formulation of policy and the publication of pamphlets and memoranda at least maintained a certain momentum.

This process was built upon the legacy of the thirties, the great rethink that had followed 1931. The wartime Research Department was inevitably a skeletal organisation, and the major weight fell upon a few Executive members. Two were of particular importance, symbolising as they did distinctive strands in the party tradition. Morrison, moderate in his proposals, spent much time in overviewing the exercises, not only in the Executive's sub-committees, but also in a series of speeches designed to educate the electorate about the need for post-war reforms. In contrast, Laski, the committed academic, devoted his energies to ensuring that the party was prepared to seize its historic moment, with policies capable of harnessing the radical sentiments unleashed by the war.

Both proposed in the first half of 1941 that the party dedicate its energies to a re-examination of policy, and on 23 May 1941, the NEC's Policy Committee decided to recommend that a special Committee on Post-War Economic and Social Reconstruction be formed.[33] This was agreed by the full NEC[34] and announced to the 1941 Conference. Subsequently, the new body took the title of 'Central Committee on Reconstruction Problems' with Shinwell as Chairman and Laski as Secretary. This body met for the first time on 30 July 1941, spawning thirteen sub-committees, including at Morrison's suggestion one on 'Social and Economic Transformation'.[35] The first fruits of the exercise were revealed in February 1942, when Shinwell presented a draft, 'The Old World and the New Society', to the full NEC.[36] This general statement was primarily the work of Laski, while five resolutions, again fairly broad in content, were drafted by Dalton and Morgan Phillips, on the basis of the statement, in readiness for the 1942 conference.[37]

During the second year of the Committee's work, reports began to emerge from the sub-committees. Thus in December 1942[38] a wealth of material was debated covering health, housing, education, local government, transport, coal and power, finance, agriculture, scientific research, social and economic transformation, international affairs and relief and rehabilitation. A drafting committee – Clay, Laski, Ridley and Shinwell, plus a later addition, Morrison – was appointed to produce a further interim report entitled 'The Labour Party and the Future'.[39] Once again, on Morrison's advice, it was kept general, rather than including specific details. On many crucial issues, the document demonstrated Morrisonian coyness: criteria of monopoly and public service were used as justifications for public ownership, while on the old delicate issue of the commercial banks, it stated that the state's relations should take on 'a more integrated form'. At the 1943 Conference Morrison was a little more precise, although hardly radical, proposing the public ownership of transport and mining and of the Bank of England.[40]

Following the 1943 Conference it was decided to terminate the Central Committee and responsibility passed back to the established Policy Committee which took control of the seven remaining sub-committees.[41] This body, with Dalton as Chairman and Phillips as Secretary, continued policy-making through to the next Party

Conference in December 1944. One of the most important
developments during this eighteen months concerned the strengthening
of liaison with the TUC. Two representatives from the party — Laski
and Collick — were already attending the TUC's Economic Committee,
and in the autumn of 1943 Phillips and Middleton met Citrine. This
meeting resulted in an agreement that TUC acquiescence would be
sought before documents were published, especially in the fields of
transport, coal and power.[42] Subsequently, Citrine and Woodcock
began in March 1944 to attend meetings of the Policy Committee.[43]
The type of consultation that developed can be appreciated from the
development of a party document on transport. Before final approval,
a meeting was called with interested unions on 2 May 1944 in order to
secure their views.[44] By then the NEC had authorised not only a
statement on transport but two others covering full employment and
coal and power. These reports could form the basis of a post-war
programme. In September, Phillips presented a memorandum on a
'Short Term Programme' with a list of possible and predictable
proposals drawn from the preceding reports.[45] This could be seen
as the initiation of the process that produced the 1945 Manifesto.
However, the next stage in the exercise involved the drafting of
resolutions for the delayed 1944 Conference.

The crucial one concerned an earlier report on full employment, a
document described by Dalton as 'largely Keynesian' with 'some
Socialist additions'.[46] The resolution based on the report was composed
mainly of generalities with only a few references to specific measures:
it spoke only of 'the transfer to the state of power to direct the policy
of our main industries ...'[47] In spite of long-standing commitments
there was no unambiguous proposal for the public ownership
of any industry. This omission generated widespread criticism in
the debate centring around a resolution moved by Mikardo,
later a prominent Labour left MP, but then a delegate from the
Reading Trades Council and Labour Party. This aimed to commit
the party to include in its election manifesto a list of industries
for public ownership: 'land, large-scale building, heavy industry
and all forms of banking, transport and fuel and power'.[48]

In spite of an appeal from the platform,[49] the resolution was carried
without a card vote, demonstrating that even the most committed
defenders of the leadership were unhappy about the apparent shelving
of long-standing commitments.[50]

This production of home policies had been paralleled by the
preparation of a document on international affairs. It is clear that

Dalton as Chairman of the International Sub-Committee exercised the dominant influence, guiding his drafts through a protracted series of debates, firstly in the sub-committee and then in the full NEC.[51] The resulting document appeared as a compromise between the *real-politik* approach of Dalton, and more traditional sentiments included at the request of Laski and Noel Baker. Dalton reflected that the latter were 'harmless additions'. When the document was debated by the Party Conference in December in 1944, there was little controversy.[52] No doubt in some respects the production of such a foreign policy document was an empty exercise with little that could bind a future Labour Government, but the example is illustrative, showing that even a document whose preparation was dominated by the hard-headed Dalton had to pay attention to the expectations of the traditionalists. Tenderness for such expectations where the preparation of documents is concerned contrasts with the lack of sensitivity shown in practice by Labour Ministers, when they came to defend the actual international policies of the Coalition Government.

These documents formed the basis for the 1945 Election Manifesto. This last episode of the lengthy process was dominated by one man, Morrison. Following his return to the NEC in December 1944, he became Chairman of the Policy Committee, and also of a new Campaign Sub-Committee. This latter body, which met for the first time in February 1945, was concerned with the Party's electoral strategy, including the development of publicity.[53] It was in the Policy Committee however that the major debate occured. A draft programme was prepared by Morrison, but he argued for the omission of any proposal to nationalise iron and steel. Dalton opposed this suggestion, drawing attention to the Reading resolution, and Morrison was defeated.[54] However, this does not show that the resolution had a major effect on the 1945 programme. The industries mentioned in the resolution had varying statuses within party commitments. Some of the industries mentioned — e.g. fuel and power — would have appeared in any Labour Manifesto. Others would not do so — the building industry had never been a part of Labour policy, while the joint-stock banks had dropped out of party pronouncements in the late thirties. Iron and steel was a marginal case, and it is clear that the Conference decision, as enshrined in the ambiguous phrase 'heavy industry', was significant then only because it was combined with two other factors; support for the proposal within the party leadership and a reasonably assured status within the party.

The preparation of policy during the war years was kept firmly under the command of relatively few people, but their freedom was obviously limited by a variety of factors — the obligations implicit in Labour's traditional commitments, the coalition spirit on reconstruction, the need to avoid affronting the expectations of party activists, and the desirability of maintaining a good relationship with the TUC. As late as 23 May 1945, at a joint meeting of the General Council and the NEC, protests from Citrine led to modifications in the Party Manifesto.[55] Above all, however, the final stages in the preparation of the 1945 programme were dominated by one consideration, that an election was at hand, and the programme should be such as to maximise the Labour vote. The interpretation of this constraint was inseparable however from basic debates about the nature and function of the party.

The Road to Power: Class Army or National Party?

In retrospect, Labour's 1945 victory appears as the peak of its self-confidence. Certainly the victory has become part of the folklore of the British left. It was the consummation of the dreams of practical administrators and of radical Utopians, of those who had suffered the disaster of 1931 and endured the restrictions of coalition. Labour strategists during the thirties had based their hopes of office on optimism about the feasibility of a parliamentary majority. By September 1939, there was little evidence that such optimism was justified, as by-election results continued to suggest that Labour stood little chance of forming an independent government in the near future. The changes in political attitudes during the war faced the party with an opportunity and a challenge. An optimal electoral appeal would involve, on the one side, the canalisation of the new radical sentiment which tended to condemn Labour leaders along with other established politicians, and on the other, the securing of support on the basis of Labour's contribution to the coalition. Labour had to wear two hats: one proclaiming iconoclastic radicalism, and the other practicality and an awareness of institutional constraints. While this duality was on one level the reflection of a specific situation, it was also an epitome of Labour's basic posture, expressing emotional opposition to the existing order, but prepared to operate within it.

This tension was underscored, of course, by the problems encountered during the coalition years. The state of the party machine gave rise to concern. It is conventional amongst Labour's opponents to attribute the 1945 result in significant part to the different states of rival organisations — the Conservatives in disrepair, conforming to the electoral truce in the spirit as well as in the letter, Labour's machine maintained in readiness for the end of the truce. This is a fallacy. Labour membership declined by almost half between 1939 and 1943 and then began to rise, while in many city seats it is clear in the early war years that the party's presence was no more than titular.[56] The number of agents dropped drastically — in the case of Yorkshire from 33 down to 11 in the first two years of the war.[57] Given such decrepitude it is clear that whatever improvements occurred as the war drew to a close were not the result of long-term planning, but of a realisation that improvements had to be made. This is demonstrated forcibly by the rush of late adoptions of candidates. Such future notables as Robens, Wyatt and Younger only secured candidacies late in 1944.

Given concern about the party's organisational health, it is perhaps not surprising that, ideological considerations apart, calls for united action by all left-wing groups received so much attention from 1943 to 1945. There was an understandable lack of confidence in Labour's ability to secure a working majority. More important, there was a scepticism about the willingness of some Labour leaders to see an early end to the coalition. Certainly Bevin and Morrison made remarks on occasions suggesting a readiness to work in a post-war coalition, but by October 1944 the NEC was declaring that Labour would fight the next election as an independent force.[58] However, the timing of such a contest was left vague, a situation that remained until May 1945. Even then it appears that Attlee, Bevin and Dalton were ready to continue the coalition until the defeat of Japan, a proposition rejected overwhelmingly by the NEC on 20 May.[59] This rejection precipitated an immediate campaign, a development with a happy outcome for Labour but opposed initially by two of its leading figures.

One reason for this opposition was perhaps the belief, widely shared within the Labour leadership, that the party could not hope for a victory with Churchill equipped to play Lloyd George's 1918 role. Such pessimism was not supported by repeated surveys carried out by Mass Observation, indicating that Conservative support had declined strongly and that Labour support had grown. Labour strength appeared particularly amongst Service voters, and also in the 21-29 age group, none of whom could have voted in 1935.[60] However, it appears that much of this Labour support was tenuous, being based on anti-Conservatism rather than positive enthusiasm for Labour's leadership.

Throughout its existence Labour has been bedevilled by two

alternative views of its proper electoral strategy, related immediately to
two sharply differing views of its own identity. To see Labour as a class
party, the political manifestation of working-class interests, is to be led
to the position that Labour's electoral success requires the efficient
mobilisation of its 'natural' class base. Against this, the view that
Labour should be a national party appealing to all electors of
progressive inclinations irrespective of their class has a well-established
pedigree, indeed it has usually been the dominant strain in the position
of the party leadership. Certainly the pre-eminence of Morrison in 1945
gave a clear indication of which strategy was central; his well-publicised
position in 1945 being that the party:

> must gain and keep the support, not only of the politically conscious
> organised workers but also of large numbers of professional,
> technical and administrative workers ... the soundest socialist appeal
> is that which is most universal in scope.[61]

This national strategy was reflected in Labour's manifesto – 'Let Us
Face the Future', the terminus of the policy-making that stretched
back to the 1931 post-mortem. The party presented itself with its
characteristic blend of cautious reformism and commitment to the
long-term goal of qualitative social change. First steps towards such a
transformation appeared in the manifesto, but it is significant that the
specific public ownership proposals – the Bank of England, fuel and
power, inland transport, and iron and steel – were justified by the
criterion of economic efficiency. Much of Labour's appeal concerned
the economy and here it offered not a socialist alternative but its own
variant of the consensus of economic management that had begun to
develop in the thirties, and had been carried further under the coalition.
Clothed in the language of rational economic organisation and the
national interest, there was the outline of a strategy aimed at the
avoidance of depression through the government-aided stimulation of
full production and high wages. The basic ambiguity between the
socialist commitment and the pursuit of short-run economic efficiency
was demonstrated in the advocacy of a vigorous anti-monopoly policy.
While this might be rational for the pursuit of short-run economic
efficiency, given the existing economic system, it ran counter to the
traditional emphasis on co-operation rather than competition.

Apart from the internal ambiguities of Labour's economic appeal,
notice should also be taken of the relatively low degree of inter-party
distinctiveness on substantive economic matters. Most of Labour's

economic goals were shared by its rivals; the party claimed, however, that only Labour could be relied on to achieve them. In many areas, distinctions concerned not substantive goals, but commitment and integrity.[62] In this connection, Labour propaganda emphasised the lost hopes of 1918, 'the hard-faced men' and the resulting economic disasters, attempting to tar the Conservatives with the wasted opportunities of the inter-war years. While commentators agree that this 'never again' aspect was of major importance, its belated impact was curious. In 1935 electors had not flocked to Labour as the result of economic deprivations: doubtless, the impact of war was vital as an intensifier of economic expectations.

In the social field, distinctions between Labour and Conservative viewpoints were even less clear. On welfare, Labour accepted Beveridge as a basis, and such distinctiveness as there was turned on Labour claims that Conservative Ministers would give only a low priority to welfare improvements. In the educational and housing fields, Labour statements were extremely general. Education had been, of course, the one major field where the coalition had introduced legislation that served to indicate the lack of distinctive Labour policy in this area. The absence of a substantive housing policy is interesting, since opinion polls showed consistently that this was a major concern of the electorate. In so far as Labour attracted support on the basis of such a concern, this was based presumably on an impression of competence and commitment.

The Labour Manifesto was set before an electorate which was, in several respects, an unknown quantity. Apart from the larger turnover since 1935, there had been major population shifts. These were the results of two major developments. One was the major expansion of suburbia, especially in the south-east. Superimposed on this were the changes produced by war, demonstrated most dramatically by the depopulation of blitzed inner urban areas. Such developments produced major problems for party organisations, blunt through lack of employment, and provided obstacles to the pursuit of any coherent strategy. Whether any strategy was feasible or not, the objective for Labour was clear — to break out of the minority position of 1935, and surpass the 'near miss' of 1929.

The resulting Labour victory, with its average swing of 12 per cent, showed how thoroughly this was achieved but beneath the immediate impression of a Labour tidal wave it is necessary to consider the anatomy of Labour victory. The national swing is an inadequate indicator of the party's advance since it masked significant variations.

One way of examining the result is to see how far Labour's advance can be understood as demonstrating the success of the 'national party' strategy.

The most obvious feature of Labour's success was that it was urban-based. The only notable exception to this was in East Anglia where the National Union of Agricultural Workers was relatively strong, and several villages had a history of economic depression and heightened class conflict. In Norfolk and Suffolk Labour gained seven seats. Elsewhere, Labour was rarely able to provide a strong rural challenge, although it is arguable that in the south-west many Conservative members survived only because Labour and Liberal fought for the radical mantle on broadly equal terms.

In urban areas, the party did manage to capture most seats which were not strongly middle-class. Most spectacularly, Labour broke the Conservative dominance in Birmingham which, after a brief flirtation with Labour in 1929, had reverted back to its Conservative unanimity. Now Labour held ten out of thirteen seats: the ghosts of the Chamberlains seemed at last to be laid. If this can be seen as a belated 'normalisation' of the working-class vote, there were other urban areas where Labour did relatively poorly. In Glasgow, where the state of the Labour machine was an open scandal, the swing to Labour was only 2½ per cent, and while Liverpool saw five Labour gains these were based on relatively low swings. In both cases, it is arguable that traditional religious divisions tended to freeze voting behaviour and prevent Labour annexation of the expected share of working-class support. A similar immobility can be found in several north-western textile towns. While Labour made several gains, these resulted often in exiguous majorities, and the party failed in Bury, Royton and the dual-member Stockport seat. The durability of traditional conservative values amongst textile workers may be significant, but it would be expected that 'never again' would have been an evocative slogan in an area of high inter-war unemployment. Even in urban areas therefore Labour's mobilisation of working-class support was uneven. At one extreme, the Birmingham case showed an apparent replacement of traditional alignments, but on Merseyside and in many cotton towns, Labour's advance was only moderate.

The emphasis by some Labour campaigners on the appeal to all progressive public-spirited electors raises the question of how far this produced Labour support amongst non-manual electors. The party made major gains in London and the south-east, in all areas except the most socially exclusive. In this region, gains included seats that had never looked possible such as Winchester, Wycombe, Norwood, Wimbledon and Gillingham. Population changes could provide part of the answer to these unexpected advances, but it is apparent that in this region the Morrison strategy worked, a success symbolised by his own capture of a suburban seat, East Lewisham. These suburban gains were the victories that turned a safe majority into a Conservative rout, yet once again the ambiguity in Labour strategy appears. In a campaign with the chief co-ordinator emphasising an appeal transcending class differences the base for Labour victory was found in a substantial, though still uneven, rise in its urban working-class support.

In attempting to reconcile the result with the previous analysis of strategy, there is a difficulty. No election this century has a more elusive quality, stemming in part from the scarcity of informed contemporary comment, and the inaccuracies in what little there is. Many of the old landmarks that had sustained the prognostications of pre-war commentators had vanished or were drastically misleading. Furthermore the campaign lacked heat, and the few attempts to generate it, Churchill's 'Gestapo' speech and the Laski Affair, appeared out of place. The drama was reserved for the declarations.

Perhaps in the absence of detailed commentaries, reliance must be placed on representative images, less objective but more evocative and possibly more revealing. One is of Attlee addressing a meeting, without dramatic oratory, outlining the major points of Labour policy and being received with calm but sympathetic attention, a sharp contrast to the barnstorming progress of Churchill. On one level, Labour succeeded because of its sobriety, its practicality, its concern with material issues.

And yet, there is another image or collection of them, of dancing in the street, of an incredulous realisation that at last the miracle had happened, of an intoxication far removed from immediate material concerns. July 1945 was the 'glad confident morning' of Labour, and the triumph of a radicalism that went far beyond the party. In their own ways, both sides had been correct in the wartime debate over party strategy. There was a place for a party that could give realistic answers to practical problems, but there was also a reservoir of idealism, a readiness to experiment. The dualism that characterised the party also characterised a large section of the electorate — 'bread and butter plus a dream'. That was the secret of 1945.

Notes

1. *LPCR 1941*, p. 77.
2. For background see below, pp. 115-16.
3. See Foot, *Aneurin Bevan Vol. I*, chs. 10-15.
4. For the TUC reaction see *Minutes of Joint Meeting of the NEC-PLP Advisory Committee and the General Council*, 28 June 1944.
5. See *NEC Minutes*, 25 April and 18 May 1945; *LPCR 1945*, pp. 81-2. The vote was 1,314,000 to 1,219,000. The opposition included the AEU, the Miners, the NUR and the NUDAW.
6. *NEC Minutes*, 24 September 1941.
7. Ibid., 9 April 1942.
8. The vote was 1,275,000 to 1,209,000. *LPCR 1942*, pp. 145-50.
9. The NEC *Minutes* give no indication of the extent of disagreement over progressive unity in 1945.
10. See Middleton's comment that it 'had not functioned as it should have done during the war period'. *Minutes of Joint Meeting of NEC-PLP Advisory Committee, and the General Council*, 28 June 1944.
11. 'Guilty Men' (1940).
12. See A. Bullock, *The Life and Times of Ernest Bevin, Vol. 2: Minister of Labour, 1940-5* (Heinemann, London, 1967).
13. See V. Allen, *Trade Unions and the Government*, pp. 201-2.
14. For mining see Angus Calder, op. cit., pp. 431-3.
15. See Bullock, *Vol. 2*, pp. 161-72, and Dalton, *Memoirs Vol. 2*, pp. 389-403.
16. *LPCR, 1942*, pp. 104-6. Also the *NCL Memorandum*, pp. 3-5.
17. Bullock, *Vol. 2*, pp. 220-4 and 235-7.
18. Calder, op. cit., p. 525-32.
19. See *NEC Minutes*, 24 February 1943. Also Donoughue and Jones, op. cit., pp. 314-5, and Bullock, *Vol. 2*, pp. 225-32.
20. For contrasting appraisals see Bullock, *Vol. 2*, pp. 298-309, and Foot, *Vol. I*, ch. 13.
21. Foot, *Vol. I*, p. 452.
22. In his *A Prime Minister Remembers* (Heinemann, London, 1961), p. 37. For background see Addison, op. cit., chs. 5 and 6.
23. 401 H.C. Debs 5th Series, Col. 526.
24. See Rodney Barker, *Education and Politics: 1900-51: A Study of the Labour Party* (Clarendon Press, Oxford, 1972).
25. 'The International Post-War Settlement', *LPCR 1944*, p. 9.
26. *LPCR 1945*, p. 114 (Dennis Healey).
27. Foot, *Vol. I*, pp. 476-89.
28. *LPCR 1944*, pp. 143-50.
29. See Paul Addison, 'By Elections of the Second World War' in Cook and Ramsden, op. cit.
30. For the general flavour of wartime radicalism see Calder, op. cit., *passim*, and also the sources cited by him on pp. 631-2.
31. For a portrait of Common Wealth see ibid., pp. 546-50. For the problems of Common Wealth's relationship with Labour see, *Minutes of Meeting between Organisation Sub-Committee and Commonwealth Representatives*, 15 November 1944.
32. For West Derbyshire, see the reports in the *Manchester Guardian*, January 1944.
33. On Morrison's role see Donoughue and Jones, op. cit., ch. 24: For Laski see Kingsley Martin, *Harold Laski, 1893-1950: A Biographical Memoir* (Gollancz, London, 1953).
34. *Policy Committee Minutes*, 23 May 1941.

35. *Central Committee on Reconstruction Problems Minutes*, 30 July 1941.
36. *NEC Minutes*, 4 February 1942.
37. *Policy Committee Minutes*, 12 February 1942.
38. *Central Committee on Reconstruction Problems Minutes*, 19 December 1942.
39. For text see *LPCR 1943*, pp. 3-6.
40. The Conference debate is in *LPCR 1943*, pp. 120-7.
41. For termination see *NEC Minutes*, 23 June 1943; *Policy Committee Minutes*, 21 July and 5 August 1943.
42. *Policy Committee Minutes*, 26 October 1943.
43. *Policy Committee Minutes*, 22 February and 21 March 1944.
44. Meeting noted in *Policy Committee Minutes*, 17 April 1944.
45. Phillips' Memorandum, *RDR 271, 'Short-Term Programme: Points For Discussion – Policy Committee Minutes*, 12 September 1944.
46. Dalton, *Vol. 2*, p. 422.
47. *LPCR 1944*, p. 161.
48. Ibid., p. 163.
49. The NEC had 'agreed that general sympathy be expressed with the Reading resolution, but that they be asked to withdraw it.' *NEC Minutes*, 11 December 1944.
50. For details see *LPCR 1944*, pp. 163-8.
51. Dalton, *Vol. 2*, p. 423.
52. *LPCR 1944*, pp. 131-40.
53. See *Campaign Sub-Committee Minutes*, 19 February 1945: also on the discussions, *NEC Minutes*, 10 January, 28 March 1945; *Policy Committee*, 27 February and 27 March, 24 April 1945.
54. See Donoughue and Jones, op. cit., pp. 331-2, and Dalton, *Vol. 2*, pp. 432-3.
55. V. Allen, *Trade Unions and the Government*, pp. 263-4. The items were concerned with improved industrial conditions.
56. See *Memorandum* attached to *NEC Minutes*, 26 September 1941.
57. *NEC Minutes*, 28 January 1942.
58. Ibid., 13 September and 29 October 1944.
59. Ibid., 20 May 1945; also Donoughue and Jones, op. cit., pp. 332-4; Bullock, *Vol. 2*, pp. 375-7. Dalton, *Vol. 2*, pp. 458-9.
60. See Tom Harrison, 'Who'll Win?', *Political Quarterly*, January 1944, pp. 21-32.
61. Cited in H. Morrison, *Autobiography* (Odhams, London, 1960), pp. 238-9.
62. See R.B. Macallum and A. Readman, *The British General Election of 1945* (University Press, Oxford, 1947).

5 LABOUR IN OFFICE 1945-1951: THE PARTY'S 'HEROIC AGE'?

The Attlee Government's record dominated subsequent strategic debates within the party. It has been seen as *the* example of successful Labour strategy, the securing of major reforms based on a high degree of consent, and achieved through the machinery of Parliament. Party critics can be discovered who questioned the Government's tenacity in certain respects, but none within the party who would reject its basic strategy. It has always been viewed in Labour discussions as an example to be emulated. Yet the record of the Attlee administration raises fundamental and difficult questions about the pursuit of socialist goals through Parliament. One difficulty concerns the extent to which Labour innovated after 1945. One Minister subsequently recalled that there was:

> a new society to be built; and we had the power to build it. There was exhilaration among us, joy and hope, determination and confidence. We felt exhalted, dedicated, walking on air, walking with destiny.[1]

This interpretation has passed into Labour folklore, the Government being viewed as enacting at least the first steps towards a socialist society. Yet there is an alternative view that much of what Labour achieved did not represent a fundamental break with the past, but its own variant of an emerging consensus on economic management and social welfare. Whatever the controversy about Labour innovations in policy matters, there can be no doubt that in matters of administration and parliamentary procedure Labour adhered firmly to the established orthodoxy. Some Conservative members may have doubted the reverence of Labour parliamentarians for the elaborate ceremonial that enshrouded their parliamentary lives. They need have had no fears. Whatever iconoclastic thoughts might have lurked in the minds of some new arrivals quickly disappeared.

Continuity was certainly reflected in the new Government's composition. It was dominated by the leaders of the thirties. The self-effacing Attlee, who had once had a reputation for flirting with left-wing ideas, was now the epitome of respectability. Morrison, the advocate of a national moderate appeal, became Lord President, Leader

135

of the Commons and the co-ordinator for Home Affairs. There could be no better agent for easing new members into the etiquette of parliamentary life. Bevin, in many ways not a party politician, went to the Foreign Office where he was to practise a continuity of policy that drove several on the Labour benches almost to despair, while Dalton, an accomplished deflater of 'Utopians', undertook the burden of the Treasury. While this triumvirate had had and would continue to have disputes based on both policy and personality, they were united by a preference for pragmatism rather than doctrinal purity. Most other Cabinet posts went to stalwarts of the 1935 Parliament, while only two appointments could arouse any expectations on the part of the left. Cripps, newly returned to the party, went to the Board of Trade, yet by 1945 he had moved away from his earlier apocalyptic Marxism to religious puritanism and a willingness to compromise. In contrast, Bevan's wartime record had shown that his radicalism was a living force. His appointment as Minister of Health could be seen as a stroke of imagination, or perhaps as a caging of the Government's most effective potential critic. At the junior level, nearly all posts went to safe, established members of the PLP. Although a majority of Labour MPs had never sat in the Commons before, only three of the newcomers were given office. One of them was an unknown former civil servant, the member for Ormskirk, Harold Wilson.

This moderate, rather aged team, found itself faced with immediate problems of a frightening magnitude. The prosecution of the war had severely damaged the British economy: its domestic capital had been depleted by £3,000 million, overseas investments had shrunk by £1,000 million, net debts were £3,000 million and exports were cut by two-thirds. The abrupt American termination of lend-lease and the subsequent negotiation of an American loan with stringent conditions marked the new Government's initiation into a continuous economic battle aimed at raising exports to 75 per cent above the pre-war level to compensate for the depletion in 'invisible' earnings. Labour Ministers became preoccupied with the need to raise production and to control inflation. This drive for economic efficiency carried implications for party orthodoxy — it was difficult to maintain a sense of direction when immediate crises dominated everything. It was difficult to build a new society when a primary task was to prevent the premature disintegration of the old.

Inevitably the complexities of office produced disparities between what Ministers actually did, and what, on some interpretations of party tradition, they were expected to do. Certainly the dominant contemporary interpretation, accepted by partisans of diverse shades, was that Ministers were struggling against great difficulties to achieve initial advances on the road to socialism. Much political debate was couched in these terms. Yet there is another, very different interpretation, that objectively, the Attlee Government did not move in the direction of socialist reform, but made the existing society more efficient and more humane, laying the foundations of a society characterised by the mixed economy and the welfare state. While this achievement can be evaluated in diverse ways, it is clearly not socialism as hitherto suggested by party orthodoxy.[2]

This fundamental and complex problem of interpretation dogs any analysis of the Government's performance. The questions asked, and the evidence submitted will turn significantly on a judgement about the nature of government policies. If Ministers presented reforms that in fact improved the existing society as measures that would facilitate its abolition, then the proposals could encounter difficulties that appear extraordinary, given their beneficial impact on the existing social order. The reasons for such ministerial misrepresentation could vary: one possibility is genuine misunderstanding, another, a Machiavellian desire to appease critical followers. It is this perennial problem in social analysis — the complex interplay between actors' beliefs and observers' judgements — that makes assessment of the Attlee Government's performance so difficult.

Party Relationships in Office

Before embarking on the thorny questions involved in an attempt to evaluate the Government's performance, it is necessary to examine the power relationships within the party, now that ministerial conventions were imposed on traditional party structures. After 1931, the distrust engendered by MacDonald's exodus had led to an attempt to lay down guidelines for the selection of a future Labour Government, involving a specific commitment to a PLP meeting whenever the possibility of forming a government was present, and also to consultations with the NEC and the General Council. In July 1945, Attlee ignored procedures worked out in very different circumstances in the early thirties. He claimed conformity with them was contrary to constitutional conventions. His immediate acceptance of the King's Commission was no doubt influenced by a well-justified belief that Morrison was ready to use the consultative procedures as a means of securing the leadership for himself.[3] Attlee's adherence to the traditional approach to government formation, and his flouting of a Conference decision on this, passed almost unnoticed in the euphoria of victory. But the adherence to traditional procedures was a significant intimation of the whole pattern of relationships between government and party. The Government dominated all such relationships, with its back-benchers, with the National Executive and with the Party Conference.

At the start of the Government's career, there existed a potential divergence between a politically experienced Cabinet and a PLP containing many idealists entering Parliament for the first time. This was not a simple matter of conservative Ministers and radical back-benchers — rather from the leadership viewpoint, it was a question of management, of channelling enthusiasm in constructive directions. Much of the necessary work was carried out by Morrison.[4] It began with the election of two back-benchers as Chairman and Vice-Chairman of the PLP. This established the PLP as a body formally separate from the Government. In order to help prevent a repeat of the unhappy experience of 1929-31, a liaison committee was established, containing the PLP Chairman and Vice-Chairman, the Leader of the House, the Chief Whip and a non-ministerial peer. This aimed at the abatement of discontent by early preventive action. Meetings were arranged where particular Ministers could clarify their policies or answer specific problems. A further attempt to promote harmonious Minister-back-bencher relationships was less successful. A systematic attempt was made to develop Subject Groups for the development of dialogues between Ministers and interested back-benchers. While some were successful, others were not. Bevin indeed was constantly at odds with a Foreign Affairs Group, which contained according to one, not unbiased source: 'all the pacifists and fellow travellers, pro-Russians and anti-Americans, and every sort of freak harboured in our majority.'[5]

Eventually the Subject Groups were transformed into Regional Groups, thereby preventing their use as mobilisers of dissent on particular issues. Finally, in an attempt to facilitate harmony, and perhaps based also on an astute judgement of the limited extent to which such a large Parliamentary Party would accept discipline, the Party's Standing Orders were suspended. The power of the PLP to withdraw the Whip remained — as did the power of the NEC to refuse endorsement to a particular candidate. But the suspension meant that a wide range of lesser dissent could be expressed without precipitating any sanctions.

Difficulties of parliamentary management were bound to increase, as the Government's responses to both international and domestic crises produced responses that seemed in conflict with some interpretations

of party orthodoxy. A perusal of Labour lobby revolts and critical
Early Day Motions suggests that concern was widespread. One authority
has claimed at least 39 occasions in the 1945 Parliament when groups
within the PLP publicly expressed dissatisfaction with government
policy.[6] These demonstrations ranged from the critical Amendment to
the Address in the autumn of 1946 condemning Bevin's foreign policy,
and supported in various ways by up to 90 back-benchers, down to
rebellions by a handful of members. Much of the dissent concerned
international and defence matters; other controversies arose over
Palestine, Ireland and a few domestic issues, e.g. civil aviation and
attempts to curb wage demands. Two characteristics of this series of
revolts need to be noted. They tended to involve a recurrent group of
members, and with a very few exceptions, they had no effect on
government policy.

A minority of back-benchers possessed few resources against a
Government defended by a reliable body of loyalists who took an
unashamed pride in the Government's achievements. The only
significant concession secured by a lobby revolt concerned the
Conscription Bill in March-April 1947,[7] when 72 Labour back-benchers
opposed a continuation of conscription. The Cabinet then cut the
proposed period of service from eighteen months to twelve, although
the cut was rescinded the following year. One reason for this temporary
concession was that most of the Government's opponents on this
occasion were not habitual rebels, and therefore any concession would
not be taken as a promise of more to come. Perhaps greater significance
should be attached to rumours of a Cabinet revolt on this occasion.
Normally, back-bench rebels found no sympathetic listeners within the
Cabinet. Although they claimed to be defending party values against
ministerial compromises, they occupied an isolated and powerless
position. Indeed, in extreme cases, their position was highly vulnerable.
During the 1945 Parliament, five MPs were expelled from the party,
four for pro-Soviet views, and one, in contrast, for his opposition to the
nationalisation of iron and steel.[8] There were also occasions when rebels
were warned informally or formally about the consequences of repeated
dissent.[9] Although the difficulties experienced by the Government
produced inevitable strains within the PLP, for most MPs any discontent
was subordinate to their belief that their primary task was to sustain a
Labour Government in office. Accordingly, although lobby revolts
sometimes embarrassed the Government, their impact was limited to
this. Ministerial control was never seriously challenged within the
Parliamentary Party.

The same lack of serious challenge to government policies can be found in the Party Conference. The Government's critics were sometimes more vocal here, but they never made much impact. They were faced by a NEC which was little more than a channel, whereby the Government could mobilise the extra-parliamentary rank and file in support of its policies. The Executive was always controlled in these years by a majority thoroughly loyal to the Government, centred around the trade union section, and a group of Ministers — Attlee, Griffiths, Dalton, Morrison, Shinwell and, until April 1951, Bevan. Since the women's representatives also reflected the attitudes of loyalist trade union leaders there was little danger of conflict between the Government and the Executive. Although Ministers were sometimes unable to attend NEC meetings, the degree of contact remained considerable and their case was always accepted by the great majority of Executive members. Critics within the NEC were few. In the early years of office only Laski was both identified with the left and unencumbered by governmental responsibilities. Later, Foot, Driberg and then Mikardo increased the number of critics, but their opposition remained insubstantial beside the vast support which accrued almost automatically to Ministers.

The Executive sustained nine defeats at Party Conferences during the Government's career, all on relatively marginal matters. In each case, the victory of the Conference did not affect the development of policy, although government spokesmen tended to suggest that any divergence was one of timing, not substance. On more central policy issues, the NEC was never in much danger. Although international issues preoccupied many of the Government's critics, there were only two card votes in this field during the Government's lifetime. Both resulted in large pro-Government majorities.[10] Similarly in 1947, perhaps the most difficult year for the Government, critical resolutions on national service and on the Government's planning strategy were easily defeated.[11] Although some sections of the party became concerned about the results of government policy on public ownership, this rarely received coherent expression at Conference. However, in 1950, a rather confused debate on the public sector of the economy was terminated when a delegate moved the previous question, a manoeuvre accepted by a majority of just under one million votes.[12] Other card votes occurred over Communist affiliation in 1946, and later in 1948 and 1949 over the expulsion of MPs. In each case the NEC was able to carry the day easily although in the two expulsion cases 1,403,000 and 1,993,000 votes were cast for the suspension of Standing Orders to allow appeals by the appellants.[13]

The NEC, and thus the Government appeared to be guaranteed a large Conference majority on all but a very few peripheral issues. Often contentious questions did not come to a card vote, owing to procedural manoeuvres or passionate appeals from the platform for loyalty. When a card vote was forced, the leadership could rely almost automatically on support from a majority of the large trade unions. Their relative domination of the Conference was increased by the repeal of the 1927 Trade Disputes Act with its 'contracting in' provision.[14] This pro-leadership phalanx has been examined earlier, but proper weight must be given to a development that strengthened its resolve after 1945. Loyalist union leaders had always been firm anti-Communists, and this commitment was strengthened by the shift in the Communist position after 1945, which culminated in opposition to the Marshall Plan. This shift was reflected within the trade union movement, through the growing alienation of many British union leaders from the World Federation of Trade Unions, a body in which Communist unions had a majority. This ended in a final international split in July 1949.[15] These developments, plus the intensification of Communist/anti-Communist battles within individual unions, led to loyalist union leaders classifying all political differences in terms of their preoccupation with Communism. Any resolution criticising government policy could be interpreted as a gambit in the Communist bid for control. In spite of these increased pressures for loyalty, some large unions remained critical of government policies, usually those with a sizeable Communist faction which was capable of allying with representatives of the Labour left to produce a majority.[16] During the Government's lifetime, USDAW*, the AEU and the NUR[16] cast critical votes on sensitive issues. Other smaller unions such as the Foundry Workers and the ETU were more consistent opponents.[17] During this period union criticisms were less overt in the loyalty-impregnated world of the Party Conference than in the parallel meetings of the TUC. There, with Communist speakers permitted, debates were more acrimonious, and card votes were sometimes closer.[18] Although the Government was always backed by a majority of union votes at Party Conferences, it is clear that the principal opposition there came frequently not from constituency delegates, but from a minority of critical unions.

*The National Union of Distributive and Allied Workers combined with the National Amalgamated Union of Shop Assistants, Warehousemen and Clerks in 1946 to form the Union of Shop, Distributive and Allied Workers (USDAW).

The readiness of both Executive and Conference to support government policies led to growing concern about the declining vitality of these two bodies. As early as June 1946, Laski tried unsuccessfully to initiate an Executive review of the problems of NEC-Government relations.[19] Further discussion of the same issues developed early in 1948, when the Executive considered a memorandum submitted by Nat Whine of the St Marylebone Party, expressing concern about ministerial domination of the NEC and claiming that the policy-making role of Conference had been superseded by the Government. These claims, and the memorandum suggestions for reform were rejected by the Executive – the rejection was the sequel to a hostile response to the memorandum by the Party Secretary.[20] Essentially, proposals to review party-Government relationships were of only academic importance so long as the central party bodies contained pro-Government majorities. Certainly the arrival of a strong Labour Government did produce problems for the vitality of party institutions, but these problems were obscured by the fact that majorities in these bodies were ready to see any issue as a matter of confidence. Thus Ministers could go through the motions of consulting party opinion assured of a favourable result.

The stability of the Government thus rested firmly on a loyalist majority in the PLP, the Executive and the Conference. This assumes that the Government itself was a monolith, yet any discussion of power relationships that ignores Cabinet debates would be defective. Overriding everything, there was the contribution of Attlee. After 1945, his hold on the party leadership was much stronger, the only substantial challenge came in the crisis-ridden summer of 1947, when Cripps was the moving spirit in an attempt to supplant him. This attempt failed as its predecessors had, partly because of Bevin's almost unshakeable loyalty, and partly because of his would-be removers' inability to agree on a successor.[21] Yet it remains difficult to assess Attlee's contribution. The images that emerge are often conflicting, the only common factor being that Attlee's leadership presents a puzzle.[22] The positive portrait presents him as a reconciler, skilled at the healing of factional differences by appropriate formulae, the living embodiment of Maxton's dictum that 'a man who can't ride two horses at once has no right to a job in the bloody circus.' Added to this there is the impression of Attlee as the skilled head of the Cabinet, avoiding irrelevant discussion and facilitating decision-making. He appears to have interfered little in the workings of individual departments, allowing Ministers to reach their own decisions. His independence of factional alignments is normally seen as a virtue – only Bevin enjoyed a special relationship with the Prime Minister. Morrison, to his eternal distress, was kept at rather more than arm's length. Attlee was very much the cat that walked alone, a ruthless butcher of the incompetent, he divulged his thoughts to no one, showing little concern when affairs went badly and little enthusiasm when they went well. Beneath the laconic inoffensive exterior, there seemed to be a leader of outstanding firmness and self-confidence requiring reassurance from no one.

This is the positive portrait, Attlee the accomplished undemonstrative party manager – and yet it is easy to construct a less favourable picture. His silences could be interpreted as demonstrating an unawareness that support required mobilisation. He never attempted to communicate the Government's strategy to the electorate. He rarely attempted to raise the spirits of the PLP, and when he did, his attempts involved metaphors straight from his upper-middle-class background. If he was not an inspiring communicator, neither did he waste any time on problems of party management. These time-consuming tasks were left to Morrison, and back-benchers approaching their leader for advice would be met with formidable formality and an abrupt response. His readiness to let Ministers run their own departments had its obverse side – when individuals ran into difficulties, support from the Prime Minister was noticeable by its absence. This may have been a skilful calculation, but concentrated attacks on individual Ministers, such as Shinwell and Strachey, weakened the Government. His absence of concern in difficult situations could be attributed to single-minded self-confidence, but it could be explained also by a lack of awareness or uncertainty about strategy. He remained above the political battle, far removed from Bevanite fervour or Morrisonian zeal for votes. So the riddle remains: Attlee was an enigma who left few traces. Was he the accomplished party manager, or the 'mouse' who arrived as leader by accident and was sustained there by the mutual jealousies of his rivals? Perhaps the riddle continues because an oversimplified answer is sought. In some situations, Attlee's personality appeared in positive terms as the great reconciler, in others as a handicap, the introverted insensitive conformist leading a reforming party.

The leadership of the apparently unremarkable Attlee appears even more striking when it is contrasted with the vivid personalities of some of his most powerful Ministers. Bevin, Morrison, Cripps, Dalton and Bevan all generated in their own ways more substantial presences. Throughout most of the Government's career, these individuals managed to work as a team. Certainly there were personal tensions. The most obvious was Bevin's almost pathological distaste for Morrison. When policy divisions arose in the Cabinet, they were explicable only in part on the basis of traditional left-right divisions.

Cabinet disputes and tensions between the Government and the labour movement were inevitable, but throughout most of the Government's life, these were contained by the predictability of loyalist support, and also by a general agreement about party policy. The weakening of the harmony stemmed from a growing uncertainty about Labour's direction. This culminated in the upheaval of April 1951. One element in the crisis was an unhappiness about the increased fossilisation of a party structure, accustomed to generating majorities for government policies and to dismissing dissent as disloyal, but more significance must be attached to the difficulties for party doctrine generated by six years of government.

The Ideal and the Real

Bi-partisanship in Foreign Affairs

The symbol of socialism was of fundamental importance to the maintenance of the Labour coalition. While various groups might argue over interpretation, it provided a basis for unity, and also a means of differentiating Labour from its rivals. In office, differences resulting from diverse interpretations of the basic socialist commitment could be glossed over no longer. The mere fact of action by a Labour Government led to Ministers defending one interpretation, and thereby excluding others. Controversy first became significant over international policy. In July 1945, many Labour back-benchers and activists believed in the feasibility and desirability of a 'socialist foreign policy', although this covered a mass of conflicting interpretations. Pre-war controversies had produced a greater awareness of the role of power in international affairs, but traditional values remained strong. In some individual cases, these might take the form of carefully articulated ideological perspectives, but more frequently they were just stock responses to familiar problems — distaste for armaments and conscription, distrust for power politics, sympathy for the Soviet Union. In contrast, participation in the wartime coalition had produced a growing acceptance by Labour Ministers of bi-partisan views on foreign policy, including alarm at Soviet ambitions in Eastern Europe.

This divergence of outlook between Ministers and a sizeable section of the party was a recipe for discontent, while the choice of Bevin as Foreign Secretary meant that the Government's international dealings would be couched in robust empirical terms with few concessions to the feelings of party critics. It is unclear whether Bevin and his colleagues decided from the outset that there was no chance of any agreement with the Soviet Union, or whether they arrived at this position as the result of failures to negotiate a settlement. Certainly Byrnes, the US Secretary of State, reflected that:

> Britain's stand ... was not altered in the slightest, so far as we could discern, by the replacement of Mr. Churchill and Mr. Eden by Mr. Attlee and Mr. Bevin. This continuity of Britain's foreign policy impressed me.[23]

Certainly Bevin demonstrated a readiness to follow the established British line of opposition to any developments threatening the European balance of power, and adhered in no way to traditional socialist precepts about the immorality of power politics. Pursuit of the traditional British policy was hampered by economic weakness, which led to protracted attempts to involve an initially reluctant United States in the defence of Western Europe. The termination of British military aid to Greece and the resulting proclamation in March 1947 of the Truman Doctrine marked the initial success of this policy; the emergence of Marshall Aid, the Czechoslovak *coup* and the Berlin airlift were subsequent landmarks in the development of the Cold War and in the emergence of that system of alliances which culminated in the formation of NATO.

It is difficult to overestimate the extent of the gulf between the international policies pursued by the Government and the expectations of many of its supporters.[24] The Government consistently worked to further what it viewed as national interests, accepting that fundamental changes in the quality of international relationships would not occur. This pragmatic approach was at odds with the belief that foreign policy could be and should be conducted according to a clearly articulated set of principles and with precise ethical goals in view. There was a similar divergence over the content of government policy. Some claimed that the Government had opposed its 'natural ally', the Soviet Union, and had entered into an alliance with the 'reactionary capitalist' United States, while others complained that no attempt had been made to secure a co-operative international community; instead, the acceptance of 'power politics' had resulted in the continuation of a high level of defence expenditure, and the continuation of conscription. However, it is crucial to emphasise that the Government's international record did not dismay all its supporters, either in the PLP or in the Party Conference. Many Labour back-benchers were not interested in international questions. A combination of loyalty and satisfaction with the Government's economic record was sufficient to guarantee their support on international issues. Often, such support was based on more positive considerations. Many Labour MPs were tied to their party by a class identification, expressed in specific economic and social demands. Beyond these class claims however, they were essentially nationalists, just as prepared to accept a bi-partisan foreign policy to withstand Stalin as their predecessors had accepted coalition to resist the Kaiser. They identified closely with Bevin and were ready to defend him from his critics. Such Labour patriotism, with its suspicions of the Soviet Union as both foreign and Communist, formed a dominant element in the outlooks of many trade union leaders who drew a simple parallel between Soviet manoeuvres in Eastern Europe and Communist manoeuvres in their own organisations.

Although it is crucial to emphasise the patriotism of significant sections of the labour movement, the idea of a socialist foreign policy had moulded the ideas and the expectations of many Labour activists. Its erosion through the practice of a Labour Government was therefore significant. The resulting critics of Bevin formed three distinct tendencies, although on some occasions they could unite into a somewhat discordant opposition.

The most significant group of critics was those who inspired the hostile Amendment to the Address in November 1946, and subsequently formed the 'Keep Left' group.[25] They tended to be new entrants to Parliament, university-educated, and sometimes with a background in journalism. They were not pacifists, nor did they wish to give general support to the Soviet Union. Rather, they saw Britain as the democratic socialist nucleus of a Third Force, which could appear as a desirable alternative to the political and economic structures offered either by the USA or the USSR. Although in some ways this conception broke new ground, it still rested strongly on traditional socialist beliefs. Most centrally, it involved the old radical belief that a nation could exercise a decisive moral influence on international relationships through its own example. This Third Force proposal became less persuasive as the Cold War intensified. Supporters of the position reached very different assessments of the emerging system of alliances. Some, for example Crossman and Michael Foot, saw NATO as acceptable. This involved a reinterpretation of the role of the United States. It was presented not as the most developed example of an aggressive capitalism, but as a progressive democracy, a fitting partner for a democratic socialist Britain. Other advocates of the Third Force refused to accept NATO, viewing it as a final surrender of all that had been implied by the idea of a socialist foreign policy.[26] Such a rift within this small group of critics showed the problems facing defenders of traditional values. The ambiguity of such values, plus the Government's responses to a deteriorating international situation, provided abundant opportunities for divergent interpretations. One central problem involved the weight and the interpretation to be given to 'democracy', and the relationship of this to 'socialism'. Those former critics who supported NATO tended to argue that existing democratic practices and institutions were of value, and were an indispensable concomitant of any socialist advance; therefore an alliance constructed to defend 'democratic' régimes should be supported.

A reformed 'Keep Left' group produced a second pamphlet in January 1950.[27] This was an attempt to reconcile traditional values and post-1945 developments. It accepted NATO and also the idea of Soviet Imperialism, but attempted to revive the Third Force proposal by relating it to the emergence of colonial nationalism. This provided a long-term basis for Labour left support of revolutionary causes, exempt from the disillusion which now dominated nearly all Labour assessments of the Soviet Union. These advocates of a Third Force formed a small rather exclusive group which was of special importance, in so far as it illustrates the difficulties of reinterpreting traditional values, and also because it became the nucleus of the Bevanite faction.

Sympathy for traditional sentiments obviously extended far beyond the relatively sophisticated advocacy of a Third Force. Most obviously there were those who were ready to take an optimistic view of Soviet intentions. This typically turned on the assumption that the differences between Communists and socialists were as nothing compared with those between socialists and defenders of capitalism. In this case, socialism, defined as the achievement of a publicly-owned economy, was seen as a more important goal than the defence of liberal democratic institutions. Pro-Soviet feeling within the party declined with the worsening international situation. From the end of 1947, Labour Ministers and party officials took steps to discredit and to prevent the expression of such viewpoints. Labour Ministers began to refer to the fundamental incompatibility between democratic socialism and Communism, while disciplinary action was taken after 37 Labour MPs sent a telegram of good wishes to the Nenni socialists who had entered a Popular Front with the Communists for the Italian elections in April 1949. One participant, Platts-Mills, was expelled and 21 others who refused to disown their signatures were warned. By July 1949, three other Labour MPs — Solley, Zilliacus and Hutchinson — had been expelled by the NEC.[28] The open advocacy of pro-Soviet views had become impossible within the Parliamentary Party.

A less distinct but more extensive source of concern about the Government's international policies was based on traditional Radical distaste for armaments and power politics. Although often there was little that was specifically socialist about such criticism, it had been a potent element in Labour condemnations of British foreign policy, at least since Versailles. Occasionally, this position appeared as pacifism, more often as anti-militarism. Some adherents to this viewpoint justified their stance on religious grounds; sometimes they contrasted their ethical socialism with totalitarian Communism. The strongest expression of this tendency came over the conscription issue. These rebels tended to be distinct from other foreign policy critics. They were often older, less educated, and argued their case in terms of overriding moral principles. There were two other aspects of this position which were important. One was the readiness to advocate dramatic gestures capable of breaking the international deadlock. The other, although negative, was of particular importance. Many Labour MPs and activists, motivated by these values, were simply unenthusiastic about the Government's policy. Certainly no alternative perspective survived unscathed for long, but this did not imply that the Government's judgement on international questions had secured wide positive acceptance within the party. Many, both MPs and activists, remained attached to traditional values which, however vague and discredited by events, still seemed more palatable than the Government's position. Although by early 1950 there was almost a total lack of open opposition to Bevin's policies, this was illusory. The lack did not indicate enthusiastic support, but the absence of any credible alternative.

The failure of many within the party to adapt is readily understandable. The international policies of the Attlee Government had shown a disregard for all traditional socialist values. But it was difficult to disown government policies, and there was always the threat of disciplinary sanctions. The other possibility was to jettison the traditional values. Such an enterprise possessed profound implications for the identity of the party, since it eroded the party's distinctiveness. Some party leaders, in attempting to replace the traditional categorisation of régimes into 'capitalist' and 'socialist', by a 'democratic/totalitarian' distinction, raised serious questions about the relationship between the party and existing British society. Obviously Labour had always demonstrated in practice a considerable willingness to accept existing institutions, but this defence of 'democracy' raised the issue in a much more self-conscious form. Earlier intimations of such a perspective can be found in the writings of Durbin with his presentation of social democracy and Communism as opposed ideologies,[29] and also in official Labour statements produced in periods such as 1939-41. The growing emphasis in party literature, after 1947, on the democratic component in Labour doctrine proved to be of major importance, since it marked one of the points from which a fundamental attempt to revise Labour's view of socialism would come. The whole Cold War experience was crucial for many in the party, in discrediting or rendering ambiguous many traditional socialist values. Yet the final emphasis must be on the continuing attraction of these same values for an articulate group of Labour MPs while for many more the old commitments died hard. Bevin's policy did not really take deep roots in Labour's collective psyche. Although the PLP accepted the Government's Korean policy with just a few isolated criticisms, it was not long before widespread doubts began to revive.[30] Dogged adherence to traditional outlooks was easily transformed into a more fervent commitment by increased American involvement in the Far East. The difficulties over international policy thus were a major factor in the development in 1950-1 of a significant intra-party cleavage.

A Programmatic Party in Power

The domestic record of the Attlee Government is a classic example of a programmatic party in office. It was concerned with the implementation of the series of proposals developed by the party between the wars. These proposals had been advocated not only for their specific benefits but also as significant steps towards the realisation of a socialist commonwealth. This blend could satisfy both practical politicians with their sights set on particular improvements, and idealists more concerned with the distant socialist horizon. The opportunity to implement such measures raised the possibility of divisions between these different groups, as specific needs were satisfied, but fundamental social change remained as far off as ever.

Two central aspects of the traditional programme will be considered in this section — welfare and public ownership. The commitment to full employment and the complex problems of economic management raise a distinct set of issues which will be dealt with below. A consideration of Labour's welfare programme must begin with an emphasis on the considerable degree of continuity. Certainly, Labour had been keen to suggest in 1945 that it was the only party with the necessary resolve in this field, a claim given plausibility by some initial Conservative reactions to Beveridge. Nevertheless, the tradition of welfare legislation on which Labour based its policies had a pedigree stretching from Lloyd George to Beveridge — while including on the way the contributions of Conservatives such as Neville Chamberlain. Many of the Government's measures were extensions and rationalisations of existing policies. It extended earlier attempts to remove the more inhumane aspects of the existing economic system. Social insurance became universal — covering unemployment, illness, old age and industrial injuries. Family allowances were maintained, and a national health service inaugurated. Taxation on the highest incomes became even heavier than in the war years; self-appointed spokesmen of the 'middle class' proclaimed its imminent extinction, and in 1950, the Chairman of the Party Conference could assert that: 'Poverty has been abolished. Hunger is unknown. The sick are tended.'[31] This claim was to become the conventional wisdom, and yet it has become clear that the impact of the welfare and taxation policies of the 1945 Government was less straightforward than this optimistic assessment suggests. Certainly the extensions of existing services and the creation of a health service were considerable achievements — they did modify the previously harsh pattern of social inequalities, but the extent of that modification was exaggerated by both supporters and opponents. The figures used in the debates about income redistribution in the late forties and fifties are now widely accepted as hopelessly inadequate, and resulting conclusions about the equalisation of wealth were unjustified. This conclusion is important since much Labour policy-making and theorising from 1948 onwards was based on the beliefs that welfare reforms had abolished 'real' poverty, and that progressive taxation could not be increased further without undermining crucial incentives.

Although the extension of most welfare services was clearly uncontroversial, Labour's introduction of the National Health Service can be seen as an exception. Once again there was a background of a Beveridge recommendation, a subsequent White Paper and schemes by Coalition Ministers of Health. In spite of this consensual prelude, this reform is of particular significance for an understanding of Labour's implementation of its programme, since it exemplifies some of the problems of a reforming government faced with an entrenched and hostile pressure group.[32]

The British Medical Association's concern at any attempt to reform

Britain's medical services had been expressed under the Coalition, and was increased by the advent of a Labour Government with a long-standing commitment to a universal, free and comprehensive health service. Moreover the Minister had no reputation as a meek conciliator, but was Bevan, wartime critic of Churchill and perennial scourge of the Labour leadership's timidity. There was no discussion of the measure between Minister and BMA prior to the Bill's publication in March 1946. In several respects Bevan's proposals followed the broad contours of the Coalition White Paper, but there was one important change. Instead of the compromise advocated in the earlier White Paper, the existing network of voluntary hospitals was to be taken into public ownership, along with the municipal ones. While this could be seen as the amendment of the Coalition proposals in a more socialist direction, Bevan made some compromises designed to ease the doctor's fears. Thus he rejected the possibility of a full-time salaried service, and suggested instead a small basic salary plus the capitation fees.

Such concessions awoke concern within some sections of the PLP, but the legislation passed readily through the Commons in the summer of 1946, leaving the Ministers with the difficult task of negotiating an agreement with the doctors. By then the BMA had aligned itself in opposition to so many aspects of the proposed scheme that it almost appeared as opposition in principle. They condemned state control of hospitals, the proposed salary structure and the proposed powers of the Minister. Eventually at the end of 1946, BMA members voted in a referendum on whether the Association should enter into negotiations with the Minister. On a poll of 80 per cent, 54 per cent opposed such a move.

This apparent deadlock was broken when Bevan made use of a significant cleavage amongst the doctors. Many spokesmen of the Royal Colleges were more favourably inclined towards the scheme than the BMA spokesmen, and some of them secured conciliatory responses from the Minister on questions of salaries, professional freedom and private practice. This manoeuvre at least produced negotiations between BMA spokesmen and the Ministry which continued throughout 1947. However these produced little agreement since the BMA leadership were concerned to secure changes of principle, rather than detail. Eventually at the end of the year, this divergence in approach became obvious, and the 'negotiations' appeared to have achieved little. The stage was set for the final confrontation with the inauguration of the new service scheduled for 5 July 1948.

The position of the Government appeared to be difficult when the

BMA held another widely publicised referendum, in which its membership opposed the existing act by a majority of nine to one. However, for the second time, Bevan was working for compromise through the élite of the Royal Colleges. An intervention by them, partly inspired by the Ministry, led to Bevan stating in Parliament that a full-time salaried medical service would never be introduced simply by regulation. This did not mark a substantive concession, but in the context of the developing argument it was crucial. It was clear that the scheme enjoyed wide popularity — a Gallup Poll had recently reported 69 per cent of respondents as favouring it. The Conservative Opposition, although keen to attack the Minister on his conduct of negotiations, was unwilling to openly criticise the principles behind the scheme. Some newspapers might present the doctors' stand as heralding the long-awaited revolt of the professional classes against 'socialist tyranny', but their long opposition could readily be presented as the intransigence of a clique defending its own privileges at the expense of the public good. A further BMA plebiscite registered a decline in doctors' opposition and its leadership, and decided to recommend participation in the service.

The government succeeded in this case in implementing the most far-reaching of its welfare proposals against the strong opposition of an interest group whose co-operation was vital. It is easy to see this example as a demonstration of the ability of a Labour Government to implement reforms even when faced with apparently insurmountable obstacles. Such a verdict draws attention to some important points. The achievement owed much to a committed Minister ready to make concessions that did not detract from the achievement of his central objectives, and able to capitalise skilfully on divisions and doubts amongst his opponents. Yet it must be emphasised that the scheme's wide popularity meant that responsibility for its initiation would probably bring considerable electoral benefits. Accordingly the Government was united in its policy and the Conservatives lukewarm and confused in their opposition. It was the BMA that appeared as a selfish sectional interest. The scheme is a classic case of the type of reform that, given determination, can be secured by parliamentarianism and interest group negotiations. It did not appear to violate the existing consensus, and disadvantaged nobody.

If the central welfare component of Labour's historic programme in many ways reflected an emerging consensus on the need to humanise society, could the same be said about Labour's plans for public ownership? Certainly this was seen widely as the most distinctive ingredient in Labour's programme, but two major qualifications must be made. First, the content of Labour's public ownership proposals had been determined to a considerable extent by the interests of influential trade unions. Accordingly a major justification for many of them had been one of relevance to the problems of a particular industry, rather than a contribution to the gradual replacement of capitalism. Thus there was fundamental uncertainty about the purpose of the Labour commitment. Second, it would be an error to suggest that the party's specific proposals represented a sharp ideological divide between Labour and its rivals. The Bank of England, coal, gas and electricity had all been the subject of reports by Conservative-dominated committees, and in these cases, plus that of transport, a close relationship with government was already well-established in 1945.

It is rather surprising to discover that Labour had paid little attention to the formulation of substantive proposals for the fulfilment of this part of its programme. Nevertheless, between October 1945 and January 1948, the Government introduced legislation to nationalise the Bank of England, coal, electricity, gas and inland transport. The co-ordination of this programme was the responsibility of Morrison as Chairman of the Cabinet Committee on the Socialisation of Industry,[33] and he collaborated closely — some critics would say too closely — with the Ministers responsible. In each of these cases, public ownership could be justified readily on grounds of efficiency, although Ministers also portrayed the measures as stages on the road to socialism. Nevertheless these measures produced little opposition in the Commons — the struggle only became bitter when Labour attempted to nationalise the iron and steel industry, an issue on which the party itself was divided.

Before examining this singular case, attention must be paid to certain common features of the earlier measures. They went only a little way beyond the dominant consensus on the control of basic utilities. Since the industries chosen were those for which it was hoped public ownership would mean an increase in efficiency, it followed that they tended to be industries which had acted as a break on economic growth, and whose condition was unsatisfactory. This was certainly the case with mining and the railways. Accordingly, public ownership became widely associated with obsolescence, whereas in fact the inauguration of government responsibility for these run-down but industrially vital sectors left expanding profitable industries untouched. It strengthened the private sector by relieving it of responsibility for industries requiring vast new investment programmes. Thus Labour's public ownership programme could be seen as an exercise in the removal of obstacles to growth within the emerging mixed economy.

The form of organisation chosen by the Government, the public corporation, reflected the influence of Morrison. He had developed this in his legislation on London's transport during the second MacDonald Government, and had championed the conception during the subsequent party battles on workers' control. This approach demonstrated the party's lack of concern with the distribution of power within industry. Each publicly-owned industry was run by a board of experts, appointed by the Minister. In fact Morrison had a significant hand in many of the appointments. Although some erstwhile trade unionists were included on the boards, they were there as managers, after severing their union connections. Relationships between managers and workers remained basically the same as under private ownership. Furthermore, the leaders of the new publicly-owned industries could hardly provoke consternation amongst defenders of private industry. Management recruits from Labour organisations were few — the head of the National Coal Board had previously been involved with one of the largest private colliery companies. This approach is a clear demonstration of Labour's adherence to the Fabian tradition — the belief that 'experts' appointed to public boards would act in a disinterested fashion, pursuing the public interest and disavowing sectional claims. Given this firm acceptance of traditional managerial hierarchies[34] and the idealistic expectations of many workers within the industries concerned, it is hardly surprising that dissatisfaction developed. This was expressed in various ways. Some resolutions appeared on Party Conference agendas demanding greater participation by workers in nationalised industries[35] — more dramatically there were unofficial strikes in both the mining and the railway industries. Perhaps most important, the disappointment led to declining enthusiasm for public ownership.

The Government showed itself equally oblivious to another traditional socialist argument for public ownership, that it would redistribute wealth. Any hope of this was obviated by the payment of compensation on a large scale. No one considered the coal industry to be efficient, yet the owners received £164 million; Dalton might describe the railways as 'a pretty poor bag of physical assets',[36] yet together with the canals, the total compensation reached £1,000 million, through the medium of 3% Transport Stock. Once again Labour had chosen to 'play fair' by the rules of the existing economic system.

In these cases, it is clear that the Government had extended its control in such a way that the security of private industry was maintained. On the one hand, responsibility was taken for 'problem

industries'; on the other, the traditional management/worker division
was preserved and any hint of confiscation was studiously avoided. The
iron and steel case seems to raise rather different issues, and requires
separate examination. Most crucially, the issue became for several
within both parties a question of the highest importance: it became
symbolic of Labour's future intentions on public ownership, while
Conservatives insisted that a line be drawn between public utilities and
the rest of industry. Many, although not all, Labour spokesmen felt
that socialisation really only began after the public utilities had been
dealt with. This was seen by some as necessitating a clarification of the
purpose of Labour's public ownership commitment — was it primarily
the rationalisation and modernisation of defective sectors of industry,
or did it centre around the development of a new economic order?[37]

For some within the Government, the efficiency argument was less
clear-cut in the iron and steel case. It could be claimed that British
prices were relatively low, and that the industry had produced plans for
expansion. Critics claimed however that the plans were inadequate and
demonstrated the essentially restrictionist approach of the steel masters.
A further difficulty stemmed from the fact that the confines of the
industry were not immediately apparent — where, for example, should
the line be drawn between iron and steel and engineering? The
Government's proposals were far less ambitious than in its previous
public ownership ventures. It envisaged the creation of a Corporation to
own the securities of the major steel companies without much change in
organisational structures. Although the Government's majority ensured
a safe passage through the Commons, it ran foul of Conservative
dominance in the Lords, being amended to prevent implementation
until after the next election. The vesting day was thus postponed until
15 February 1951. By then, Labour's majority had been slashed to six,
a predicament providing endless fuel for constitutional arguments as to
whether the Government still had a mandate to proceed with the
measure. Constitutional niceties apart, subsequent events demonstrated
that the Government lacked the power and the will. The Steel
Federation refused to co-operate and only one member of the new
Corporation came from the industry.[38]

This case had been quoted as a demonstration of the limits of
parliamentary socialism. Once, so the argument goes, the consensual
parts of Labour's programme had been fulfilled and the struggle began
in earnest, Labour collapsed before the ferocious opposition of the iron
and steel capitalists. Obviously, Labour did fail on the steel issue, but it
is doubtful whether this case must be interpreted in these terms. That is

not to argue against the contention that a commitment to
parliamentarianism imposes great limitations on socialist policies, only
that the steel case cannot play the important part in the argument that
is sometimes assigned to it. First, attention must be paid to some factors
that obviously affected the outcome but which were clearly contingent.
The Government's own divisions on the issue, the decision to take steel
last of all the nationalisation measures, the fatigue of many Ministers
and the uncertain survival prospects of the Government after February
1950 — all these factors obviously weakened the Government's
position in its dealings with the steel industry, yet none of them was
inevitable. Second, it is vital to consider whether the issue did represent
the crucial struggle for economic power portrayed by many of the
protagonists. How far this portrayal rested on sincere belief and how
far on each side on a desire to 'inspire the troops' is unclear. Certainly
steel was seen as important, but as a symbol of party morale perhaps,
rather than as a political Rubicon. The dramas of 1948-51 were
re-enacted in an extremely muted fashion in 1965, but when steel was
finally nationalised after March 1967, no one proclaimed the death of
private enterprise. In a strange way, those who use the steel case to
demonstrate the impossibility of parliamentary socialism seem to take
at face value the more theatrical pronouncements of parliamentarians.

The implementation of so much of Labour's traditional programme
inevitably produced difficulties. In the case of welfare, the fulfilment
of pledges left a vacuum — what, if anything, should be proposed now?
Perhaps attention should be paid to other policies such as education,
where the distinctive contribution of the Government had been
minimal. The public ownership measures of the Government had ended
with rather more than 20 per cent of the economy run directly by the
state. Now, the ambiguity about Labour's commitment to this
technique had to be faced — was it a tool to be used to increase
economic efficiency, in which case its application would be selective, or
a means of effecting a qualitative social change? Certainly the
Government's policies in this field had contained little that supported
the latter interpretation. Here, more than anywhere, the rift was
apparent between the short-term impact of the party's traditional
measures and the aspirations that they had been intended to promote.

'We Are All Keynesians Now'

The implementation of the traditional party programme was not the
only domestic source of problems raised by office for the commitment
to socialism. The continual need to react to immediate and

unanticipated economic crises led to policy expedients that had little connection with party orthodoxy. These still required legitimation within the party, and thereby affected Labour interpretations of its traditional values. Two issues are of particular importance here – the complexities of economic management and the crucial choices made by Labour Ministers; and secondly the problem of government relationships with the private sector of the economy. Faced with the need to modernise industry, to raise production and to increase exports, the Government inherited an armoury of economic controls, far beyond the dreams of any socialist planner. Typically, Labour's planning intentions were notable for their vagueness. Morrison, as the Minister responsible for co-ordinating planning, spoke of the combination of 'large-scale economic planning with a full measure of individual rights and liberties'; from the beginning, official pronouncements suggested that economic controls and democratic rights were in a state of incipient tension.

Morrison presided over a planning machine inherited from the Coalition which centred around the Cabinet and appropriate committees. In the early years of the Government, responsibility for drawing up an overall plan lay with the Official Committee on Economic Development, but responsibility passed to a Central Economic Planning Staff in 1947. At first, the armoury of physical controls covered all aspects of economic activity but those relating to production and manpower quickly became marginal. Most weight was then placed on controls over resource allocation, in attempts to channel scarce resources to the sectors most crucial to the export drive. At first this was done largely on a short-term basis without the guidance of any overall plan. Even at the peak of the Government's utilisation of direct controls, there were significant gaps in the fields of personal incomes, profits, exports and manpower.[39]

The crucial point about the Government's use of direct controls is that it did not attempt to plug these gaps, but shifted away from its existing reliance on controls. There was always much vagueness in its planning proposals, and rhetoric did not disguise the lack of techniques. It is clear that many Labour Ministers preferred exhortation to compulsion. They saw the use of controls not as indicative of an alternative economic system, but as a necessary instrument in a situation of shortages. There was also a question of responsibility. Ministers were at least formally responsible for the administration of controls, and were not adverse to terminating them, if this meant they could escape direct liability for economic errors. The fuel crisis of 1947 hardly served as an attractive advertisement for the efficiency of planning, and while some within the party drew the conclusion that controls should be extended and more rigorously administered,[40] several influential figures favoured a flight from controls. From 1948 onwards, the Government relinquished most of its control over private industry, and by 1950, the Government's annual economic survey contained little to justify the title of 'planning'. One factor in this 'bonfire' of controls was obviously the attitude of private industry, a question dealt with below, but a further issue of importance relates to a recurring theme. The discussion of Labour's nationalisation programme emphasised how this could be interpreted in two ways, through the criterion of efficiency and as a means of advancing socialism, and that Labour's governmental practice suggested an abandonment of the latter. Similarly the use of direct controls could be seen either as indicating the way to a new economic system or as a means of alleviating shortages within the existing system. Labour's flight from controls indicated that the choice had been resolved in favour of the latter interpretation, with Labour succumbing to that market morality which was condemned by much of its traditional rhetoric.

This outcome was influenced perhaps more than anything by the existence of an alternative. Keynesian theory has had a profound effect upon the development of post-war politics. By holding out the prospect of a mixed economy with full employment, the approach could serve as a counter to traditional socialist doctrines about the inevitable decay and collapse of capitalism. The theory provided an approach to economic issues that transcended pre-war party divisions. The underlying principle concerns the utilisation of fiscal techniques, not to balance government expenditure but to avoid inflation or deflation through the balance of savings and investment. Obviously these demand management techniques permitted variations based on political values. Thus taxation changes could be assessed for their redistributive effect, as well as their role in terms of the Keynesian framework.

Keynesian techniques had been absorbed into government economic thinking from 1941, but did not become dominant for the Attlee Government until 1947.[41] Originally, the major economic problem had been viewed as a question of ending the manpower gap, but this came to be superseded by the judgement that the problem was one of suppressed inflation. The summer of 1947 was perhaps the most difficult period in the whole life of the Government. Preceded by a bitter winter that paralysed industry, the Government attempted to honour its long-standing commitment to restore full sterling convertibility. This was a total failure and was suspended after less than a month. The Government's long-term response to the crisis shows their acceptance of the Keynesian framework. Plans were made to foster increased exports, to restrict consumer spending still further, and to cut public investment. Perhaps most damaging of all to the Government, the housing programme was cut.

The Keynesian approach is evident in Dalton's last budget in November 1947, and the remedy of cuts in public expenditure and increases in taxation dominated the budgets of his successor, Sir Stafford Cripps. It is a fascinating paradox of party development that this former prophet of inevitable capitalist collapse should preside over a strategy representing a major acceptance of existing economic practices. Given the weak state of Britain's overseas balance, the preoccupation of Ministers with increased production and the reduction of inflation is understandable, but this meant inevitably that any concern with socialist economic measures came a very poor second. The Government's first priority was economic survival which meant the survival of existing economic arrangements. Thus Cripps presided over a shift from direct to indirect taxation. Productivity had to take precedence over equality. Indeed Cripps spelt out his blunt belief that further redistribution was dependent on the creation of further wealth. This was a rejection of the traditional socialist belief that the problem of production had been solved. His successor at the Treasury, Gaitskell, went even further in an attempt to educate his party into the 'realities' of administering an ongoing economic system, saying that there could be no objection to profits that were honestly earned.

In spite of the rigours of the Government's austerity programme, it is clear that this would have been inadequate if assistance had not been forthcoming from the United States in the shape of Marshall Aid. This arguably prevented draconian cuts in the standard of living and a major rise in unemployment, but equally the acceptance of Marshall Aid was not without obligation. Throughout the Government's career, economic problems were greatly exacerbated by a high level of defence expenditure, and it has also been claimed that increased dependence on American support was a constraint on the possible production of radical policies. Ministerial attacks on Communists and fellow travellers, and the abandonment of the more egalitarian economic policies could not help but reassure Congressmen anxious as to whether British Labour was merely a half-way house to Communism.[42]

Labour's economic strategy after 1947 marked in practice an abandonment of any claim to be constructing a new economic order. In seeking higher production, the Government abandoned its equality aspiration, came to accept the need for reasonable profits and relied on the motivation of self-interest.[43] Keynesian theory can be seen as a significant medium whereby Labour was socialised into accepting the mixed economy. There was no fundamental change in the structure of economic penalties and rewards. There was full employment, however, and this explained much about the ready acceptance of existing practices.

This acceptance raised a major doctrinal problem for the party, namely its attitude towards the private sector of industry. Government involvement in the administration of the economy raised the problem of policy towards industrialists whose co-operation was essential for the fulfilment of economic targets. One particularly crucial area concerned the administration of economic controls. Here the Government made frequent use of the services of leading figures in the industries concerned, either by employing them within the planning machinery, or delegating the administration of controls to appropriate trade associations. This demonstrates a remarkable — although typical — act of faith by Labour in industrialists' ability and readiness to behave in a disinterested fashion. Such 'administrators' formed a powerful group favouring the abandonment of such controls. Furthermore the administration of controls by trade associations or dominant firms led to a freezing of economic structures, inhibiting innovation and throwing a cloak of acceptability over the maintenance of industrial inefficiency.[44]

While the party had spent much time in the thirties discussing candidates for public ownership, it had spent very little time on developing policies for private industry. In many sections of the party, there seemed to be a tacit assumption that the issue was unimportant since the private sector would soon become marginal. Yet the drive for economic efficiency inevitably raised the question in a pressing form after 1945. Should a Labour Government seek an efficient private sector through the removal of obstacles to effective competition? The Government did enact some rather innocuous anti-monopoly legislation, a step clearly at variance with traditional socialist condemnations of the competitive ethic. A more important development concerned the development of government intervention in some industries as a means of promoting greater efficiency. This had been foreshadowed in the thirties, and after 1945 could be justified as part of the production drive.

The early development of government policy towards private

industry fell under the control of Cripps at the Board of Trade. It seems clear that he envisaged the maintenance of a viable private sector. Thus in October 1945 he established a working party on cotton, the first of several looking at particular industries. The report stressed that the working party's terms of reference required the submission of 'proposals based on maintaining private enterprise'.[45] These working parties gave rise to the most distinctive Labour proposal on the private sector, the creation of Development Councils for particular industries or groups of industries. They were to contain equal numbers of employers and employees plus a few independent members. Such a proposal, enshrined in the 1947 Industrial Organisation and Development Act, related closely to the pre-war drive towards collaboration and rationalisation. Typically their creation was dependent on the existence of a significant degree of consent in the industry, and any goals were to be pursued through persuasion.[46]

This exercise in collaboration was a failure; only four Councils appeared during the Government's lifetime. This reflected extensive opposition from industrialists which mirrored in turn the increasing general hostility of private industry towards the Government. There is no doubt that a large section of private industry saw Development Councils as a Trojan horse for the furtherance of government control. In addition, distaste for extensive government intervention increased along with optimism. In the immediate post-war years, a return to pre-war depression was widely anticipated and many industrialists therefore viewed government intervention with a tolerance that diminished as their faith in the viability of free markets was renewed.

This particular friction between government and private industry must not be permitted to disguise the basic change that came over Labour's attitude towards private industry. The earlier vacuum was replaced by an emerging relationship wherein a private sector, responsive to national considerations, was treated as an appropriate and necessary partner for a Labour Government. Most important, this treatment was largely on industry's own terms. Labour Ministers' concern with production led to respect for industrialists because of their strategic position within the economy.

It could be argued that Labour acceptance of Keynesian techniques and its collaboration with private industry were precipitated by the need to combat major and immediate economic difficulties. Equally, it could be claimed that this outcome was implicit in Labour's past performance and beliefs — the Fabian belief in the neutral expert, the development of Mondism, the reliance on consensus — all foreshadowed

this attempt to operate the existing economic system. While there is
much truth in this, the dualism of Labour's 1945 position must be
emphasised. Perhaps the scales were weighted in favour of collaboration,
a weighting increased by crisis, but even moderate leaders did speak for
a time with apparent sincerity about the promotion of a new economic
system. The acceptance, in practice, of the mixed economy raised major
difficulties for party doctrine. This was particularly the case since the
achievement of full employment, plus the enactment of the traditional
programme met many of the substantive needs that had fuelled Labour's
radical inclinations.

Collaboration and Loyalty – the Government and the Unions

The Government's dependence upon the co-operation of industrialists
led to a close relationship with them, accepting that their control of
scarce resources gave some leverage over government policy-making. By
embracing the spirit of a pluralist society, the Government inevitably
raised problems for the traditional special relationship between the
Labour Party and the trade union movement. The largely successful
attempts after 1931 to ensure that the Party and the TUC remained in
harmony on crucial issues meant that in 1945 there appeared to be
extensive agreement between the two sides of the Labour alliance. Yet
this relationship was not one of total trust. A further legacy of 1931
had been a search by trade union leaders for alternative political
channels for solving their problems. This had been rewarded by the
increased status given to trade union leaders after 1940 because of their
essential role in the war effort. Increased status was matched by a
proliferation of the points at which unions and government interacted.
Unions were no longer marginal bodies, but were close to the
formation of economic and industrial policy. Naturally the General
Council were concerned to maintain their elevated status after 1945,
and while such aspirations would be regarded benevolently by a Labour
Government, it could be argued that the long-term maintenance of such
a position would be prejudiced by an excessively partisan identification
with such a government. There were thus factors on the TUC side
that favoured government treatment of the unions as an important,
friendly, but distant interest group.[47]

Union-Government distinctiveness was aided by the Government's
composition. Apart from Bevin, union representation in the Cabinet
was unimpressive. By 1951, a Cabinet of 17 included only 4 trade
unionists, and in the remainder of the administration the proportion
was 18 out of 66. It appears that leading Ministers were aware of a need

to offer posts to younger trade union MPs, but were inhibited by generally unfavourable assessments of their potential.

There were also factors making for a close relationship between union leaders and the Government. A crucial one was the Government's readiness to meet long-standing TUC demands. The most significant example was the early repeal of the 1927 Trade Disputes Act, providing Bevin with the opportunity of appearing not as the defender of a bi-partisan foreign policy, but as the vigorous defender of trade union interests. The changing membership of the General Council also led to a closer relationship with the Government. Citrine left the TUC in 1946 to join the Coal Board, being succeeded by Tewson, while between 1945 and 1947 ten other members left the General Council. Although political moderates, these leaders had sharp memories of MacDonald. While ready to give general support to a Labour Government, they retained an independence of judgement. When a new leadership group emerged on the General Council, it was dominated by Deakin of the TGW and Lawther of the Mineworkers. They were less critical of government policies, and saw their role as the protectors of moderate Ministers against the attacks of the left. Their hostility to criticism deepened as the fight against Communists intensified inside individual unions. The ease with which any dissent could be labelled as Communist-inspired aided this group in its control of Congress, and in the short run, made union support for government policies even more reliable. However, the behaviour of Deakin and his followers increased the bitterness of the left towards what they regarded as excessive conservatism and authoritarian bureaucracy.

The emergence of this loyalist union leadership coincided with growing Ministerial perceptions of economic crisis, which led them to make new, far-reaching demands upon the TUC and its member unions. These involved some notion of wage restraint as a means of reducing inflation. During the immediate post-war period, General Council were clearly opposed to any wages policy,[48] but as difficulties became more acute in 1947, Ministers began to make veiled suggestions. In the August crisis Attlee appealed to workers just to maintain differentials, and this was followed by an appeal to the General Council by Cripps on the question of wages stability. By December 1947, the General Council had gone so far as to publish an 'Interim Report on the Economic Situation', recommending moderation and restraint in the formulation of wage demands, but early in February 1948 a White Paper was published, laying the principal responsibility for inflation on rising wages. The General Council, aggrieved at an absence of prior consultation, was angered further by Cripps' lack of courtesy at a subsequent meeting, but such was the loyalty of the new TUC leadership that the principle of wage restraint was accepted.[49] No doubt loyalty was strengthened by Cripps' subsequent concessions on price controls and dividend restraint. Many within the TUC were extremely concerned about these developments,[50] although for two years the restraint seemed effective.[51] The Deakin group was aided by the fact that some of the policy's most vocal critics were leaders of Communist-dominated unions, and therefore criticism could be dismissed as politically motivated. The absurdity of this interpretation was demonstrated in 1950. Concern at the continued operation of the policy plus the inflationary effects of the Korean War led to an attempt by the General Council to forestall criticism by presenting a diluted wage restraint policy to the 1950 TUC. However, even this anticipation was inadequate and the wage restraint proposals were defeated.[52] The period of maximum loyalty was at an end.

The growing tensions were reflected in another direction, that of industrial stoppages.[53] During the early years of the Government, the incidence of strikes had been very low but the Government continued, with the General Council's acquiescence, to maintain the Conditions of Employment and National Arbitration Order 1305. This permitted the prosecution of strikers in essential services. After several years disuse the Government reactivated the Order, prosecuting ten gas workers in October 1950, and seven dockers the following February. These decisions succeeded in uniting all sections of the trade union movement against the Government. Some opposed 1305 on principle, while many others were affronted by governmental insensitivity and lack of consultation. The resulting agitation led to the termination of the Order in August 1951. Once again however, this episode shows the Government's characteristic adoption of a 'national interest' standpoint rather than support for the sectional claims of trade unionists. Indeed the attitude of Labour Ministers towards industrial action was generally hostile. Stoppages were frequently attributed to Communist agitation, and appeals were made to workers to loyally support *their* government.[54]

Two themes of the greatest importance emerge from a consideration of party-union relationships during this period. One concerns the role of the unions within a mixed economy with full employment, and is raised in an acute form by the debate over wage restraint. Should unions be subject to controls in the wider public interest, or did such controls involve an emasculation of union power? Was there anything sacrosanct to a socialist in the maintenance of unhindered collective bargaining, or did such an approach merely serve to maintain the inequities of the existing economic system? These issues, although raised by the Attlee Government's dealings with the unions, were barely perceived at the time. The difficulties became more apparent only when the Wilson Government attempted much more extensive controls. A satisfactory examination of this issue turns upon a prior assessment of the type of economic system that has emerged since the war. Contemporary Labour assessments tended to portray the 1945 Government's policies as first steps towards radical social change. On this interpretation, it could be argued that individual unions should abandon their competitive, sectional goals. On the other hand, the interpretation developed in this chapter is that the developing mixed economy was still dominated by private claims — the old market morality survived intact. If this is so, then appeals for restraint could be interpreted as attempts to curb union power in a full-employment situation.

This consideration links to the second theme. In the short term the ultra-loyalty of the General Council's dominant group meant that widespread concessions were made by unions in response to government demands, while the high exposure given to the Communist 'threat' meant that opposition was readily discredited. This artificial consensus however masked the tensions within the trade union movement. With prominent leaders acting as agents of government policy in many respects, one requirement for a more critical union leadership was met; the other awaited the expunging of the equation between criticism and Communism. Government-union relationships were characterised by the solid support generated by Bevin's participation in the Government, and given unstintingly by Deakin, Lawther and their supporters. Such commitment, plus the radical innovations in the undertakings offered by the TUC, prepared the ground for future conflicts. The origins of the traumas of the sixties can be found in the apparent near-unanimity of the late forties.

The Next Stage: Party Policy-making in Office

The formulation of future policy proposals by a party in office is invariably difficult. Leaders are immersed in ministerial duties and lack the time to develop a new programme. Preoccupation with both the crises and the trivia of office can produce a loosening of party ties. For Labour, after 1945, the problems were particularly severe. Much of its traditional programme had been implemented, while the crises of office had produced several deviations from traditional expectations. Party policy-makers were faced with a fundamental problem over the future of Labour's socialist commitment. Need it be redefined in the light of governmental experience and how should it be pursued?

This question of the party's future direction was tied to another central difficulty, that of producing a programme that would have the same electoral appeal as 'Let Us Face The Future'. The party's electoral strategists were confronted after 1945 by new problems. Instead of searching for the breakthrough to majority status, they were confronted with the problem of retaining their 1945 position. In so far as the government's by-election record offered any illumination, it was reasonably encouraging. No seats won in 1945 were lost in subsequent by-elections, but this success covered a multitude of swings. Labour retained a series of apparently vulnerable seats — Heywood, Gravesend, Hammersmith South and Sowerby — but in some contests, for example, Bexley and Edmonton, the 1945 majority was drastically cut.

Labour's spectacular 1945 gains had been based on an electoral coalition that included a substantial degree of middle-class support. The need to maintain this coalition produced two very different strategic responses within the leadership, with their distinctive implications for a future party programme.[55] Several advocated a strategy based on class interests. The party should maintain a close relationship with the working class, admitting and welcoming the domination of British politics by class issues. This image of the party has always had a wide circulation amongst both the party's supporters and opponents. While its strongest advocate amongst Labour leaders happened to be Bevan, it is clear that various programmatic conclusions could be derived from this position. The view of Labour as the advocate and defender of working-class interests could be held by moderates who considered themselves to be voicing the demands of their mass support. Equally the image of a class-based party could be seen as implying radical policies on the assumption that legitimate class claims could be met only by thorough social reconstruction.

The alternative image of party and electorate was that championed by Morrison. He argued that Labour could only maintain its majority if it presented itself as an umbrella for all voters with progressive inclinations. Here the programmatic implications were more precise. Since Morrison assumed that Labour was guaranteed its natural working-class support, there was no need to offer them special inducements to vote for the party. The programme should be such as to attract the crucial moderate voters which meant for Morrison that its content should be pragmatic and classless in its appeal. This idea of the crucial centre voters was one which came to dominate the thoughts of electoral strategists from both parties. The implications for Labour were far-reaching, raising the sensitive issue of the relationship between party principles and the preferences of centre voters. How far should party principles be redefined or discarded in the struggle for their allegiance?

Morrison dominated the formulation of future policy, from his position as Chairman of the NEC's Policy Committee. Although the Policy Committee had discussed the need for research work on the new programme as early as May 1946,[56] the principal work was done between the 1948 and 1949 Party Conferences. The debate over future policy was begun by Morrison at the 1948 Conference when, in a speech on the next election, he emphasised that:

> Whilst in the next programme it will be right to give proper consideration to further propositions for public ownership, do not ignore the need, not merely for considering further public ownership, but for allowing Ministers to consolidate.[57]

Consolidation was to become the key word in Morrison's approach. Another Labour Government would seek to digest fully the achievements of the 1945 administration, devoting considerable attention to the improvement of existing publicly-owned industries. It must be emphasised that consolidation did not involve necessarily any abandonment of the view that the party's purpose was the gradual achievement of socialism; it merely implied a breathing space. However, this was sufficient to produce a heated debate about the future of the party.

The principal battleground was the NEC's Policy Committee. At a meeting in July 1948, it resolved to set up seven sub-committees to cover aspects of future policy.[58] Morrison chaired two of these, significantly on the Administration of Nationalised Industries; and to consider possible candidates for public ownership. In contrast, Bevan, his principal protagonist, was placed in charge of a Sub-Committee on Privately-Owned Industry. Bevan's interest in this subject demonstrates clearly that the controversy was not between consolidators and all-out nationalisers. He certainly accepted that a mixed economy would exist for the foreseeable future. Differences were rather concerned with the balance between public and private industry, with the desirability of maintaining a reforming momentum and over differing conceptions of electoral strategy. It is indicative of the symbolic importance attached to the public ownership issue that this became the principal battleground.[59]

During the remainder of 1948, Morrison's Sub-Committee on possible nationalisation candidates considered a variety of possibilities — commercial insurance, chemicals, water, shipbuilding, motors, cotton, aircraft and oil distribution were all discussed. The consideration of specific industries was favoured by those supporting further public ownership on the grounds that the alternative, a set of criteria, would permit Morrison and his supporters to escape any commitments. However the 'shopping list' approach permitted the erosion of each proposal on its own particular grounds. Thus chemicals fell because of trade union opposition: shipbuilding was left undecided. By January 1949, the Policy Committee had approved a draft, the summation of over a hundred previous papers, amounting to almost 600,000 words. This was followed in February by a joint Cabinet-NEC discussion at Shanklin[60] and the approval of a revised draft by the full NEC a month later. The document, 'Labour Believes In Britain', undoubtedly reflected Morrison's general position, but contrary to his views, a small list of public ownership proposals was included — cement, sugar, meat slaughtering, water and industrial assurance. This peculiar mixture could be attributed in part to the way in which individual candidates were considered, the survivors being those against which no persuasive arguments had been brought. Cement, for example, had been the subject of a Research Department paper[61] as late as February 1949, and had been included after support from Charles Key. Morrison fought particularly hard to remove the commitment on industrial assurance, but a proposal of his for a fact-finding enquiry was defeated at the March NEC meeting.

This was the position at the time of the 1949 Conference.[62] Both sides could claim some influence on the document. Its general tone was clearly consolidationist, but the small shopping list was at least a concession to the alternative viewpoint. However, Morrison was not defeated yet. Following the Conference, the industrial assurance case was considered again by the NEC.[63] An expert committee was set up; the Policy Committee considered a possible alternative — 'mutualisation'; a lengthy discussion was held with representatives of the Co-operative Insurance Society, who were opposed to the scheme. Eventually the whole issue came before the Policy Committee in November, in the shape of four alternatives — 'nationalisation', 'mutualisation', 'control' and 'withdrawal'. Only three members backed the original proposal and mutualisation was passed by six votes to four as a compromise. This

was approved subsequently by the full NEC.[64] This prolonged
controversy over what was really little more than a form of words
showed how fundamental and sometimes vaguely defined issues had
become encapsulated into a small question.

The ease with which Morrison secured most of his goals is
understandable given the composition of the NEC. However, he was
aided, undoubtedly, by the failure of anyone on the left of the party
to offer a thorough analysis of the Government's performance. The
pamphlets produced by the 'Keep Left' group were restricted to the
advocacy of more direct controls, some extension of the public sector,
and above all, more audacity and determination. There was no
examination, however, of the assumptions behind the Government's
economic strategy, the failure to change the pre-existing managerial
hierarchies in the newly nationalised industries, or the readiness with
which existing economic practices and incentives had been accepted.

When electoral battle was joined early in 1950, the Labour
campaign placed little emphasis on the public ownership proposals.
Most weight was placed on the Government's record in the fields of
employment and welfare, policy areas that lay inside the emerging
consensus on economic and social policy. Churchill later described the
campaign as 'demure', a verdict accepted by many commentators, but
others have portrayed a more combative contest with class feelings
higher than in 1945.[65] Certainly, the consolidationist approach did not
succeed in maintaining its 1945 level of middle-class support. Labour's
overall majority shrank to a perilous five, and opinion polls indicated
that its share of the middle-class vote had declined from 21 per cent to
16. In contrast, Labour had kept intact and perhaps even expanded its
working-class support. Such an interpretation was supported by the
variations in the swing. Over the whole country this was 2.9 per cent,
but in many Home Counties suburban seats, it was between 7 and 8
per cent. It was such constituencies that accounted for a considerable
proportion of Labour losses, and several more could be attributed not
to changes in voting, but to the abolition under the 1948 redistribution
of Labour strongholds in the depopulated centres of cities.

The loss of middle-class support could be explained perhaps by the
continuing post-war austerity and the accompanying feeling of
middle-class deprivation. More fundamentally, the factors that had
radicalised a section of the middle class in 1945 no longer obtained.
Those who had been shocked out of complacency by the social mixing
precipitated by war had now returned to a settled pattern of life in
which significant reference groups and cultural norms worked in favour

of an identification with the Conservative Party.[66] In contrast, the
absence of many proposals in Labour's programme might have assisted
in the maintenance of working-class support, since the lack of policy
was balanced by the wide use of retrospective appeals. While such a
strategy tapped an identification of Conservatism with the deprivations
of the thirties, such an approach was clearly a declining asset for a
supposedly progressive party. It is ironic that Labour's consolidationist
campaign ended with its working-class support intact, but with
diminished support amongst those voters for whom the appeal had been
devised.

The 1950 result led to each side in the controversy drawing
appropriate conclusions. The left claimed that dilution of the party's
socialism was bound to produce electoral difficulties, since the party
could not hope to win a competition in respectability. Once again,
however, it was Morrison who took the initiative. As early as March
the NEC discussed a memorandum by him – 'The Recent General
Election and the Next'.[67] This showed his concern with the loss of
middle-class support and the rise in Conservative voting, warning
Labour spokesmen to be 'careful in policy and speeches not to stimulate
what might be a quiet Conservative rank and file'. But it was on the
question of nationalisation that the statement became really
controversial. He claimed that the first priority should be given to
improving the existing public sector, and made a critical onslaught on
the shopping list:

> At the last election, we were in difficulty because we had to meet
> the differing views of the members of the Executive, and this
> weakened the consistency of our programme. We rather invented
> a further socialisation programme. This was not supported by many
> Trade Unionists, and was difficult to present in the campaign.[68]

Morrison denied that this meant an abandonment of socialism – rather
further extensions must depend on securing public support on the basis
of a strong case. However, he did attack those who took the view that
'the electorate having apparently not been keen on a further
socialisation programme at this stage, the remedy is to feature these
proposals in bigger type than ever.'[69]

This clarion call for more consolidationism was discussed
subsequently by the National Council of Labour in April, and then at a
joint meeting of NEC members and Ministers at Dorking in May.[70] Here
Morrison met opposition not just from the few representatives of the

left, but also from others concerned at the apparent dilution of traditional values, and concerned to maintain the party's impetus. Pressure for consolidation came, however, from the TUC Economic Committee – their suggestion being that attention be devoted to the state of the existing public sector, and that the proposals for extension should be dropped.[71] Obviously the consolidationist position enjoyed influential support, but equally it produced reservations from people who would not be identified normally with the left. Morrison soon made a significant advance. When the NEC met in July, he produced a formula on public ownership for insertion in the policy statement being prepared for the 1950 Conference. This formula was accepted, and thus replaced the shopping list.[72] Rather it was agreed that the next election manifesto would consider public ownership when existing concerns were operating against the national interest. Obviously this compromise could be interpreted as justifying vast or minimal extensions of public ownership. The advantage in Morrison's eyes was that it released the party from specific commitments. When the document 'Labour and the New Society' was debated at the 1950 Conference, Morrison referred to the shopping list industries as not dropped – 'they are within the field of eligibility'.[73] The formula was an efficient means of maintaining unity in the short term.

The most interesting feature of this debate is the way that the problem of electoral strategy became compressed into a debate about the party's commitment to public ownership. There is no reason to believe that this issue determined Labour's fate: at the side of housing, rationing or social welfare, such a claim seems weak. The debate was as much about the party's future identity as over electoral strategy. Experience of independent office with its achievements and difficulties had produced a crisis. By 1950, consolidation was not just a proposal, but a description of a government that had exhausted its ideas. The diverse interpretations of the post-1945 experience had prepared the way for a clash. This debate over the party programme was the first engagement in a lengthy war.

The 1951 Resignations: a Climax and a Starting Point

In April 1951, Bevan, recently transferred to the Ministry of Labour, resigned from the Government along with the President of the Board of Trade, Harold Wilson, and a junior Minister, John Freeman. These resignations, policy differences and personality clashes were to dominate Labour politics for more than a decade.[74] The passions aroused related closely to the problems faced by Labour in office, and to the debates, sometimes strident, sometimes muffled, about the Government's responses.

The explosion had been a long time in the making. The basic cause can be regarded as the divergence between theory and practice that marked government policies. The more proximate causes were specific manifestations of this general question. For a considerable time, there had been controversy within the Government on the desirability of curbing expenditure in the Health Service. Pressures for such restrictions had come inevitably from the Treasury, but also from some leading Ministers. Bevan fought to prevent the imposition of any restrictions, and, to some degree the argument could be seen as a round in the perennial war between the Treasury and the spending departments. On another level, however, the controversy concerned the strength of the Government's commitment to reform — how far should the pursuit of such reforms be restricted by Treasury orthodoxy?

This dispute was exceeded in both complexity and intensity by the controversy resulting from the Government's general support for American policy in the Far East. The original, almost unanimous PLP decision backing the Government's firm decision to join in the military opposition to North Korea was punctured by a series of reservations, as American forces advanced northwards and China was drawn into the conflict. Labour Ministers began to be oppressed by the imminence of a Third World War. They were firm in their belief that a Labour Government could reduce the excesses of American diplomacy, but also believed that such influence depended on Britain being seen to do its share in the defence of the West. The result of this analysis was a dramatic escalation in Britain's defence budget. For 1950-1, this had been fixed at £700 million (7½ per cent of the national income). In response to American pressure, this was raised initially in September 1950 to a three-year programme of £3,400 million and then in January 1951 to £4,700 million or 14 per cent of the national income. This second increase brought the crisis within the Government a stage nearer. Both Bevan and Wilson argued that the proposal was incapable of realisation due to the impossibility of securing the necessary physical resources.[75] This controversy was paralleled by a second related one, stemming from pressure on the Government to support an American resolution tabled in the United Nations branding China as an aggressor. This produced heated Cabinet debate and considerable agitation within the wider party. Not only Bevan but also Dalton opposed any move likely to produce a total breach between China and the West. But an original Cabinet decision against support for the resolution was rapidly reversed.

The world crisis produced a crisis in the party which was exacerbated by internal developments. The original leadership group was now in obvious decline. Cripps' ill health had led to his resignation in October 1950, Bevin was visibly failing and left the Foreign Office in March 1951, Dalton had never recovered from his temporary absence from office. It was obvious that Attlee's leadership would end in the next few years. The question of the succession was beginning to be discussed. Given the depletions in the Old Guard, there were two obvious candidates: Morrison, the perpetual locum for Attlee, now in his sixty-third year, and Bevan, still the Minister with the most radical appeal. By 1950, these two rivals had become symbolic of divergent approaches to policy-making. There was however a newly emerged rival to both men. Hugh Gaitskell, a product of Winchester and New College, had entered the Commons in 1945. A protégé of Dalton, he had achieved office rapidly, and had risen via the Ministry of Economic Affairs to become Cripps' successor. Gaitskell's political values and strategic outlook are dealt with below, but two factors of immediate significance should be emphasised. The rise of Gaitskell to the Treasury produced strong opposition from Bevan, apparently not because he had hoped for the office, but because he saw Gaitskell as no more than an elected civil servant, unable to sympathise with working-class aspirations. Furthermore, in a tired administration, Gaitskell was now an unflagging advocate of policies likely to produce left-wing opposition: he insisted more than most of his colleagues on the need to support American policy and to oppose Communism in all its guises.

The combined policy and personal differences came to a head with Gaitskell's 1951 budget. This was designed to cope with a worsening economic situation as inflation increased, vital raw materials became scarce, and Treasury insistence on curbing public expenditure became more clamorous. Towards the end of March the Cabinet discussed a proposal to impose charges on teeth and spectacles; Bevan and Wilson opposed this, but several others spoke in favour. Attlee, the great reconciler, was in hospital throughout the Cabinet crisis and Morrison, his deputy, was a generally firm supporter of Gaitskell. For almost a month the dispute remained unresolved but well publicised. Gaitskell was firm, Bevan at times wavered, but eventually on 21 April, eleven days after the budget was introduced, the three Ministers resigned. In his resignation speech Bevan widened the issue to include the basic questions of foreign policy and party strategy, the need above all to avoid the destruction of the party's commitment to socialist reform through excessive attention being paid to immediate difficulties.[76] Some observers suggested that such a widening represented a subsequent rationalisation aimed at mobilising support within the party. This is absurd. The sources of the explosion lay deep in the party fabric, in the development of its distinctive ideology and the experience of office. More personally, the basic problems ventilated by Bevan in his speech had preoccupied him for months before the breach, and the exposition was consistent with his past record.

The content of Bevanism belongs to the subsequent chapter on the debates in opposition. The crucial point at this stage is simply that the formal unity of the party remained largely unimpaired down to the election in October 1951. Much Labour criticism of the resignations had been fuelled by a fear that their consequence would be another 1931-type disaster. Yet compromises were readily secured, enabling the party to fight the election in reasonable unity. Certainly, when the NEC considered a draft policy statement in July 1951, attempts were made by Bevan and his supporters to amend the document drastically in accordance with their views, but all such attempts were defeated overwhelmingly.[77] In contrast, the drafting of an election manifesto was left to a sub-committee of four — Bevan, Dalton, Watson and Morgan Phillips. They successfully produced a compromise: for example on rearmament, the need for some level was accepted, but no figure was given.[78]

More broadly the manifesto was essentially consolidationist. It was dominated by four immediate issues — peace, employment, the cost of living and social justice. The appeal was essentially backward-looking, comparing Labour performance since 1945 with the Conservative's inter-war record. There were very few new proposals and no commitments on public ownership. The reforming idealism of 1945 had vanished: the word socialism was not mentioned.

In spite of the earlier explosions and the lack of programme, Labour did much better than many of its leaders anticipated.[79] Its total vote actually exceeded that of the Conservatives by a quarter of a million, but the party lost on balance twenty seats, giving the Conservatives a workable majority of seventeen. It appears that a major factor in the defeat was the drastic drop in the number of Liberal candidates, with many former Liberal voters shifting to the Conservatives in spite of some Labour attempts to attract them.

In many ways the 1951 defeat was a 'blessed release'. Ministers were tired, traditional policies had been implemented, momentum had run down. The resignations had demonstrated the tensions and confusions that had developed through six years of office. Now the party appeared to have the opportunity, with its mass support still intact, to consider the lessons of office. Inevitably, the stark fact of internal cleavage dominated such considerations, moulding them into a certain pattern, and with the background noise resulting from personal acerbities often drowning the debate over issues.

In Retrospect

How is the performance of the Attlee Government to be appraised in the light of this examination of specific problems? The process of appraisal occurs of course with reference to some ideal standard. If the assessment is restricted to Labour's formal implementation of its 1945 programme, then in most respects the party achieved what it set out to do. It was indeed Labour's 'heroic age' with Ministers dutifully implementing its traditional remedies for the ills of society. If, on the other hand, the comparison is widened to the consequences of that implementation, then the problem becomes much more complicated. When the remedies had been implemented, did the result match Labour expectations?

The answer to this question depends on the policies considered, and also on the groups whose expectations are being assessed. The maintenance of full employment and the development of universal welfare provision were undoubted achievements, although it is highly questionable how far such developments can be described as socialist. Nevertheless, such humanisation within the confines of a mixed economy was the sum total, more or less, of the aspirations of many within the party. This, in substantive terms, was what they understood by socialism — their demands appeared to have been met and thus they became an essentially conservative force, concerned to protect such achievements and with little interest in further reforms. Such satisfaction obviously provided a large proportion of the weight behind the consolidationist position.

The effect of the party's public ownership measures was much more ambiguous. As shown earlier, management-worker relationships in the industries concerned remained essentially untouched and there were demonstrations of disillusion on the part of some of those involved. These produced little response with the party, except an addition to the consolidationist case: publicly-owned industries must now be 'socialised' before any further extension of the public sector was undertaken. The content of such further 'socialisation' remained obscure, although it clearly did not include any major overhaul of

power relationships within these industries.

It would be easy to say that the performance of the Government was welcomed by the 'realistic practical' members of the party, and that such disillusion as existed by 1951 stemmed from Utopianism. In this perspective, the basic problem facing the party was one of reinvigoration. A new programme had to be constructed to replace the old. It was the exhaustion of this that had led to uncertainty and controversy. On this assessment, there was nothing in the post-1945 experience to justify any further examination of Labour's basic strategy: rather experience had shown that the parliamentary and administrative machines could be employed to introduce far-reaching reforms, that a combination of determination and guile could bring recalcitrant interest groups to heel.

This interpretation leaves a major problem unresolved. Defenders of the basic strategy have argued in the light of the 1945-51 experience that socialist measures could be implemented on the basis of consent, provided that the electorate had been persuaded of their necessity. However, if the reforms of the period are regarded not as socialist but as a means of ameliorating existing society, broadly acceptable to all groups, then this case is non-proven.

The essential acceptance of the basic strategy by all groups within the party meant that disputes over the lessons of office and future policy were constrained by electoral, parliamentary and administrative considerations. While groups varied in their diagnoses of the situation, and in the weight attached to such factors, they were all continuing and unquestioning advocates of the strategy. This inevitably restricted the scope of any reappraisal of party policy. Given this situation, debates within the party were bound to be like many family quarrels. Since the raising of fundamental strategic issues would question the basic purpose of the party, this did not happen. All disputants paid their respects to the successes of the Attlee administration, yet tensions obviously had resulted from the performance of the Government. Most fundamentally, these concerned the extent to which the Government in its practice had consigned the party's ideals to a theoretical museum. Until 1945, the party had balanced pragmatism with socialist idealism. While it had been predictable that in any crucial choice pragmatism would triumph, now that it had done so, the abandonment of any commitment to radical transformation could not be admitted.

It was not merely that the party had run out of determination by 1951. Rather its mission had been accomplished. Its traditional prescriptions had been implemented, to the satisfaction of its supporters, and also judging by the general lack of subsequent reversal, with the acceptance of its formal opponents. This period might have been the party's heroic age, but like many feats of heroism it had a devastating effect on the hero.

Notes

1. Hugh Dalton, *Memoirs Volume 3: High Tide and After* (Muller, London, 1962), p. 3.
2. For an attack on the traditional view see Miliband, op. cit., ch. 9.
3. See Donoughue and Jones, op. cit., ch. 25.
4. Ibid., ch. 27.
5. Dalton, *Vol. 3*, p. 23.
6. R. Jackson, *Rebels and Whips* (Macmillan, London), p. 47 – for dissent see chs. 3 and 4.
7. Ibid., pp. 59-61.
8. Ibid., pp. 202-17.
9. The NEC Minutes contain sometimes lengthy charge sheets for dissident MPs.
10. See *LPCR 1948*, pp. 184-200 and *1950*, pp. 141-50. The minority votes were 224,000 and 881,000.
11. *LPCR 1947*, pp. 134-53 on Planning. Minority vote 1,109,000; pp. 108-13 on National Service. Minority vote 571,000.
12. *LPCR 1950*, pp. 87-92.
13. *LPCR 1948*, pp. 120-1 and *1949*, pp. 119-27.
14. See Martin Harrison, *Trade Unions and The Labour Party Since 1945* (Allen and Unwin, London, 1960), ch. 1.
15. See V.L. Allen, *Trade Union Leadership: Based On a Study of Arthur Deakin* (Longmans, London, 1957).
16. See Bagwell, op. cit., pp. 630-1.
17. See H.J. Fyrth and Henry Collins, *The Foundry Workers* (AUFW, Manchester, 1959), and on the ETU, Harrison op. cit., pp. 182-5.
18. See the debates on the WFTU, *TUC Report 1948*, pp. 439-51; *1949*, pp. 321-39. Also on 'Trade Unionism and Communism', ibid., pp. 349-60.
19. *NEC Minutes*, 27 June 1946.
20. *NEC Minutes*, 25 February 1948, Whine Memorandum attached, and also the reply by Morgan Phillips.
21. See Donoughue and Jones, op. cit., ch. 30, and Dalton, *Vol. 3*, ch. 29.
22. For example, see Michael Foot, *Aneurin Bevan Vol. II 1945-60* (Davis Poynter, London, 1973), pp. 25-30.
23. James F. Byrnes, *Speaking Frankly* (Heinemann, London, 1947), p. 79.
24. See Richard Rose, *'The Relationship of Socialist Principles to Labour Foreign Policy'*, unpublished, Oxford D.Phil. thesis, 1960.
25. *430 H.C. Debs 5th Series*, Cols. 525-94, and *Keep Left* (1947).
26. See for example, the debate in *Tribune*, 20 May 1949, between Michael Foot (for) and Mikardo (against).
27. *Keeping Left* (1950).
28. Jackson, op. cit., pp. 65-9 and 203-7. Also *NEC Minutes*, 23 March 1948 (i.e. before the incident), and the accompanying memorandum on party discipline. This noted 'certain MPs whose general political activity makes it difficult to distinguish them from the Communist Party.'
29. See Evan Durbin, *The Politics of Democratic Socialism* (Routledge, London, 1957), New Edition.
30. As demonstrated in the first commons debate on Korea, *447 H.C. Debs 5th*

Series, Cols. 485-596.
31. *LPCR 1950,* p. 77 (Sam Watson of the Durham Miners).
32. See Foot, *Vol. II,* chs. 3 and 4. Also Peter Jenkin 'Bevan's Fight with the B.M.A.' in M. Sissons and P. French (eds.), *The Age of Austerity, 1945-51* (Penguin, Harmondsworth, 1964.)
33. Donoughue and Jones, op. cit., pp. 354-6.
34. See R. Brady, *Crisis in Britain* (University Press, Cambridge, 1950), p. 564.
35. For example, *LPCR 1948,* pp. 167-72 and *1949,* pp. 127-31.
36. *431 H.C. Debs 5th Series,* Col. 1809.
37. See, for example, Dalton's comments in his *Memoirs Vol. 3,* p. 138. For Morrison's attempt at a compromise see Donoughue and Jones, op. cit., pp. 400-3.
38. See A. Rogow and P. Shore, *The Labour Government and British Industry 1945-51* (Blackwell, Oxford, 1955).
39. Donoughue and Jones, op. cit., pp. 348-54; Rogow and Shore, op. cit., ch. 2.
40. See for example *Keep Left.*
41. On the shift see S. Beer, *Modern British Politics* (Second Edition, Faber, London, 1969), pp. 189-200.
42. See David Coates, *The Labour Party and the Struggle for Socialism* (University Press, Cambridge, 1975), pp. 68-9.
43. The 'new line' is demonstrated clearly in the policy statements, 'Labour For Higher Production' (1947) and 'Production, the Bridge to Socialism' (1948).
44. See Rogow and Shore, op. cit., ch. 3.
45. Brady, op. cit., p. 543.
46. Rogow and Shore, op. cit., pp. 76-82.
47. For a discussion of these features see V. Allen, *Trade Unions and Government,* ch. 15.
48. As demonstrated in Deakin's comments, *LPCR 1947,* p. 144.
49. See Beer, op. cit., pp. 200-8; and Allen, *Trade Unions and Government,* pp. 283-6. Also *TUC Report 1948,* pp. 287-93 and 565-74.
50. Even in 1948, 2,184,000 votes were cast for the critical ETU resolution.
51. Opposition at the Party Conference was negligible. See *LPCR 1948,* pp. 141-50; *1949,* pp. 139-48.
52. *TUC Report 1950,* pp. 467-73.
53. See Allen, op. cit., pp. 283-6.
54. For example, see the debate on the use of Emergency Powers on the 1949 dock strike, *467 H.C. Debs 5th Series,* Cols. 461-576.
55. The two approaches are portrayed in Foot, *Vol. II,* ch. 7: and Donoughue and Jones, op. cit., chs. 33 and 34.
56. *Policy Committee Minutes,* 27 May 1946.
57. *LPCR 1948,* p. 122.
58. *Policy and Publicity Committee Minutes,* 7 July 1948.
59. The deliberations can be followed in *Policy and Publicity Committee Minutes,* 19 July, 15 November 1948, 14 and 21 February, 14 March 1949; *NEC Minutes,* 9 and 23 February, 23 March 1949.
60. Described in Donoughue and Jones, op. cit., p. 445.
61. *RD 276;* its inclusion was noted in *Policy and Publicity Committee Minutes,* 21 February 1949.
62. Key speeches on the document can be found in *LPCR 1949,* pp. 152-7 (Morrison), and pp. 169-72 (Bevan).
63. *NEC Minutes,* 5 June 1949.
64. For these later developments see *Policy and Publicity Committee Minutes,* 26 September, 17 October, 12 December 1949; *NEC Minutes,* 23 November and 21 December 1949.
65. On the campaign see H. Nicholas, *The British General Election of 1950*

(Macmillan, London, 1950); also the comments of Foot, *Vol. II*, pp. 277-82.
66. See M. Bonham, *The Middle Class Vote* (Faber, London, 1954).
67. *NEC Minutes,* 22 March 1950. There was also a memorandum by Morgan Phillips.
68. Memorandum: 'The Recent General Election and the Next' — in *NEC Minutes.*
69. Ibid.
70. On Dorking see Donoughue and Jones, op. cit., p. 457, Foot, *Vol. II*, pp. 288-9; also the summary of the discussions attached to the *Minutes of the Policy and Publicity Sub Committee,* 19 June 1950.
71. *Report of the Joint Meeting of the Policy and Publicity Committee and TUC Economic Committee held on 7th July 1950;* contained in *Minutes of the Policy and Publicity Committee,* 12 July 1950.
72. *NEC Minutes,* 26 July 1950.
73. *LPCR 1950,* p. 114.
74. For different interpretations see Foot, *Vol. II,* ch. 8; Donoughue and Jones, op. cit., pp. 484-91. The latter leans heavily on the Dalton Diaries. Dalton was by no means an objective observer. See his *Memoirs, Vol. III,* pp. 362-70.
75. For Wilson's position see Paul Foot, *Vol. II,* ch. 8; Donoughue and Jones, Harmondsworth, 1968), pp. 87-99.
76. *487 H.C. Debs 5th Series,* Cols. 34-43.
77. *Policy Committee Minutes,* 16 July 1951; *NEC Minutes,* 25 July 1951.
78. See Dalton, *Vol. III,* pp. 375-6.
79. David Butler, *The British General Election of 1951* (Macmillan, London, 1952).

6 THE TRAUMAS OF OPPOSITION 1951-1955

In October 1951, Labour went into opposition with mixed feelings. Exhaustion and uncertainties about policy were balanced by optimism about the future. It was thought that a Conservative Government would be incapable of maintaining the high level of employment and the welfare provisions that had been two of Labour's proudest achievements. Such crass optimism indicated a lack of awareness of the type of society that was emerging. Such views about the likely policies of a Conservative administration were founded on a belief that the principal changes in post-war British society would be reversed. When the Churchill Government showed little readiness to do this, and indeed took special pains to deal generously with public sector wage demands, one of the principal props behind Labour's expectation of a rapid return to office disappeared. Indeed, after an early crisis, the Conservative Government presided over a period of economic growth, in which it appeared that the prescription of 'setting the people free' was technically preferable to the Labour emphasis on planning.

The apparent success of Conservative economic strategy in 1953 and 1954 left the Labour Party with two major problems — one doctrinal and one electoral. The ease with which the Conservatives had managed the mixed economy raised questions about many of the party's traditional appraisals. If the Attlee Government had implemented socialist reforms, then presumably the Conservative Party had accepted the resulting society, and could operate its economy with a high degree of competence? Such competence however carried implications for Labour's electoral prospects.

The loss of optimism was made more serious by the internal state of the party. The resignations of April 1951 had produced a freezing of alignments; groups of Bevanites and loyalists freely traded insults, while other parliamentarians worked assiduously to blur differences. The loss of direction was only one cause of this internal warfare. The barely disguised struggle for the leadership produced further hostility. Bevan remained the obvious standard-bearer of the Labour left, but his opponents found it more difficult to agree on a champion. Morrison was the initial choice, but he suffered a series of reversals. An unhappy period as Foreign Secretary was followed by defeat in the 1952 NEC elections. Although he returned to that body a year later, through a specially created place for the Deputy Leader, he never recovered his old dominance in the inner counsels of the party. He gradually forfeited the crucial support of trade union leaders, who came to see him as a spent force, and no barrier against the left. Similarly, his prestige declined in the Parliamentary Party, as his command over the Commons appeared to falter.[1] Loyalists within both the unions and the PLP began to look elsewhere. The choice gradually crystallised as Gaitskell, an assiduous cultivator of links with trade unionists, and a dedicated opponent of Bevan. During the early years of opposition, their intense rivalry, based on policy differences, style and personality, became a recurrent motif in party affairs.

The internal atmosphere of the party during these years was one of bitterness and intolerance. Party Conferences became theatres in which the representatives of Good and Evil mixed declarations of principle and imputations of base motives to the background of partisan demonstrations from the floor. The meetings of the PLP and the NEC were sometimes occasions for the trading of juvenile insults. Labour journals attacked factional rivals with abandon. On occasions the fabric of the party appeared close to disintegration, but a kind of unity was maintained.

A Guaranteed Majority: the Rule of the Moderates

The most important single fact about the internal politics of the party during these years was that the loyalists or moderates could almost always rely on a majority in all the party's decision-making bodies. The power configuration of office was carried over into opposition, except that the majority's utilisation of its position now involved less sophistication. When appeals to shared values failed, the crude power of a vote or the threat of discipline was employed.[2]

This domination was reflected in the PLP, most sharply in the annual elections to the Parliamentary Committee. During the 1951-5 Parliament, this body was dominated by moderate ex-Ministers, frequently reduced to offering the mildest criticisms of Conservative policies, because these coincided so closely with what they themselves had done. Only Bevan from November 1952 to April 1954 offered an alternative viewpoint which the convention of collective responsibility prevented him from expressing publicly. Apart from this, the unanimity of the Parliamentary Committee was rarely ruffled by policy differences. The most significant exception was German rearmament. This cut across the conventional cleavage, and Dalton, Callaghan, Robens and Ede all opposed such a development.[3]

The moderation of the Committee was an accurate reflection of the temper of the majority of Labour back-benchers. During the 1951 Parliament, almost all lobby revolts were connected with the Bevanite controversy, and all but one involved international or defence issues.[4] The composition of any rebel demonstration was normally predictable, and never large enough to offer any threat to the position of the Parliamentary leadership. Furthermore, when rebel demonstrations became too vocal, the moderate majority could be mobilised in support of disciplinary sanctions. Early in March 1952, 57 Bevanites and assorted individualists staged a revolt on defence policy. Subsequently at a PLP meeting, Attlee moved a resolution condemning the rebels, reimposing the PLP's Standing Orders and requiring individual signatures of each member's acceptance. However, many critics of the rebels were concerned about the divisive effect of such a resolution, and a 'compromise' was subsequently carried by 162 votes to 73.[5] This reimposed Standing Orders without condemning past behaviour. Although this took the edge off the leadership's initiative, crucial restrictions had been imposed on dissent. These were fortified by 188 votes to 51, through a ban on unofficial groups. Although these examples show how a majority could be mobilised easily against the critics, the failure of the more extreme proposal in March 1952 showed that powerful forces existed in the PLP opposed to any sanctions likely to cause an ultimate rupture.

The same uncertainty amongst the moderate forces could be seen in March 1955 when an attempt was made to expel Bevan for repeated 'disruption'. The occasion was a lobby revolt on nuclear weapons preceded by a speech from Bevan which was interpreted widely as an attack on Attlee. The expulsion proposal produced division within the normally monolithic Parliamentary Committee with Morrison pressing firmly for it, but Attlee uncertain. The proposal was carried there by nine votes to four and went to the PLP meeting. Once again, the forces of compromise emerged. The expulsion proposal was carried by the inoperable majority of 29, and a compromise asking for censure was lost only by 14. The issue then shifted to the NEC, where the trade union opponents of the left were more directly represented, but even here a compromise emerged, this time through an amendment asking not for Bevan's expulsion, but for a Committee to interview him and seek assurances as to his future behaviour. This amendment, moved by Attlee himself, was carried by one vote, to the dismay of those committed to Bevan's expulsion. However, following an apology by Bevan, an attempt by Attlee to secure NEC approval of this outcome was defeated in favour of a tougher condemnatory motion.[6]

It is apparent that the loyalist majority in the PLP had more sensitivity towards the need to maintain unity than some of the loyalist zealots within the trade unions. The pressure for squashing the critics came largely from the latter source, and was mediated through some parliamentarians, most notably Gaitskell and Morrison.[7] The motivations of this loyalist bloc have been examined in the previous chapter: the fundamental pattern of trade union loyalties remained constant through to 1955. The triumvirate of Deakin, Lawther and Williamson continually agitated for strong measures against the left, sometimes expressing dissatisfaction with Attlee for his alleged weakness in dealing with critics. Such an alignment tended to produce a belief that the left secured little support from trade unions. This is an error. Left-wing Conference resolutions secured some support from the NUR, the AEU and USDAW, while more constant backing was given by some smaller unions.[8] Nevertheless the solidarity of the triumvirate was a basis for the mobilisation of support for the leadership within the Party Conference with the result that the left secured no victories at all during the period.[9] However, one procedure that could not be controlled by the loyalist union leaders was the election of representatives to the NEC's Constituency Section. During the last two years of the Attlee Government a critical minority had begun to develop amongst these representatives, and by 1951 this included Bevan, Driberg, Mikardo and Castle. The following year, the nucleus received dramatic publicity when Crossman and Wilson replaced Morrison and Dalton. Now Bevanite representatives occupied all but one of the seven places, the exception being the diplomatic James Griffiths.[10] The sensation was compounded by the fact that Gaitskell had stood for the constituency section, and had achieved a vote little more than half that of the lowest successful candidate. Nevertheless the six critics were still greatly outnumbered by the combined strengths of the trade union representatives and the women, who functioned generally as their delegates. Furthermore the 1952 successes meant that the left's most articulate spokesmen were prevented from offering their own views at Party Conferences, and were compromised to some extent through their formal responsibility for the pronouncements of a body where they were in a minority.

This situation presented the Labour left with an acute problem of tactics. The crucial party forums were dominated by opponents who were ready for and usually capable of imposing restrictions on the rights of minorities. One possible solution for the left was involvement in decision-making in the hope of affecting outcomes. The successes in the NEC elections and Bevan's membership of the Parliamentary Committee seemed more likely to generate complicity in policies determined by opponents. An alternative was agitation outside the established institutions as a means of changing their composition or affecting their decisions. Bevan and his followers utilised *Tribune* as a propaganda weapon, publicising their NEC candidates, debating policy and attacking their opponents. Some attempts were made to organise within the constituencies, but essentially the left's grass-roots activities never extended beyond the holding of 'Brains Trusts', which provided a platform for virtuosity, but little scope for the development of influence over events. Even these marginal attempts produced a torrent of denunciation from loyalists demanding investigations into the extra-parliamentary activities of left-wing MPs.[11]

Generally, the Bevanites made little attempt to influence the conduct of trade union affairs, yet it was obviously here that the key to loyalist domination lay. Eventually, in the summer of 1954, Bevan faced the problem, declaring his intention of resigning from the constituency section of the NEC to contest the party treasurership against Gaitskell. This office had become a matter of political controversy in the previous year, when Morrison had stood against the popular but ailing incumbent Arthur Greenwood in his bid to return to the NEC. He had had the backing of the triumvirate, but support had rallied behind Greenwood, partly on doctrinal anti-Morrison grounds and partly from distaste at the blatant manoeuvring of the big battalions. At the last minute, Morrison had withdrawn his candidacy; victory was uncertain, it was feared that defeat might kill Greenwood, and the way back to the NEC through the Deputy Leader loophole seemed guaranteed. This withdrawal was a milestone in the disillusion with Morrison as a hammer of the left.[12] During the following year, Greenwood died leaving a vacancy. Gaitskell was rapidly nominated and secured the support of the two general unions, the NUM, and not without acrimony, the AEU. There is no doubt that Bevan saw the contest as an attempt to demonstrate to the union rank and file that their leaders were casting votes without any worth-while consultation. Yet no attempt was made to organise the left within key unions. Bevan did secure the support of USDAW and the NUR but Gaitskell secured the treasurership by a majority of more than two to one. The following year, the contest was repeated, but Bevan's reliance on spontaneous union democracy was clearly optimistic. He lost the support of both the NUR and USDAW and the defeat was now by a devastating margin of five to one. There seemed no way out of loyalist domination.[13]

In 1955 nothing seemed more secure than the control of the party by a coalition of trade union and parliamentary loyalists. There might be occasional disagreement about the extent to which the control of dissent should be taken; on a few occasions, the alliance could be split by policy differences. However, it seemed a basic fact about the party that this control was immutable, and not the product of contingent circumstances.

The Debate Over Socialism

Although a loyalist majority was usually guaranteed, it was not always clear what views it would be employed to advance. Doctrinally, this period was a tail piece to the achievements of the Attlee Government, although there were developments, sometimes barely noticed, that pointed to subsequent major changes.

Bevanism: the Illusory Alternative

The Bevanite faction and its supporters emerged from the controversies over the policies and the electoral strategy of the Attlee Government. They were a response to loss of momentum, bi-partisanship and a desire on the part of some Labour leaders to avoid offending middle-class sensitivities in the interests of electoral success.[14] In spite of such a beginning, the faction failed to produce any significant perspective on the party's problems.

One glaring difficulty concerned the significant differences within the ranks of the parliamentary left. About thirty MPs attended Bevanite meetings, and about the same number could be relied on to support any Bevanite initiative. Generally this paralleled another division. The committed members of the faction tended to be less at odds with official policy. Indeed, some — most notably Wilson — had very few points of difference. Bevan himself, although distinguishable in style from the cautious posture of much of the party leadership, was anxious to build on the achievements of the Attlee Government. The first Bevanite pamphlet, 'One Way Only', showed how wide the area of agreement was between the leading Bevanites and the official party leadership. It covered the acceptance of NATO, the acknowledgement of Soviet dictatorship and imperialism, the readiness to agree to some level of rearmament. Bevanite pronouncements even indicated a need for care and flexibility in the application of public ownership techniques. While Bevan and his immediate lieutenants mobilised the broader left through the employment of socialist rhetoric, they had little time for anything smacking of Utopianism. They advocated an increase in the distinctiveness of Labour's commitment, but did not propose any fundamental rethink of strategy.[15] However, the use of traditional rhetoric, and the resulting mobilisation behind the Bevanite banner of the disparate army of the left, had the result of exaggerating the differences between the Bevanite leadership and the official leaders of the party.

This disparate army recruited from many sources. Within the PLP it included those motivated by pacifist or anti-American sentiments. Many of those were inveterate individualists, sometimes with striking parliamentary gifts, but not interested in participating in any collective formulation of policy. Others were unimpressive tenacious adherents to traditional prescriptions. Beyond the Commons, Bevanite appeals rallied support from two very different groups. Within the constituency parties, they energised the constant fund of traditional idealism. Of course, this response was not the only one within local parties. There were elements who responded vehemently to what they considered as disloyal criticism. Within the unions, Bevanism evoked the strongest positive response in those organisations with significant Communist factions, a factor that weakened the Bevanites considerably. It was easy to present Bevanite 'disruption' as a Trojan horse for Communist infiltration, although in policy terms the Bevanite leadership position was far closer to the Labour moderates than to the Communist Party.[16]

The weakness was particularly acute in the international field. The first significant characteristic of Bevanite policy preoccupations was that they concentrated on international and defence issues to the virtual exclusion of almost everything else. Given the pulverisation of traditional party beliefs on international questions, this is rather surprising, although it could be argued that debates on foreign policy did not risk raising the sensitive issue of party strategy in the same direct fashion as any thorough analysis of domestic policy. It was unfortunate for the Bevanites that it was international policy that enabled loyalists to maximise their support by pointing out the readiness of Communist spokesmen to back Labour left positions. Yet Bevan and his closest colleagues criticised Labour foreign policy from within a framework that varied little from that employed by Bevin and Morrison. When Bevan opposed the extent of rearmament or the adherence of Britain to SEATO, these criticisms did not mark deviations in principle from post-1945 policies, but rather concern about specific applications. There was no condemnation of American policy as a whole but an unhappiness with the uncritical acceptance of American strategy, particularly in the Far East, that was evinced by some Labour spokesmen.

The only occasion on which the Bevanites came close to achieving a majority on an international question was over German rearmament. The proposed rearming of the Federal Republic evoked opposition from the Labour left of a characteristically heterogeneous variety. Leading Bevanites claimed that opposition was quite compatible with general support for the Western Alliance, and would prevent a further growth in international tensions.[17] In contrast, some parliamentarians based their dissent on a generalised distaste for armament, while some unions were influenced by a strong Communist campaign against rearmament. So far, this was the usual left-wing foreign policy coalition, but it was strengthened on this issue by a wide spread of moderates from the PLP and the unions who were ready to oppose German rearmament as a stage in the re-emergence of militarism. This opposition was based on patriotic sentiments that normally had little overlap with the sensitivities of the left. The specific strengthening of the critical coalition was reflected in the PLP and on the NEC. It meant that the party's acceptance of German rearmament was a protracted affair. In the end, a narrow acceptance was facilitated by international developments, aided by a sustained campaign within the party.[18] Even then the majority at the 1954 Conference was only a quarter of a million.

Much of the left's criticism of international developments during these years involved responses to particular situations in the light of a varied collection of traditional values. Some leading Bevanite figures attempted to reconcile traditional aspirations with the broad contours of post-1945 policy in an attempt to produce a viable compromise, but these were only peripheral developments. The left's preoccupation with international questions served only to highlight the devastation of traditional outlooks produced by the Labour record in this field. Much of the left's case was an emotional response rather than an alternative policy, and was doomed to rejection in all decision-making bodies.

This concern with international crises reflected both the historic preoccupations of the Labour left and also the continuing pressure of world events. However, the problem of future home policy was, if anything, more urgent. Did the Labour left produce anything distinctive here? On one level, they could be regarded as those who were ready to press on with further instalments of public ownership as the next stage in the transition to the socialist commonwealth. The

debate with Morrison and his followers had been essentially over the
rate of progress. Both parties to the dispute had accepted the broad
strategy of gradual transformation of existing society towards socialism,
and the advocacy of an early and large expansion of the public sector
was not restricted to the Labour left. Furthermore, the argument
tended to be restricted to a dispute over the application of agreed
criteria, most commonly economic efficiency. Spokesmen of the
parliamentary left rarely advanced any alternative case for public
ownership based on the redistribution of power. Even less attention was
given to proposals for the radical restructuring of existing publicly-
owned industries. While some trade unions — most notably the NUR —
advocated some form of workers' control, this received minimal
attention amongst Labour parliamentarians. Basically, the left did not
reconsider its attitude to the extension of public ownership in the light
of experience. It merely demanded more without considering problems
of implementation and purpose.

This lack of reappraisal reflected a more fundamental weakness. The
Labour left, with the possible exception of Bevan, had failed to develop
any theoretical appreciation of the type of society that had emerged
as the result of wartime and post-war changes. This deficiency was
prevalent in the party, but it posed particular problems for the
advocates of further extensive reforms. They were vulnerable to
claims that the economic system had changed dramatically, with the
Government now able to control private industry if desired, and the
old equation between ownership and control apparently disproved.
Claims that extreme poverty had disappeared and the achievement of a
reasonable rate of economic growth placed the burden of proof on those
who wished to introduce widespread structural reforms. In the
optimistic climate of the early fifties, it was difficult to develop a case
for further extensive public ownership based on the promotion of
greater economic efficiency.

The failure to develop a critical appraisal of the domestic
achievements of the Labour Government raises the whole question of
the role of the Bevanites. Some of the reasons for failure were highly
specific. The personalisation of disputes that flowed inexorably from
the domination of the left by articulate, forceful spokesmen diverted
attention from the work of policy reappraisal. The difficulties of
reaching agreement within an army of individualists have already been
noted. These were exacerbated by the liking of some left-wingers for
elaborate tactical manoeuvres, and in contrast by the distaste of others
for any collective work. These contrasting conspiratorial and anarchic

tendencies left little opportunity for substantive policy-making.

There was little inspiration available. The Labour left in the early fifties remained in thrall to two ghosts – an emotional traditionalism, and a Stalinism whose intolerance and rigidities were perceived even by the previously sympathetic. The old gods had failed the left – the intellectual poverty of Bevanism reflected in part this barren heritage. It also reflected the parliamentary commitment of its principal spokesmen. Given the need for electoral consent and the decline in relative deprivation amongst traditional Labour supporters, the prospect for future radical reform looked bleak. Bevanism was not an alternative to official policy. Its spokesmen did not question the party's basic strategy, and within this, the range of options was restricted greatly by electoral imperatives in a period of relative prosperity. Bevanism was rather a symptom of the tensions produced within the party by its acceptance, in practice, of existing economic arrangements.

Two Schools of Moderation

The failure to analyse recent changes in British society that characterised the Labour left was equally true of a majority of its opponents. Consolidationism was after all an admission of present satisfaction and future uncertainty. Many leading Labour figures had seen the achievement of their policy ambitions. They lacked the energy and the inclination to begin formulating a further set of objectives. Morrison spent much time emphasising the need for proposals to be practical, while Attlee, more and more preoccupied with the maintenance of harmony, made very few statements on future policy. This lack of concern about the future was echoed by trade union leaders such as Deakin and Lawther. They found their position under a benevolent Conservative Government tolerable, and did not wish to see it disrupted by the pursuit of divisive policies. One influential school of thought within the party's dominant moderate group was extremely cautious, the product of advancing age, uncertainty and the contentment of many trade union leaders. Such complacency was a long-term threat to the party's vitality. How could it present itself as a progressive alternative if its major purpose was to defend the reforms of 1945-51?

While the left produced no real answer to this question, an alternative perspective began to emerge from the discussions of younger moderates, a position implying the rejection of many traditional Labour attitudes. Although the seed-time of this new perspective can be located in the early years of opposition, it did not achieve a full flowering until another electoral defeat had awoken the party to a need to rethink traditional conceptions. By then, this revisionist perspective had been developed, and also, as we shall see, enjoyed the support of key individuals, especially Hugh Gaitskell.

Revisionism involved a radical discontinuity in Labour doctrine, but not a total break with what had gone before. The element of continuity lay in the fact that there had always been a strand in party thought that had stressed the positive attachment of the party to parliamentary democracy. This could take several forms: sometimes it was an instinctive defence of the British 'way of life'; sometimes it took the form of the defence of individual rights against executive power. However in the thirties, a small group developed within the party who remained self-consciously dedicated to moderation, and implacably opposed to what they regarded as Marxist irrelevancies. Such writers as Dalton, Jay and above all Durbin, formed a marked contrast with the apocalyptic visions of Cripps and Laski.[19] The prognoses of the latter might have had a far greater influence on a generation of activists, but the moderate perspective proved to be a more accurate preview of the post-war behaviour of Labour Ministers. Durbin gloried in the pursuit of consensus:

> Those of us who believe in democracy, have faith in moderation, and search for agreement in the field of politics, have behind us the long and splendid tradition of British political thought and practice.[20]

This position was elaborated and sharpened in the light of post-war experiences to produce the revisionist perspective. The committed social democrat experienced no doctrinal difficulties on account of the Cold War. Such developments as the Czech *coup* could be used as evidence for the judgement that social democracy and Communism were fundamentally opposed. Scope was provided for a more sensitive analysis of post-war society than anything generated by the traditional framework. The adoption of Keynesian techniques and the growth of the Welfare State suggested that predictions of capitalist collapse were misguided, and that, while the mixed economy contained unacceptable imbalances of wealth and status, these could be eradicated without a fundamental attack on existing structures. This at least represented an attempt to come to terms with recent developments, basically through an admission that much had been achieved without a drastic extension of public ownership. Since such an assessment had profound implications for Labour orthodoxy, it is not surprising that the full perspective developed slowly.[21]

The first elaborations of this position were taking place under the auspices of the Fabian Society prior to the defeat of the Attlee Government. A series of discussions led to the publication, in 1952, of 'New Fabian Essays', a series of attempts to point the way forward on major questions.[22] Some of the contributors — Crosland, Jenkins and Albu — were to become leading exponents of the revisionist case. However, four more years were to elapse before revisionism acquired a 'Bible' capable of measuring up to the earlier works of Laski and Tawney. Crosland's 'The Future of Socialism'[23] was a thorough and unapologetic presentation of the revisionist case. It emphasised the extent to which traditional goals had been achieved, or shown to lack significant content.

Although publication of this work fell outside the period covered in this chapter, it is fitting to include a full appraisal of the revisionist position here, since it was developed during the first years of opposition, and was so obviously a product of that period of relative stability. Accordingly, it contained an optimistic evaluation of the existing economic system. The revisionists' democratic commitment and their assessment of post-war developments led to the conclusion that significant economic changes could be obtained through existing institutions. Furthermore, they were sanguine about the growth potential of the mixed economy, and believed that with efficient management a satisfactory standard of living could be achieved. Overall there was a tendency to pay comparatively little attention to economic matters; it was implied that Labour's central concerns in this area had been largely met with the achievement of full employment and the apparent end of acute poverty.

This assessment had profound implications for party doctrine, especially when linked to a basic revisionist principle. This rejected the idea that socialism was an ideal goal to be approached through a gradual transformation of society. Rather, social reform consisted of the continuing adaptation of an inevitably pluralistic society in order to realise more fully ideals such as equality and individual liberty. Such a reinterpretation of Labour's commitment to socialism plus the optimistic economic judgement greatly reduced the contribution of public ownership measures. The tradition that they were an indispensable technique for the realisation of a socialist commonwealth was undermined by the revisionist refusal to talk about progress towards a socialist society. A supporting argument for extending public ownership had been that of efficiency, but revisionists seemed reasonably happy with existing economic arrangements. They spent considerable time arguing that ownership rarely mattered, and that countervailing institutions, whether governmental or trade union, could produce a high level of social responsibility within the private sector. By viewing private industry in this way, revisionists came to defend existing market morality. They accepted self-interest as a crucial feature of any worth-while economic system, and thereby denied in the most basic fashion the relevance of the traditional socialist values of fellowship and co-operation. Such a denial was of course only an explicit acknowledgement of the practice of the Attlee Government. Similarly, an extreme empiricist position was taken on economic wants, with revisionists arguing through from the decline in relative deprivation to a claim that the existing economic order was broadly acceptable.

This acceptability produced a problem of partisanship. Labour was confronted with the problem of reviving its progressive commitment, and this had to be solved through the advocacy of non-economic reforms. Thus, considerable emphasis was placed on 'equality', by which was generally meant equality of opportunity, plus whatever safeguards were required to prevent the emergence of a meritocratic élite. Accordingly, much thought was given to proposals for educational reform, a sphere that had been largely neglected by the Attlee Government. Basically, the positive proposals of revisionists can be seen as an attack on the ascriptive elements in British society which were presented as causes of economic inefficiency and offensive social distinctions. They proclaimed Sweden as a worthy example for British Labour to emulate, regarding it as a society where social democracy had adapted itself successfully to material affluence in such a way as to appear the natural governing party.[24]

There was no guarantee, of course, that the revisionists' progressive claims on non-economic matters would strike a responsive chord amongst Labour's traditional supporters. If the latter were now largely satisfied with their material situation, and the party wished to retain both a progressive dynamic and its traditional support, then there could be difficulties. Certainly, the desired compatibility seemed very unlikely in two areas of reform favoured by the revisionists. They revolted strongly against the puritanical strand in the party tradition, and against what they saw as excessive cultural commercialisation. Yet in their advocacy of libertarian reforms and cultural excellence, it can be argued that they were expressing a minority liberal viewpoint. This is significant because of their basic empiricism. They appealed frequently to 'what the ordinary man wants' as a justification for opposing radical economic policies, yet in some non-economic areas, which they believed would become more significant politically, they seemed ready to advocate positions which did not enjoy majority support.

There was much within the revisionist perspective that bore the hallmark of traditional moderate Labour policy. The belief that existing administrative institutions were politically neutral, the readiness to seek consensus, the commitment to incremental change: all would have been familiar to earlier generations of Labour moderates. The divergence appeared through the rejection of the episodic view of social transformation combined with the comparatively positive judgement on the economic system. These aspects raised problems for the party's socialist identity: many revisionist proposals seemed indistinguishable from the more progressive brands of liberalism.

In some respects revisionism seems a moderate's natural response to post-war developments, building as it did on certain central features of party tradition. It also provided one answer to the problem of future policy that took notice of the Attlee Government's record, accepted the constraints of parliamentarianism, was aware of the need for something more than the defence of existing achievements and attempted some reappraisal of British society. It was thus a much more thorough response than those of the left and the advocates of consolidation.

The Search for a Policy

Policy-making was complicated by the intense factional divisions and by the general loss of direction. Work on future policy began soon after the 1951 defeat. In December 1951 the Executive decided to set up four sub-committees on the suggestion of Morgan Phillips. These covered nationalised industries, privately-owned industries, agriculture and rural life and social services.[25] Members were co-opted and meetings held at intervals during the following year, while in May 1952 a further sub-committee on financial and economic policy, charged with a degree of overlordship, was inaugurated. However, the policy document, 'Facing the Facts', produced for the 1952 Conference was of a general character and made little use of the detailed reports produced by the sub-committees.[26]

The debate on this document at the 1952 Conference took place amidst clear evidence that several trade unions were prepared to support any relatively positive statement on public ownership. At the 1952 TUC a resolution moved by Bryn Roberts of the National Union of Public Employees demanding an extension of social ownership had been carried against the advice of the General Council by a margin of 1,300,000 votes.[27] Following this, the NEC found it prudent to accept a lengthy resolution asking for a party programme and including an instruction that the Executive 'draw up a list of the key and major industries to be taken into public ownership during the five-year programme'.[28]

The resolution became the responsibility of the new Executive. This now contained six Bevanites. Furthermore, Morrison was now deposed and the Chairmanship of the Policy Committee had passed to the more conciliatory James Griffiths. The Executive immediately began to erect the necessary machinery. At its December meeting, it considered a series of documents on the problems of policy-making. Many questions were left open, but it was agreed at this early stage that the central thrust of any policy document must be the solution of the national economic problem, with particular attention devoted to achieving higher investment.[29] Some discussion was held on candidates for public ownership. When this question passed to the Policy Committee, it was agreed to form working parties on possible candidates: engineering and aircraft, chemicals, textile machinery and shipbuilding and ship repairing. In addition, the existing sub-committees on agriculture, economic policy and social services were to continue their work.[30]

A difficulty soon emerged over the composition of the working parties. The original suggestion had been that there should be three representatives from the NEC and from the General Council (who were concerned of course with parallel deliberations on the basis of the Roberts resolution), plus two experts. However, the General Council refused to join the working parties and a joint NEC-General Council meeting on 8 January 1953 only underlined the degree of suspicion and animosity within the labour movement. Although Tewson raised objections of time-tabling, Lincoln Evans of the Steel Workers bluntly commented that there was no virtue in nationalisation as such. Williamson thought that 'ICI was first class' and Deakin protested at anti-TUC sentiment in the party. The eventual outcome was to accept Tewson's suggestion that representatives of each working party have informal discussions with the TUC Economic Committee.[31]

The most important of these working parties was that on engineering and aircraft. This included one Bevanite, Mikardo, but he was balanced by Tiffin of the T & GW, and Brinham of the Wood Workers. After consultations with the TUC, recommendations were made that the policy on mining machinery and machine tools should include the acquisition by the state of a controlling interest in a few large firms. The question of the aircraft industry and its possible nationalisation was a more difficult one. Eventually the working party decided, in the absence of Mikardo, that it was opposed to outright nationalisation: once again, the recommended solution was that of a controlling interest in some firms. Only if aircraft companies were adjudged to have acted contrary to the national interest was a complete take-over suggested.[32]

The work of the other working parties proved less complex. That on shipbuilding was dominated by moderate trade unionists, and came rapidly to the conclusion that no form of public ownership could provide a satisfactory solution to the industry's problems. Instead a Development Council would be an appropriate means of producing the necessary co-operation. After initial inclusion in the policy document, this was dropped as unworkable.[33] In the case of textile machinery, an early difficulty arose because members decided that no decision on public ownership could be taken without some investigation into the future production prospects of the textile industry. A request that the working party consider the future of the whole textile industry was ruled out by the Policy Committee on the grounds of time. The Textile Workers' Union spokesmen pointed out that their organisation now had some division of opinion on the desirability of nationalising the whole industry. In view of the complexity of the problem, no firm recommendation emerged.[34] The Working Party on Chemicals recommended the acquisition of a controlling interest in some major firms, an approach which led to further debate on the full NEC.[35]

Apart from these controversies over the extent and form of public ownership a controversy developed within the Agriculture Sub-Committee over the advisability of nationalising land. At the Sub-Committee's January meeting a resolution against public ownership on a large scale was carried by five votes to four.[36] However at the end of March, this decision was opposed within the Policy Committee from two positions. One advocated the public ownership of all agricultural land, while the other, that of Bevan, restricted any take-over to rented land.[37] The decision was deferred to the next Policy Committee meeting in mid-April. Here fears of electoral damage were voiced: Phillips spoke of widespread electoral opposition to wholesale nationalisation, and of the need to secure the co-operation of the farmers. Eventually two votes were taken. Griffiths moved that Labour's policy of obtaining control of the use of land be pursued through the powers initiated by the Attlee Government, while a Wilson amendment urged the nationalisation of all rented agricultural land. The amendment was defeated by eight votes to three with Griffiths' motion then carried by eight votes to none.[38]

These proposals formed the basis for the policy draft for consideration by the full NEC although another important element had emerged from the deliberations of the Sub-Committee on Financial and Economic Policy. This body had worked on the basis of papers presented by Gaitskell and Crosland on the problems facing sterling with respect to the dollar, and their analysis of Britain's economic problem provided a foundation of the policy draft.[39]

After prior consideration by the Policy Committee[40], the draft was debated by the full NEC over the weekend of 24-26 April. Once again one of the most debated sections was that on agriculture with Bevan and some others continuing to urge the public ownership of all rented land. Two attempts to amend the draft in this respect, by Bevan and Wilson, were lost by thirteen votes to nine. A motion by White backing public ownership when necessary to ensure full use of land and high output was carried however by fifteen votes to seven, and became part of the document. There was also considerable discussion of the section on chemicals, and it was agreed to endorse the recommendations provisionally pending further discussion with the TUC.[41] A meeting was held between NEC representatives and the TUC Economic Committee on 13 May. The TUC then reiterated its view that they supported public control of the chemical industry, but felt that any specific policy decision should follow a fact-finding enquiry. In the light of these discussions the NEC agreed on 19 May to accept the deletion of references to a controlling interest in leading firms, leaving only a broad commitment to 'a substantial degree of public ownership'.[42]

At the NEC's final consideration of a revised draft on 21 May, Bevan and his supporters made a series of attempts to amend the draft in the direction of an alternative document produced by him. Specific proposals included the taking of leading chemical firms into public ownership, the development of new state enterprises in engineering, the acquisition of key firms in machine tools and mining machinery, the nationalisation of rented land, the introduction of more direct controls, and a capital gains tax. All attempts at amendment were defeated, the strength of the minority varying between four and seven members.[43]

The document was then published under the title 'Challenge to Britain', with its proposals for unspecified extensions of public ownership in engineering and chemicals. The lack of clarity here allowed some Bevanite Executive members to support the proposals publicly, although the foregoing account shows that they regarded them as inadequate. Nevertheless, the document represented some minimal advance for the left, in comparison with the parallel TUC Interim Report on Public Ownership. This restricted concrete proposals for further nationalisation to the water supply industry, but was accepted at the 1953 TUC by a majority of just over a million.[44] The acceptance of such a moderate document indicated that the Party Conference was unlikely to amend 'Challenge to Britain' in a more radical direction. The Conference debates again showed the domination of the moderate majority as the old Executive battles were re-enacted on the Conference floor.[45] A series of attempts to radicalise the sections of the document on engineering, aircraft, mining machinery, machine tools and chemicals failed, with minorities ranging from 1,400,000 to just over 2 million. In these votes it is obvious that some large unions were opposing the Executive. Similarly an attempt to re-insert a commitment to land nationalisation into the document failed, although securing over 1,750,000 million votes. The only part of the document to be significantly amended was that on education. This followed a debate in which concern was expressed at the document's moderation by a variety of speakers including Deakin and Gaitskell.[46] Otherwise consultations continued with the TUC on the industrial aspects of the document.

The discussions continued[47] until the party was confronted with the need to produce an election manifesto using 'Challenge to Britain' as a basis. The debates in the Policy Committee were on the basis of papers from the Research Department which provided an added impetus towards moderation. For example, it claimed that taxation was progressive enough, and that while there might be a case for a capital gains tax, it was better to avoid any precise commitment.[48] The manifesto indicated that the party would 'bring sections of the chemical and machine tool industries into public ownership'. This, plus a commitment to start new public enterprises where necessary, was the sole evidence of the protracted internal debate over public ownership. Taxation proposals remained vague, and overall the manifesto indicated the problems of justifying radical proposals when faced with an apparently prosperous economy.[49]

Overall, the formulation of domestic policy during this period reveals some important features. Most fundamental, there were the varied and complex ways in which the moderate majority within the Executive were able to assert themselves when faced with a comparatively strong Conference resolution on public ownership — apart from the power of the vote, the consultations with the TUC, the avalanche of background papers, the gearing of proposals to immediate economic needs, and the cultivated ambiguities of the policy document all played their part. However, this process did mean that the moderates did make some concessions to the left, most obviously the commitments on chemicals and machine tools, whose sheer imprecision provided a good basis for political misrepresentation in the heat of an election. The outcome was thus a compromise in so far as it was not totally to the moderates' liking. Finally, it is important to emphasise that the document was firmly in the same mould as past documents. The arguments had been between the advocates of 'Consolidation' and 'Full Speed Ahead'. Revisionism had not entered into the currency of the policy debate. These debates were an attempt to produce a successful programme without any serious questioning of party purposes and values.

The Failure of Traditional Responses

In 1951, it had still been easy to portray Labour as the party of the future. The loss of seats had been accompanied by a rise in the party's aggregate vote. Buoyed up by predictions of Conservative failure, little time was spent after the 1951 defeat in rethinking electoral strategy, although some moderates did warn against extremism. The first breach in this optimism came in May 1953, when in a by-election, Labour managed to lose a seat, Sunderland South, to the Government. The Regional Organiser submitted a report to the NEC containing a succinct statement of Labour's problems:

> One of the difficulties we had to face was the absence of any particular issue apart from the Cost of Living and the Budget ... We have to find something to awaken the electorate.[50]

The search during the next two years was unsuccessful. Perceptions of economic prosperity were heightened by a liberal Budget in April 1955, and Labour went into the campaign without a 'cause', having only belatedly patched up its factional differences.[51] The party's campaign lacked co-ordination. The machine was controlled by Morgan Phillips, and it appears that the principal leaders never met collectively to discuss strategy. The party went through the motions like a football team playing an end of season game that is of no significance. There was little public interest in the campaign: meetings were small and controversy a rarity. Turnout fell from 83 per cent in 1951 to 76.8 per cent, but more dramatically the Labour vote fell by one and a half million. With a Conservative drop of only 400,000 this meant that Labour's share of the total vote declined from 48.8 per cent to 46.4 per cent. The Conservative majority rose from seventeen to sixty, although a small part of this reflects the advantage given by a further redistribution. The swing was slight, only 1.8 per cent, but it was enough to place Labour firmly in opposition, draining away its electoral optimism and producing a more fundamental reappraisal of policy. It also made a change in the leadership imminent. Attlee was obviously too old to lead the party into another election. The time had come for a generational change at the top.

It was now obvious that the party had to come to terms with its own achievements. It was equally apparent that the personalised bitterness of the previous four years had not only damaged the party's prospects, but had diverted attention away from the fundamental problems. The clarification of these problems and the attempt to provide a solution were bound to create new difficulties raising questions about the party's purpose and strategy. The seed-time of revisionism had ended; now a debate about fundamental issues might begin.

Notes

1. See Donoughue and Jones, op. cit., chs. 36 and 37.
2. As demonstrated in Arthur Deakin's 'Fraternal Greetings' to the 1952 Conference. See *LPCR 1952*, pp. 125-7.
3. Saul Rose, 'The Labour Party and German Rearmament: A View From Transport House', *Political Studies*, 1966, pp. 133-44.
4. Jackson, op. cit., pp. 113-33.
5. Foot, *Vol. II*, pp. 362-6 – also *NEC Minutes*, 13th March 1952.
6. On the 1955 explosion see *NEC Minutes*, 23 and 30 March 1955; Foot, *Vol. II*, ch. 12; Donoughue and Jones, op. cit. pp. 533-4; Dalton, *Vol. 3*, pp. 409-10. Leslie Hunter, *The Road to Brighton Pier* (Arthur Barker, London, 1959).
7. For an example of moderate fears see Morrison's Memorandum, *Considerations Arising Out of the General Election 1951* in *NEC Minutes*, especially the statement: 'We are driven to go in for a lot of undesirable manipulation so that the Conference can be a vote-winning and not a vote-losing occasion.'
8. Harrison, op. cit., especially pp. 212-14.
9. On German rearmament the failure was by 3,270,000 to 3,022,000 – and 3,281,000 to 2,910,000.
10. For Griffiths' role see his *Pages From Memory* (Dent, London, 1969).
11. For attacks on 'Brains Trusts' see *NEC Minutes*, 28 January and 25 February 1953. The initiative had been taken by the decaying National Council of Labour.
12. See Donoughue and Jones, op. cit., pp. 522-5.
13. See Harrison, op. cit., pp. 315-19 and Foot, *Vol. II*, pp. 437-40, 449, 491-2.
14. In general on the faction see Foot, *Vol. II*, chs. 8-13.
15. See 'One Way Only' (1951): also Bevan's own *In Place of Fear* (MacGibbon

The Traumas of Opposition 1951-1955   201

and Kee, London, 1961, new edition).

16. See for example the comment of Ernest Jones of the NUM on the German rearmament agitation. *LPCR 1954*, p. 103.
17. See their pamphlet *It Need Not Happen: The Alternative to German Rearmament* (1954).
18. For the campaign and associated questions see *NEC Minutes*, 26 May 1954.
19. See Hugh Dalton, *Practical Socialism for Britain* (Routledge, London, 1935). Douglas Jay, *The Socialist Case* (Faber, London, 1937), and Evan Durbin, op. cit.
20. Durbin, op. cit., p. 321.
21. For a general uncritical survey see Stephen Haseler, *The Gaitskellites* (Macmillan, London, 1969).
22. R.H.S. Crossman (ed.), *New Fabian Essays* (Turnstile Press, London, 1953). This was not wholly revisionist. The contributors included Ian Mikardo.
23. C.A.R. Crosland, *The Future of Socialism* (Cape, London, 1956).
24. These positions can be found in *The Future of Socialism*. In some cases they are presented more sharply in Crosland's *The Conservative Enemy* (Cape, London, 1962).
25. *NEC Minutes*, 12 December 1951 and *Policy Committee Minutes*, 3 December 1951.
26. *Policy Committee Minutes*, 18 February, 21 April, 19 May 1952.
27. For debates see *LPCR 1952*, pp. 87-112, and *TUC Report 1952*, pp. 438-48.
28. *LPCR 1952*, p. 91.
29. *NEC Minutes*, 13 and 14 December 1952. See also the memorandum *R.169* 'Policy Formation: General Directive'.
30. *Policy Committee Minutes*, 15 December 1952.
31. *NEC — General Council Joint Meeting Minutes*, 8 January 1953.
32. See *Minutes of Working Party on Engineering and Aircraft*, 17 and 26 February, 9 March 1953 and the discussion of its recommendations in the *Policy Committee Minutes*, 16 March 1953.
33. The Working Party's conclusions were also discussed by the Policy Committee at its meeting on 16 March 1953. The proposal was abandoned two years later. *Policy Committee Minutes*, 14 March 1955.
34. *Minutes of Working Party on Textile Machinery*, 11 February and 9 March 1953. Trade union doubts were expressed at the latter meeting.
35. *Working Party on Chemicals Minutes*, 29 January 1953.
36. *Agriculture Sub-Committee Minutes*, 26 January 1953.
37. *Policy Committee Minutes*, 30 March 1953.
38. Ibid., 20 April 1953.
39. *Sub-Committee on Financial and Economic Policy Minutes*, 30 January 1953.
40. *Policy Committee Minutes*, 20 April 1953.
41. *NEC Minutes*, 24-26 April 1953.
42. Ibid., 19 May 1953.
43. Ibid., 21 May 1953.
44. *TUC Report, 1953*, pp. 363-93 (Debate) and Appendix A, pp. 475-526 (Report).
45. Consideration of the document occupied most of the Conference. The debate on public ownership can be found in *LPCR 1953*, pp. 100-19 and pp. 122-9.
46. Ibid., pp. 166-77.
47. They involved continuing attempts to dilute commitments. See, for example, the discussion initiated by Gaitskell in *Policy Committee Minutes*, 14 February 1955.
48. See *Policy Committee Minutes*, 14 March and 18 April 1955. Also the memorandum *R.495*, 'Plans For An Election Manifesto'.
49. See 'Forward With Labour'.

50. *NEC Minutes,* 24 June 1953.
51. See David Butler, *The British General Election of 1955* (Macmillan, London, 1955).

REVISIONISM AS PARTY POLICY 1955-1959

Revisionism emerged as a major tendency within the party after the 1955 defeat. If filled the generally acknowledged vacuum in party policy in part because there was no significant rival, but also because of the election of Gaitskell as Party Leader in December 1955. The party leadership had already committed itself to a fundamental review of party policy and over the next three years a series of nine policy documents emerged from the Executive, marking the substantial acceptance of many revisionist views as official policy. This revolution in policy was accomplished openly, and without a major upheaval. The factional feuding that had marked the first period of opposition was now greatly reduced. Bevan entered into an uneasy truce with Gaitskell. The left was exposed in an ideological nakedness that had previously been concealed by his personality.

This period also saw three developments which had a potential for curbing the growing revisionist dominance. Concern over the proliferation of nuclear weapons began to be expressed widely, and pressure for the unilateral renunciation of the British bomb developed inside and outside the party. This was an issue with a potential appeal much greater than any cause championed by the left since before 1939. Furthermore, the sterility of left-wing thought appeared to be at an end. The revelations of the twentieth CPSU Congress and the Soviet invasion of Hungary provoked an exodus of finally disillusioned intellectuals from the British Communist Party. This linked with a less precise radicalisation within the universities precipitated in particular by the Suez invasion to produce a broad, ill-defined 'New Left' movement. This had an ambivalent relationship with the Labour Party, but provided reappraisals of socialist thought from a radical position. Such changes stood little chance of impinging on the internal processes of the party, unless the domination of the moderate majority was reduced. However there were signs of movement here. Deakin had died suddenly in May 1955; his successor, Tiffin, lived only a few months and was succeeded by Frank Cousins. This unexpected elevation did not produce, contrary to popular myth, an instant change in the political position of the T & GWU, but what did emerge gradually was that the union's large vote was no longer available to the party leadership in *all* circumstances. The dominance of the moderates was reduced just by a fraction.

These countervailing developments all proved to be of crucial importance in the development of the party, but in this period, Gaitskell's control was, if not unchallenged, at least completely certain. An analysis of this must be therefore the starting point for an understanding of this period.

The Arrival of Gaitskell

In retrospect, the resignation of Attlee after the 1955 defeat seems inevitable. At the time, it appeared very protracted. Many commentators have suggested that Attlee's behaviour was motivated by a wish to ensure that Morrison's support had declined enough to rule out any possibility of his success. Dalton precipitated the first stage in the debate over the leadership in June 1955 by suggesting the resignation of the older members of the Parliamentary Committee in the interests of the party's future.[1] Attlee was specifically excluded from his proposal, but Morrison was not. As a result Dalton, Ede, Shinwell and Glenvil Hall moved to the back-benches, and Whitely retired unwillingly as Chief Whip. Although some of the newcomers on to the Parliamentary Committee were hardly youthful, such a change was bound to aid Gaitskell and hinder Morrison. It appears that even at this stage Gaitskell was reluctant to oppose Morrison, but gradually accepted the argument that the older man might fail to defeat Bevan. Eventually, when Attlee announced his resignation in December, most of Morrison's once powerful support had shifted to Gaitskell. The result of the leadership contest was decisive — Bevan received little more than the standard left-wing support, seventy votes. The remainder of the PLP opted overwhelmingly for Gaitskell. His 157 votes contrasted sharply with Morrison's pitiful forty. This victory on the first ballot established Gaitskell as an apparently unchallengeable leader, and marked the end of Morrison's influence.[2]

Gaitskell rose to the leadership and was sustained there by an alliance of revisionist intellectuals and loyalist trade union leaders.[3] Even before entering Parliament, he had been a protégé of Dalton, and had worked closely with other committed social democrats. The support of influential trade union figures began during his period at the Ministry of Fuel and Power, developed while he was at the Treasury, and became even more significant in opposition. He became regarded as the best prospect for the continuing domination of the party by the alliance of political and industrial moderates. He appeared to take notice of the opinions of union spokesmen; he certainly could not be faulted on his attitudes towards the Cold War and internal party discipline.[4]

His approach to party leadership was in marked contrast with that of his predecessor. Whereas Attlee's main concern had been to check Labour's divisive tendencies by offering leadership that was unattached to any group, Gaitskell used his position to promote a specific and controversial interpretation of Labour doctrine. Furthermore, he viewed policy ambiguities with distaste, thereby rejecting a time-honoured method of healing differences. His theory of leadership and his ideological position were intimately connected.

Doctrinally, he blended the caution of a former civil servant with the fervour of the committed revisionist. He rejected the view that the task of an opposition is to oppose, thereby feeding the 'Mr Butskell' image of weak partisanship, and producing dissatisfaction in those sections of the party that distrusted statesmanlike opposition. This feature of his style was fed further by his lack of familiarity with back-bench life. He had achieved office only nine months after entering the Commons, and since then had always spoken from the Front Bench. There were some issues — often non-economic — where he demonstrated a high degree of emotional partisanship; for example over Suez. He could also reach emotional heights in expanding his view of socialism, although he made little use of traditional rhetoric.

Certainly in his conception of socialism there was no central place for public ownership: it was a matter of enquiry as to whether any application of this technique would assist in the realisation of socialist ideals. It was the pursuit of these — above all of equality — that characterised his outlook. Such ideals were to be pursued through the parliamentary process, not as an inescapable necessity, but as something desirable in itself.

Gaitskell conceived one of his roles as educational. The party must amend its doctrine to take proper account of the practice of the Attlee Government. Above all, this meant for Gaitskell a conscious acceptance of the mixed economy and appropriate changes in party rhetoric. He considered that the electorate would become discontented with any party that spoke with one voice to the party faithful, and used another to the wider electorate. Furthermore, he believed that the effectiveness of the party in government would be damaged if no attempt was made to keep rhetoric in line with what the leaders saw as feasible policies. Gaitskell's view of appropriate policy, in its emphasis upon electoral and administrative constraints, obviously carried major implications for traditional doctrines.

His approach to this task involved frontal attacks on what he regarded as illusory expectations. In this enterprise he had mixed fortunes. There proved to be a major difference between changing the substantive content of policy, and seeking to discredit and remove the central symbols of the party. It was this taste for a clean sweep that produced difficulties. The history of Labour policy-making is essentially one of moderate policies attached to potentially radical symbolism. Gaitskell's difficulties arose from an inability to be satisfied with the moderate policies. A charitable verdict on this approach would be that he overestimated the rationality of political movements. A less positive one would be that he had an imperfect appreciation of the function of symbols and myths within a political party, failing to see that they provided an efficient means of maintaining unity. Obviously these different verdicts found echoes within his party. To many on the left, he appeared as the spokesman of an unrepresentative faction, only distantly related to the roots of the party, and dedicated to the undermining of its traditional commitments. To his supporters, he was a courageous and principled moderniser, placing a low evaluation on his own popularity, and seeking to persuade by rational argument rather than by the employment of anachronistic slogans. To the reconcilers, he was an agent of disunity, bent on unnecessary confrontations which could be avoided by the use of ambiguous formulae. This unwillingness to compromise highlighted a central aspect of Gaitskell's approach to politics, his ruthlessness. He had, in the words of one colleague, 'a will like a dividing spear'.[5] The advice of those who were normally allies could be sharply disregarded if it appeared to lead towards an unpalatable compromise. Throughout the Bevanite arguments he had been a committed adherent to the view that dissent should be firmly punished, and as leader he presided over a series of purges and proscriptions at the grass roots.

This commitment to party discipline was one major reason why Gaitskell had secured the support of right-wing trade union leaders. Yet his rapport with the party's trade union element was not without its tensions. He saw nothing peculiar in being both party leader and remaining closely identified with a small, mostly university-educated group known as 'the Hampstead Set'. His closest associates also included a few ideologically congenial trade union leaders such as Birch of USDAW and Greene of the NUR. There is no doubt that this aura of social exclusiveness created problems inside the Parliamentary Party, not just with the committed left, but also with more politically sympathetic members who resented the existence of what appeared as a closed élite circle. The existence of the 'Hampstead Set' did not mean that Gaitskell was ill-equipped to communicate with the party rank and file. Although critics enjoyed the image of the stiff, rather aloof Wykehamist, this was a misunderstanding. On some occasions he showed himself ready and willing to enter into emotional communion with party activists. Moreover, he was able to capitalise effectively on the deferential component of the leadership-rank and file relationship which has always had a bizarre prominence in a supposedly radical party.

Difficulties about Gaitskell's confrontationist approach rarely developed during his first three years as leader. Such concern as there was tended to be subterranean; much of the potential for an explosion was there, but certain crucial ingredients were missing. One of these was the presence of a focus for discontent. Whereas Bevan had previously provided this, he now entered gradually into a working arrangement with Gaitskell. He had returned to the Parliamentary Committee in June 1955, and following the upheavals of December, he opposed Griffiths for the deputy leadership vacated by Morrison. Although unsuccessful, he received 111 votes, far more than the standard left-wing complement, and evidence of the desire within the party for unity.

The election of Gaitskell as leader meant that a replacement had to be found for the treasurership in 1956. Bevan was an early candidate, while the moderate alliance attempted to find a new champion. The search was protracted, the choice eventually falling on George Brown. The situation was complicated however by the perennial controversy over the use of the Engineers' vote. It was resolved in this instance by a decision to nominate their own candidate, Pannell, a committed Gaitskellite. The dual foci for moderate support created a new situation, made even more interesting when the NUM decided to support Bevan. So did the NUR and so, on the eve of the vote, did USDAW. The eventual result was Bevan, 3,029,000, Brown, 2,755,000 (including the T & GWU and the GMW), Pannell, 644,000 (including the AEU). The left congratulated itself on 'the most significant shift in British politics since 1951'. It was important in so far as it marked a split in the triumvirate, resulting in defeat for the two General unions, but it could not be counted as a victory for the left. Rather it was an indication of a general desire for compromise.[6]

The absorption of Bevan into an arrangement with the moderate leadership was carried the crucial last stage at the 1957 Party Conference — and this time there could be no illusion on the part of the left. By then, the question of Britain's possession of nuclear weapons had become a central issue within the party. After considerable deliberation, Bevan agreed to speak for the Executive defending official policy against the unilateralists, and against many of his old supporters. His speech was a typically sophisticated argument, backing neither the unilateralists nor the crude Cold War warriors. As such it was in keeping with the subtlety of his past thinking. However, he did not shrink from attacking what he presented as the Utopianism of the unilateralists. The consequences of this for the party were far-reaching: it produced peace for a time. The left was in disarray, Bevan was linked with Gaitskell at the cost of much personal happiness. But the long-term cost was considerable. An observer not in sympathy with the left wrote of being 'present at a murder — the murder of the enthusiasm that built the Labour movement'.[7]

The decline of opposition was reflected in all sections of the party. The Parliamentary Committee remained dominated by supporters of moderate policies and opposition to the PLP was sparse and ineffective. Those NEC members who had been elected on the Bevanite ticket in 1952 were now occupying diverse positions. Wilson, and to some extent Crossman, had preceded Bevan in reuniting with the moderates. Mikardo, Driberg and to a lesser degree Castle remained opponents of many majority positions. Anthony Greenwood, a later addition to the constituency section, had a left-wing reputation but was in fact a reconciler. The constituency section of the Executive was not a hotbed of left-wing dissent. There were some doctrinal opponents of Gaitskell, but others differed from him on questions of tactics and style rather than policy. The remainder of the Executive could be relied on generally to support any moderate position. The trade union section was dominated by Watson, leader of the Durham Miners and a close associate of Gaitskell. The only exceptions to this rule were the election in 1956 of Padley as the USDAW representative, an advocate of moderate policies, but a devotee of traditional rhetoric, and more peculiarly, the brief membership of Casasola of the Foundry Workers, a long-term promoter of left-wing causes, and a well-publicised convert to the Communist Party after his retirement.

There were new forces at work in the Conference in this period. The change in the Transport Workers' leadership has already been noted. In 1958, the union opposed the Executive on education policy, a hint of future developments. Elsewhere amongst the large unions forces seemed to be moving in favour of the moderates. The AEU, the NUR and USDAW all experienced leadership changes. Carron, Greene and Birch all threw their personal influence in favour of moderation. Their task was assisted by the declining influence of the Communist machines in these organisations, resulting in large part from the events of 1956. Although there were forces favouring moderate control, the margins in these three unions tended to be small. This unreliability plus the changed position of the T & GWU Secretary meant that the moderate domination was less firmly based than in the days of the Deakin-Lawther axis.

During the crucial period of policy reformulation, therefore, Gaitskell enjoyed a generally secure control over the party. His principal rival had reached an uneasy arrangement. Moderates dominated the Parliamentary Party, while in Conference and on the Executive, although alignments lacked the immobility of 1951-5, majorities in favour of the leadership could be virtually guaranteed.

Creeping Revisionism

The Executive's Policy Committee began to consider the state of the party's policy in July 1955, and decided to advise a long-term research programme concentrating on specific topics.[8] These preliminary discussions were based on a Research Department paper that was strongly revisionist in its position. It saw the party's problem as one of convincing the electorate:

> that there is an important role for a democratic socialist party working within a framework of a 'successful' and expanding economy,

while it echoed Gaitskell in suggesting that:

> we may have to think rather more about aims, and about the kind of society we are interested in, and perhaps rather less about means, institutions and techniques.[9]

Before the 1955 Conference, the Policy Committee had drawn up a list of ten areas for research, with the aim of revising policy to take account of recent social changes.[10] After a preliminary airing at the 1955 Conference,[11] this programme was considered in more detail by the Policy Committee.[12] Three documents were prepared for the 1956 Conference, on equality, on personal freedom and on housing, each having been the responsibility of a Study Group.

The equality document was of particular interest to Gaitskell. He chaired the Study Group, and introduced the resulting draft to the Policy Committee and then to the full Executive in June 1956.[13] It produced little controversy either there or at the 1956 Conference.[14] Perhaps this was to be expected, since a document advocating greater equality would be difficult to oppose. The Conference debate on the rather imprecise document demonstrated considerable uncertainty about the content of the equality aspiration. Some speakers interpreted it as equality of opportunity, while others spoke more broadly about equality as denoting a common humanity. There was no discussion of equality, as equality of power and influence, indicating a characteristic revisionist optimism about existing power structures. This was demonstrated in the document's specific proposals, which were restricted for the most part to taxation reforms. It was implied that the equality aspiration could be realised largely through marginal adjustments to the existing economic order.

Although the implications of 'Towards Equality' could be regarded as profound — a traditional socialist aspiration could be realised within existing economic arrangements — it was the other two documents that provoked the controversy in 1956. The Study Group on 'The Individual and Society' produced a draft for the Policy Committee in May.[15] The first difficulty arose over the dissatisfaction of trade union spokesmen about the draft's criticisms of the practice of 'sending to Coventry'. The concern was enough to produce a marked moderation of the statement on this question. Subsequently, a dispute developed over the published document's general acceptance of existing state security procedures: Driberg refused to speak on behalf of the Executive at the 1956 Conference,[16] and there was a strong difference of opinion in the debate. Although a critical resolution was defeated by 850,000 votes,[17] echoes of this controversy reverberated in the Executive for several months.

The third 1956 document, 'Homes of the Future', produced considerable debate within the Executive about its most distinctive proposal — the municipalisation of privately rented housing. Inevitably, such a proposal raised doubts in some quarters about its electoral wisdom. When Anthony Greenwood presented the report of the Study Group to the Home Policy Committee in May 1956,[18] he admitted that there was a difference of opinion over the pace of municipalisation. Some members of the Group presented a case for an early vesting day, whereas others wished the process to be more gradual. At this stage, party officials were asked to prepare a draft, allowing a future Minister considerable flexibility. Gaitskell was the next to voice concern about the municipalisation proposal, arguing that the draft failed to justify the proposal adequately.[19] Doubts about the proposal remained after its acceptance at the 1956 Conference.[20] They surfaced again in the autumn of 1958 when the party published a glossy compendium of its policy proposals, 'The Future Labour Offers You'. This departed from the original proposal by suggesting that municipalisation would be applied only where private landlords had clearly failed.[21] The pressures for a shift to a less ambitious proposal were clearly considerable.

If the equality document had marked a first injection of revisionism into policy reformulation, the preparation of documents for the 1957 Conference was a much more significant episode. The programme included a review of the existing public industries, but more important a Study Group considered the party's future policy on public ownership. A third group dealt with the development of a National Superannuation Scheme, but it was inevitably the production of policy on public ownership that occupied the centre of the stage.

The Study Group, including Gaitskell, Griffiths, Bevan, Wilson and Mikardo, began to meet in December 1956, and based its discussions on a Research Paper, 'The Ownership of Industry'.[22] This argued that in large firms, private ownership was no longer performing any worth-while function. At this early stage the Study Group decided that individual firms, rather than whole industries, would provide the medium for an extension of public ownership. The Research Paper, after revision, formed the basis for a policy statement with the added suggestion that it was undesirable to include any detailed statement on the pace and method of public ownership, since this would arouse 'vehement opposition'. Contact with the TUC was maintained in the preparation of the document, the TUC Research Officer was present at the Study Group meetings, and a meeting was held with the TUC's Economic Committee. The draft was then presented to the NEC and approved for publication, apparently with little controversy.[23]

The absence of major opposition was rather surprising although the document was an interesting example of mobilising support on the basis of ambiguity.[24] Its introductory analytical section reflected the original Research Paper, being a detailed examination of changes in the structure of private industry, focusing on the emergence of large firms and the irrelevance of shareholders, and couched in language capable of generating support from the most committed advocates of public ownership. The substantive proposals, however, were not just anti-climactic in their moderation, but in one case antipathetic to extensive sections of the party. Apart from the inevitable proposals to renationalise iron and steel and road haulage, the document did not recommend any specific acts of nationalisation, but rather the state purchase of shares in large firms. This obviously involved a positive acceptance of the acquisitive motivations of private industry, a conscious enshrining in party policy of that market morality that the Attlee Government had accepted in practice. It was a rejection of the traditional belief that the socialisation of industry would change economic relationships fundamentally. Furthermore, the document rubbed salt into the wound by remarking that many firms were serving the economy well, reflecting again the characteristic revisionist optimism about the state of the economy.

The conclusions of the document encouraged a crop of different interpretations. Gaitskell seemed ready to suggest that a Labour Government would take over only inefficient firms, while Mikardo wrote of how a determined government could use the share-buying technique to extend the public sector dramatically.[25] However the belief was widespread within some sections of the party that the proposal was not another approach to public ownership, but a substitute for it. When Conference debated the document, the strength of opposition to a further programme of public ownership on the 1945 pattern became apparent. Revisionist thinkers and less reflective speakers concerned about electoral consequences combined to oppose those who condemned the document as a retreat from socialism. In his concluding speech Gaitskell developed a very full elaboration of the revisionist case on public ownership: any extension must appear immediately relevant to the ordinary elector, backed by specific reasons and not presented as an end in itself. What really determined the acceptance of the document, however, was the position of the six largest unions. Only the NUR opposed it, and therefore an overwhelming victory was guaranteed by a majority of more than four million votes.[26] Within two years therefore party policy on public ownership showed a major shift in the direction favoured by the revisionists. This development was obviously assisted by the strong desire for a united party. It was widely expected that a general election was imminent and unnecessary divisions must be divided.

The election did not come however, and the Executive produced three more policy statements for the 1958 Conference. This completed the restatement process, as it had been decided not to proceed with the tenth document on automation. One of the three documents, on agriculture, reflected the 1953 position on land nationalisation, and attempts to press for a positive commitment at the 1958 Conference were opposed successfully on grounds of electoral expediency.[27] The other two documents were closely linked with revisionist concerns. A

Study Group on Education produced a draft in a policy area, seen by
revisionists as one of the main areas of future reform. During its
preparation, controversy developed over the future of the public
schools, although it appears that no one on the Study Group urged a
complete take-over. The more decisive proposal, advocated by Michael
Stewart, was for a 75 per cent acquisition of the places, but this was
rejected in favour of postponing any clear commitment until 'substantial
changes in the distribution of wealth and public opinion have occurred'.[28]
Inevitably this sensitivity towards electoral considerations produced
opposition at the Party Conference, and a more radical approach was
defeated by less than 500,000 votes. Caution had triumphed narrowly,
but it was indicative of future difficulties that the T & GW vote was
cast against the platform.[29]

The final document in the series, 'Plan for Progress', emerged from
the work of a Study Group on the Control of Industry.[30] A meeting
with the Economic Committee of the TUC had been held at the very
beginning of the Group's work and throughout the development of the
document TUC representatives were closely consulted. Finally, the
Economic Committee went through the whole document and made
more suggestions.[31]

The close relationship with the TUC in the development of this
document requires some examination of changes in that body's
attitudes in the late fifties. The apparent success of Conservative
economic policies down to 1955 had affected the behaviour of the
unions. The conciliatory approach of the Government had been
matched by the desire of many union leaders to remain on reasonable
terms with all governments.[32] This 'era of good feeling' ended in
autumn 1955, with a balance of payments crisis and a credit squeeze.
Ministers began to express concern about the impact of excessive wage
demands, while at the 1956 Congress Cousins led an attack against
wage restraint as an instrument of policy. Industrial stoppages became
more frequent and unemployment mounted. Early in 1958, the
Government attempted to hold the line against wage increases, the
testing ground being the London busmen. Eventually in June, the
General Council faced the problem of whether to seek an extension of
this stoppage, but decided not to do so because of the political
implications. The busmen were defeated, a symbolic victory for the
Government.

Although the General Council remained politically moderate, these
economic strains inevitably had an impact upon its outlook. In
retrospect, they can be seen as early manifestations of Britain's

economic malaise. In 1958, the TUC reaction could be found in the Labour document 'Plan for Progress'. The principal emphasis was on the need to end the reliance on deflationary techniques. The basis for an expanding economy was presented as the utilisation of appropriate planning techniques aimed at fostering the necessary level of investment. Union support would be based on more equitable social and taxation policies. There were two crucial elements in this perspective. Firstly, an increased growth rate was presented as a prerequisite for all other economic and social benefits. It was not possible to meet demands through redistribution. Secondly, the document suggested that Labour's primary concern was not to transform the mixed economy, but to operate it more efficiently than its opponents. Attacks on 'capitalism' were clearly out: the Keynesian Revolution had left its mark on party policy.[33] The revision of policy to accord with practice was accepted with little criticism. At the 1958 Conference, union leaders vied with one another in their readiness to support the document.[34] The delegate who protested that he was 'not interested in working capitalism more efficiently than the capitalists themselves', seemed a survivor from an earlier age.[35]

This period of policy reformulation marked a major advance for the revisionists. Major features of their position were now enshrined in policy documents, especially in the crucial areas of public ownership and economic strategy. Proponents of such developments now occupied key places in the policy-making process, and had been aided by the overwhelming desire to unite for electoral victory. There was just enough ambiguity in the policy documents to disguise the full extent of the change. Doubts were mostly stilled, while hope of electoral success remained, but the absence of widespread criticism did not indicate a positive acceptance of the changes by all sections of the party.

The Labour Left and The Bomb

The Labour Left was certainly in no position to offer a challenge to the revisionist case: its theoretical poverty was apparent, while its support declined from 1955 to 1957, as leading Bevanites took the path of reconciliation, and the strength of the trade union left was weakened by the disarray of the Communist machines. The 1957 Conference was the lowest point of all, with the overwhelming adoption of 'Industry and Society' and Bevan's attack on unilateralism. 'The left of the party looked for a moment as if it had exterminated itself. Without its incomparable leader, it was unlikely to regather strength for years.'[36] Attempts were made by some of the remaining left-wing MPs to check the decline by reviving a defunct organisation, 'Victory for Socialism'. This came to the attention of the Executive early in 1958, and when attempts by reconcilers to avoid conflict failed, the leaders of VFS were warned of the folly of introducing 'distractions' into the party.[37] The hostility of many within the leadership cannot really account for the failure of this initiative. A few policy pamphlets were issued but with little impact. The truth was that by 1958 the purely Labour left with its lack of theoretical awareness and its preoccupation with party manoeuvrings no longer dominated radical debate. The major developments were not centred on the party, a significant portent for Labour's future.

The events of 1956 had created a broad rather incoherent New Left movement centred originally around two journals, one, the *New Reasoner,* run by disillusioned ex-Communists, and the other, the *Universities' and Left Review,* by a younger, more amorphous group. The gradual uniting of these two groups, symbolised in January 1960 by the inauguration of the *New Left Review* did not indicate any clarification of perspective. The preoccupations of the New Left were diverse and sometimes contradictory: attempts to develop Marxist analyses after the frozen years of Stalinism rubbed along with appeals to traditional English radicalism, or variants of Existentialism. Subjects covered included not only obvious economic and international problems, but questions of cultural and philosophical significance. The movement was an emancipation of left-wing thought from the stultifying choice between Stalinism and acceptance of NATO and the mixed economy. It gave critics of revisionism at least a chance to develop an alternative perspective that paid some attention to recent changes.[38]

There was one question however that the New Left seemed incapable of resolving — its attitude towards the Labour Party, still the focus of the loyalties of the majority of the working class, but now becoming more and more revisionist. The ambiguities of the relationship showed with particular clarity as the unilateralist issue became more central both to the New Left and to the internal politics of the party.[39] Crucially, the unilateralist movement developed outside the party's official channels. In February 1958, the Campaign for Nuclear Disarmament was launched, and at Easter the Campaign began its series of annual Aldermaston marches. Spokesmen of liberal, anti-establishment Britain, as well as self-conscious socialists, participated in the movement, an upsurge of radical feeling unparalleled since the Popular Front agitations of the thirties. As then, the Labour

Party seemed marginal to the agitation. Prominent party figures — Castle, Greenwood and Foot — spoke on unilateralist platforms. *Tribune* proclaimed itself 'The Paper that leads the Anti-H Bomb Campaign'. But many who participated in the campaign were antagonistic, not just to the Conservative Government, but to what they saw as the torpor of the existing party system. During the war, a similar radical revolt had been capitalised on by the party in 1945, and it was not surprising that spokesmen for the Labour left attempted to divert unilateralist sentiment into internal party battles, arguing that the only way unilateralist hopes could be realised was through effecting a change in party policy. No doubt, most Labour politicians who backed unilateralism were genuinely committed, but they also viewed the strength of the agitation as something that could improve their position within the party.

The unilateralist tide began to wet the feet of the party leadership, producing some modifications to its firm defence of the British deterrent. Thus, early in 1958, a joint Party-TUC meeting attempted to meet the challenge of the unilateralists, with Bevan occupying a position between those of Gaitskell and the unilateralists who were strengthened now by Cousins.[40] The resulting joint document, 'Disarmament and Nuclear War', proposed a unilateral suspension of nuclear tests, but did not include Bevan's proposal that the party would oppose a first use of nuclear weapons by Britain. Such modifications to party policy were marginal. The majority within the Executive and the Shadow Cabinet remained fully committed to NATO and all that that implied. The essentially tactical nature of such amendments was readily apparent. They helped the Executive to another easy victory over the unilateralists at the 1958 Conference,[41] but the problem of unilateralist pressure became even more urgent. This was demonstrated by the growing evidence of support for such a policy amongst the unions. In June 1959, the perpetually loyal GMW supported a unilateralist resolution at its conference, an aberration quickly corrected at a recalled meeting. In the interim, another NEC-General Council meeting had produced another tactical concession, 'the non-nuclear club', proposing a collective renunciation by all countries except the USA and the USSR.[42] This probably helped to restore the Municipal Workers' to their characteristic orthodoxy, but played little part in the party's internal debate.

Unilateralism had become a major concern of Labour's leadership by mid-1959. A TUC memorandum pontificated that 'while it is not the habit of the TUC to attach much importance to movements and demonstrations of this character, it is suggested that the success of this year's march from Aldermaston is a phenomenon which cannot altogether be disregarded.'[43] Its attraction in union circles was indicated by the vote of over 2.5 million against the official position at the 1959 TUC.[44] Inevitably the Labour left gained by the emergence of this issue, although the strengthening of the left was almost in spite of itself. The small, ageing parliamentary left was buoyed up by forces that it could not control, and with which it was in imperfect sympathy. Many within the New Left viewed all Labour parliamentarians with suspicion or even hostility, and the latter responded by compressing the argument into internal party terms.

The Road to Power?

The debate over the future of the party did not concern itself just with a restatement of policy; criticism was also expressed in the 1955 post-mortem about the state of party organisation. Immediately after the defeat, the Executive appointed a committee under Wilson's chairmanship to examine this. Its report was considered by the Executive in September; both Morgan Phillips and the National Agent, Len Williams, claimed that it contained inaccuracies.[45] In spite of some opposition, it was decided to publish a revised version for debate at the 1955 Conference. The state of party organisation in many constituencies was condemned as deplorable. There was little attempt to concentrate crucial resources such as full-time agents in key marginals, while the almost total lack of any party machine in many safe Labour seats suggested a gulf between Party structure and its grass-roots support. Yet it would be misleading to contrast this situation with an earlier 'Golden Age' of party organisation. Labour in 1955 had about the same number of agents as in 1950. It was rather that the gap between Labour's amateurish machine, ever mindful of financial difficulties, and the increasingly professional Conservative organisation was becoming wider. Little was done to remedy the situation in the following four years, although some attempt was made to concentrate resources in crucial constituencies. In general, however, the opposition of the senior Transport House staff to major changes prevented the kind of radical transformation that could be advocated on the basis of the report's findings. The unwillingness of officials to change their approach to propaganda was demonstrated by Labour's sparse attempts to mobilise support. In contrast to a well-planned efficient and expensive Conservative advertising campaign extending from 1957 to September 1959, Labour spent most of its time addressing the committed. Only

£22,500 was devoted to a brief national poster campaign. This is not to argue that lack of professionalism was the key to Labour's problems in the late fifties. Its difficulties were clearly more deep-seated than communications and mobilisation of voters. Nevertheless it is clear that revisionist 'modernisation' was far less effective in the field of party organisation than that of policy-making. One reason was that many who would ally with revisionists on policy matters were opposed in principle to the use of mass advertising techniques, and were obsessed with the need to keep a careful watch on party funds.

During the 1955 Parliament, by-election results gave some encouragement to the Labour Party with three gains from the Conservatives. However, the popularity of the Government, low in 1957, subsequently recovered, and when the election campaign began in September 1959, it was widely expected that Labour would lose. Although the expansion of the economy had suffered a setback after 1955, by the late summer of 1959 the economy was expanding again. Certainly there remained pools of unemployment, especially in Lancashire and the West of Scotland, but in many industrial areas, full employment led to higher incomes and new levels and patterns of expenditure. For many electors 'Conservative Freedom' did seem to work.

The whole process of rethinking Labour policy since 1955 had left the party highly vulnerable to this situation: once the basic argument had been defined as who could run the mixed economy more efficiently, then there was no real answer to an efficient Conservative performance. A subsidiary strand in Labour's strategy could be called 'the appeal to the liberal conscience'. Labour spokesmen had sought to emphasise the immorality of Conservative policy over Suez, and the cynicism and anachronism of its outlook on colonial affairs. This won plaudits from liberal commentators but evoked almost no electoral response.

The conduct of the campaign showed that Labour at least intended to fight in a more positive fashion than in 1955. Its effort was spearheaded by a four-member Campaign Committee under Crossman. Its television presentation was widely accepted as pre-eminent, and during the early stages of the contest the party appeared to be gaining ground. Its election manifesto was a testimony to the revisionist advance. Public ownership was a marginal element; socialism was the 'Great Unmentionable'; the party competed in the 'prosperity stakes' with the Government, and as a result, over most of the country it lost ground.

Labour's total vote was even 190,000 down on the bleak year of 1955, and with a rising poll and an increased Liberal vote, its share of the vote fell by 2.6 per cent to 43.8. The results showed significant regional variations. Two regions, South-east Lancashire and West Scotland, swung against the Government, and these provided Labour with five gains. However, the party lost 27 seats to the Conservatives, located mostly in two regions. Nine of them were in London and the south-east, and seven in the West Midlands, with particularly heavy swings to the Conservatives in several seats in the latter region. This diversity suggested a fairly simple explanation for this loss of Labour seats. The issue was simply 'money'; industrial areas with rising expectations had turned towards the Government, those that felt left out had not.

This interpretation is clearly crude: the relationship between increasing affluence and voting loyalty is extremely complex, mediated as it is through a screen of other cultural and community traditions. However, it was this verdict that determined the nature of Labour's post-mortem. The issue here was not really whether Labour could have won in 1959 with a different policy. In the aftermath of that golden, somnolent summer, all formulae for victory, revisionist or traditional, consensual or confrontationist would have been blunted by the widespread optimism about Britain's economy. Rather the question raised was whether Labour could hope to win in the future – how should it adapt itself in a situation where the traditional prophecies about capitalist decay seemed so totally refuted? Accommodation with existing structures and values had gone most of the way; should it be taken further? Was the party's weakness that it had not been revisionist enough?

Notes

1. Dalton, *Vol. 3*, pp. 413-22.
2. See Donoughue and Jones, op. cit., ch. 39; Dalton, *Vol. 3*, ch. 45; Foot, *Vol. II*, pp. 494-6.
3. See W. Rodgers (ed.), *Hugh Gaitskell* (Thames and Hudson, London, 1964) for a strongly positive portrait – and for a scathing attack, Tom Nairn, 'Hugh Gaitskell' in *New Left Review*, 25, May–June 1964, pp. 63-8.
4. For example, see his Stalybridge speech reported in *The Times*, 6 October 1952.
5. John Strachey quoted in Foot, *Vol. II*, p. 295.
6. Ibid., chs. 14 and 15.
7. Ibid., p. 577. The debate is in *LPCR 1957*, pp. 163-83. For the pre-Conference deliberations see *NEC Minutes*, 27 and 29 September 1957.
8. *Policy Committee Minutes*, 18 July 1955.

9. Memorandum *R.522*, 'A New Research Programme'.
10. *Policy Committee Minutes*, 22 September 1955.
11. *LPCR 1955*, pp. 111-29.
12. *Home Policy Committee Minutes*, 14 November and 5 December 1955; *NEC Minutes*, 23 November 1955.
13. *Home Policy Committee Minutes*, 18 June 1956; *NEC Minutes*, 27 June 1956.
14. *LPCR 1956*, pp. 117-32.
15. *Home Policy Committee Minutes*, 14 May 1956; *NEC Minutes*, 6 June 1956.
16. *NEC Minutes*, 30 September 1956.
17. *LPCR 1956*, pp. 117-32.
18. *Home Policy Committee Minutes*, 14 May 1956.
19. See his note, *Re 74* − also *NEC Minutes*, 6 and 11 June 1956.
20. *LPCR 1956*, pp. 98-115.
21. *Home Policy Sub-Committee Minutes*, 16 February 1959.
22. *Minutes of the Study Group on the Ownership and Control of Industry*, 17 and 20 December 1956, 12 February 1957. See memorandum *Re 114* 'The Ownership of Industry' − and the revised version *Re 134*.
23. *NEC Minutes*, 25 June 1957.
24. See *Industry and Society, passim*. Bevan's attitude remains an enigma to which Foot's biography offers no solution.
25. In *Tribune*, 26 July and 13 September 1957.
26. *LPCR 1957*, pp. 128-61.
27. *LPCR 1958*, p. 133 (the contribution of Tom Williams).
28. *Home Policy Sub-Committee Minutes*, 14 April 1958 − and the Stewart Memorandum *Re 375. NEC Minutes*, 14 May 1958.
29. *LPCR 1958*, pp. 85-114.
30. See the reference in the memorandum *Re 219*, 'Programme of Work', discussed at the Home Policy Sub-Committee, 19 November 1957.
31. *NEC Minutes*, 25 June 1958.
32. See the General Council's statement after the 1951 election that they would try 'to work amiably with whatever government is in power', *TUC Report 1952*, p. 300.
33. See 'Plan for Progress', *passim*.
34. *LPCR 1958*, pp. 141-73.
35. Ibid., p. 163 (Trevor Park, MP for South-east Derbyshire, 1964-70).
36. Foot, *Vol. II*, p. 579.
37. See *NEC Minutes*, 26 February 1958.
38. See also E.P. Thompson (ed.), *Out of Apathy* (Stevens, London, 1960).
39. See Frank Parkin, *Middle Class Radicalism* (University Press, Manchester, 1968), especially chs. 4, 5, 6.
40. *Joint Meetings of TUC and Labour Party International Committee Minutes*, 13 February and 6 March 1958. See also Foot, *Vol. II*, pp. 595-8.
41. *LPCR 1958*, pp. 186-224.
42. *NEC Minutes*, 24 June 1959.
43. *TUC Memorandum*, dated 26 May 1959 in NEC Minutes.
44. *TUC Report 1959*, pp. 395-415 − text of 'Disarmament and Nuclear War − The Next Step', is at pp. 220-3.
45. *NEC Minutes*, 28 September 1955.

8 CONFRONTATION AND COMPROMISE 1959-64

In October 1959 Labour entered a third successive Parliament in
opposition, surrounded by prophecies of its long-term decay at the
hands of an increasingly affluent electorate. Five years later, the party
returned to office, albeit with a small majority, having refuted the
predictions of pundits, political opponents and some supporters. The
apparent stability of 1959 proved to be an illusion — it was not only
the leaders of the parties that changed. In retrospect 1959 seems an
Indian Summer of self-confidence. It was perhaps the time of the last
great British illusion. In the early sixties, this perished before an
increasing awareness of economic decline and institutional obsolescence.

Such developments were bound to improve the chances of Labour if
only on the basis of 'Time for a Change'. The 1959 defeat produced a
protracted crisis within the party, as various responses to defeat were
debated. The crisis was deepened by the growing strength of the
unilateralist cause and by the emergence of the leadership as an issue.
In essentials, the arguments resulted in victories for the moderates,
although these were often coated in a diplomatic ambiguity. The
cessation of hostilities was facilitated by an awareness of the party's
improving electoral prospects. It is also arguable that such a
development was assisted by the unexpected death of Gaitskell in
January 1963, and by the election of Wilson, the arch-reconciler, as his
successor.

Four Crises

During the two years succeeding the 1959 election, the party passed
through four interconnected crises, each symbolic of a basic uncertainty
about future strategy and doctrine. Two of these concerned policy —
the future of public ownership and of unilateralism: another was
concerned directly with Gaitskell's leadership, while the fourth
involved the structure of the party, especially the relationship between
the Conference and Labour MPs. The fact of defeat removed a vital
constraint. Already opposition to Gaitskell and his revisionist colleagues
was developing: now it could be expressed in an uninhibited way.

The first initiative came however from the revisionists. On the
Sunday after the election, a small group gathered at Gaitskell's house,
and several of those present suggested that defeat resulted from the

incomplete nature of the earlier policy restatement.[1] Some suggestions in the Press hinted at a further attack on the principle of public ownership, and an attempt to loosen the widely perceived connection between the party and the working class, perhaps through a loosening of ties with the unions.

Such reactions to defeat eventually became the focus of controversy late in November, when the party held a two-day post-mortem Conference at Blackpool. Gaitskell broke his silence to treat delegates to a thorough presentation of the revisionist case.[2] He began by suggesting that the party's defeat could not be attributed to the campaign, but rather to long-term economic and social changes. The relative decline of traditional industries, the absence of any fear of unemployment, changes in consumption patterns, all contributed in his view to a declining Labour vote. His response was predictable — the party should modernise itself both organisationally and doctrinally. It should not pose as a class party — doctrinal purity should be replaced by a readiness to reflect popular preoccupations:

> our object must be to broaden our base, to be in touch always with ordinary people, and to avoid becoming small cliques of isolated doctrine-ridden fanatics, out of touch with the main stream of social life in our time.[3]

Above all, he claimed that the party lost votes through its identification with public ownership and the belief that the party wished to nationalise everything. Once again, he cited the distinction between ends and means, with public ownership just one possible means for the realisation of socialist values. The policy restatement before 1959 was of course compatible with this perspective; now however Gaitskell proposed an extension of revisionism, to include not just policy but also the party's basic symbolism. He attacked the wording of the existing Constitution on this question, and suggested its amendment. By attacking 'Clause Four' in this way, he unleashed a major debate within the party. Several speakers at the post-mortem referred to this proposal — some defended it as a necessary piece of modernisation, while others deplored what they regarded as an attempt to erase the party's socialist commitment.

It is difficult to understand what Gaitskell hoped to achieve by raising the issue of Clause Four. This was the best example of his readiness to seek total victory without apparently attaching any importance to the emotional appeal of traditional symbols. This controversy split the coalition that had supported him into three distinct groupings. There were of course those who went along with his suggestions, but there were two normally friendly groups that objected to this 'symbolic revisionism'. Some older trade unionists opposed any change in Clause Four. Their everyday political practice showed that they accepted the mixed economy as permanent, but having entered the party at a time when socialism and public ownership were identified closely with one another, they found it difficult to erase a memento of that formative period. More frequently, moderate figures opposed the venture because they regarded it as tactically ill-conceived. It was simply not worth an argument, since for several years the party had existed amicably with a combination of specific policies that implied acceptance of the mixed economy and a constitutional clause that did not. Such ambiguity was valuable — so why destroy it?

This wide alliance of forces opposed to such a change, buttressed of course by the hard-core left, was sufficient to block the proposal for constitutional amendment. At first, it appeared that revisionism would triumph even on this symbolic level, since the NEC in March 1960 approved a new twelve-point draft as part of the Constitution: a draft that recognised a place in the economy for private enterprise. The approved version involved some modification of Gaitskell's original proposals. Jennie Lee successfully moved an amendment that removed a reference to the need for 'a substantial measure of common ownership ...'. Instead, the amended version committed the party to 'an expansion of common ownership substantial enough to give the community power over the commanding heights of the economy ...'.

This was a characteristic example of a reconciling formula. A more critical amendment was moved by John Boyd of the Engineers and seconded by Harry Nicholas of the Transport Workers. This proposed the deletion of the phrase, 'Recognising that both public and private enterprise have a place in the economy' in favour of, 'We recognise that for some time to come there will be a mixed economy.' This proposal was defeated by sixteen votes to eight,[4] but it became apparent that the issue could not be settled so readily. The opposition of two members of the trade union section was significant. The moderate concern at Gaitskell's attack on Clause Four was nowhere stronger than in the decision-making bodies of the large unions with their preponderance of old-style loyalists, and those who regarded the whole argument as irrelevant. Only USDAW and the GMW were ready to see the draft inserted into the Constitution — the other four largest unions went on record as opposed. By July 1960, it was clear that defeat for such a proposal at the Party Conference was almost certain, and the NEC decided to demote the draft from the status of a constitutional amendment to 'a valuable expression of the aims of the Labour Party'.[5]

The first crisis, for what it was worth, ended in a defeat for the revisionists. It was impossible for them to attack the party's traditional symbolism without endangering the stability of the moderate alliance. This was a bizarre episode – the crisis was induced by the party's leader. Although Labour did face a major strategic problem, Gaitskell chose to concentrate on an issue that was both irrelevant and costly. It produced tensions between his supporters and it also generated suspicions about the more substantive parts of the revisionists' programme. At no time was the revisionist concern with getting to the root of issues demonstrated in a less favourable light.

One reason for the compromise over Clause Four was that by the summer of 1960, the leadership faced another challenge over defence. By then, the attraction of this policy had had a dramatic effect on the positions of four of the large unions – USDAW, the T & GW, the AEU and the NUR all became committed to unilateralism. Despite this rising tide, the NEC remained overwhelmingly multilateralist. During the 1960 summer, a new Joint Declaration on Defence was prepared by the party and the TUC. Attempts were made in the NEC to amend this in a unilateralist direction. These efforts led by Castle, Greenwood and Nicholas were defeated overwhelmingly with the strength of the minority varying from three to five. A similar division of opinions can be found in the pre-Conference deliberations of the NEC.[6] There can be no doubt that once again the resulting controversy was symbolic of far more than the question of 'The Bomb'. This had become almost academic with the Government's cancellation early in 1960 of the Blue Streak programme, but beneath detailed questions of deterrence, there lay the unresolved and ever-simmering question of the party's attitude towards a NATO-oriented foreign policy. By now the unilateralist question encapsulated all the fundamental problems about socialist foreign policy that had bedevilled the party since the mid-thirties.

These underlying issues meant that unilateralism was an excellent basis for reforming the moderate alliance that had been so strained by the Clause Four controversy. Many moderates could be persuaded back into their old allegiance by reviving the prejudices of the Cold War. This is exactly what happened in the 1960 Conference debate on defence. In his concluding speech Gaitskell referred to 'the pacifists, unilateralists, and fellow-travellers that other people are.'[7] He defended NATO, arguing that unilateralism should really be equated with neutralism. Although such appeals revived the moderate alliance, they did not prevent the narrow passage of two unilateralist resolutions and the defeat of the official policy statement.[8]

These Conference defeats for the official policy meant however that the controversy over defence policy became linked with two other crises. The public lack of harmony between the Conference and the majority of Labour MPs meant that the question of Conference authority was at the forefront of the debate. Moreover the whole argument had now become entangled with the question of Gaitskell's future as leader. Could he maintain his control over the party?

The dominant theory of intra-party democracy had always placed primary emphasis on the decisions of Conference. Certainly, there had always been qualifications about timing and changing circumstances, but it was accepted that a basic change in the Conference position on a major issue was of fundamental significance. This had certainly been argued by Labour leaders at the time of the German rearmament controversy, on the grounds that an adverse Conference verdict would produce difficulties for the PLP.[9] Perhaps it is plausible to argue that such predictions of chaos could be used by leaders as a tactical weapon — the principle of Conference supremacy was acceptable and even useful so long as they felt assured of a Conference majority. Nevertheless it is true that until 1960, the opinion that Conference had a dominant or at least a major voice in policy formulation enjoyed wide currency. There was a very confused debate on the constitutional issue at the 1960 Conference, when the NEC accepted a resolution offering a moderate version of the 'supremacy of Conference' thesis, but it did so in such a way as to emasculate its meaning. This tightrope act was in fact the consequence of a defeat for the hard-line moderates within the Executive.[10]

The traditional view was challenged directly by Gaitskell in his speech at the end of the 1960 Conference debate on defence, with a claim that PLP acceptance of the unilateralist verdict would be intellectually disreputable and electorally impossible.[11] Thus the Party leader and the PLP majority attempted to defy the Conference verdict, demonstrating their own authority by their deeds. To some degree perhaps, the readiness of the parliamentary left to engage in open warfare had been increased by the death of Bevan in July. A unifying factor had disappeared.

The events of the next twelve months showed that the moderate majority in the PLP was able to adhere to a multilateralist position.

There existed no mechanism whereby the Conference verdict could be imposed on recalcitrant MPs when the latter had a clear majority. Moreover, an attempt to ensure that the NEC acted as the advocate of the Conference decision in its dealings with the PLP and the General Council was defeated overwhelmingly.[12] This was demonstrated as early as November when Gaitskell was confronted with a challenge to his leadership. Initially this came from the unilateralist Greenwood, but subsequently the challenge passed to Wilson. His opposition to Gaitskell was not based, of course, on agreement with the Scarborough decision, but on concern with Gaitskell's confrontationist style of leadership.[13] However, the contest ended in a reaffirmation of support for Gaitskell by 166 votes to 81. Similarly Brown was elected to the vacant Deputy Leadership. The solid base enjoyed by Gaitskell in the PLP and his dominance of the Shadow Cabinet led to comparatively little tolerance being shown to unilateralist MPs. The openly dissident minority gradually declined in prominence during the winter until it was reduced to five individualists who were deprived of the Whip.

If Gaitskell and multilateralism reigned securely in the Parliamentary Party, there still remained the question of the 1961 Conference. Could the unilateralist victory be reversed, or would there be a further year of open disunity? Two processes were crucial in the resolution of this conflict – the formulation of a new defence policy within the party, and the subsequent decisions by the large unions.

The early months of 1961 saw a series of debates on the policy question centred around a joint NEC-TUC 'Committee of Twelve'.[14] This discussed three documents, an official draft, 'Policy for Peace', a unilateralist statement produced by Cousins, and a third reconciling document, 'the Crossman-Padley compromise'. The last document differed only marginally from the official draft on the question of the first use of strategic nuclear weapons. This fine point of difference demonstrates how far the internal party struggle had become concerned with Gaitskell's style of leadership, his unwillingness to allow even symbolic concessions. It is also interesting that many party unilateralists were ready to accept this superficial compromise as a token of Gaitskell's defeat, although it was still essentially multilateralist. When the debate came before the full Executive, an alliance of unilateralists and reconcilers lost by 15 votes to 13.[15]

The adoption of the uncompromising official policy again showed Gaitskell's desire for unambiguous victory. The failure of his opponents to produce any dilution of defence policy meant that a further impasse could be avoided only if the Conference verdict was changed.

This reversal happened basically because USDAW, the AEU and the NUR all retreated from unconditional unilateralism.[16] However the change did not represent approval of Gaitskell's strategy, but rather a desire for unity. In fact, each of these unions returned ambiguous verdicts when discussing unilateralism; the primary emphasis was on a unifying policy rather than a clear commitment. Since the leaders of each of these unions were committed multilateralists, the ambiguity led to support for the leadership. In October 1960 Gaitskell had promised to 'fight and fight and fight again'; a year later he reversed the Scarborough decision although suffering defeats on other defence issues.[17] This reversal occurred not because of his total opposition to unilateralism, but because of the readiness of some trade union leaders to pursue multilateralism through appeals for loyalty and ambiguous phrases.

By October 1961, the party had reached the end of its period of introspective crises. Clause Four remained untouched, the one revisionist failure. Elsewhere they triumphed — unilateralism ceased to be a threat, Gaitskell's dominance was virtually unchallenged, and the PLP majority had demonstrated its freedom from Conference control. The one defeat was of little importance, since it carried few implications for policy. The major lesson of these crises was that Gaitskell and his allies controlled the party, but that their success was built in part on the cultivation of what was to them a distasteful ambiguity.

The End of Electoral Optimism

Labour's 1959 defeat was the final act in the burial of a party myth. Until then, it had been possible to argue that Labour was the party of the future, that 1950 and 1951 had been temporary setbacks and that 1955 stemmed from weak organisation and internal feuding. When the party lost seats for the fourth successive election, such excuses ceased to be convincing. A more radical reappraisal was required.

The old optimism had been founded on a simple theory of class voting. Labour was deemed to be the party of the working class, and the majority of the electorate would be converted over time into a natural Labour majority, as they came to recognise where their true interests lay. Some Labour strategists, most notably Morrison, had argued for the cultivation of 'progressive' middle-class support, but all had taken the naturalness of Labour's mass working-class vote for granted. Now the inevitability of Labour decline began to be predicted.[18]

This change in the assessment of Labour's basic position was attributed to a number of developments that were not always clearly separated. An obvious one was the increasing material prosperity of a significant proportion of manual workers leading to a decline in feelings of relative deprivation. From 1951 to 1958 the average real earnings of the industrial worker rose by more than 20 per cent. Such a change could be associated, especially in the case of younger voters, with the arrival of a Conservative administration. It was a living riposte to Labour evocations of 'The Hungry Thirties'.

The basic equation of affluence with a declining propensity to vote Labour bristles with difficulties. Afflence *per se* does not alter the industrial position of the individual worker. He remains subject to factory discipline, and prone to the fear that his earnings are not protected by any professional qualifications. Indeed many affluent workers experience work situations typically associated with high levels of Labour support. They are employed in large plants with remote management and a high level of unionisation. The effect of affluence on political allegiance cannot be considered apart from a wide range of industrial and cultural experiences. The entire past experience of a particular work force is likely to colour assessments of its situation. Perhaps more weight should be attached to the disintegration of traditional working-class communities where common occupational, domestic and recreational experiences helped to mould and maintain a common political outlook. By the late fifties, such communities were frequently in decline, especially in the decaying inner areas of cities. In some cases, new communities were of comparable social homogeneity, and here Labour strength remained relatively unimpaired. Arguably, problems arose from the increasing heterogeneity of social experience, a possible but not inevitable result of increasing affluence. A distinct but related process concerns the relative decline in the manual work force. Some children of manual workers climbed the educational ladder, often blending a new life style with uncertain political and social allegiances.[19]

Obviously the problem of the relationship between changing economic and social experience and party affiliation is a complex one, yet after the 1959 defeat many Labour politicians were ready to pontificate on the implications for Labour strategy on the basis of extremely limited evidence.

Three aspects of the debate were of particular significance. The revisionists argued that Labour was failing to capture crucial marginal voters because of an inadequate appreciation of recent economic and social changes. This suggested that party doctrine and proposals should be highly malleable, and determined to a large extent by assessments of majority electoral preferences.[20] This was challenged by a combination of practicality and principle. One claim was that such dilution would render a Labour Government impotent, since dictation by transient electoral preferences would remove the necessary socialist ingredient. Any worth-while Labour victory would be achieved only on the basis of socialist policies even if it involved a lengthy period in opposition. From a more self-consciously ethical position it was argued that abandonment of principle involved a compromise with what was, by socialist standards, an immoral society. This view of Labour strategy was presented to the 1959 post-mortem by Michael Foot:

> In order to win an election, we have to change the mood of the people in this country, to open their eyes to what an evil and disgraceful and rotten society it is.[21]

This prescription relates closely to a second aspect of the debate, the place of Labour within the party system. Revisionists wished to see the party as a persistent contender for office. By moulding itself to majority preferences, it would emerge hopefully as the natural governing party, thereby emulating the Swedish social democrats. In contrast, an alternative vision saw Labour as generally opposition-orientated. It could preserve its radical credentials but would be ready to take office at moments of crisis. This was expressed, cogently, by Crossman's claim that:

> the prime function of the Labour Party ... is to provide an ideology for nonconformist critics of the Establishment, and a political instrument for interests and social groups which are denied justice under the 'status quo'.[22]

Finally, revisionists claimed that Labour's appeal was weakened by excessive identification with a sectional class interest. Part of this claim was pragmatic; traditional working-class communities were in decline and therefore the identification produced a less secure electoral base. Related to this there was a belief that potential white-collar Labour voters were discouraged by the party's identification with the sectional claims of trade unionism. This sometimes involved the suggestion that militant union activities were harmful to the party. Such pragmatic reservations blended with doctrinal judgements. Since revisionists tended to see Labour's future radicalism expressed more and more in non-economic terms, the centrality of class support based on socio-economic factors could be expected to diminish. The whole revisionist perspective placed a low weight on class divisions. They believed that a firm left of centre progressive majority could be mobilised across class lines within the British electorate. These reflections acquired particular relevance in the light of an unexpectedly high Liberal vote in 1959, and some subsequent high Liberal polls in by-elections. The mediocre support for Labour candidates enabled revisionists to claim that the party was failing to profit from disenchantment with the Government, since potential supporters were being discouraged by Labour's sectional associations.

Such prescriptions clearly contraverted several of the party's basic symbols. The whole history of the party's growth and the central links with individual unions and the TUC meant that the loosening of such identification would be extremely difficult. The strength of the revisionist position was that it offered a relatively coherent diagnosis of Labour's electoral problems plus a means of responding to them. As with policy, the revisionist response had the virtue of being positive. Opponents failed to offer anything of equivalent scope. Occasionally a claim was made that the meekness of some Labour leaders had weakened the attachment of working-class voters, and that a more radical policy would rally this support. While such a strategy would probably strengthen the fervour of Labour activists, it seemed unlikely to offer an immediate recipe for Labour revival. It was difficult to produce a persuasive short-term case in a climate characterised by widespread satisfaction with the economy and a belief that class conflict was declining.

The post-mortem raised fundamental questions about Labour strategy with a particular immediacy. It was inevitable, given the parliamentary orientation of all Labour politicians, that the revisionists should offer the persuasive answer to electoral difficulties, but since it implied changes in the party's central characteristics, persuasiveness did not lead automatically to action. Once again the party experienced the tensions implicit in its dual commitment to parliamentarianism and formal socialist ideals.

The Forging of a Compromise

One of the major problems facing the party after October 1959 was what to do about policy. Many believed that the restatement process of the late fifties had been overdone, and had produced confusion. There was a general preference for broad statements rather than further detailed surveys. Policy-making developed almost independently of the crises analysed above, and provided an essential basis on which the warring groups could agree at least not to differ. The key to this compromise was the gradual development on the Executive of an alliance between committed Gaitskellites and reconcilers, giving birth to a policy that was essentially moderate, and yet with just enough ambiguities to serve as a unifying force.[23]

The first stage in this process ended paradoxically at the divisive 1960 Conference, when a document 'Labour in the Sixties' was commended to Conference by the Executive, and produced the most united debate of the week.[24] The document had its origins shortly after the 1959 defeat, when Peter Shore, head of the Research Department, had suggested that a future policy statement should avoid complexities and concentrate on a few basic principles and issues. Its preparation was influenced by the need to produce something that would counteract the growing disunity. Primarily the work of Shore and Morgan Phillips, its major importance lay in its emphasis on the idea of 'scientific revolution' as a justification for planning and public ownership.[25] The Conference debate also included an undertaking by the Executive that it would prepare policy statements on both home and international problems – in the event only the domestic statement was issued. Work on this began at the November 1960 meeting of the Home Policy Committee, with the setting up of a Working Party under Wilson's Chairmanship. This had a politically mixed membership of pro-Gaitskell and reconciling figures.[26] The development of the document went through several vicissitudes. It appears to have begun as a Research Department paper, that placed considerable emphasis on issues then being debated by the New Left, especially the extension of democracy beyond formal political institutions, and questions of culture and the mass media.[27] The deliberations of the Working Party produced in March 1961 a 15,000 word draft that still placed considerable weight on such questions. This was then passed back to the Home Policy Committee and eventually in May came before the full Executive. The document was not accepted, but instead was referred to a group composed of the party's officers. This unusual step, coupled with the fact that the Treasurer, Nicholas, was unavailable, meant that the remaining members of the group were a balance of Gaitskellites and reconcilers, Gaitskell and Brown, Crossman and Wilson. They greatly revised the draft, excising the remainder of the references on cultural and kindred topics. Gaitskell contributed a section on land, Wilson those on planning and taxation, while Crossman dealt with education and welfare. Agreement among these four was reflected on the full

Executive when the document was discussed finally at the end of June. Only Mikardo seems to have raised much opposition over the public ownership section, although more criticism seems to have arisen on the shelving of municipalisation.[28]

This absence of major opposition should not be understood as indicating that the specific items in the document, published as 'Signposts for the Sixties', reflected a balance of the various tendencies within the party. As so often, the introductory rhetoric had a radical tinge. It emphasised the concentration of private economic power, and the deterioration of public services. There were obvious links with Galbraith's 'private affluence/public squalor' antithesis. When the proposed remedies are examined, it is clear that the acceptance of the mixed economy is, if anything, more wholehearted than in the pre-1959 restatement. The principal proposal concerned the application of 'planning' to the economy in order to secure a higher growth rate. The fundamental problem was perceived not as economic control, but the modernisation of the mixed economy:

> If the dead wood were cut out of Britain's boardrooms and replaced by the keen young executives, production engineers and scientists who are at present denied their legitimate prospects of promotion, our production and export problems would be much more manageable.[29]

Given this perspective, it is hardly surprising that proposals for public ownership were restricted and tentative. Apart from steel, the suggestions were not for the public ownership of industries but for state holdings and competitive public enterprises. There were no other firm commitments, although aircraft and pharmaceuticals were mentioned as possible areas for government intervention. This timidity was reflected in other sections of the document. Municipalisation was omitted, although a proposal for a Land Commission to purchase the freehold of building land, was introduced. The section on the public schools moved marginally beyond the non-intervention of 1958; it accepted that some unspecified means of integration would be introduced. The document was fundamentally revisionist in content, although with a few symbolic concessions to the left. It seems probable that the growing control of Gaitskell and his supporters over the document's development was assisted by the increasing awareness that the Scarborough defence decision was bound to be reversed and that Gaitskell's control of the party was guaranteed. Inevitably, the debate on the document at the 1961 Conference produced criticism of the section on public ownership, and of the omission of municipalisation, with almost 2.5 million votes cast for one implicitly critical resolution on public ownership. In spite of this, the 'compromise' succeeded. A revisionist document became the basis of the party's appeal.[30]

The success of the 'compromise' was a testimony to the party's desire for unity and electoral success. It also reflected the bankruptcy of the Labour left. Its theoretical poverty had been evident before 1959; it had acquired a revived prominence because of the unilateralist upsurge, but this did not solve its basic problems and weaknesses. When this cause went under, it collapsed like a house of cards. The reconcilers were now committed to their working arrangement with Gaitskell; spokesmen of the left remained to engage in public speculation that 'Signposts for the Sixties' contained something for them. Beyond the specifically Labour left, the vigorous, yet ill-defined New Left was disillusioned by the events of 1961. The ambiguous, uncertain relationship with the party now had to be clarified – after the acceptance of 'Signposts for the Sixties', the *New Left Review* reflected despairingly on its defeat:

> The things we have been fighting for during the last five years are rejected with scorn, and without comment by the Party leaders, and apparently mean nothing to the bulk of the Party delegates ... The question is – what are we going to do about it? What *can* we do about it?[31]

The devastation of the left appeared more complete because the early sixties witnessed the growth of a strong revisionist organisation, the 'Campaign for Democratic Socialism'. This had two aims, the protection of those with revisionist views in key party positions, and the packaging of revisionist values for mass consumption. From its inception following the Scarborough Conference, CDS attempted to give the impression of a movement active at the party's roots, representing not just a small group of intellectuals, but a wider, less coherent range of moderate opinion. Much of its activity was based on the assumption that party policy-making paid excessive attention to the demands of an unrepresentative left-wing minority, whose influence was attributable largely to assiduous organisation. Accordingly CDS spent much time attempting to mobilise party moderates, and dissuading them from accepting compromise solutions. In this respect they were as committed as the most inflexible members of the left.[32]

Despite its attempts to appear as a movement of ordinary party members, CDS exhibited a concentration of influence in the party's highest echelons. Public support was secured from 45 MPs, while Shadow Cabinet support was proportionately stronger. Brown, Callaghan, Healey and Gordon Walker all had connections with the organisation, but apart from the last named, they did not participate intensively in CDS activities. The major burden was taken by back-benchers and by a number of candidates who came into the PLP during the 1959 Parliament or in 1964. This last group included Taverne, Rodgers, Shirley Williams and Dennis Howell. To some extent, their adoptions in winnable seats can be accredited to CDS organisation aided possibly on some occasions by party officials who seemed less than neutral. In spite of CDS claims to represent the broad mass of party moderates, many, although not all, of their key parliamentarians remained close to the stereotype revisionist — Oxbridge-educated, and with a life style far removed from the typical Labour voter.

Since CDS was concerned not just with the broad propagation of revisionist values, but also with the reversal of the Scarborough decision, the organisation sought influence within the decision-making bodies of the large trade unions. Several union leaders supported CDS, including Carron of the AEU, Hayday and Williamson of the GMW and Watson of the NUM. Despite such impressive backing, it is doubtful whether CDS influence was crucial to the multilateralist victory. More weight should be given to the general disposition towards unity. Similarly, while CDS attempted to organise within local parties, it is difficult to assess its success. One analysis suggests that the number of constituency parties supporting multilateralism in 1961 was actually less than in 1960.[33] Whatever the reality, there can be no doubt that factionalists of all shades saw CDS as significant.

Although it is clear that the policies favoured by CDS in fact dominated 'Signposts for the Sixties', several revisionists remained unhappy about the frequency with which 'traditional' sentiments were employed at party gatherings. Even the compromise over rhetoric struck them as regrettable. The forging of the 'compromise' was carried a major step forward in 1962 when Gaitskell became separated from most of his closest supporters over the issue of British membership of the European Community. The doctrinal significance of this question will be considered later; at this stage all that need be emphasised is that the emergence of the question produced a further unification of Labour ranks. While Labour divisions on this issue cannot be comprehended wholly in terms of traditional cleavages, it is reasonable to claim that most revisionists were in favour of entry as a relevant and 'progressive' step. Gaitskell, in contrast, moved to a position, if not of total opposition, at least of dramatically emphasising the difficulties. His speech at the 1962 Conference evoked applause from his former opponents, and regrets from his supporters. In this, he united the party, not as an act of calculation but as a result of his own nationalism, an emotion shared by the bulk of the party. Ironically, the great confrontationist's last major political statement was one that blurred factional divisions.[34]

By the end of 1962, although the Labour Party was broadly united behind a revisionist programme, there remained one major problem, the relationship between a future Labour Government and the trade unions. The 1958 document on economic policy had contained a vague reference to union co-operation on wages. This assumed an expanding economy presided over by a Labour Government pursuing socially just policies. With the deterioration of the economy after 1959 the question of wage restraint soon became of immediate importance. By 1961, the earlier optimism had given way to a 'pay pause'. A less rigorous emphasis on restraint continued in government policy after the severe conditions of 1961 had eased. The question of governmental control of incomes had become more prominent than at any time since the Cripps wage freeze.

Economic difficulties also involved the Macmillan Government in a flight to planning that would influence the contours of economic policy for the next decade. Particular emphasis was placed on the National Economic Development Council, a body intended to act as a forum for government, unions and industrialists to debate their views, about the prospects for, and obstacles to, higher rates of growth. The General Council's decision to participate in the NEDC was approved by the 1962 TUC.[35] This was an occasion for argument between integrationists and those wishing to have no connection with institutions created by a Conservative Government. By then, however, the TUC's position owed much to the views of its General Secretary, George Woodcock, especially to his belief that trade union influence should be expanded within the administrative machine. The outstanding question of trade union attitudes to wage restraint was discussed in 1963, at both the Party Conference and the TUC.[36] In the unity-dominated atmosphere of the party, agreement was readily secured on a long resolution advocating an expanding planned economy with 'an incomes policy to include salaries, wages, dividends and profits'. Such an aspiration left open the questions of a Labour Government's policy on wages in a stagnant economy, and more basically whether profits and dividends were controllable in the type of mixed economy accepted by the party. The same unity had not been so evident at the TUC, where a motion was carried by 380,000 votes declaring 'complete opposition to any form of wages restraint'. Hence the compromise with the unions was only skin-deep. Reluctance to abandon the traditional goals of trade unionism under a Labour Government remained a powerful emotion.

The development of this spirit of unity through the phases of policy formulation, the Common Market debate and the imprecision over income policy was aided by growing optimism about electoral prospects. After a poor by-election record in 1960, the party began to recover the following year and from June 1962 started to gain seats. At first this process was attributable to the way in which a revived Liberal Party was eating into the 1959 Conservative vote, but eventually the Labour advance began to assume a more positive form. With such rising expectations, who could spend time debating the precise nature of the commitments in 'Signposts for the Sixties' or enquiring into the substance of the idea of an incomes policy?

The Arrival of Wilson

Gaitskell's unexpected death in January 1963 produced no important change in the content of Labour's 'compromise'. The contest for the leadership saw two pretenders to the mantle of Gaitskell, Brown and Callaghan, opposed by Wilson, the reconciling pragmatist. After an inconclusive first ballot with Wilson in first place, Callaghan dropped out and Wilson defeated Brown by 144 votes to 103.

Wilson had always belonged in substantive terms to the moderate wing of the party.[37] He was a devotee of Keynesian techniques, and optimistic about the neutrality of existing political and administrative institutions. Such a perspective had been very evident in his work at the Board of Trade under Attlee, and was borne out by most of his later speeches on economic problems. During the early sixties it became embodied in his favourite themes of planning, modernisation and the harnessing of scientific developments to productive purposes. These features were related closely to the growing Labour emphasis on socialist techniques as the means of managing technological change.

His presentation of socialism was vague. Whereas Gaitskell had attempted to redefine the party's socialist goals in detail, Wilson equated socialism with 'applying a sense of purpose to our national life — economic purpose, social purpose and moral purpose. Purpose means technical skill.'[38] He disavowed, more openly than many

Labour leaders, what he saw as the anachronistic irrelevancies of
Marxism. He offered instead a more efficient and meritocratic variant
of existing society. This dismissal was linked with an almost Webbian
emphasis on national efficiency that placed him firmly within the
Fabian tradition.

Although the efficiency element loomed particularly large, ethical
justifications were not forgotten. His values were moulded to a large
degree by that protestant nonconformity that has always been
prominent in the attitudes of British Labour.[39] In some ways its
rhetoric contrasted with the advocacy of a more efficient society, but
in one crucial respect there was an identical implication, a tendency to
see class conflicts as deviant and as soluble, given good intentions. Both
the efficiency and nonconformist perspectives secreted a preference for
consensual politics.

Wilson's quintessential moderation did not prevent many within the
party from seeing his quest for the leadership as a posthumous challenge
to Gaitskell. Most obviously this judgement was based on his old
association with Bevan, although his intimacy with the left had been
short-lived. It was his perception of the leader's role as reconciliatory
that had led him to challenge Gaitskell in 1960. He saw the leader's
task as the preservation of the heterogeneous coalition that was the
Labour Party by the avoidance of unnecessary divisions over 'theology'
Furthermore, there existed a stylistic rift between Wilson and the
revisionists, attributable in part to his self-conscious provincialism, his
readiness to elevate the views of grass-roots opinion above the polished
judgements of urbane metropolitan commentators. He preferred
Huddersfield Town to Belgravia.

The twenty months following Wilson's election as leader were
dominated by expectations of an election. He pursued the revisionist
goal of a broad left-of-centre coalition. By 1963, there had been some
reform of party organisation to allow a more efficient pursuit of this
strategy, involving the formation of a Campaign Committee envisaged
as a central co-ordinator. A more significant development saw the
acceptance by the party, in some individual cases unwillingly, of
marketing techniques similar to those that had distinguished the
Conservative's 1959 campaign. In Labour's case, this involved an
attempt to identify a relatively broad band of target voters and the
subsequent tailoring of policy proposals to their apparent needs.[40] Thus
propaganda on public ownership was tied to the themes of regional
improvement and scientific development, while more broadly, socialism
was portrayed as the means of humanising the scientific revolution. The

proposal for the nationalisation of development land was kept vague, and connected to the need for more houses. Wilson seems to have viewed the crucial voters as the liberally-inclined and socially mobile who had tended perhaps to vote Labour in 1945, but whose support had subsequently been lost. His identification with efficiency and meritocracy placed him in a strong position to bid for their votes, contrasting the supposed aristocratic amateurism of the Macmillan and Home Governments with Labour's meritocratic readiness to reward ability. This domination by the 'equality of opportunity' motif meant that references to fellowship and other moral collectivist virtues had a declining place.

Wilson's style received its most complete exposure at the 1963 Scarborough Conference, a veritable pageant of unity,[41] staged with the particular help of the Labour left. They were ready to see him as, if not one of their own, then at least much better than any feasible alternative.[42] This apparent unity and certainty over policy was to be a misleading prelude to the experiences of Labour in office. Apart from the lack of clarity over incomes policy, there were other portents of future difficulties. One stemmed from Labour's adherence to the modernisation theme — in his Scarborough speech, Wilson asserted that 'there is no room for Luddites in the Socialist Party.'[43] The implications of this for the trade unions were to become stark as the Wilson Government's attempts to modernise and rationalise industry came up against what it viewed as less than wholehearted co-operation from the unions.

Such problems were only dimly perceived in the protracted prelude to the 1964 election. Labour's manifesto generally followed the pattern laid down in 'Signposts for the Sixties'. The party remained united and optimistic, although the narrowness of the eventual victory had been foreshadowed by an apparent loss of impetus during parts of the campaign. Eventually the large Conservative majority of 1959 was found to have just disappeared: Labour 317, Conservative 303 and Liberals 9. It was much more a Conservative defeat than a Labour victory. While the Conservative share of the poll fell by 6 per cent, Labour's proportion rose by only 0.3 per cent and the actual Labour vote was 11,000 fewer than in the disaster year of 1959. In contrast, on a turnout down by 1.6 per cent the Liberal vote had risen sharply from 5.9 to 11.2 per cent of the total. Labour's hold on office looked extremely tentative.[44]

The significance of this result for the party can be assessed only when an attempt is made to penetrate below the theatre of the immediate campaign. One feature which repeated a characteristic of the 1959 result concerned the marked variations in the pro-Labour swing in different regions. Generally it was higher in urban areas, but within this category there were striking contrasts. At one extreme, Merseyside constituencies averaged 8.5 per cent swing against the Government while above average shifts could be found also in most other parts of the north-west, much of London, and around Glasgow. In contrast the Black Country moved slightly to the Conservatives if anything, even if the individualistic Smethwick result is ignored. While some commentators suggested that some strong pro-Labour movements could be attributable to the attraction of specific Labour proposals, especially on housing and land, such variations can perhaps be analysed more fully in a longer-term perspective.

This can be approached through a comparison of Labour's 1964 position with the almost identical aggregate result of February 1950. Across the whole country, Labour was marginally worse off in 1964 (1.1 per cent), but this superficial macro-comparison hides the very different developments in various regions. Labour had gained ground in Inner London (0.7 per cent), Lancashire (2.7 per cent) and Scotland (4.1 per cent), but had lost relatively heavily in the Midlands (4.2 per cent). More specifically Labour was worse off by over 6 per cent in Birmingham, Leicester, Bradford and Stoke-on-Trent, but stronger in Glasgow (7.7 per cent), and Liverpool (4.8 per cent). Even allowing for intervening boundary changes it is clear that in 1964, Labour captured areas of these two cities where it had failed in 1945. To some degree demographic changes can explain these advances. For example, in the unexpected 1964 gain of Glasgow Pollok, former middle-class exclusiveness had been invaded by municipal estates. While such changes should not be ignored, they were obviously not restricted to cities showing a secular trend to Labour. Possibly the long-term growth of Labour strength in Liverpool and Glasgow is explicable partly through the erosion of traditional religious differences that weakened the Conservative hold on some socially mixed or even largely working-class seats.

The equally deviant behaviour of many West Midlands seats is comprehensible to some extent in economic terms. The region had enjoyed an above-average prosperity even in the comparatively difficult economic climate of the early sixties. Once again it is important to emphasise regional factors. In Birmingham at least, manual workers had shown a traditional reluctance to support Labour candidates, while the immigration issue was probably more salient there than anywhere else.[45] Labour attempted to present a contemporary image, but its narrow success rested on the peculiar impact of regional differences, plus some revulsion against governmental incompetence. In spite of the Conservatives' recent upheavals, Labour had just secured office; it was not yet the natural governing party.

The Opposition Years — A Retrospective Comment

The opposition years were years of alternating crises and surface unity in which contending factions shifted between bitter feuding and the temporary subordination of differences to electoral considerations. Although several contested issues could appear trivial to the observer, they symbolised in their own distorted way the party's strategic dilemma.

Labour's traditional perspective was under strain by 1951. Its measures had produced benefits, but had never looked like effecting a radical transformation of society. The choice then was to relinquish the transformation goal or to rethink the basic strategy. The three previous chapters have shown how the first alternative, revisionism, developed and eventually dominated party policy, if not all party rhetoric. Such a response was natural and persuasive, as it accepted wholeheartedly Labour's parliamentarianism, and produced a coherent critique of the society that had developed since 1940. It was a modern adaptation of the major pro-system consensual strand in the party tradition.

Whatever its deficiencies, revisionism had little positive challenge within the party. There were those who accepted it in their practice or with their intellects, but who dissented on grounds of party management from too overt a pronouncement. No real challenge came from the Labour left except a defence of traditional values. The fundamental reason for this sterility was not that Labour left parliamentarians failed to perceive any problem. Rather they were imprisoned by their acceptance of the same basic strategy. They too adhered to the politics of electoral considerations, and to the belief in the neutrality of existing institutions that were central features of revisionism. In an era of comparative economic prosperity, the Labour left was characterised by emotionalism, compromises and opportunism. This failure was matched by the growth of the extra-parliamentary New Left, ready to consider alternative strategies, although uncertain on their practical details. Practical weaknesses apart, however, the growth of this movement meant that the revisionist-dominated party had lost contact with recent developments in socialist thought.

Labour, by 1964, had accepted the mixed economy as permanent, and under Wilson's leadership, it presented itself more sharply than ever as the agent of modernisation and the advocate of meritocracy. Even its central emphasis on planning had ceased to be distinctive, after the Macmillan Government's interventionist response to the deterioration of the economy. Labour's traditional emphasis on welfare had become subordinate to the pursuit of efficiency, while the socialist commitment was rarely mentioned. This optimism about the mixed economy and the elevation of successful management to the centre of Labour's commitment did not prevent many within the New Left from backing the party in 1964. Labour, the political vehicle of the organised working class, still dominated any strategic discussion, whatever the implication of its policies. Such naivety seems bizarre in retrospect, and yet it contains an important truth. The commitment to modernisation and efficiency was dominant but not total. The place of the unions within the party structure meant that Labour's acceptance of the ground rules of the mixed economy was subject to one vital constraint. If the rules were followed in a situation of stagnation rather than expansion, then tensions between political leaders and union leaders would be inevitable in the final analysis.

There was no substantive reason to believe that Labour in 1964 had any intention of challenging the existing distribution of power. The maxim was 'Business as Usual – only more Efficient.' Compared with 1945, its programme was a flimsy blend of optimism, rhetoric and sparse proposals. The party evoked the image of 'Thirteen Wasted Years' – it might have applied this a little nearer home.

Notes

1. This is dealt with in the unpublished sections of the *Dalton Diaries,* October 1959.
2. *LPCR 1959,* pp. 105-14. This contrasts with the speeches of Castle, ibid., pp. 83-6 and Bevan pp. 151-5.
3. Ibid., p. 109.
4. *NEC Minutes,* 16 March 1960.
5. See *NEC Minutes,* 13 July 1960, and Morgan Phillips' prior suggestion that it would be wise to drop the proposed change.
6. *NEC Minutes,* 25 May and 22 June 1960 for discussions on the defence document.
7. *LPCR 1960,* p. 201.
8. The majorities were 407,000 and 43,000 for the unilateralist resolutions, 297,000 against the NEC statement and 332,000 against a multilateralist resolution.
9. See *LPCR 1954,* p. 108 – 'If the Executive motion were lost today, we would be in a chaotic situation in the House of Commons' (Morrison).

10. See *LPCR 1960*, pp. 159-68, and *NEC Minutes*, 2 October 1960. The defeat was by eleven votes to twelve.
11. *LPCR 1960*, p. 201.
12. By twenty votes to four. See *NEC Minutes*, 23 November 1960.
13. See Paul Foot, op. cit., pp. 126-32.
14. See *NEC Minutes*, 21 December 1960, 25 January 1961, also *Minutes of Joint Meeting of NEC, Parliamentary Committee and General Council*, 24 January 1961.
15. *NEC Minutes*, 22 February 1961.
16. For details see Parkin, op. cit., pp. 127-32.
17. See *LPCR 1961*, pp. 162-94. The defeats were on Polaris bases, and the training of German troops in Wales. On the anatomy of voting at the two conferences, see also K. Hindle and P. Williams, 'Scarborough and Blackpool: An Analysis of Some Votes at the Labour Party Conferences of 1960 and 1961', *Political Quarterly*, July—September 1962.
18. See for example, Mark Abrams and Richard Rose, *Must Labour Lose?* (Penguin, Harmondsworth, 1960).
19. See J. Goldthorpe *et al., The Affluent Worker. Political Attitudes and Behaviour* (University Press, Cambridge, 1968). Also Brian Jackson and Dennis Marsden, *Education and The Working Class* (Routledge, London, 1962).
20. For example see Gaitskell's post-mortem at the 1959 Conference, *LPCR 1959*, pp. 107-8. See also Morgan Phillips' *Report* on the election, submitted to the NEC, 28 October 1959.
21. Ibid., p. 122.
22. R.H.S. Crossman, 'The Affluent Society 1959', reprinted in his *Planning for Freedom* (Hamish Hamilton, London, 1964), p. 91.
23. See the Memorandum *R.D. 18* presented to the Home Policy Sub-Committee, January 1960.
24. See the document 'Labour In The Sixties' — and the debate, *LPCR 1960*, pp. 133-52.
25. For the background, see Phillips' *Memorandum Sec. No. 104* discussed at the NEC, 13 July 1960 — and the amended version, *Sec. No. 109*, presented to the NEC on 27 July 1960.
26. *Home Policy Committee Minutes*, 7 November and 5 December 1960.
27. See *R.D.96*, 'Outline For Policy Statement'.
28. On this see especially Anthony Howard, 'A Documentary Story', *New Statesman*, 30 June 1961. Also *LPCR 1961*, p. 30.
29. 'Signposts For The Sixties', p. 10.
30. See *LPCR 1961*, pp. 101-21 and 125-56.
31. 'Missing Signposts', *New Left Review 12*, November—December 1961, p. 10. See also W. Norman, 'Signposts For The Sixties', ibid., 11, September—October 1961, pp. 45-9.
32. See Lord Windlesham, *Communication and Political Power* (Cape, London, 1966), chs. 4 and 5. Also the CDS newsheet *Campaign* and Dick Taverne, *The Future of the Left* (Cape, London, 1974), chs. 1 and 2.
33. See Hindell and Williams, op. cit.
34. See *LPCR 1962*, pp. 154-94 (debate) — and pp. 245-51 (policy statement).
35. See *TUC Report 1962*, pp. 381-91.
36. *LPCR 1963*, pp. 189-201 — and *TUC Report 1963*.
37. See Paul Foot, op. cit. — and for an evocation of the optimism of the early Wilson period, Anthony Howard and Richard West, *The Making of The Prime Minister* (Cape, London, 1965).
38. Speech at Birmingham Town Hall, 19 January 1964, in his *The New Britain* (Penguin, Harmondsworth, 1964).

39. See his interview with Brian Blake in Richard Rose (ed.), *Studies In British Politics* (Macmillan, London, 1966).
40. David Butler and Anthony King, *The British General Election of 1964* (Macmillan, London 1965) and Richard Rose, *Influencing Voters* (Faber, London, 1967).
41. For Scarborough, see particularly his 'scientific revolution' speech, *LPCR 1963*, pp. 133-40.
42. The almost uncritical support of the left is captured in Michael Foot, *Harold Wilson: A Pictorial Biography* (Pergamon, Oxford, 1964). But optimism was not restricted to the Labour left; see Perry Anderson, 'Critique of Wilsonism', *New Left Review*, 27, September–October 1964.
43. *LPCR 1963*, p. 134.
44. Butler and King, op. cit.
45. Nicholas Deakin (ed.), *Colour and The British Election of 1964* (Pall Mall Press, London, 1965).

9 '... THE SECOND TIME AS FARCE' — LABOUR IN OFFICE 1964-1970

The 1964 Labour Government presided over a nation whose difficulties were obvious. The Indian Summer of the fifties had been succeeded by widespread pessimism. The economy was in a state of continuing crisis, with low investment and declining international competitiveness. The Labour Party's attempt to mobilise support on the basis of vague discontent with national decline had left open the question of a Labour Government's response to the crisis. There was no clear response, let alone any remedy that had a socialist pedigree. The Government began with a vague optimism unsupported by a clear substantive programme. There could be no sharper contrast with 1945. The contrast continued through the next six years. The earlier experience had been the heroic — and sometimes agonised — climacteric of British social democracy. The later experience witnessed its decline into mere rhetoric, worldly pragmatism and an open worship of the most traditional symbols of British society. Despite its problems, the Attlee Government had maintained some sense of identity with its working-class base and a feeling that great changes were being enacted. After 1964 there were no equivalents. British social democracy did not provide a second instalment.

The Impotence of the Party

One of the most striking contrasts between the 1945 and the 1964 administrations concerns the relationship between the party and the Government. Under Attlee a close relationship had been maintained, with party institutions employed as apologists and mobilisers. In contrast, difficulties mounted after 1964 as party bodies began to criticise the Government. Such differences became acute after the 1966 election. The Government's flouting of many party principles provoked hostile reactions in the Conference, in the National Executive and in the Parliamentary Party.

The reliability of the Conference was affected significantly by changes in union attitudes. The ultra-loyalty that had characterised the Deakin-Lawther axis was absent. Hugh Scanlon's election in 1967 as President of the Engineers, and successor to Carron, epitomised the emergence of a new kind of union leader, prepared to work with a Labour Government, but opposed vehemently to policies that appeared to strike at union power. Together with Jack Jones, the successor to Cousins at the T & GW, he provided the spearhead of union opposition to several government policies. This development was backed by significant shifts in the affiliated memberships of individual unions. These reflected a changing industrial structure and also some union amalgamations. The decline of traditional industries meant that the combined affiliated membership of the Railwaymen, the Miners and the Textile Workers fell by more than half a million between 1955 and 1970.[1] In contrast the Transport Workers and the Engineers expanded,[2] while even more dramatically the left-orientated Supervisory Staffs vote rose from 2,000 in 1956 to 66,000 in 1970. Such developments did not just assist the critics. The strongly pro-Government Electricians also grew significantly.

The changing balance plus the emergence of sensitive issues produced twelve Conference defeats for the Executive and by implication for the Government (see Table 1). This record contrasted with the docility of Conference under the Attlee Government. These defeats covered many key government policies, but they did not influence subsequent ministerial decisions.

Table 1: Twelve Conference Defeats

Year	Issue	Majority
1966	Unemployment	152,000
	East of Suez	538,000
	Vietnam	1,207,000
1967	Greece	269,000
	Vietnam	119,000
	Acceptance of principle of Prices and Incomes policy, but opposition to execution	196,000
1968	Prices and Incomes	3,974,000
	Reference back on Pit Closures	1,071,000
	Immediate withdrawal of prescription charges	Show of Hands
	End of Wages Stop	Show of Hands
	Amendment to resolution backing Labour Government involving deletion of clause 'subject to the reservations involved in the policy decisions of the TUC'	565,000
1969	Economic policy	1,153,000

Conference was not dominated, of course, by the Government's critics. Leading Ministers registered their oratorical triumphs, and diminished temporarily the tide of dissatisfaction. Wilson's annual set speech was an exercise in the instant mobilisation of the rank and file, through which a fleeting sense of unity and *élan* could be rediscovered. While there were occasional attacks on 'dinosaur thinking in our own party ... the attitudes of the Social Democratic Federation',[3] the principal emphasis was on Labour as the party of change, responsibility and patriotism ('This is a proud country ... which has no time for those who knock Britain when we are up against it.') – and on the need to unite in the face of Conservative criticism. Other major figures had their Conference triumphs, especially Callaghan with his eleventh-hour defence of pre-devaluation economic policy in 1967.[4]

The problem of securing compliance with Conference decisions remained. Formally, the task lay with the Executive, but from October 1964 the NEC usually acted as a mobilising agent for policies determined elsewhere. Fourteen ministers served on the Executive during the Government's lifetime, and this firm nucleus in favour of government policies was bolstered by the loyal support of most trade union section members. The repeated re-election of Ministers to the constituency section showed that doubts about policies did not lead automatically to the rejection of the Ministers responsible, although the few changes did strengthen the critics. Similarly, it might have been thought that the radicalisation of some trade union leaderships would be reflected in the trade union section. But, although one consistent supporter of left-wing causes, Alex Kitson of the Scottish Commercial Motormen, entered the section in 1968, the election of trade union nominees still had a largely non-ideological character.

The exceptions to the general harmony came largely in the most sensitive policy areas. The Executive developed a distinct position on prices and incomes, prescription charges, Greece and above all, on trade union reform. From 1968, emphasis was placed on the holding of joint meetings between Executive members and appropriate Ministers to discuss points of difference.[5] Once again the development of pressure through the Executive produced no substantive changes in government policies. Even when the Executive recorded critical votes, these were normally no more than a passing embarrassment for the Government, but the mere fact of divergent opinions indicated a lack of the solidarity that had characterised the party after 1945. Perhaps the most serious rift came in March 1969 when the Executive passed a critical resolution on trade union reform by sixteen votes to five.[6]

The Government could rely normally on the loyalty of the PLP. Apart from the singular case of 'In Place of Strife', with its threat to the party-union link, the parliamentary critics were normally identifiable with the Tribune Group. In some ways this was a direct descendant of the old Bevanite faction. Some of the older members, such as Foot and Mikardo, had participated in most revolts since 1945. The left-wing entrants of 1964 introduced a rather different note. Several did not conform to the stereotyped image of the white-collar intellectual critic, but came from shop-floor trade unionism. Their criticisms of government economic policy were based frequently on their own industrial experience. The Tribune Group maintained more coherence than its predecessors in the 1945 Parliament. Obviously this was aided by the principal diet of controversy with the repeated clashes over economic policy. Instead of being confronted with the sterile alternatives of Cold War politics, they faced a Government that was clearly departing from many traditional values, and in much of their opposition they enjoyed the support of a significant section of trade union opinion.

Parliamentary critics who were normally in a minority could make little impact; extra-parliamentary critics who lacked significant resources faced the same problem. But there was a more debilitating factor. However deep the gulf between Ministers and critics, they remained members of the same party. Since Ministers made policy, this limited the range of critics' objections and strategies. In the end they had to retain some confidence in the good faith of their leaders.[7]

Wilson's Leadership

The fact that it was Wilson who led the party during this period in office is important, not because he determined the direction of party development, but because he acted as its most widely perceived representative. He was the prism through which assessments of the party were filtered. The central feature of his strategy was to transform the party into the natural party of government. Throughout his Premiership, he attempted to mobilise support on the basis of national symbolism, especially through his propensity to indulge in economic chauvinism. In speaking of Labour's programme for Britain's industrial regeneration to the Economic Club of New York, he asserted: 'Given the response of which our people are capable, be under no illusions, we shall be ready to knock hell out of you.'[8] References to the 'Dunkirk Spirit', to the need to unite in the building of a 'new Britain', combined in an attempt to achieve what had been a goal of his predecessor, the termination of a widespread identification of the party with a particular class, and its replacement by an identification with the interests of the nation as a whole.[9]

This commitment obviously produced problems of party management. It was another episode in the long-standing battle of Labour leaders against the 'sectionalism' of many of their followers. Wilson's conduct of this battle was ambiguous. During the Gaitskell period he had appeared as the exponent of the art of compromise at all costs. The necessary policy changes could be made without arousing primeval passions. Such a strategy was followed to a limited degree in the years in office. There were occasional sops to the left, such as Harold Davies's Vietnam mission, but this was not his dominant strategy. On issues such as deflation and most significantly of all trade union reform, his relationship with critics was not one of compromise and cultivated obscurity, but of confrontation, a sometimes brutal recital of the facts of life.

In considering his success as a party manager it is necessary to draw a distinction between the party rank and file and his immediate colleagues. His popularity with the first group remained high – his Conference speeches became annual acts of reassurance that the Government had not departed from its principles. They blended together a welter of statistics, examples of the wonders of technology, nationalism and moralising idealism. And the audiences loved every minute of it. Yearly, there were Press predictions that Wilson would have a more difficult Conference, and each time they were falsified. His hold over the mass of organised Labour was unbroken, although it could be argued that by the later years of the Government, most of those whose principles had been affronted had withdrawn from active party work. Thus the rapturous receptions were not just testimonies to Wilsonian skill and rank and file deference, but also to the exit of the disillusioned.

This control was certainly not reflected at the highest level. Unlike the Attlee Government, the Wilson administration was notable for its recurrent open quarrels. Although the 1945 Government's apparent unity of purpose had concealed personal and doctrinal differences, the Wilson years were punctuated by a series of resignations often characterised by personal acrimony. Cousins, Herbison, Brown, Gunter – all indicated in their own ways, flaws in the Government's performance. Especially in the last two cases, it is clear that personal tensions between Wilson and the Minister concerned were significant.

In no case did a resignation lead to the development of a vociferous opposition group within the party. Cousins was soon to rid himself of his parliamentary shackles, Herbison was temperamentally a loyalist, Brown and Gunter could hardly hope to appeal to the most critical groups on the party's left. Indeed it was the left who were ready to mobilise behind Wilson, to protect him from the presumed machinations of the unrepentant Gaitskellites.[10] During his Government's career, it is ironic that Wilson, the self-confessed enemy of 'theology', profited from the support of the party's traditional theologians who thought not so much of his pragmatic present, but more of his Bevanite past. Wilson is credited with the remark that 'A week is a long time in politics': some of his supporters showed that for them fifteen years was no time at all.

The continuing abrasiveness of the highest level of the party reflected the essential isolation of Wilson — 'The Cat that Walks Alone'. The acrimonies of the Bevanite years lived on. In office Wilson paid for his earlier independent strategy; his earlier isolation from any faction now meant that he lacked a dependable basis of support. The result was a tendency to surround himself with advisers who acted as a necessary reassurance, but also as an insulator against disturbances from outside. Also it seems that he kept in office, sometimes for long periods, those whom he found congenial and reliable. This picture of an isolated, dependent, rather unsure leader contrasts with Attlee, the seemingly mild product of Haileybury, the impeccable bourgeois who was a ruthless butcher of incompetent colleagues and an isolate whose independence seemed to be based on an inner certitude. Wilson, however much he might talk of Yorkshire forthrightness, found the sacking of Ministers extremely difficult, and his isolation bred insecurity and suspicion of conspiracies.

Wilson's insecurity and his continuing hold upon the diminishing party rank and file can be understood to a large degree by seeing him, as he saw himself, as an outsider. This did not mean that he was in any way an iconoclastic scrutiniser of existing institutions or practices. It was rather that he continued to behave as if he were 'king for a day', as if the trappings of office were not really meant for people like him. Perhaps this reflects one of the basic appeals of the Labour Party — not the changing of society, but a mechanism whereby, albeit briefly, 'we' can inhabit 'their' world and exercise 'their' power. Yet it was almost as if the miracle of the take-over was in itself sufficient, that the mission of Labour was to expel those who exercised power by family tradition, and to replace them with 'our people'. Under Wilson, the party became, as it never had been before, the party of meritocrats, an association whose competitive overtones carried basic implications for the traditional values of co-operation and equality. It is likely that the outsider image, whatever its political moderation, deepened the tensions at the top of the Government, since some of the Prime Minister's most crucial colleagues were clearly not outsiders. There was a world of difference between the polished dry urbanity of Jenkins and the self-conscious provinciality of Wilson, who had conquered the metropolitan citadel and remained unsure of his ability to hold it. There was a world of difference also between Wilson and those Labour back-benchers who shared the Gaitskellite inheritance; the old guard of CDS and their younger supporters. Once again their differences with Wilson were not substantively political, so much as stylistic and temperamental. They were, or aspired to be, insiders, not outsiders temporarily on the inside.

It is peculiar that parallels between Wilson and Lloyd George should have been suggested, when a more apt one is surely with Lloyd George's enemy and destroyer, Stanley Baldwin. Both Baldwin and Wilson attempted as they saw it to re-educate their parties; both had a better relationship with their rank and file than with their immediate colleagues; both in their own ways appear as isolated rather unsure men: both blended periods of stagnation with dazzling passages of tactical virtuosity. It would be reasonable to label Wilson, as Churchill labelled Baldwin, 'a consummate politician' — yet the limits of this strength were in both cases narrow. There was little original vision. They were both conventional men, doing a rather unimaginative best in perplexing situations, suspicious of doctrine, concerned to capture the solid worthy centre of British politics. Baldwin succeeded in confirming his party's position as the national party: Wilson attempted to emulate the success of Baldwin, and failed. Perhaps the most outstanding feature of Wilson's Premiership was this failure. As with MacDonald and Gaitskell, the residue of traditional radical sentiments proved too powerful. This failure demonstrated once again the central dilemma of Labour leadership.

The Victory of Orthodoxy: Labour in Economic Crisis

The initial economic strategy of the Wilson Government was based on a crucial assumption about the compatability of two principles. The mixed economy could be operated efficiently by a Labour Government, and this efficient operation would permit the provision of substantial benefits for Labour's supporters. But what if the search for profitability necessitated the withholding of such benefits? This was the crucial dilemma posed by the experience of the sixties. It had already been implicit in the economic difficulties faced by the Attlee Government, but now the problem of trying to satisfy working-class demands while remaining committed to the discipline of the mixed economy emerged starkly.[11]

In 1964 Labour showed little evidence of any coherent economic strategy. Conservative Chancellors were condemned for their addiction to 'stop-go'; the Labour alternative involved 'planning' for growth based on increased investment and rising productivity. This was held to be compatible with the maintenance of the existing exchange rate. The 'planning' motif also appeared in a second aspect of economic policy, a radical modernisation of industry. This was to be based on government intervention in specific industries, but precise proposals on public ownership remained limited to steel. The drive for growth based on a modernised economy was seen as a prerequisite for any expansion of welfare provisions.

There was, of course, no suggestion of any fundamental change in the structure of the economy. The expectation of a constructive partnership between government and industry left any public ownership measures as aids to modernisation, not as invasions of existing power structures. The emphasis on 'planning' was supposed to indicate a divergence between the parties. Labour's allegedly coherent strategy was supposed to contrast with Conservative nostalgia for *laissez-faire*. This studiously ignored the Macmillan Government's adoption of indicative planning. While Labour spokesmen basked in their advocacy of planning, Conservatives reiterated the rhetoric of free enterprise. But in reality the difference was small. Another possible point of difference was supposed to be Labour's advocacy of 'equality', but this barely showed in Labour's programme. There were references to more equitable educational, taxation and welfare systems, but these were largely dependent on the drive for efficiency.

The most striking feature of the perspective was its blind optimism. This preoccupation with economic efficiency had left Labour Ministers ill-prepared to deal with a situation dominated by a deteriorating balance of payments. When faced with this, they elevated the defence of the exchange rate to the first priority and relinquished the commitment to growth. This inevitably led to attacks on Labour's social proposals. In the first eighteen months, the drift to orthodoxy was disguised and limited. It was restricted to a temporary import surcharge, some restrictions on credit and public expenditure and the first dents in the voluntary incomes policy. In March 1966 these permitted a successful electoral appeal. But Nemesis was at hand. The seamen's strike and speculation against the pound were the prelude to a savage deflation in July 1966: public expenditure cuts, a wage freeze and tax increases.[12] Inevitably there was a significant rise in unemployment, but devaluation was postponed for only sixteen months. This final collapse of the Government's policy necessitated further deflation in the quest for a trade surplus at the new parity. The measures involved slashing cuts in social expenditure including, most painfully for party activists, the reimposition of prescription charges. Budgetary policy showed little regard for party orthodoxy. Reduced spending was sought not by increasing direct taxation, but through indirect tax increases. Labour's egalitarian sentiments received a marginal acknowledgement through a special once-and-for-all charge on investment income. By the end of 1969, the Government had achieved its surplus at the expense of deep party divisions and unprecedented electoral disenchantment.

This surrender to orthodox pressures virtually destroyed the commitment to growth. This was symbolised by the destruction of the much-publicised National Plan, the child of George Brown's Department of Economic Affairs. Subsequent verdicts on the Plan have tended to be coloured by the fact of its early abandonment and the inability of a new government department to defend it.[13] Yet beyond the unfortunate circumstances of its conception and stillbirth there was a basic problem. The Plan was no more than a permissive incantation, without instruments of implementation. One somewhat disillusioned participant in the exercise has reflected that 'this was not a weakness of planning as such. It was a lack of political will.'[14] The implication that all would have been well if the task had been approached with greater tenacity fails to pay proper attention to the earlier history of Labour planning. The record after 1945 suggests a deep-seated inhibition against getting involved with far-flung sections of the economy and against the use of compulsion. Typically, the National Plan was founded on targets drawn up by the industries themselves. 'Planning by consent' could hardly be carried any further.

This tender regard for industrialists' interests was reflected elsewhere. Public ownership measures were insignificant. Apart from steel, all that emerged was a Bill to nationalise the docks. Its passage was terminated by the 1970 dissolution. The image of the episodic socialisation of the economy that had marked Labour debates on public ownership after 1945 was now wholly absent. Elsewhere, the Government employed public funds to rationalise key areas of the economy. From January 1966, the Industrial Reorganisation Corporation was charged with the promotion of efficiency and profitability by sponsoring appropriate mergers.[15] The methods were persuasion backed by funds, or in some cases direct intervention. As in similar ventures after 1945, the agency was staffed largely by leading industrialists. The Government also aided ailing private firms; it assisted in the construction of aluminium smelters; it attempted to prevent the decline of shipbuilding; it promoted a merger in the computer industry and assisted innovations in machine tools. While such expenditures and interventions were presented to Labour audiences as examples of 'socialism in action', they were nothing of the sort; that is unless 'socialism' is so stripped of meaning that it signifies no more than the bolstering of a private economy by public funds, and token attempts to inspire marginal gestures by firms in the direction of a governmentally defined national interest.

If government-industry relationships were devoid of socialist content, there was no compensating pursuit of Labour's notional commitment to 'equality'. While apologists and critics have wrangled over whether the Government affected a more equitable distribution of income,[16] it is clear that any improvement was at best highly marginal, and attributable to the unintended rather than the intended consequences of government policies. It is obvious that the Government never began an attack on economic inequalities and indeed its whole strategy made such a move dependent on increased economic efficiency.

Overall, the Government's economic record was one of failure, even measured against the vague optimism of 1964. When compared against any expectation of a socialist economic policy, the record is at best irrelevant and at worst a disaster. Why did it happen? Many explanations emphasised contingent factors. If these had not been present, then much more would have been achieved. Several such explanations turn around the postponement of devaluation: 'The fact that we did not devalue for three years, and then, having tried for three years not to devalue, that we were forced to, is probably the single most damaging fact about the Government.'[17] Although many economic commentators have seen this as the key factor, others have suggested that an earlier devaluation would still have necessitated a heavy deflation in order to protect competitiveness against rising real wages.[18] It remains a political question as to why the existing parity was defended so resolutely. The initial decision was apparently based partly on fears that Labour would be labelled as the 'devaluation party' and partly on American pressures.[19] The defence of the parity also seems to have acquired a symbolic significance for Wilson and Callaghan as indicative of their strength of purpose. If the rationale behind the 1964 decision at least possessed some tactical plausibility, this is not true of the subsequent refusal to reconsider. Part of the explanation no doubt lies in the personalities of individual Ministers. Perhaps it is not surprising that the relatively iconoclastic Brown came to support a change in the exchange rate, while the more conventional Wilson and Callaghan remained opposed.[20] Support for devaluation seemed tied to a readiness to think divergently. There are no grounds for assuming that Labour politicians will do this simply because they belong to a party of the left. Many of them are not innovators, and are prepared to show respect to the idols of the established order. With Labour so keen to prove itself a party of 'responsible government', it was natural for Ministers to attempt to demonstrate their responsibility by defending a symbol of national prestige. It is ironic that this dedicated pursuit of respectability produced an economic record that destroyed the reputation for competence sought so eagerly by Labour Ministers. Essentially an emphasis on the failure to devalue is an emphasis on a failure to think divergently within the confines of the mixed economy.

The development of orthodox policies was clearly influenced by the Government's dependence on foreign loans. Often government policies seemed designed to demonstrate orthodoxy. On occasions, 'inadequate' proposals generated a sterling crisis. Sometimes constraints were applied more directly. Wilson has referred to a series of early encounters with the Governor of the Bank of England, during which sweeping cuts in public expenditure were demanded as the price of foreign confidence.[21] In the post-devaluation period, assistance from the International Monetary Fund was clearly dependent on the Government pursuing appropriate policies.

The operation of such constraints has been presented frequently as indicative of the conspiratorial malevolence of financial interests towards a Labour Government. Such an explanation is clearly inadequate, and underestimates the potency of the constraints. One clear problem with the simple malevolence theory flows from the interpretation of Labour's economic policy developed here. Why should a policy whose central purpose was to modernise the mixed economy provoke the wrath of financiers? Basically the answer must be sought in Labour's dual personality. The central commitment was clearly to economic efficiency, but there was also the subordinate welfare commitment. Although now in a secondary position, this retained a tenacious hold on the party through the link with the unions and its incorporation into traditional rhetoric. This dimension of Labour's personality had to be repressed if financiers were to be reassured. No doubt this demand was fuelled by ideological hostility, but it was also influenced by another more persuasive factor. Both financial interests and multinational companies had abundant reasons for nervousness about sterling. Why should groups motivated by profitability hold reserves in a currency whose prospects seemed so uncertain? And why should they have confidence in the future of an economy whose government's willingness to modernise seemed compromised by its welfare commitments and by its unreadiness to combat rising industrial costs by taking a firm stand against trade union power? Although Labour leaders had turned resolutely towards modernisation, their continuing base in the organised working class made the shedding of its welfare commitment extremely difficult. The commitment did not involve any radical challenge, but it ensured that the surrender to orthodoxy would be painful.

The Special Relationship Under Strain

Although a harmonious party-union relationship has always been central to the conception of a labour movement, there have always been tensions over goals, tactics and personalities. Normally these have been subordinated to the demands of unity, but the tensions have been greater under Labour Governments. While in terms of party rhetoric the unions have been presented as one indispensable instrument for the creation of a better society, from the governmental viewpoint they have been regarded as a powerful sectional interest. The special status of the unions in the party could clash readily with ministerial preoccupations about the need to secure co-operation from all significant groups. Assessments by Labour Ministers of the technical or electoral desirability of economic policies might conflict with the demands of union leaders.

These problems certainly existed after 1945, as the Attlee Government's response to economic crisis led towards the Cripps wage freeze, but the degree of conflict was much greater after 1964. The deterioration of party-union relations under Wilson had several causes. The Attlee Cabinet had included some influential trade unionists, most notably Bevin, who fulfilled a dual function. They could reassure dubious trade union leaders and were able to indicate the limits of such leaders' tolerance to Cabinet colleagues. Union representation in the Wilson Cabinet was quantitatively and qualitatively inferior. Brown and Gunter carried relatively little weight in industrial circles. They had always been associated with the movement's political wing, and suffered perhaps from having followed white-collar occupations in a culture that placed a high premium on experience of manual labour.

The attitudes of the large unions had also shown significant changes. In some cases, increasing opposition was attributable to the emergence of new leaders who reflected an increased rank and file awareness of economic pressures, but elsewhere moderates found themselves driven to oppose government policy on sensitive questions such as trade union reform and the control of wages. One final factor making for increased tension was a changed evaluation of union critics. After 1945, it had been easy to dismiss them as 'Communists' or 'Communist-inspired'; after 1964 this was much more difficult. The exodus of many union spokesmen from the Communist Party in the late fifties had unfrozen debate, as many critical viewpoints could no longer be dismissed so arbitrarily. Nevertheless, some unions showed an increasing commitment to the right. The ETU, purged of its Communist leadership, had moved by 1965 to an unblemished right-wing position, while the NUR was increasingly loyal, especially on incomes policy.

Underlying these changes there was something far more basic: the condition of the economy and the associated roles of the Labour Government and the unions. The attempt to 'modernise' industrial structures provided deep union opposition, initially because of government support for 'rationalisations' that were often euphemisms for contraction, and then through an attempt to control union behaviour directly by legislation. More immediately, relationships were strained by the Government's response to inflation. The choice of deflation and wage controls, no matter how disguised by rhetoric, produced a major rift.

The potential for dissent was revealed initially over incomes policy. Increasing government anxiety over inflation led to a switch from voluntary restraint. It has been shown how Labour's pre-election statements on incomes were a masterpiece of ambiguity and how crucial issues had been left undiscussed. In September 1965, the voluntary approach was eroded by the granting of statutory powers to the Prices and Incomes Board, the initiation of 'early warning legislation', and the granting of powers to the Minister to delay the implementation of any wage or price increase while the Board's enquiries were continuing. These first erosions required a lengthy exercise in persuasion by Brown before the General Council accepted them, but the subsequent Party Conference witnessed vocal opposition by several unions, including the T & GW.[22] The shift to statutory

controls in July 1966 produced greater union antagonism, but it is
indicative of the old loyalty ethos that concern was expressed only
hesitantly at Party Conferences. However, by 1968, with the TUC now
firmly opposed to statutory controls, a resolution critical of the
incomes policy was carried overwhelmingly:[23]

Table 2: Votes on Principal Resolutions Critical of Government Policy
        on Prices and Incomes

	Mover	For	Against
1965	ASSET	2,540,000	3,635,000
1966	T & GW	2,471,000	3,925,000
1967	Boilermakers	2,535,000	3,860,000
1968	T & GW	5,098,000	1,124,000

Such massive opposition was composed of various elements. There were
those who argued that it was wrong to control wages in an economic
system where other types of income could not be restricted. This
obviously reflected the continuing debate as to whether an incomes
policy could function as a socialist instrument within a mixed economy.
More narrowly, several union spokesmen portrayed statutory control of
wages as a decisive erosion of traditional union rights. Their opposition
was an instinctive reaction against government intervention. Whatever
the reasons, it was significant that by 1968 the vast majority of unions
opposed a central element of the Government's economic strategy. The
extent of the disenchantment was demonstrated at the 1969 Party
Conference, when Scanlon and Jones supported the reference back of
the party document 'Agenda for a Generation' because of the section
on prices and incomes and its claims for 'the vital importance of an
effective prices and incomes policy'.[24] Although the attempt failed by
a margin of 1.25 million votes, such opposition was a dramatic indication
of how far the ambiguities and optimism of 1964 had been dispelled.

The instinctive reactions and dismay masked a crucial doctrinal
problem — was an incomes policy an instrument of socialist planning, or
a technique for blunting the unions' power, aimed at the creation of a
more competitive economy by restricting wage increases? Union
resistance could be interpreted as irrefutable proof of their conservatism,
or as the defence of the organised working class against the subtle
enticements of a new corporatism. Such problems had been perceived

dimly at the time of the Cripps wage bargain; now they were more prominent, although continuing confusions reflected in part the almost infinite elasticity of terms such as 'planning' and 'socialism'. The Labour rhetoric of the early sixties had reduced the content of socialism to little more than its equation with government intervention in the economy, with the question of the purpose of intervention hardly discussed.

The incomes policy debate was pregnant with implications for the future of the labour movement, although internal debate was hindered by both theoretical poverty and pressures towards unity. Other features of the Government's policies could not be disguised so readily by doctrinal ambiguities. Most important, this applied to the question of full employment. As a result of the 'July Measures' unemployment averaged 512,000 in 1967 and, after a further deflation, 543,000 in 1968. It was widely argued that Ministers had come to accept the Paishite thesis that the economy could avoid serious inflation only with a margin of unused capacity greater than that previously regarded as tolerable. Such a shift in priorities led inevitably to union criticisms. These were highlighted at the 1967 TUC, when a resolution deploring the use of traditional deflationary techniques was carried against the advice of the General Council, while the latter body was ready to support another resolution critical of the Government's record on employment.[25] A further indication of TUC disengagement from government strategy was provided by the inauguration in 1968 of an annual TUC Economic Review. The first one, by placing expansion as the first priority, expressed clear rejection of the Government's economic priorities.[26]

The Government's failure to protect the traditional union interest in full employment produced opposition across the full spectrum of TUC opinion. It was not simply a question of the impact of deflationary policies; the Government's commitment to modernisation produced further unemployment, especially in less prosperous regions. This was so particularly in the mining industry, where the Government introduced a programme of extensive pit closures. Between 1964 and 1969, the northern region lost 45 per cent of its mining jobs. These draconian measures, inflicted on one of the most loyal blocs of Labour supporters, inevitably produced critical reactions. The NUM came into open opposition at the 1968 Conference, when it moved the reference back of the appropriate section of the NEC report.[27] This was because of an alleged failure by the Government to act on a 1967 Conference resolution calling for an overall fuel plan. In spite of a plea from the platform, the reference back was carried by one million votes.

One result of the commitment to modernisation was friction between the Government and particular groups of workers, a tension understandable in terms of the party's traditional concern with the protection of working-class interests. However, the Government's dedicated pursuit of efficiency produced another type of tension. There can be no doubt that Wilson, in his commitment to industrial efficiency, was always ready to proclaim that such an objective required changes by unions. In his 1963 Scarborough speech, he had proclaimed 'no place for restrictive practices or for outdated methods on either side of industry'. This disregard for established patterns of union behaviour became far more obvious after March 1966, when he made a series of appeals to trade unions to exercise restraint and to modernise their structures. He advised the AEU National Committee that 'the sooner your rule book is consigned to the industrial museum, the more quickly the union will be geared to the challenge facing industry and the nation.'[28]

Such remarks based on a combination of concern about the economy and a taste for industrial efficiency were indicative of the imperfect sympathy prevailing between Ministers and union leaders. This acquired a further dimension in May and June 1966 when the National Union of Seamen struck for seven weeks.[29] This was seen widely as a test case for the Government's incomes policy. Wilson's reaction to the stoppage provoked much criticism in the labour movement. He condemned the strike as one 'against the State, against the community', but after the NUS had rejected the Pearson Report on the dispute, he widened the attack. Previously he had avoided any explanation of industrial stoppages as the result of 'subversive' influences, but now faced with the economic consequences of a protracted strike, he claimed that the militancy of the Seamen's executive was due to Communist conspiracy, or as he expressed it retrospectively: 'The moderate members of the seamen's executive were virtually terrorised by a small professional group of communists or near-communists.'[30]

The national Press, despite consistent editorial attacks on the seamen, found nothing substantive to support these allegations. Certainly his campaign produced the first major rift between the Prime Minister and the Parliamentary left, but this did not prevent similar statements being made on later industrial disputes. Gunter, the Minister of Labour, was no stranger to this type of denunciation, while Wilson seems to have accepted a 'conspiracy theory', that opposition to structural industrial change was frequently fuelled by subversive influences. The overall view of industrial relations that emerges from Wilson's memoirs is one of grievances resulting from necessary changes that would be capable of settlement by 'reason' and 'statemanship', but where exacerbation by subversives produced confrontation, sometimes with damaging economic consequences. Ministers accustomed to the instinctive loyalty of Deakin and Lawther lamented the passing of 'reliable' trade union leadership. Gradually the relationship between unions and Government came to occupy a significant place in their thoughts.

This issue had been barely considered by Labour in opposition. It was hardly surprising; the place of the unions had not been a question of strong partisan debate since the General Strike, while the intimate party-union links were likely to prevent discussion of anything that could be interpreted as trade union reform. Even the most moderate of union leaders were likely to see such proposals as an attempt to erode a hard-won status. Such reforms were unmentionable in Labour circles. However, a Labour Government was sensitive to other influences. By 1968, industrial disputes appeared to be securing increasing public attention. This raised the possibility of union reform as an electoral issue, while it is clear that many Ministers were concerned about the impact of stoppages on their post-devaluation economic strategy.

As early as April 1965, the Government had initiated a Royal Commission on Trade Unions and Employers' Associations, the Donovan Commission. Its Report, published in mid-1968, offered little comfort to any ministerial hopes of union reform. It reasoned that a reduction in the incidence of unofficial stoppages should be pursued through a reform of existing bargaining procedures: only if this failed should consideration be given to the possibility of obtaining a reduction through legislation. The non-interventionist character of the Report provided a problem for the Government. By mid-1968, it was all too apparent that the compulsory incomes policy was so unpopular that it was probably increasing the number of stoppages. Yet Ministers believed that any abandonment of compulsory powers necessitated a substitute, not least to reassure foreign bankers of the Government's firmness. Donovan, however, failed to produce any basis for bargaining with the TUC. One factor assisting reform, however, was the disappearance in April 1968 of the Ministry of Labour, and the emergence of a new Department of Employment and Productivity. The replacement of a department distinguished for conciliation was underlined by the appearance of Barbara Castle as head of the new Ministry. She illustrated the doctrinal complexities surrounding the issue of union reform. While she had a record of support for most left-wing causes reaching back to the thirties, she had always been a strong economic interventionist, advocating rational direct planning as the road to socialism. In contrast, she saw little in union addiction to differentials and sectional rivalries that was compatible with her vision.

By the late autumn of 1968, she had decided that unofficial strikes could be dealt with only by legislation, a viewpoint that understandably gained support from the modernisation-minded Wilson.[31] When the White Paper 'In Place of Strife' appeared in January 1969, it contained only three penal proposals: a compulsory cooling off period of twenty-eight days in certain disputes, a compulsory strike ballot before some official stoppages, and the imposition of solutions by the Minister in intractable inter-union disputes. In each case there was the brooding sanction of fines, and presumably imprisonment for non-payment. Although its defenders advocated the reform as a move towards more rational industrial relations, it is significant that the White Paper was conceived in an atmosphere of panic. Early in December there had been a violent flow of funds out of the City, based partly on a further instalment of deflation, but also on fevered rumours about the Government's imminent collapse.At the same time, Ministers felt their credibility undermined by industrial troubles.

Although the penal proposals formed a very small part of the White Paper, the fact remained that these were the first suggestions of this type advocated by any peacetime government for almost a century. Part of the answer to the question of how a Labour Government came to advocate them lies in the nature of their overall economic policy, but there were more immediate considerations. Beliefs about the preferences of the electorate were important, while the party tradition was ambiguous on the role of the unions. Many Labour MPs were unwilling to underwrite virtually all union practices, while the ambiguity of the rhetoric of 'planning' permitted the mobilisation of some support. Considerable opposition was inevitable of course, within the Cabinet, the PLP, the NEC, and from the General Council. At first criticism was deceptively mild. It is clear, however, that a number of Ministers opposed the proposals. Callaghan, formerly the dedicated deflationist, now emerged as the unions' champion, seeing the proposals as inherently unworkable. The former T & GW official, Marsh, and Mason, the ex-miner, offered similar opposition, the criticism of practical men against the ruminations of theoreticians.

The deceptive acquiescence of the PLP vanished abruptly on 3 March when the Commons debated the White Paper.[32] Fifty-seven Labour MPs opposed the government openly, and between thirty and forty are believed to have abstained. Although many of the rebels were habitual critics of government policy, several others were stalwarts of the Trade Union Group, who were concerned at any hint of penal clauses. The general discipline of the Parliamentary Party was starting to collapse, as another government proposal to reform the House of Lords ran into determined opposition. In order to stem the tide, the Government decided to introduce a short Bill on industrial relations. The decision, taken on 14 April, was announced by the Chancellor on the following day, in his Budget speech.

Previously, opposition had been expressed both within the NEC and on behalf of the General Council. At the Executive's March meeting, a resolution declaring the unacceptability of legislation based on the White Paper was passed by sixteen votes to five. This was an extreme case of the separation between 'party' and 'government' that was becoming more frequent on sensitive issues. On this occasion the majority included Callaghan. This rebuff was matched by growing resistance from the General Council. The style of the resistance was affected by the retirement of Woodcock on 1 March and his succession as General Secretary-Elect by Victor Feather. He was far more of a Labour Party figure than his predecessor, and was concerned with the avoidance of any major rift in the labour movement.

The announcement of the proposed legislation in the Budget speech had been designed to present it as a trade-off with the promised termination of a compulsory incomes policy, but the presence in London of an IMF delegation haggling over terms for further credits led to suggestions that the early legislation was yet another example of Labour principles being discarded to appease international bankers. The Chancellor's speech alleged that Britain's 'competitive position had been damaged by irresponsible industrial action',[33] while Wilson, addressing the Parliamentary Party, depicted the Bill as 'essential to our economic recovery, essential to the balance of payments, essential to full employment'.[34]

In fact, the proposed legislation did not contain even the penal proposals of the White Paper: the compulsory ballot had been discarded. For both sides in the argument, the proposals were symbolic. The battle concerned not their specific content, but their implications for government-union relations.

Throughout May, the General Council attempted to prevent the introduction of the proposed Bill and produced its own 'Programme for Action'. This was rejected by the Government because of the TUC's lack of powers for dealing with unofficial stoppages. Eventually, a special Congress on 5 June voted overwhelmingly for the TUC proposals, but failed to influence the Prime Minister. He appeared resolved to play for a victory, not a compromise. In a speech on the same evening, he applied Baldwin's stricture on the Press — that they sought power without responsibility, the prerogative of the harlot throughout the ages — to the trade unions.

Despite this apparent dedication to total victory, the opposition within the Parliamentary Party had grown. Early in May, agitation over the Bill had become interlaced with manoeuvres to change the leadership, but when these collapsed, the back-bench opposition remained stronger than ever. On 7 May, Douglas Houghton, the PLP Chairman and widely respected as a conciliator, issued a statement opposing the proposals: 'No good that any contentious Bill of this kind can do to industrial relations or the economy, will redeem the harm we can do to our Government by the disintegration or defeat of the Labour Party.'[35]

This was condemnation from a position of impeccable loyalty: it was not so much the Bill's content as its likely impact on party stability that concerned him. Certainly Houghton reflected accurately the growing concern in the PLP. For example, Tom Bradley, PPS to Roy Jenkins and a figure with strong moderate credentials, attacked the proposals in his *alter ego* as President of the Transport and Salaried Staffs Association. It was claimed by mid-May that 61 Labour MPs were pledged against the Bill, enough to keep the Committee Stage in the full House, exposing it to delay and destruction.

Parliamentary discontent became significant just at the moment when a clash between Government and General Council seemed inevitable. At a Cabinet meeting on 17 June the Chief Whip, Robert Mellish, intervened and claimed that there was no chance of any penal legislation passing through the Commons. According to one source, this precipitated a dramatic shift in ministerial alignments. Those who had always been hostile reasserted their position, while others changed in the light of Mellish's statement. One claim is that 'at the end, Wilson and Castle were virtually isolated.'[36] But Wilson has suggested that:

a majority of the Cabinet had expressed either their opposition to the Bill, or at least strong reservations, about it. But after Cabinet, one or two colleagues spoke to me, some telephoned, one or two sent me brief notes and others did so in the afternoon. If, they said, I was insisting on legislation, they were with me all the way.[37]

It is clear, however, that the TUC negotiators believed Wilson and Castle to be in an exposed position. Only a face-saving formula was needed to reach agreement. When the General Council's representatives met Wilson and Castle the following day, discussion centred on an appropriate TUC replacement for the conciliation pause. Although determined to resist any rewriting of TUC rules, the negotiators agreed to a 'solemn and binding undertaking' aimed at the provision of enhanced status for the TUC in the handling of inter-union disputes. The TUC was granted the substance of its case through a crucial distinction. When the TUC held unofficial strikers responsible, then trade unions concerned were obliged 'to take energetic steps to obtain an immediate resumption of work'; if a different judgement was formed, then the TUC's role was restricted to 'considered opinion and advice'. The whole impact of a conciliation pause was lost, since there was nothing automatic about these prescriptions. The TUC would look specifically at each case.

The settling of this dispute — arguably the most traumatic party crisis since 1931 — healed the breaches within the PLP, but inevitably left the Government open to the gibe that 'although they may still wear the trappings of office, the power resides elsewhere'.[38] In so far as this comment suggests that Labour's parliamentary leadership was the creature of the unions, it was mistaken. The settlement was not the result of dictation by one section of the labour movement. The crisis had developed because the delicate balance between trade unionists and politicians, realists and dreamers, radicals and moderates that is the secret of Labour's viability, seemed threatened. The ultimate constraint did not come from the TUC, but from within the PLP and then the Cabinet. While some MPs objected to the proposals on grounds of principle, many were opposed on grounds of practicality. The proposals were inoperable, and would devastate the party. There is a parallel here with the earlier Clause Four controversy, with the ideological debate engulfed by doubts about the political wisdom of such proposals. Frequently, speakers on the proposals seemed to deal not with their actual limited significance, but with appropriate dramatic interpretations.

More basically the crisis highlighted some crucial developments within the labour movement. Wilson's public criticisms of trade union activity could be interpreted as an important step in his strategy of remoulding Labour as the National Party. The final failure to hold the party behind such a move indicated that many Labour parliamentarians were prepared to resist any move that threatened the historic links with the unions. The resistance did not always indicate a close affection for existing trade union behaviour. Many critics of the proposals undoubtedly accepted ministerial strictures about militant trade unionism, but were more influenced by the risk of party divisions. Labour remained closely attached to its traditional class base, with attempts to redefine this relationship being deflected by a mountain of sentiment.

The crisis also highlighted some ambiguities central to the Labour tradition. Attention has been drawn already to the problems created by Labour's proclamation of the modernisation message. Most important, the vision of an efficient society led to attempts to regulate the behaviour of trade unionists in the public interest. This crucial policy development reflected several sets of ambivalent attitudes. Firstly, there was nothing new in tensions between Labour parliamentarians and militant trade unionists — MacDonald's embarrassment over the General Strike, the use after 1945 of the Communist label to attack strikers: both fitted in with the Wilson Government's behaviour. These attacks were based on a distinction between 'responsible' and 'irresponsible' industrial action that has always been prominent in Labour thinking. Such contrasts had been grounded traditionally on some presentation of the national interest. After 1964, this was connected closely with the drive for modernisation and the ambiguities within the Labour advocacy of 'planning' came into full view. The rhetoric of 1964 had left open the question of whose interests the modernisation and the planning were intended to serve. The unwillingness of the Government to change the existing power structure, and its acceptance of the rewards and penalties central to the operation of the mixed economy, suggested that the planning rhetoric merely served to hide Labour's accommodation with the existing economic structure. This judgement indicates yet another problematic area. Labour thinkers had failed to produce a coherent analysis of recent changes in economic and social structures; their failure included any appraisal of the role of trade unionism. Those within the party who defended the unions against governmental criticisms often seemed unsure about what they were defending. How far could a defence of free collective bargaining be justified in socialist terms?

The June 1969 settlement prevented further confrontations between politicians and trade union leaders. The prevention of strife is very different however from the establishment of a positive community of interest. On incomes policy and industrial relations reform, union leaders of almost all political persuasions found themselves opposed to the Government. The use of orthodox deflationary policies, the dismissal of opponents of drastic industrial changes as 'Luddites', the readiness to condemn industrial disputes as 'irresponsible' — all indicated a crisis within the labour movement. For the first time for many years, a significant section of the trade union movement appeared more radical than the politicians. As government spokesmen talked about the need for co-operation to cope with industrial change, so the leadership of the Engineers and the Miners moved significantly to the left. Unofficial stoppages, such as those in the previously quiescent Yorkshire coal-field in 1969, could be seen as a rejection of the ethic of co-operation.[39] The experience of 1964-70 left a basic problem for the future of party-union relations. Was the old Labour alliance losing its cohesion? The forces of tradition still worked strongly in favour of harmony, but the conflict between the modernising economic concerns of the politicians and the unions' desire to defend their positions appeared to leave a reduced scope for the traditionally ambiguous compromise.

Labour's Search for an International Role: Liberalism, Nationalism and Self-interest

The Government's preoccupation with economic crisis was paralleled by another distinctive but related problem, the need to redefine Britain's international relationships. The Suez débâcle had highlighted a pre-existing reality: no longer did 'going it alone' seem a plausible option. The theatre of imperial grandeur began to be viewed by leading politicians as an anachronism. Attention shifted to other options: an increased emphasis on the American alliance, a belief in a remodelled Commonwealth as a basis for British influence, or a drive for a closer association with leading European states through membership of the EEC. By 1964, the imperial trappings were threadbare, there had been one unsuccessful application to the European Community, the association with the United States remained close. Britain's role remained unresolved.

No one but the most naive expected that an incoming Labour Government would produce any 'socialist' innovations in foreign policy. Its 1945 predecessor had fought against declining party opposition, and a more pervasive lack of positive acceptance, to forge and to cement the Atlantic alliance. It had also established a somewhat misleading reputation for anti-colonialism based exclusively on its granting of Indian independence. Chauvinistic rhetoric was employed only rarely, but national interests were pursued firmly, often accompanied by justifications in principled terms. Typically these revolved around the desirability of expanding Britain's benevolent influence.

After 1964, the conduct of foreign policy was the responsibility of Ministers — Gordon Walker, Stewart and Brown — who were in this tradition. All prized the American connection, although they had different evaluations of the relative merits of European and Commonwealth entanglements. Wilson also played a major part in the making and the presentation of international policy. Although in his Bevanite period, he had made a number of speeches critical of American policy, such attitudes found no reflection in his more recent statements. From Kennedy's election, Wilson's comments on the United States were almost wholly favourable. The image presented by the 'New Frontier' rhetoric harmonised closely with Wilson's own emphasis on modernisation and a renewed sense of national purpose.

Ministers believed firmly in the centrality of the American alliance. One facet of the relationship sought by Wilson concerned the ability of a sympathetic British Government to act as a brake on the more provocative American proposals. This claim to influence was central to the Government's defence of its general support for American policy in Vietnam.[40] For more than two years Wilson pursued the chimera of a negotiated Vietnam settlement with himself as the honest broker.[41] The attempt failed, in part because Johnson and the Washington 'hawks' saw such gestures as marginal, and basically irrelevant to their pursuit of a military solution. Nevertheless such Labour peace initiatives could be useful as symbolic concessions to Labour critics.

Many of the Labour critics of the Government's attitude on Vietnam drew their inspiration from the same liberal values as were used by the Government to justify their position. Although critics spoke often of the need for 'a socialist alternative', much of their criticism was fuelled by those same sentiments that had provided a basis for the pre-1914 opposition to Sir Edward Grey. Distaste for militarism and power politics, pleas to stop the killing, calls for a public dissociation were the staple diet of the critics' case. Sometimes dissociation was presented as part of a radical initiative but more often it was viewed simply as a question of clean hands. Such critics based their case on the belief that American policy was immoral — the rejection was religious rather than political, based often on instinct rather than any study of the underlying facts.

This dominant liberal criticism was supplemented by a more recognisably socialist perspective that presented the Vietnamese struggle as an episode in the revolt of the Third World against imperialism. This had obvious affinities with the old Bevanite position as elaborated in 'One Way Only'. The hostility to government policy in Vietnam was apparent amongst the hard-core Labour left from early 1965, and produced Conference condemnations of government policy in 1966 and 1967.[42] Such criticisms made no difference to a government that deviated from total support of the United States only over the bombing of the Hanoi and Haiphong oil installations.

It is a significant comment that most of the criticism by Labour politicians of the American alliance was restricted to the Vietnam issue, and was fuelled by liberal sentiments. There was little development inside the party of a perspective that presented the United States as the champion of a new form of economic imperialism, based on multinational corporations and military reinforcements. Such an approach had deep socialist roots, but its failure to develop amongst Labour politicians is a significant testimony to the way in which critical outlooks were dominated by radical liberalism. Certainly, Ministers expressed occasional concern about the growing economic penetration of Western Europe by American firms, but this was expressed in terms of national economic independence.

Increasing disenchantment with the American connection did not produce a dramatic change in the Government's foreign policy, but it did help to produce a search for alternative means for the exercise of international influence. The prelude to the 1964 election had found Labour presenting the Commonwealth as a significant factor in world affairs. It is, at first sight, strange that a supposedly social democratic party should present itself as the custodian of an imperial legacy. Yet an appreciation of this commitment illuminates the distinctive way in which Labour has been a nationalist party. The essential belief was that a bloc reflecting 'British standards' would be a force for good in world affairs. This position was at the basis of many Labour commendations of the Commonwealth. The nationalism might be based on liberal values, but it was still nationalism.

Despite this initial optimism, the Government found itself entangled with a range of problems resulting from the imperial legacy.[43] Rhodesia was the most dramatic. Prior to October 1964, Labour's position had been one of supporting independence only if constitutional changes were made to end white minority rule. The Government's immediate response to Rhodesia's declaration of independence in November 1965 was to abjure force and rely on sanctions. The survival of the Rhodesian Government led to African criticism of the British Government and to two attempts at negotiation in December 1966 and October 1968. On both occasions Wilson moved a considerable way towards the Rhodesian position, but failed to secure agreement. The second attempt generated widespread Labour criticism. Stalwarts of the left combined with revisionists. The latter saw the proposal as a deviation from liberal constitutional principles, and also from liberal values on race relations. On a highly sensitive issue, the Government had fallen below the standards set by its professed liberal idealism.

The same preference for *real-politik* can be seen in government policy towards South Africa. Condemnations of apartheid were balanced by self-conscious worldliness concerning the importance of Britain's trade links. Although an arms embargo was imposed in October 1964, towards the end of 1967 demands for a series of new arms contracts produced a crisis in the party.[44] Strong ministerial pressure for a relaxation of the embargo was blocked by a back-bench demonstration. Nevertheless, it is significant how far the Government's preoccupation with its version of harsh reality moved it away from its professed principles. The idealists' agony was apparent: 'a Labour Government that had sold armaments to South Africa would have ceased to be a Labour Government; it is as simple as that.'[45]

Problems stemming from Britain's imperial past were not restricted to international affairs. The development of Labour policy towards Commonwealth immigration reveals the same victory for opportunism over idealism. The Government moved quickly towards more rigorous control of entry and in August 1965 a White Paper announced a ceiling of eight and a half thousand new entrants a year. Criticism developed in some sections of the party,[46] but was limited by fear of electoral consequences and by parallel attempts to legislate against discrimination. Little more was heard of the question until after devaluation. The switch of Callaghan to the Home Office brought a new style into the field.[47] He did not project himself as a self-conscious defender of liberal values, but as an advocate of practicality and common sense opposed to the lofty pretensions of theoreticians and experts. This change coincided with an unofficial Conservative campaign aimed at preventing the arrival in Britain of Asians threatened by Kenya's Africanisation policies. Many of them had chosen to retain British passports after Kenyan independence, and were not subject to existing controls. Eventually the Government decided to restrict their entry. A Bill was rushed through the Commons against the opposition of a minority from all parties. Firm supporters of liberal principles combined against what they viewed as a panic surrender to prejudice. But within Labour's ranks, many were ready to support the Bill from 'the ordinary working-class point of view'.[48]

This was probably the Government's greatest deviation from its professed principles. Seven months later, the Prime Minister could proclaim to the Party Conference that: 'We are the Party of human rights ... the central theme of this Government's actions since the day we took office,'[49] but Rhodesia, South Africa and the Kenyan Asians were testimonies to the Government's readiness to ignore its professed liberalism. As a result many who had endured the rigours and miscalculations of the Government's economic strategy were disillusioned.[50]

These controversies turned around the liberal component in the party's international perspective, but nationalism was of course another powerful element. It fuelled the tortuous debate over Britain's defence commitments. Of course, there had always been Labour back-benchers who had advocated radical reductions in defence expenditure, and they had always been opposed by those who saw a 'responsible' attitude on defence as a characteristic of any governing party. Throughout the life of the 1964 Government, the Minister of Defence was Dennis Healey, a devoted defender of NATO. It might be expected therefore that controversy over defence would take a traditional left-right form. This did not happen because of the continuing economic crisis and the gradual acceptance of Britain's changing world role. Inevitably the economic constraint precipitated a detailed government review of overseas commitments, and by February 1966 there was official recognition of the need to contract non-European forces.

The uncertain content of government policy led to critical comments and demonstrations from Labour back-benchers. They were not mollified by Wilson's impassioned defences of Britain's overseas commitments.[51] These critics were not limited to the hard-core left. There were also back-bench revisionists who regarded the question as one of modernisation versus traditionalism.[52] They considered large-scale defence cuts to be preferable to reductions in social expenditure. Some were relatively new members who saw their role as a responsible questioning of traditional practices inside and outside the party. They regarded ministers as excessively cautious and conventional. This 'unholy alliance' of defence critics was destroyed in 1967. After further paring down, the East of Suez role was finally ended by devaluation. The significance of the final decision is debatable since the general direction had probably been determined earlier. But in politics, where symbolism often carries much more weight than substantive changes, the post-devaluation cuts were vital. They ended revisionist criticism and left the perennial left-wing critics to turn their attention to NATO.

It is the tardiness with which the Government pursued reductions that is particularly striking. It was not just that Ministers remained attached to traditional national goals. In this they did not differ from earlier Labour generations. They also showed a stubborn loyalty to the most traditional means of achieving them. Even within the national consensus Labour Ministers failed to think in divergent terms.

A similar adherence to traditional symbols can be seen in many of Labour's reactions to the development of the European Economic Community. As shown above, Labour reactions to the original 1962 application for membership had centred around Gaitskell's nationalist rhetoric. Patriotic pronouncements were linked frequently to liberal protestations that membership of a 'rich man's club' would produce a decline in British influence amongst less developed nations. An additional argument emphasised the damaging effect that Community membership would have on Labour's commitment to economic planning. Membership of an essentially capitalist union would undermine Labour's pursuit of 'socialism in one country'. This spirit of opposition dominated Labour attitudes until 1966, although there were individual ministers and back-benchers who remained passionately pro-Market. Officially the party position was one of support in principle, with appropriate safeguards; an umbrella that allowed opposites to formally unite.

After the 1966 election the government position shifted rapidly to one of positively seeking membership, a change no doubt facilitated by the collapse of the Government's economic policies.[53] The European arena offered a potentially attractive balance to the growing disillusion within the party. It also offered an antidote to fears about the harmful effect of American multinationals on the British economy. The support of the Cabinet and the PLP had to be cultivated assiduously through the winter of 1966-7. It seems that six Cabinet Ministers remained unconvinced, while 35 back-benchers voted against the formal application in May 1967.[54] Although the application was blocked by the French, it had become a central issue within the party. Whereas at the 1967 Conference the pro-Marketeers carried the day, two years later, the outcome was a vacuous compromise.[55]

There is no doubt that between 1967 and 1970, Labour enthusiasm for the Market declined. Committed supporters continued to claim that living standards would rise, that there was no economically viable alternative, and that membership would involve some realisation of the party's internationalist values. The zealots were often revisionists and presented their position as part of Labour's commitment to modernisation. The alternative position was strengthened, in part because some large unions became more concerned about the possible consequence of entry, but also because, in a PLP where the committed on both sides were relatively few, the great uncommitted mass tended to shift to a more sceptical position. The principal arguments against entry each tapped a strand in the Labour tradition. Some were narrowly economic. It was persuasive to suggest that working-class living standards should not be sacrificed on the altar of a middle-class intellectual enthusiasm. Other critical responses tapped the nationalist strand in Labour's tradition. Sometimes these were no more than an uncomplicated patriotism with populist overtones, but other presentations possessed a quality reminiscent of Orwell's writings. Entry would prevent the realisation of 'British socialism'. Whether this cherished ideal was seen as concerned with economic planning or whether it involved a broad image of an egalitarian community, it was veiled in respect for national values. Such criticisms were linked frequently with condemnation of the Community's anti-socialist ideology, although why this label was more applicable to the Community than to Britain remained obscure. This dismissal also reflected a Utopian strand in Labour's tradition. An ill-defined socialist ideal was employed to condemn an available alternative, but little positive guidance was offered. It is not surprising that some opposition arguments were based on liberal principles. Some were centred around institutional problems. Community membership would involve the acceptance of decisions that could not be subject to parliamentary control. Never before, perhaps, had Labour politicians demonstrated so forcibly their commitment to parliamentarianism. A second liberal argument involved an attempt to turn the pro-Market internationalist claim on its head. Genuine internationalists would not restrict their energies to a narrow Community. This argument often had a nationalistic underpinning: British moral influence should have as wide a stage as possible and should not be restricted to the Community. The adherence of the Labour left to the varied nationalistic arguments is revealing. Praise for 'our way of doing things' came from speakers given to class-conscious rhetoric on economic matters. It is often noted that the European question does not fit snugly into left-right divisions. In part this is surely because it illuminates the frequently disguised nationalism of the Labour left.[56]

The Wilson Government's international record lacks the stark simplicity of its 1945 predecessor. Instead of the collapse into the Cold War and the unilinear progression towards the Atlantic alliance, there was a series of attempts to redefine Britain's international role — the American alliance, the Commonwealth, Europe. All were explored but nothing was decided. The groping for a new certainty bore little resemblance to any distinctive party perspective on international affairs. Anything that could be dignified as 'socialist' had long since ceased to count in Labour foreign policy: now even those liberal principles that had provided the essence of many earlier Labour positions were disregarded in the face of political and economic 'necessities'.

Towards Safety First

The narrowness of Labour's 1964 victory compelled party leaders to devote considerable time to the cultivation of further electoral support. This had an inevitable effect on the Government's decisions. Particular attention was paid to the fostering of Labour's image, in so far as it reduced criticisms by the Labour left. The quest for greater electoral popularity appeared doomed, when in a January 1965 by-election the Government lost a supposedly safe seat at Leyton, but a revival seems to have developed later in the year. Evidence of this was provided in January 1966 when the Government retained a 1964 gain, Hull North, with a sizeable increase in its majority.

The following general election campaign in March 1966 was built around Labour's claims of responsibility and efficiency.[57] 'You know Labour Government Works' epitomised its appeal. There was little emphasis on detailed policy proposals. The manifesto, 'Time for Decision', emphasised the Government's record and added little to the proposals of 1964. The only significant innovations were the public ownership of ports, the creation of a National Freight Authority and public participation in the aircraft industry. All were variations on the central Labour theme of economic modernisation through government intervention. In contrast, the Conservative platform showed the first signs of a retreat from economic intervention. However, Labour's emphasis on continuity and responsibility dominated the election, with Wilson's final television broadcast stressing stability and national unity. In the short term this strategy was successful. Compared with 1964, Labour's aggregate vote rose by more than half a million on a lower turnout, and the Labour margin over the Conservatives widened to 6 per cent, the largest since 1945. The party now held 110 more seats than its principal rival. Its gains included such unlikely places as Hampstead, Cambridge and Exeter.

This first ever clear Labour triumph under normal peacetime conditions should perhaps be attributed to two factors, approval of Labour's performance in office and concern about the Conservative alternative. In 1945, Labour had won on the basis of a programme opposed to the Churchillian cult of personality; now it secured victory on account of the personal appeal of its leader, and an aura of competence and responsibility. Such an emphasis had been accepted readily by most Labour activists, prepared to abstain from criticism in order to achieve a clear majority. *Tribune,* for so long the gadfly of the leadership, praised the 1966 manifesto as 'in essence, a socialist one', while Michael Foot presented the election as a watershed equivalent to 1945: 'one of the essential dates in the forward march. It is an opportunity which only incorrigible sectarians and nihilists, the best allies of the forces of reaction will not wish to seize.'[58]

The 1966 campaign was the latest example of a continuing strand in the Labour tradition, the drive for governmental credibility. MacDonald had sought to acclimatise his colleagues into a full acceptance of the mores of Parliament and office; Morrison had attempted to construct a majority coalition of the 'useful people'; Gaitskell had tried to purge the party of what he viewed as anachronistic dogma. Now Wilson tried to construct an image of efficiency.

On 31 March 1966, the zenith of Wilson's 'competence and responsibility' strategy was reached. The Government's subsequent by-election record was one of almost unparalleled disaster.[59] Nineteen English seats were defended. Eleven of these were lost to the Conservatives and one to the Liberals. By the end of September 1967, defences of Labour seats had changed from the 'backs to the wall' posture characteristic of almost all governments into token attempts to prevent a rout. The position deteriorated still further in 1968. An anti-Government swing of over 21 per cent was sustained at Dudley, while in the May 1968 local elections, Labour councillors were returned only in a derisory 450 seats. With an almost equivalent disaster at the 1969 local elections, the Labour base in local government was almost totally destroyed. Retrospectively, the first half of 1968 represented the nadir of Labour's electoral fortunes, but eighteen months later Labour was still haunted by the spectre of a disaster of 1931 dimensions. Losses had included not just the obviously vulnerable marginals such as Cambridge and Wellingborough, but also apparently secure seats such as Dudley and West Walthamstow. The belief that Labour had established almost a prescriptive right to some of these seats was possibly one cause of their loss since, in many Labour strongholds, party organisation was weak because it had been considered unnecessary. Now that the Government's unpopularity made such seats vulnerable, the lack of resources was exposed.

Disillusion with the Government was not restricted to its marginal supporters, but penetrated deep into traditionally loyal working-class ranks. Often this manifested itself in apathy and abstention. Broadly, it can be attributed to discontent with the Government's economic record. It was not so much a question of dissatisfaction with specific government policies, but a broad belief that its economic record was inadequate. This disenchantment was far greater than anything experienced by the Attlee Government. It reflected the failure of the Wilson administration to generate an identification between Ministers and traditional Labour voters. Such a failure could be seen particularly in the impact of the Government's commitment to modernise traditional industries. The continuing contraction of the cotton industry led to some local branches of the Textile Workers' Union reconsidering their attachment to the party. This was an extreme example of the dismay created in traditional Labour circles by the pursuit of rationalisation. The resolute implementation of a programme of pit closures did not produce such a radical reaction from mining communities, but it was likely to weaken a long-standing identification. Moreover, the contraction of traditional industries eroded the bases of some of Labour's most reliable support. The patterns of industrial and community loyalties that had formed the bulwark of Labour strength were being superseded, sometimes as the result of deliberate government action.

Such erosions were perhaps of particular importance in Scotland and Wales. Economic difficulties had a particularly severe impact: pit closures and the economic vulnerability of such 'fringe' areas produced perhaps an even deeper disenchantment than elsewhere. Both areas were Labour strongholds. In 1966 they provided 78 Labour seats, over 20 per cent of the party's parliamentary representation. Many Welsh seats and a few Scottish ones had records of continuous Labour representation dating back to 1918 or 1922. Disillusioned Welsh and Scottish Labour voters had their own alternative to abstention or a Conservative vote. They could support the appropriate Nationalist party, and they began to do this in considerable numbers.

Carmarthen can perhaps be dismissed as atypical, with an unusually high proportion of Welsh speakers and a record of electoral unpredictability, but Rhondda West and Caerphilly were two of Labour's most solid South Wales seats. For decades the party had been identified with such communities, but now the rigours of government

Table 3: Labour By-Elections 1966-70

Wales

| | | March 1966 | | By-Election | |
		Labour Vote	Nationalist Vote	Labour Vote	Nationalist Vote
14 July 1966	Carmarthen	46.2%	16.1% (3rd place)	33.0%	39.0%
9 March 1967	Rhondda West	76.1%	8.7%	49.0%	39.9%
18 July 1968	Caerphilly	74.2%	11.1% (3rd place)	45.7%	40.4%

Scotland

| | | March 1966 | | By-Election | |
		Labour Vote	Nationalist Vote	Labour Vote	Nationalist Vote
9 March 1967	Glasgow Pollok	52.4%	—	31.2%	28.2%
2 Nov. 1967	Hamilton	71.2%	—	41.5%	46.0%
30 Nov. 1969	Glasgow Gorbals	73.0%	—	53.4%	35.0%
19 March 1970	South Ayrshire	67.2%	—	54.1%	20.3%

policy produced a weakening of the identification.

The Nationalist performance in Scotland was more uneven, although the same broad trends were apparent. Hamilton, held by Labour since 1918, was a sensation, but later results suggested that Scottish Labour, in spite of well-publicised organisational defects, had succeeded in containing the Nationalist challenge. Nevertheless this threatened a long-term weakening of Labour's position. Since 1922 Labour had usually dominated the Celtic electorate; now its hold appeared less secure.

This 'Celtic factor' clearly helped to expedite the flight of disillusioned Labour voters in Wales and Scotland. In some parts of England there was an equivalent exacerbating factor. In the spring of 1968, the agitation over the admission of Kenyan Asians and the Birmingham speech of Enoch Powell revived immigration as a central political issue. There is considerable evidence to suggest that Powell's views enjoyed wide support amongst Labour voters. An already weakened economic identification with Labour could be further undermined if the issue became salient. Labour's recovery from the electoral disasters of 1968 was protracted. Any successful appeal to the electorate required the reconstruction of something approaching the 1966 electoral coalition. This task required judgement about timing and style.

Policy preparation had continued during the years of government, although early tensions had arisen as Research Department officials opposed ministerial deviations from proposals developed before 1964. As economic difficulties grew these frustrations became enshrined in a resolve that the next manifesto must contain 'socialist' commitments less susceptible to evasion.[60] The work of the Research Department resulted in the publication, in 1968, of what was labelled vaguely 'a mid-term manifesto', 'Britain: Progress and Change'.[61] This began by supporting the Government's basic economic strategy, but then moved on to advocate high taxation as a means of increasing welfare benefits, and to imply that a Wealth Tax was needed to reduce 'glaring and unacceptable inequalities'.[62] Such suggestions were no doubt unwelcome to some Ministers, but the need to avoid further controversy at a time of considerable discontent led to the document being presented to the 1968 Conference.[63] This, plus the acquiescence of the NEC's Home Policy Sub-Committee, led to the Research Department using the document as the basis for the production of an election programme.[64] The reconciliation of its proposals with government decisions was supposedly facilitated by the formation in

December 1968 of a Co-ordinating Committee. This included Ministers, executive members, and party administrators. In practice, its work tended to be restricted to minor questions, but it gave Ministers the chance to air their doubts about proposed policies.

After the 1968 Conference, some members of the Research Department combined with members of the Executive in an Economic Strategy Group,[65] which subsequently added its backing to the Wealth Tax proposal. Two lengthy documents, 'Labour's Economic Strategy' and 'Labour's Social Strategy' secured Executive support but enjoyed only the ambiguous status of discussion documents. Proposals for 'serious consideration' of a Wealth Tax and extensions of public ownership were included in a further Executive statement, 'Agenda for a Generation'.[66] This provided a basis for the debates at the 1969 Conference. Once again its status was obscure. The text contained a denial of manifesto status. Supporters of the more radical proposals were ready to believe that their inclusion in such a document made their omission from any subsequent manifesto highly unlikely.

The relatively unexpected dissolution followed a winter in which little had been done to reduce the ambiguities.[67] The production of a manifesto was left to a drafting committee of twelve, drawn largely from the NEC and the Cabinet. The first meeting saw a long discussion on the extent to which the manifesto should contain specific future commitments. A group of officials was asked to produce a draft and the committee had just one more meeting prior to the manifesto coming before the full NEC. This second meeting saw the clash between Ministers opposed to detailed commitments, and some NEC members and officials unhappy about vague generalities. Typically these differences became encapsulated in one specific issue, the proposal for a Wealth Tax. Wilson and Jenkins were opposed strongly to this, and the advocates of vagueness won the argument with the insertion of the formula: 'We shall ensure ... that there is a greater contribution to the National Revenue from the rich.'[68] The contents and style of the manifesto were a defeat for those who had fought for specific radical proposals.[69] Earlier documents had never had a definitive status, unity pressures were inevitably at their height in a pre-election situation, and it was virtually impossible to force policy commitments on a leader who was determined to resist them.

Labour leaders' dreams of a successful appeal to the electorate as a moderate party of government were threatened more by the parlous condition of the party organisation. In the early sixties there had been some willingness to employ modern campaign techniques, but behind the glossy facade there lurked the rusty penny farthing attacked by the Wilson Report. This obsolescence was condemned strongly in October 1965 through the 'Plan for an Efficient Party' campaign. This enjoyed support across the party's normal political divisions, and attacked on a wide front. 'Cosy squalor and amateurism' were said to be the party's main qualities. The grass-roots organisation was condemned as obsolescent, and unattractive to potential young recruits. The interested newcomer 'may go for months without hearing anything authoritative about the party's problems and actions ... for years without ever discussing "socialism"'.[70]

The deficiencies of Transport House were presented sharply: it was 'bureaucratic', 'amateur', with poorly paid staff characterised by a high turnover. Eventually the agitation produced NEC support for an enquiry under the chairmanship of Simpson of the Foundry Workers' Union. This was a protracted non-event. Two reports appeared in 1967 and 1968 — and then the NEC engaged in a slow digestive process.[71] The few proposals were largely inconsequential. In part this reflected the rigid financial orthodoxy of many Labour administrators. The long decline in party membership became a catastrophic fall precipitated by mass disillusion with the Government's record. One estimate of individual membership in 1970 placed it between 310,000 and 385,000.[72] In many constituencies Labour had become a stage army decimated by disillusion. Its structure and ethos frequently recalled a bygone age, with veteran collectors religiously gathering small subscriptions.[73]

The collapse was dramatic but it was the finale to a long decline. Was the kind of grass-roots party life that had once characterised at least some local parties an anachronism? Were the weaknesses incapable of remedy through structural changes and good intentions? Obviously, it is easy to be deluded about a past 'Golden Age' of party organisation and of involvement in Labour politics. Often such claims possess no more substance than equivalent claims of socialist purity. Nevertheless, some local parties had succeeded in the past in developing a vigorous community extending beyond the narrowly political. A persuasive case can be constructed to demonstrate that the decay of local party life stems from fundamental social changes. A wider range of leisure pursuits and means of achieving local prestige have made 'the party' increasingly peripheral within most communities. On this diagnosis, local activists can be equated with the embattled stalwarts of declining religious groups, battling against changing cultural priorities and fondly believing that revivalism, the modernisation of premises or appropriate social inducements will bring back the 'faithful'.[74]

Some within the party leadership welcomed such a deterioration. The belief that local organisation mattered little in an age of mass campaigning implied that the dissenting tendencies of some local parties were too great a cost to pay for a dubious increase in organisational strength. This alternative image of a dominant leadership and a reduced rank and file was a logical corollary to Labour's commitments to electoral success and governmental credibility. The centrality of these concerns inevitably increased with the fulfilment of Labour's traditional programme and the resulting ideological vacuum. Immediately after 1945, it made some sense to regard Labour as a mass party — or at least to suggest that it had the potential to become one; but Labour activities had withered along with its traditional vision.

Despite these difficulties Labour entered the 1970 campaign with optimism. The large gains in the May local elections suggested the return of support in the wake of apparent economic recovery. The style of the campaign was captured in Baldwin's 1929 slogan 'Safety First'. The manifesto was significant for its lack of proposals. Considerable space was given to attacks on the opposition, and to boosting Labour's achievements since 1966. This was another instalment in the strategy of establishing Labour as the party of government, a more extreme manifestation of the 1966 appeal. 'Socialism' was rarely mentioned by party leaders. Their emphasis was on the record of a government willing to forgo immediate popularity in the quest for economic health. For much of the campaign the strategy appeared successful, and the Conservative victory came as a surprise to most observers and participants. Labour lost 68 seats to the Conservatives, and regained 6 by-election losses from them. In other directions Labour lost one seat to the SNP, took one from the Liberals and recouped all by-election losses to the minor parties. Sixteen seats were lost that had been Labour at general elections since at least 1945.

The dimensions of defeat were more in keeping with Labour's by-election performance than with the immediate expectations of victory. The party retained almost its 1966 level of support in some industrial areas such as Merseyside and Tyneside, but in the cotton towns and above all in the Powell heartland of the West Midlands, it lost votes heavily.

These considerations were the immediate 'nicely calculated less or more' of the campaign, but in the longer perspective of Labour development, the electoral record of the party in the late sixties indicated more basic problems. Once again a working Labour majority had failed to survive one term of office, while its natural support had become disillusioned to an extent that had not happened after 1945. But even more significance should be attached to the style of Labour's 1970 campaign. Its Baldwin-like quality was an almost comical epitaph on the final exhaustion of Labour's social democratic inspiration. It was no longer a question of the party offering criticism within the existing institutional framework, but rather a muting of dissent. The tensions that had plagued the party since 1966 were to be stilled by a benevolent sunshine campaign.

This sterility is crucial, but the failure of 'Safety First' was equally important. By 1970 nobody pretended that socialism was on the party's agenda. The best that one sympathetic commentator could offer was 'there is no greater guarantee of this country's internal stability and security than a solid Labour majority in the House of Commons.'[75]

In essence, Labour's purpose was to preside efficiently over the mixed economy, and to expand support beyond its traditional working-class base, becoming thereby a 'national party'. Such traits have always been present in the Labour position: the ambivalence between practicality and idealism, the tension between class and nation, the doubt over whether to aim for a lengthy tenure of office or to be satisfied with rare interludes of reforming zeal. During the sixties the party's official appeal was more purely national, practical and governmental than ever before. On these criteria it failed. It suffered from negative evaluations of its competence, it failed to expand support beyond its traditional base, and it lost office. In spite of all, in electoral terms, Labour remained the party of the majority of the working class. This identification had been loosened but Labour had not discovered any alternative — neither had a majority of the working class.

The Government's record had a devastating impact on the party. The surrender to economic orthodoxy, the confrontation with the trade unions, the lack of principle in international affairs all left their mark. The experience of the six years produced two major legacies. Most clearly it was evident that the social democratic inspiration was dead. It had been nurtured after 1931, it had had its heroic hour after 1945, and it had failed to give guidance since then. It had been built around a belief that major reforms could be achieved piecemeal within the existing system, and it had held together a motley coalition with its blend of short-term benefits and future-orientated idealism. Now the vision had withered, the potential for major reforms seemed virtually dead and the coalition showed signs of disintegration. But the second legacy was negative — a limited degree of organisational decay. Certainly activists had quit in droves, but the unions remained loyal, and in the 1970 defeat Labour's electoral base remained largely intact, although hardly enthusiastic. The vision might have died, but the organisation lingered on. This continuing organisational dominance might be derided as a wasting asset, but it remained of major importance. By 1970, few socialist intellectuals could find anything positive to say about the party. The contrast with the thirties is revealing. The latter-day equivalents of Laski, Cole and Tawney gave their support to growing but still very small groups to the left of the party, or retired to an independent agnosticism.[76] Labour was unlikely to undergo a theoretical renaissance, but it remained with its working-class base, a dominant element in any left-wing strategy. The vision was dead — but what about the instrument?

Notes

1. By 1970 the figures were NUM 304,760; NUR 175,266; Textile Workers 59,610. The analysis of trade union attitudes owes much to Lewis Minkin. See his 'The British Labour Party and the Trade Unions: Crisis and Compact' in *Industrial and Labour Relations Review*, Oct. 1974, pp. 7-37.
2. To one million and 813,616 respectively.
3. *LPCR 1966*, p. 163. He also referred to seeking 'vainly to find the answer in Highgate cemetery'.
4. *LPCR 1967*, pp. 192-201.
5. NEC consultations with the Government on prices and incomes and prescription charges are referred to in *LPCR 1969*, pp. 28-9.
6. Peter Jenkin, *The Battle of Downing Street* (Charles Knight, London, 1970).
7. For a sceptical estimate of the Parliamentary left's influence in this period see Paul Foot, op. cit., pp. 304-24.
8. Harold Wilson, *Purpose in Power* (Weidenfeld, London, 1966), p. 71.
9. For a valuable analysis see Peter Jenkin, 'The Wilson Years' in *New Statesman*, 30 July 1971, pp. 133-9.
10. Wilsonian pragmatism generated considerable hostility amongst the self-conscious revisionists. This was demonstrated in *Socialist Commentary*, especially in 1967 and 1968.
11. See W. Beckerman (ed.), *Labour's Economic Record* (Duckworth, London, 1972). Also the review 'Labour and the Economy' by Andrew Glyn and Bob Sutcliffe in *New Left Review*, 76, Nov.–Dec. 1972, pp. 91-6, and K. Coates, *The Crisis of British Socialism* (Spokesman Books, Nottingham, 1971), ch. 5.
12. For 'July Measures' see *732 H.C. Debs, 5th Series*, cols. 627-54. For Wilson's version see his *The Labour Government 1964-70. A Personal Record* (Weidenfeld, London, 1971), pp. 249-53 and 256-62.
13. See, for example, George Brown, *In My Way* (Gollancz, London, 1971), chs. 5 and 6.
14. Roger Opie in Beckerman, op. cit., p. 172.
15. On industrial reforms see A. Graham in Beckerman, op. cit., ch. 5.

16. Note the contrasting claims in P. Townsend and N. Bosanquet (eds.), *Labour and Inequality* (Fabian Society, London, 1972), and Michael Stewart in Beckerman, op. cit., ch. 2.

17. Crossman quoted in *Financial Times,* 29 September 1970.

18. See the contrasting views of Beckerman, op. cit., esp. pp. 67-74 and Glyn and Sutcliffe, op. cit., pp. 92-3.

19. On the early attitude towards the pound see Henry Brandon, *In the Red* (Deutsch, London, 1966).

20. Note Callaghan's appeal to 'solid citizens' to withstand the lure of 'gimmicks', *LPCR 1967,* pp. 196, 199.

21. Wilson, *The Labour Government,* pp. 37-8.

22. *TUC Report 1965,* pp. 465-96 and Appendix A, pp. 564-7; *LPCR 1965,* pp. 221-47.

23. For these debates see *LPCR 1966,* pp. 207-48; *1967,* pp. 163-201; *1968,* pp. 122-54.

24. *LPCR 1969,* pp. 259-61.

25. *TUC Report 1967,* pp. 507-22.

26. *TUC Economic Reivew,* 1968.

27. *LPCR 1968,* pp. 278-83.

28. Wilson, *The Labour Government,* p. 226.

29. For contrasting accounts see ibid., pp. 227-41, and Paul Foot, op. cit., pp. 172-8. Also his 'The Seamen's Struggle' in R. Blackburn and A. Cockburn, *The Incompatibles: Trade Union Militancy and the Consensus* (Penguin, Harmondsworth, 1967), pp. 169-209.

30. Wilson, *The Labour Government,* p. 236.

31. This account relies heavily on Peter Jenkin, *Downing Street.* See also Eric Silver, *Victor Feather, TUC* (Gollancz, London, 1973), and Eric Heffer, *The Class Struggle in Parliament* (Gollancz, London, 1973).

32. For the debate see *779 H.C. Debs, 5th Series,* cols. 36-166.

33. *781 H.C. Debs, 5th Series,* col. 1006.

34. Wilson, *The Labour Government,* p. 643.

35. Cited in Jenkin, *Downing Street,* p. 119.

36. Jenkin, *Downing Street,* p. 154.

37. Wilson, *The Labour Government,* p. 657.

38. Edwart Heath cited in Jenkin, *Downing Street,* p. 159.

39. For the changes in the Yorkshire coal-field see Arthur Scargill, 'The New Unionism' in *New Left Review,* 92, 1975, pp. 3-33.

40. See Wilson, *The Labour Government, passim* and Paul Foot, op. cit., pp. 198-218.

41. This role is reviewed in Peter Jenkin, 'The Wilson Years'.

42. *LPCR 1966,* pp. 255-73 and *1967,* pp. 223-6 and 231-6.

43. These questions are dealt with in detail in Wilson's book — see also P. Foot, op. cit., pp. 237-48 and ch. 8.

44. For divergent accounts see Wilson, *The Labour Government,* pp. 470-6, and Brown, op. cit., pp. 170-4. Also the judgement of Peter Jenkin, *Downing Street.*

45. *New Statesman,* editorial, 22 December 1967.

46. See *LPCR 1965,* pp. 212-20. The government position was supported by 4,736,000 to 1,581,000 — the minority included the T & GW.

47. See the portrait in Jenkin, *Downing Street,* pp. 80-3.

48. See especially the speeches of two Labour peers (and ex-MPs), *289 H.C. Debs,* cols. 961-5 (Lord Wigg); cols 1018-22 (Lord McLeavy).

49. *LPCR 1968,* p. 170.

50. See John Rex, 'The Race Relations Catastrophe' in Tyrell Burgess (ed.), *Matters of Principle: Labour's Last Chance* (Penguin, Harmondsworth, 1968).

51. For his admission of error in this see Wilson, *The Labour Government,* p. 243.

52. See, for example, John Mackintosh, 'Defence and the Backbencher', *Socialist Commentary*, March 1967.
53. See Uwe Kitzinger, *The Second Try* (Pergamon, Oxford, 1968).
54. *746 H.C. Debs, 5th Series,* cols. 1653-6. Most of the rebels were members of, or sympathetic to, the Tribune Group.
55. *LPCR 1967,* pp. 269-86; *1969,* pp. 309-23. The T & GW spearheaded the opposition, while the GMW were resolutely in favour.
56. For a later, critical analysis of this Labour nationalism see Tom Nairn, *The Left Against Europe?* (Penguin, Harmondsworth, 1973), esp. chs. 4-6.
57. See David Butler and Anthony King, *The British General Election of 1966* (Macmillan, London, 1966).
58. *Tribune,* 25 March 1966 – cited in Paul Foot, op. cit., p. 310.
59. See David McKie, 'By-Elections of the Wilson Government' in Cook and Ramsden, op. cit.
60. Background to the party's policy-making is supplied in David Butler and Michael Pinto-Duschinsky, *The British General Election of 1970* (Macmillan, London, 1971), pp. 58-61 and 149-50.
61. See *LPCR 1968,* pp. 29-33 (background) and Appendix 4, pp. 339-43 (text).
62. Ibid., p. 341.
63. Ibid., pp. 191-204.
64. *LPCR 1969,* pp. 28-33 *passim.*
65. Ibid., p. 29.
66. For the text see *LPCR 1969,* Appendix 4, pp. 380-93.
67. *LPCR 1970,* pp. 36-7. This noted that the Conference endorsement of the 1969 document was 'vigorously taken up by the Home Policy Sub-Committee in discussion with individual ministers and particularly in the discussions in the Policy Co-ordinating Committee'.
68. 'Now Britain's Strong, Let's Make it Great to Live In'.
69. For one version of the manifesto debate see *Sunday Times,* Insight Column, 31 May 1970.
70. See supplement in *Socialist Commentary,* October 1965, 'Our Penny Farthing Machine', and the 'Plan for an Efficient Party Campaign' manifesto. Also Butler and Pinto-Duschinsky, op. cit., pp. 47-58.
71. This can be traced in *LPCR 1966,* pp. 274-5; *1967,* pp. 237-53 and Appendix 4, pp. 333-52 (Interim Report). *1968,* pp. 219-30 and Appendix 11, pp. 362-80 (Report). *1969,* pp. 7-9.
72. Butler and Pinto-Duschinsky, op. cit., p. 265.
73. For one view see Paul Foot, 'The State of the Labour Party', *Sunday Times,* 29 September 1968.
74. On this see Barry Hindess, *The Decline of Working Class Politics* (McGibbon and Kee, London, 1971) – and the critical examination by R. Baxter, 'The Working Class and Labour Politics' in *Political Studies,* March 1972, pp. 97-107.
75. *New Statesman,* 19 June 1970, p. 858.
76. See, for example, the R. Williams *et al., May Day Manifesto* (Penguin, Harmondsworth, 1968).

10 POSTSCRIPT

After its June 1970 defeat, Labour lacked a programme, its links with the unions were strained, and its traditional support showed signs of disintegration. The party attempted to meet these problems in the context of an industrial situation unparalleled since the nineteen-twenties. Already, trade union militancy had grown in the face of economic difficulties and the policies of the Wilson Government, and it was given a further impetus by the industrial policies of the Heath Government. Legislation on industrial relations and a determination to control public sector wages produced a series of industrial crises. Sometimes the unions were defeated, as with the Postmen, but there were also significant union victories. Most notably the miners humiliated the Government with their successful six-week stoppage at the beginning of 1972. It was not just the fact of victory that was important, it was also the means employed. The miners adopted systematic, abrasive and effective picketing, a tactic symbolised by the successful mass picket of the Saltley fuel depot.[1] Direct action succeeded here as it did in some of the factory occupations that were the response of some groups of workers to threats of redundancy. Similar tactics were also adopted by some Labour councils who defied the Government's Housing Finance Act, and pegged council house rents at their old levels. Such resistance became epitomised in the resistance of the Clay Cross councillors, and their incipient martyrdom.[2] Saltley and Clay Cross, the motifs of direct action, carried radical implications for an embattled Labour Party. After six years of office with its devastated hopes, some groups of workers had reasserted themselves by extra-parliamentary methods. For the first time since the General Strike, the hint of an alternative to parliamentarianism appeared on the agenda and required some response from Labour politicians.

The leadership that had to respond was largely the same one that had led the party during the six years of government. The same people dominated the Shadow Cabinet, but the National Executive showed some shift to the left. By 1973, only Healey and Williams out of the twelve constituency and womens' representatives were associated unequivocally with revisionist policies. There were some reconcilers who responded to radical initiatives, while others had impeccable left-wing credentials.[3] There was every chance that policy statements would

287

express a more radical viewpoint.

The greatest single need was to renovate the Labour alliance through the development of agreed positions on questions of particular interest to the unions. The increased drive for harmony was symbolised by the creation of a Liaison Committee in January 1972. This had six members each from the NEC, PLP and the General Council[4]; it formed an interesting parallel with the upgrading of the National Council after 1931. By February 1973 harmony had developed sufficiently to allow the birth of a 'compact'. The party committed itself to a range of policies. The Industrial Relations Act was to be repealed, there were to be permanent price controls and a commitment to a major redistribution of income and wealth. Increased investment was to be promoted by public enterprises, and the public supervision of private investment. But there was no clear position on the question of incomes. This 'compact' provided a resting place in the continuing debate between parliamentarians and trade union leaders — but crucial issues were left unresolved. It might serve as a formula to salve the wounds of the sixties — but would it survive the stresses of office? Would it be viable if Labour took office in an economic crisis?

The wider re-examination of policy through the Executive's Home Policy Committee and an extensive network of Sub-Committees was on an elaborate scale. But there was no attempt to discuss the basic assumptions behind the party's approach. No one within the party questioned Labour's commitment to parliamentarianism or its reliance on existing administrative agencies. Few questioned the political commitment of Labour's leaders. There was no debate about the dominant perspective, but an attempt to promote more radical proposals within that perspective. This was particularly true in the field of public ownership. Successive Conferences saw debates in which resolutions favouring more public ownership were carried, sometimes against Executive advice. Between 1971 and 1973, Conference supported the public ownership of banking, insurance and building societies, the building industry, finance houses, road haulage, shipbuilding and ship repairing.[5] Such pressures had their inevitable impact on an Executive that contained more sympathetic members than for several years. The 1972 Policy Document, 'Labour's Programme For Britain', proposed to renationalise, without compensation, undertakings denationalised since 1970; it advocated the extension of public ownership to cover North Sea Oil, ports, pharmaceuticals, financial institutions, banking, shipbuilding and ship repairing, aircraft and building land. There was some uncertainty about the means of implementation. Certainly, they were not restricted to industry-wide take-overs. Emphasis was placed on the establishment of a State Holding Company. This feature of the policy was developed further over the next twelve months. For the 1973 Conference, the revised document proposed a National Enterprise Board to purchase controlling interests in profitable firms. Controversy centred around the declaration that this would involve 25 large companies, a suggestion opposed by most parliamentary leaders.

While this indicated the continuing timidity of many of the party's leaders, it diverted attention from the most crucial point. This was the ambiguity of the whole exercise.[6] The rhetoric of socialism enjoyed a restoration after 1970, even in the speeches of many who had been the most conservative of Ministers. But it was not just that there was no debate over Labour's theoretical assumptions. It was doubtful also that the primary justification of any extension of public ownership was to be progress towards a socialist society. The most plausible interpretation of the proposals was that they would strengthen the existing partnership between the state and private industry. Existing economic structures were to be made more efficient and where possible, more humane. Beneath the radical rhetoric, it promised 1945, or more pertinently, 1964 all over again. The commitment to efficiency contrasted with the promise 'to bring about a fundamental and irreversible shift in the balance of power and wealth in favour of working people and their families'. Once again, the old Labour dualism was evident. It promised agonies if Labour regained office.

The attempts to restore relations with the unions and to develop a coherent programme were the crucial features of this opposition period, but for the first two years they were overshadowed sometimes by the protracted redefinition of Labour's attitude to the Common Market.[7] Labour's growing hostility to the EEC continued in opposition as the Government applied successfully for membership. The crucial shift occurred in the extra-parliamentary party: and by mid-1971 few trade unions remained in favour of entry. The ultra-loyalist Municipal Workers were a notable exception. By October 1971, the party was strongly against entry on the existing terms: many pro-Market MPs were reluctant to accept this and 69 of them supported the principle of entry in a crucial Commons division in October 1971.[8] This had a significance far beyond the immediate issue, as most of the rebels were associated with the revisionist wing of the party, epitomised by their principal spokesman, Roy Jenkins. Their general influence was weakened by this opposition to a clear conference decision and their support for a Conservative Government in a crucial vote. One reason for the shift to the left on industrial policy was possibly general revisionist weakness stemming from their pro-Market stand. Their discomfort was taken a stage further in April 1972. The Shadow Cabinet supported a proposal for a referendum on the issue, and Jenkins and two supporters resigned from the Shadow Cabinet. The party's position appeared to have hardened still further when the 1973 Conference voted to boycott the European Parliament. Yet the official position remained one of seeking a renegotiation of the existing terms. All attempts to secure a clear commitment of principle against the Market failed.[9] As with industrial policy, there had been a shift away from the policies followed when in office, but the change was not as dramatic as appearances might suggest.

The principal consequence of the European debate was undoubtedly the waxing and waning of the influence of various factions inside the party. While the revisionists lost ground and the committed left made some advance, the principal advantage went to the reconcilers, typified by Wilson. They bowed to the dominant mood, but did not sacrifice all freedom of manoeuvre. Their flexibility helped to maintain a degree of unity at a time when a post-mortem on the years in office was always likely to tear the party to pieces. Time spent debating Europe deflected attention away from potentially more dangerous issues. Less time could be spent discussing the party's new programme, while a controversy in which Labour spokesmen appeared as the protectors of the national interest diminished the impact of those class-based issues seen by so many Labour leaders as potentially embarrassing.

Labour's position in the constituencies showed little improvement. There was no significant revitalisation of party life and the party's by-election record was uninspiring. Only one gain was made from the Government — Bromsgrove in April 1971 — and anxiety was generated by Labour decline in some seats. Rochdale fell to a strong local Liberal, and Liberals made significant advances in such strongholds as Chester-le-Street (Labour since 1906) and Manchester Exchange. In Scotland, a steady Nationalist advanced culminated in the loss of Glasgow Govan in November 1973. The Liberal advance could be attributed in some cases to resentment at the insensitive bureaucracy of some entrenched Labour councils: the Nationalist campaign similarly could capitalise on Scottish Labour's organisational weakness and general conservatism. Crucially, for a supposed party of the left, Labour support seemed to be contracting at a time of acute government unpopularity. The mantle of 'the real alternative' seemed to be falling to the Liberals and the Nationalists.

Considerations of a rather different kind were raised by the Lincoln by-election of March 1973.[10] The revisionist Taverne reacted to his local party's refusal to re-adopt him by resigning his seat to fight as an independent 'Democratic Labour' candidate. He enjoyed strong backing from the Press and defeated the official candidate heavily. Inevitably this raised the question of Labour's supposed drift to the left. Taverne had emphasised this question and his success could only re-awaken doubts about the electoral popularity of the party's programme.

Initially such pessimism seemed justified by the circumstances of the first 1974 election.[11] The second miners' strike in two years, the three-day week, the Conservative theme of 'Who Governs' — all seemed to foreshadow a defeat for Labour. The manifesto showed some dilution of the radical proposals developed since 1970 — but the tone and the contents were more radical than anything produced by the party since 1945. Public ownership was to be extended into 'mineral rights ... shipbuilding, ship repairing and marine engineering, ports, the manufacture of air frames and aero engines' while the idea of a public holding was to be applied to section of 'pharmaceuticals, road haulage, construction, machine tools ... North Sea and Celtic Sea oil and gas'.[12] There was vagueness on banking, insurance and building societies. The public ownership proposals were advocated on grounds of economic efficiency: there was only a subordinate place for arguments about a radical transfer of power. In other directions, the party promised an expansion of welfare provisions, a Wealth Tax and a renegotiation of Common Market terms with the presentation of the results to the electorate.

The campaign was dominated by a paradox. An election held in a national coal strike had been expected to generate widespread bitterness. But this did not happen. On the national level the contest was as genteel as most of its predecessors. For most Labour leaders, class-based rhetoric took a marked second place to suggestions that the nation's problems could be solved best by conciliation. Many leaders devoted little time to the more radical proposals.

The result was almost as surprising as 1970. Labour with 301 seats was well short of an overall majority, but had five more seats than the Conservatives. But the party's total vote was over 300,000 less than its major rival, and at 37.2 per cent of the total was unprecedentedly low for a post-war election. This was almost 6 per cent, and over half a million less than in 1970. Overall it was a parliamentary situation reminiscent of the 1920s. Simple explanations are likely to be grossly misleading. It appears that Labour did best in urban England, but in rural areas, and more generally in Wales and Scotland, it lost ground, in part because of tactical voting. Thus, the party captured several marginal urban seats: it appears that despite the consensual approach of Labour's leaders, its traditional urban vote responded strongly to the underlying class issue. The shift was inflated in the West Midlands by Enoch Powell's maverick behaviour. Labour's dual personality was reflected in the results. Its minority victory was produced by the loyalty of hard-core Labour support: despite the style of the campaign the context had kept marginal voters away.

The new Government blended the claims of left and right. Michael Foot entered office for the first time at the Department of Employment: Benn — for many commentators, the modern equivalent of Bevan — went to the Department of Industry, charged with the enactment of Labour's public ownership proposals. These appointments were balanced by the placing of Healey at the Exchequer, and other prominent revisionists in important ministries. The Government began by removing the more doctrinal legacies of the previous Government, but the deteriorating economic situation dominated by accelerating inflation soon became the major issue. The Government's minority position was clearly untenable, and in September Wilson announced a second election.[13]

A centrepiece in the Government's appeal was provided by the elaborated 'social contract' with the unions, an attempt to confront the problem of inflation while remaining opposed to any form of statutory incomes policy. The issue was debated at the 1974 TUC. After some controversy, it was agreed that in view of the general direction of the Government's economic and social policies, wage claims should be centred around the maintenance of real income levels. The debate revealed varied interpretations of the agreement. Dignified by its committed defenders as an attempt to develop a solution based on consent, it could be presented as a sweetened form of restraint facilitated by the special relationship between a Labour Government and the unions.[14]

The election was a low-key affair in which Labour leaders resurrected much of the Safety First rhetoric that had marked the 1966 and 1970 appeals: '"Business as Usual" — with all that that implies in terms of caution and conformity.'[15] These bromides did not produce a decisive parliamentary majority. Labour gained 17 seats from the Conservatives and withstood a concerted Nationalist challenge in Scotland. The Liberals receded from their peak of February but although Labour now led the Conservatives by 43 seats, the growth of Nationalist groups

restricted the overall majority to three. Although Labour's share of the
votes rose to the still low level of 39.2 per cent, its total vote actually
fell by over 180,000. For Labour, the outcome was an obvious
disappointment. The wafer-thin majority indicated that any
implementation of radical proposals would be difficult, and the
economic crisis remained the major priority. Nevertheless, the optimism
of the Parliamentary left remained high. The 1974 entrants included
several whose views were firmly on the left of the party. In a few cases,
they were well to the left of anything normally found in the PLP.

When the 1974 Conference met at the end of November, there were
some criticisms of the Government, most significantly over economic
policy.[16] But the disagreements were limited and muted; as always, the
first conference under a Labour Government was notable for expressions
of loyalty and a general desire to give the Government a fair chance. It
was not the increasingly difficult economic situation that produced the
first major dispute, but the issue that had so dominated discussions
after 1970 – the Common Market. After protracted negotiations, the
Government decided to support the new terms. They were rejected
however by a Special Conference by a majority of the PLP and by a
Cabinet minority.[17] The referendum debate became one between a
minority of the Labour leadership backed by the majority of activists
and trade union leaders, and a majority of Labour leaders supported by
minorities within the party but also enjoying the support of most
Conservatives, Liberals and the overwhelming bulk of industry and the
Press. Many within the party took little part in the debate, yet it was a
dispute not just about Europe, but about the future orientation of the
party. The commitment of Jenkins to the pro-European position and the
equally firm opposition of Benn and Foot symbolised this. It was the
occasion for the open reassertion of revisionist power. The sizeable
majorities in favour of membership constituted a major setback for the
left. They had been vanquished by a weapon that they themselves had
forged. Revisionists could argue now that the left's views were
unrepresentative of most Labour voters, and had secured a
disproportionate influence inside the party. The left's response could
only be that they had been damaged by the grotesque imbalance in the
financial support accruing to the two sides. Revisionists rapidly made
their presence felt. Benn was transferred from the Department of
Industry, along with all the junior Ministers.

The recriminations were soon submerged by the growing economic
crisis. By the beginning of July inflationary pressures had produced a
run on sterling, and the Government responded with a promise of early

measures. These emerged after consultations with the General Council, and centred around the idea of a £6 restriction on pay increases, with a vague threat of sanctions if the limit was breached. The policy was presented as an agreed response to crisis that would ensure the protection of essential trade union interests. Left-wing criticism was limited. The Tribune Group was divided; some were ready to accept the measures as an immediate response to crisis, but others argued that the proposals were based on a false diagnosis, and that they involved choices that should be unacceptable to a Labour Government. Thirty-six Labour MPs opposed the policy in the lobby.[18] Most large unions came out in support. The acquiescence of traditionally loyal unions such as the GMW was predictable: more crucially, Jack Jones had been closely involved in the development of the policy and the Transport Workers backed their General Secretary. The NUM followed suit after bitter internal disputes and a coal-field ballot. Opposition came most notably from the Engineers, from NUPE and some radical white-collar unions. This division of forces guaranteed a majority for the policy at the TUC. This duly appeared – the '£6 policy' was supported by 6,945,000 to 3,570,000,[19] a more decisive verdict than the original General Council vote of 19 to 13.

Support was still more complete at the Party Conference. Certainly delegates appeared concerned about many aspects of government policy. Many of the floor speeches were critical, and Healey was displaced from the NEC in favour of Eric Heffer. But although the Chancellor suffered this personal rebuff, his policies met with overwhelming endorsement.[20] The trade union commitment remained firm, while Foot's continual participation in the Government gave the proposals a *cachet* of respectability for many potential critics. Indeed, the Government appeared secure as long as it retained the support of Foot and Jones.

Their acquiescence inevitably divided the left, a cleavage demonstrated dramatically at the Conference Tribune Rally. Jones' furious intervention in a critical speech by Mikardo, and Foot's heated defence of the Government were elemental events with as much potential significance as Bevan's confrontation with the unilateralists eighteen years earlier. Beneath the personal acerbities, the confrontation symbolised a central Labour dilemma. Almost inevitably the trade union leader is forced at times of crisis to consider the welfare of his members. The threats of inflation and unemployment relegate considerations of ideological purity to the margin. Any question 'in principle' concerning the desirability of the mixed economy crumbles into irrelevance beside problems of immediate gains and losses.

In contrast, there is the reaction of the self-conscious ideologues. No matter how well-intentioned are the motives behind emergency measures, they still involve an acquiescence in the unpalatable but inevitable demands of the existing mixed economy. Declining living standards and public expenditure cuts have the same impact when they are enforced by Labour politicians with the consent of trade union leaders. Once again, the enthusiasms of opposition notwithstanding, the agony of a party seeking successes within the existing order, but with at least some of its spokesmen committed to replacing it, is exposed harshly.

A Labour Government has entered office once again with a declared determination to avoid a collapse into orthodoxy, but once again the hopes have died, leaving the Government to preside over rising unemployment and cuts in living standards. Such a predicament invites comparisons with the second MacDonald Government. Then, Labour Ministers were equipped only with Utopian aspirations and a willingness to endure. There had never been a coherent programme. Now the one coherent programme has long since been implemented, and the ideals and aspirations are tarnished by decades of employment as manipulative symbols. Nevertheless they still have some power. In October 1975 Michael Foot employed his oratorical gifts on a troubled Conference. The Government's collapse into orthodoxy was sanctified by the use of all the traditional values. It was a notable triumph, paralleling another one 45 years earlier. Then, Ramsay MacDonald had cast his last spell over a Labour Conference. His Government's paralysis had dissolved into dreams of future splendour and justifications of present impotence. Now the wheel seems to have come full circle.

This loss of vision was underlined by the result of the unexpected leadership contest of March 1976. Wilson's sudden retirement precipitated Labour's first-ever change of leader while in office. This was a final gesture in his continuing attempt to install Labour as the natural party of government. The number of candidates was double that in any previous contest, but the machinery worked smoothly. There was very little tension between the rival groups, and eventually Callaghan secured his anticipated victory:

	1st Ballot	2nd Ballot	3rd Ballot
Callaghan	84	141	176
Foot	90	133	137
Healey	30	38 (eliminated)	
Jenkins	56 (withdrew)		
Benn	37 (withdrew)		
Crosland	17 (eliminated)		

The most significant feature of the successive ballot was the limited support obtained by candidates whose reconciling gifts were questionable. Those most strongly identified with a distinctive ideological position, and those whose ability to maintain a satisfactory relationship with the trade union leaders was uncertain, found it difficult to gain support. The failure was most marked in the mediocre performance of Jenkins. The heir to Gaitskell's mantle found it impossible to expand his base beyond the committed revisionists. Some of his supporters had cherished the dream that they would come to dominate the party after years of Wilsonian ambiguity. Now this was revealed as an illusion; Labour in its choice of leader was clearly reacting against the memory of Gaitskell, as it has always reacted against that of MacDonald.

The final ballot brought together two reconcilers, although Foot retained many of his radical associations. He almost monopolised the committed left-wing vote, but his support stretched far beyond that. Indeed there were a few revisionists who were prepared to support him on account of his libertarian principles. One of the contest's most interesting aspects was the strong performance of someone, who no matter how orthodox his performance in office, had relatively impeccable left-wing credentials.

Yet the majority of the PLP chose Callaghan, a reconciler without the disturbing rhetoric. In some ways, he followed the Wilson recipe for a Labour leader. Both have been past masters at maintaining contact with most sections of the party. There are, however, crucial differences. Unlike his three immediate predecessors, Callaghan has not had a university education. He is one of the last of those Labour politicians whose contact with the party's 'natural constituency' has not been weakened by the acquisition of those cultural traits that result almost inevitably from exposure to higher education. He turned this asset to good use in his rise through the party. The classic case of his 'commonsense' opposition to academic fantasies was of course, *In Place of Strife*. But this strength was much more than a matter of style. He had entered Labour politics through the trade union movement, and had always cultivated the support of trade union leaders. Since 1967, he had always been successful in contests for the Party Treasurership, withstanding repeated challenges from the left. He also remained close to the party machine. For many of the faithful, perhaps even more than Wilson, he was 'one of ours' who could stand up to 'them' on equal terms. In this closeness to the party's roots, he perhaps resembled Henderson more than any previous leader. And like Henderson, his avuncular exterior did not always hide a readiness to replace cajolery by harsher methods. In 1955 he had been ready to support Bevan's expulsion. Unlike Henderson he was clearly ambitious. He had grafted his way upwards serving the longest apprenticeship of any Labour leader — over twenty-four years in the Cabinet or on the Parliamentary Committee.

His performance in three major offices — Chancellor, Home Secretary and Foreign Secretary — demonstrate how far his attachment to the party is that of the initially disadvantaged, rather than that of the intellectually convinced. His triumphs — holding the line in Northern Ireland, selling the 'renegotiated' terms of entry to the EEC — have been triumphs of communication and tactics. His failures have stemmed in part from his orthodoxy. This, as epitomised in his Chancellorship, is not unusual in Labour politicians, but another dimension is perhaps more singular. The party has always contained its share of working-class conservatives and enthusiastic patriots, but hitherto such values have only had a limited expression at the party's highest level. Earlier leaders have generally expressed some commitment to social democratic or liberal values. Callaghan has rarely offended conservative instincts, either inside or outside the party. His targets have tended to be the 'good liberals', demonstrated most forcibly in his restrictions on the entry of Kenyan holders of British passports. In many respects he is an accurate barometer of the responses of the bulk of Labour's support. But for the first time the party has acquired a leader who makes no pretence even to a critical view of established practices and values. The great reconcilers of the past offered at least a distant prospect of change; Callaghan offers 'Safety First' naked and unashamed. This is an eloquent testimony to the exhaustion of British social democracy.

What then, can be said about Labour's failure? Most immediately, its survival as a government is affected by the relatively complex parliamentary situation. Such factors must affect the calculations of Labour politicians. More basically, are we on the threshold of major changes in the politics of the left? A basic distinction should be made between organisation and doctrine. Many discussions tend to ask questions about the possibility of an organisational rift; most typically, will the intense differences between left and right within the party help to produce a major realignment in the centre of British politics? Clearly there are powerful factors militating against such a change, at least in the short and medium terms: the brute fact of the existing party, the long-established belief that there is no salvation elsewhere. The fear that any split would be disastrous to the forces of progress, the self-interest of many politicians and party bureaucrats. The forces making for inertia are considerable.

Whatever view is taken about Labour's organisational stability, it is difficult to deny its doctrinal sterility. The reforms of the Attlee Government helped to produce a reformed and humanised capitalism

that appeared reasonably successful for fifteen years. This apparent
success created obvious problems for Labour, but the economic
deterioration of the sixties and the seventies has produced many more.
We have seen how Labour's commitment to social transformation
became translated into a commitment to rationalise and modernise an
ailing industrial structure. Its pursuit had produced tensions not just
with the Labour left, but also with the trade unions. There has been
little hope of a coherent programme: the radical dreams of 1973
have wilted before the rigours of office. References to socialism are for
internal consumption only. They provide no indication of what a
Labour Government will actually do.

The fusion between specific reforms within the existing economic
order and its replacement was always uneasy. Obviously, the first
component has been the dominant one; but now even the appearance
of a synthesis is no longer feasible. Indeed, some of the party's earlier
achievements within the mixed economy seem threatened. The choice
appears restricted to reform or retrenchment — both within the system.
With increasing economic difficulties, Labour Ministers have breached
the post-war economic and social settlement. They appear now as the
agents of widespread unemployment and truncated public expenditure.
Rhetorical references to socialism cohabit with a commitment to an
economic system that seems unable to satisfy even Labour's moderate
aspirations.

A claim that the post-war bloom of Keynesian capitalism has faded
does not imply, of course, any belief in an early apocalypse, but simply
an expectation that Labour will have to make difficult fundamental
choices in a harsh economic climate. As economic difficulties have
increased, various possible responses have emerged. One is a more
thorough commitment to revisionism,[21] the expectation that the
rigours and realities of economic crises will extinguish Labour's Utopian
expectations. Instead, the party will be committed — in principle as well
as practice — to the views expounded by Labour moderates over the last
twenty years. There will be no suggestion that the party is the
instrument of a radical transformation, but rather an explicit acceptance
of the realities of the situation, with attempts to secure specific and
feasible reforms. Although the extinction of the party's residual radical
idealism amounts to little more than an acceptance of existing practice,
there remains the question of its future viability. In the past, revisionist
Ministers have shown a willingness to abandon reforms in favour of
economic salvation. Faced with a critical economic situation, this
approach could involve not just the jettisoning of idealistic aspirations,

but the abandonment of any hope for reform.

This revisionist outcome implies the final deliberate extinction of the decaying social democratic perspective, basing this on a claim that the party should not even appear to function as an instrument of fundamental change. Acceptance of the same diagnosis by many committed to radical values has produced a significant disengagement from the party. This has taken several forms. For some, it has involved a commitment to one of the sects whose growth in recent years has been notable, although in absolute terms they remain small. Alternatively, many have shifted into a radical scepticism, a belief that Labour's socialist potential is nil but that the sects offer only a sterile political theatre.[22] Others have abandoned traditional political activities for participation in particular causes that offer challenges to accepted power distributions, procedures and modes of thought. Clearly the disengagement has a highly corrosive effect on the party. Once, Labour could serve as an umbrella for all those who have abandoned it: but the diverse forms of disengagement underline the fragmentation of the disillusioned. Beyond their flight, there looms the party, still dominating the left.

This dominance provides one justification for the continuation of an unhappy disillusioned left within the Labour alliance. Its spokesmen claim that economic crisis provides a golden opportunity for radical reforms.[23] Yet the weaknesses of Labour's left are apparent from its past record. This is not just because of its traditionally minority position, but also because of its inability to conceive of a coherent alternative strategy. It has been wedded to parliamentarianism, albeit with radical embellishments. Thus in its battles it has suffered from a self-inflated handicap, accepting its opponent's criteria for success. There has been little readiness to suggest that parliamentary action is only one dimension, and that a challenge to existing power structures should be generated on a variety of fronts. Equally there has been little realisation that any such challenge requires a mobilised and educated base, rather than the manipulated rank and file characteristic of Labour politics. Given these limitations it is hardly surprising that Labour's left has underwritten in practice if not in symbols much of the behaviour of Labour moderates. It is obviously an open question whether it could provide the basis for a more fundamental challenge, beginning within the dominant existing institutions, but not necessarily ending there.

The outbreaks of trade union militancy in the early seventies hinted at this one possibility, since industrial action would provide one more dimension to a radical challenge. But this is to provide only one illustration of a general proposition. It is evident from everything in the preceding chapters that trade union attitudes are a most crucial ingredient in the formation of party attitudes. The chastened but steely moderation of the thirties, the Cold War conservatism of the first post-war decade, the growth of trade union radicalism as the economy deteriorated – all left indelible marks on party policy and attitudes. How will the trade unions respond to the economic difficulties, and to the severe policies of a Labour Government? If anything is clear, it is that the growing sects on the party's left have secured minimal influence inside the unions. However valuable their theoretical analyses, political debates amongst trade unionists take as their terms of reference Labour, and to a lesser extent Communist, positions.

Is it likely then that the trade union movement will continue to accept 'realistic' policies, thus paving the way for a revisionist outcome? There are significant factors promoting union acquiescence. Trade union leaders are linked to Labour politicians by perceived common interests and shared memories, and seductive appeals for loyalty. The belief that this party is *our* party has emerged dented but basically intact from the confrontations of the last twelve years. Attempts to generate union support for government policy have involved some return to the tactics of the Cold War period. In some unions, for example the Miners and the Engineers, traditional appeals have been employed in attempts to redefine the debate over economic policy as one between moderates and Communists. In these two crucial unions, the attempts have met with initial success. The moderate majority on the Miner's Executive has reformed, and the growing left-wing dominance has been checked.[24] More spectacularly, postal ballots for seats on the Engineer's Executive have been accompanied by widespread media publicity and have resulted in impressive moderate victories.[25] Thus the union best equipped to offer a frontal challenge to government policy has acquiesced, and the balance on the Executive of the most important critic has shifted significantly. Such early responses are important – but for how long will they continue?

It is difficult to believe that they will survive continuing economic problems. Previous attempts have collapsed in the face of lesser pressures. Moreover, the political climate has been more favourable in the past. Apart from the scepticism produced by earlier failures, the use of Cold War symbolism to construct a moderate coalition on wage restraint is likely to be an inadequate barrier against concern over declining living standards. If such a strategy failed when Cold War tensions were at their height, how much less effective is it likely to be 25 years on? But if the logic of the Government's economic policies generates new tensions and conclusions within the Labour alliance, what does this suggest for the future?

The degree of tension would be affected by whether Labour continues in office. If it does then the problem is likely to emerge starkly; if not, then it will probably be obscured to some extent by the feasibility of united action against Conservative excesses. Nevertheless, the dilemma still remains. Despite the powerful connections of interest and emotion, a contradiction seems to be emerging between the modernising role of Labour politicians and the defensive commitments of trade unions. This is bound to disrupt the working of the Labour alliance, and to make the complete revisionist solution impossible. Yet the resulting strife holds no promise of easy advance for the Labour left. This reflects in part its blinkered restrictive traditions, but it also reflects the basically defensive nature of much trade union opposition. As yet, there is little here that can provide the foundation for an alternative approach.

Yet there exists an undeniable vacuum. The failures of the last 25 years underline the exhaustion of British social democracy. Certainly it retains a tough, resistant quality enshrined in institutions and practices. But the post-war economic and social consensus that the Labour Party helped to forge is now under attack. Having achieved these goals, the political practice of Labour has degenerated into a cynical manipulation that constitutes a systematic denial of its own expressed values. Once this offered at least the expectation of change: now this has ceased to be a credible possibility. The 'glad confident morning' of 1945 lies far behind.

This degeneration, and the lack of a widely accepted alternative on the left, can appear as a barren prospect. The way seems clear for the development of conscious reaction or more credibly of a manipulative managerialism possibly exercised through the medium of the Labour Party. It may be that the decayed social democratic perspective represents a peak of aspiration: that never again will a movement of the organised working class proclaim any commitment towards qualitative social change, and that a still dominant Labour Party will continue to utilise its threadbare symbolism as a means of integration and control. As such, currents of opposition will be essentially defensive and containable. The possibility of continuing decay must not be ruled out; but the absence of any immediately apparent and widely supported alternative does not rule out all future developments. British social democracy did not develop full-blown as a perspective; it grew slowly and unevenly out of decaying Gladstonian Liberalism. Again, why should not another equally protracted but equally crucial change occur? This is the uncertain future, but from this vantage point the development and decay of British social democracy can be charted clearly.

Notes

1. See Scargill, op. cit.
2. See D. Skinner and J. Langdon, *The Story of Clay Cross* (Spokesman Books, Nottingham, 1974). Also *LPCR 1973*, pp. 207-10 and 218-19.
3. For example, Joan Maynard in the womens' section and John Forrester (TASS) in the trade union section. Two other later left-wing recruits to the trade union section were Sam McCluskie of the Seamen (1974) and Emlyn Williams of the Miners (1975).
4. For its background and its pronouncements see *LPCR 1972*, pp. 44 and 351-3; *1973*, pp. 47-8 and 355-6; *1974*, pp. 69-70. On the general problems see also Minkin, op. cit., pp. 29-37.
5. For the debates see *LPCR 1971*, pp. 209-52; *1972*, pp. 175-93 and *1973*, pp. 160-88.
6. On the 1972 programme see Glyn and Sutcliffe, op. cit.; on the 1973 version Coates, *Crisis of British Socialism*, ch. 1.
7. For the development of the controversy see *LPCR 1970*, pp. 188-200; *1971*, pp. 312-61 (the Special Conference of 17 July) and 114-44; *1972*, pp. 195-217; *1973*, pp. 281-94; *1974*, pp. 249-59.
8. For the Labour rebels see *832 H.C. Debs*, cols. 2211-16.
9. In 1973 by 3,316,000 to 2,800,000: see *LPCR 1973*, p. 294.
10. See Taverne, op. cit.; also John Ramsden and Richard Jay, 'Lincoln: The Background to Taverne's Triumph' in Cook and Ramsden, op. cit., pp. 264-315.
11. See David Butler and Dennis Kavanagh, *The British General Election of February 1974* (Macmillan, London, 1974).
12. 'Let Us Work Together: Labour's Way Out of the Crisis', especially pp. 10-11.
13. See Butler and Kavanagh, *The British General Election of October 1974*.
14. See *TUC Report 1974*, pp. 420-40 (debates); also Supplementary Report A, pp. 284-91.
15. *New Statesman*, 27 September 1974, p. 404.
16. *LPCR 1974*, pp. 278-85. A critical resolution was defeated on a show of hands. There was also controversy over the release of the Shrewsbury pickets, pp. 296-301; Clay Cross, pp. 306-10, and the Government's attitude towards the Chilean Government, pp. 310-14. The only card vote involved the defeat of a critical resolution on Clay Cross by 4,378,000 to 1,173,000.
17. For the PLP's attitude see *Guardian*, 10 April 1975 and the Commons vote of 9 April in *H.C. Debs, 5th series*. The vote at the Special Conference was 3,724,000 to 1,986,000. For a claim that all but 97,000 of the minority came from ten large unions see *Guardian*, 28 April 1975.
18. For the debate see *896 H.C. Debs*, cols. 46-174 and 301-440.
19. *TUC Report, 1975*.
20. *LPCR 1975*.
21. For example Peter Jenkin, 'The Future of the Labour Party' in *Political Quarterly*, October 1975, pp. 373-84.
22. As portrayed in Trevor Griffiths, *The Party* (Faber, London, 1974). See also

Coates, *Crisis of British Socialism*, especially ch. 8.

23. For a recent statement of policy firmly within the broad social democratic framework see Stewart Holland, *The Social Challenge* (Quartet Books, London, 1975). Also Ken Coates, 'Socialists and the Labour Party' in R. Miliband and J. Saville (eds.), *The Socialist Register 1973* (Merlin Press, London, 1974), pp. 155-78.

24. In a coal-field ballot the £6 policy was rejected only in the left-wing heartlands of Scotland and South Wales.

25. By 24,838 to 12,115 in Scotland and by 45,569 to 20,685 in the Manchester and Birmingham Division (the latter removed a sitting member), *Guardian*, 19 November 1975. However a Communist Assistant General Secretary retained his position by 142,759 votes to 142,698. *Morning Star*, 26 November 1975.

SELECT BIBLIOGRAPHY

This study has been dependent upon Labour Party sources: pamphlets, Conference Reports, and above all the Minutes of the National Executive Committee. In addition, periodicals such as *Tribune, New Statesman,* and *Socialist Commentary* have been valuable. The following are some of the more important secondary sources consulted.

M. Abrams and R. Rose, *Must Labour Lose?* (Penguin, Harmondsworth, 1960)

P. Addison, *The Road To 1945* (Cape, London, 1975)

V.L. Allen, *Trade Union Leadership: Based on a Study of Arthur Deakin* (Longmans, London, 1957)
  Trade Unions and the Government (Longmans, London, 1960)
  'The Reorganisation of the TUC 1918-27', *British Journal of Sociology,* XI, 1960

P. Anderson, 'Critique of Wilsonism', *New Left Review,* 27, Sept.-Oct. 1964
  'The Left in the 1950s', *New Left Review,* 29, Jan.—Feb. 1965
  'Problems of Socialist Strategy' in P. Anderson (ed.), *Towards Socialism* (Fontana, London, 1965)

R. Page Arnot, *The Miners: Years of Struggle* (Allen & Unwin, London, 1965)
  The Miners in Crisis and in War (Allen & Unwin, London, 1960)

C.A.R. Attlee, *The Labour Party in Perspective* (Gollancz, London, 1937)
  As It Happened (Heinemann, London, 1954)
  A Prime Minister Remembers (Heinemann, London, 1961)

P.S. Bagwell, *The Railwaymen* (Allen & Unwin, London, 1963)
  'The Triple Industrial Alliance 1913-22' in A. Briggs and J. Saville (eds.), *Essays in Labour History,* 2 (Macmillan, London, 1971)

R.Barker, *Education and Politics 1900-51: A Study of the Labour Party* (Clarendon Press, Oxford, 1972)

R. Bassett, *Nineteen Thirty-One: Political Crisis* (Macmillan, London, 1958)

R. Baxter, 'The Working Class and Labour Politics', *Political Studies,* March 1972

F. Bealey (ed.), *The Social and Political Thought of the British Labour*

Party (Weidenfeld, London, 1970)

F. Bealey and H. Pelling, *Labour and Politics 1900-06* (Macmillan, London, 1958)

W. Beckerman (ed.), *The Labour Government's Economic Record 1964-70* (Duckworth, London, 1972)

S. Beer, *Modern British Politics,* 2nd edn. (Faber, London, 1969)

J. Bellamy and J. Saville (eds.), *Dictionary of Labour Biography,* Vols. I and II (Macmillan, London, 1972 and 1974)

A. Bevan, *In Place of Fear,* 2nd edn. (MacGibbon, London, 1961)

R. Blackburn and A. Cockburn (eds.), *The Incompatibles: Trade Union Militancy and the Consensus* (Penguin, Harmondsworth, 1967)

B. Blake, 'The Family Background of Harold Wilson' in R. Rose (ed.), *Studies in British Politics* (Macmillan, London, 1966)

G. Blaxland, *J.H. Thomas: A Life for Unity* (Muller, London, 1964)

W. Blewett, 'The Franchise in the United Kingdom', *Past and Present* (32), 1965
The Peers, The Parties and The People: The General Elections of 1910 (Macmillan, London, 1972)

M. Bonham, *The Middle Class Vote* (Faber, London, 1954)

R. Brady, *Crisis in Britain* (University Press, Cambridge, 1950)

H. Brandon, *In the Red* (Deutsch, London, 1966)

A.F. Brockway, *Inside the Left* (Allen & Unwin, London, 1941)
Socialism Over Sixty Years: The Life of Jowett of Bradford (Allen & Unwin, London, 1946)

G. Brown, *In My Way* (Gollancz, London, 1971)

A. Bullock, *The Life and Times of Ernest Bevin Vol. 1: Trade Union Leader 1881-1940* (Heinemann, London, 1960)
Vol. 2: Minister of Labour 1940-45 (Heinemann, London, 1967)

J.F. Byrnes, *Speaking Frankly* (Heinemann, London, 1947)

A. Calder, *The People's War* (Cape, London, 1969)

Lord Citrine, *Men and Work* (Hutchinson, London, 1964)

P.F. Clarke, *Lancashire and the New Liberalism* (University Press, Cambridge, 1971)

H.A. Clegg, A. Fox and A.F. Thompson, *A History of British Trade Unions Since 1889: Vol. I 1889-1910* (Clarendon Press, Oxford, 1964)

D. Coates, *The Labour Party and the Struggle for Socialism* (University Press, Cambridge, 1975)

K. Coates, *The Crisis of British Socialism* (Spokesman Books, Nottingham, 1971)
'Socialists and the Labour Party' in R. Miliband and J. Saville (eds.):

The Socialist Register (Merlin Press, London, 1974)

M. Cole (ed.), *Beatrice Webb's Diaries 1912-24* and *1924-32* (Longman, London, 1952 and 1956)

H. Collins, 'The Marxism of the Social Democratic Federation' in Briggs and Saville, *Essays in Labour History*, 2

C. Cook, *The Age of Alignment: Electoral Politics in Britain 1922-29* (Macmillan, London, 1975)

C. Cook and J. Ramsden (eds.), *By-elections in British Politics* (Macmillan, London, 1973)

Colin Cooke, *The Life of Sir Richard Stafford Cripps* (Hodder & Stoughton, London, 1957)

S. Crimps, *Can Socialism Come by Constitutional Means?* (Socialist League, London, n.d.)

A. Crosland, *The Future of Socialism*, 2nd edn. (Cape, London, 1964)
The Conservative Enemy (Cape, London, 1962)

R.H.S. Crossman, *Planning for Freedom* (Hamish Hamilton, London, 1964)
(ed.), *New Fabian Essays* (Turnstile Press, London, 1952)

H. Dalton, *Memoirs Vol. I – Call Back Yesterday* (Muller, London, 1953)
Vol. II – The Fateful Years (Muller, London, 1957)
Vol. III – High Tide and After (Muller, London, 1962)
Practical Socialism for Britain (Routledge, London, 1935)

N. Deakin (ed.), *Colour and the British Election of 1964* (Pall Mall Press, London, 1965)

B. Donoughue and G. Jones, *Herbert Morrison: Portrait of a Politician* (Weidenfeld, London, 1973)

R. Douglas, 'The National Democratic Party and the British Workers' League', *Historical Journal*, Sept. 1972

R. Dowse, *Left in the Centre* (Longmans, London, 1966)

P. Duff, *Left, Left, Left* (Allison & Busby, London, 1971)

E. Durbin, *The Politics of Democratic Socialism* (Routledge, London, 1957)

G. Elton, *The Life of James Ramsay MacDonald* (Collins, London, 1939)

Michael Foot, *Aneurin Bevan Vol. I 1897-1945* (MacGibbon, London, 1962)
Vol. II 1945-1960 (Davis Poynter, London, 1973)
Harold Wilson: A Pictorial Biography (Pergamon, Oxford, 1964)

Paul Foot, *The Politics of Harold Wilson* (Penguin, Harmondsworth, 1968)

Paul Foot, *The Politics of Harold Wilson* (Penguin, Harmondsworth,

1968)

'The State of the Labour Party', *Sunday Times,* 29 September 1968

H.J. Gyrth and H. Collins, *The Foundry Workers* (AUFW, Manchester, 1959)

Hurtwood As Told Through His Writings and Correspondence (Longmans, London, 1965)

A. Glynn and R. Sutcliffe, 'Labour and the Economy', *New Left Review,* 76, Nov.–Dec. 1972

J. Goldthorpe *et al., The Affluent Worker: Political Attitudes and Behaviour* (University Press, Cambridge, 1968)

V. Gollancz (ed.), *The Betrayal of the Left* (Gollancz, London, 1941)

J. Graubard, *British Labour and the Russian Revolution 1917-24* (Harvard University Press, Cambridge, Mass., 1956)

R. Gregory, *The Miners and British Politics 1906-14* (Oxford University Press, London, 1968)

J. Griffiths, *Pages From Memory* (Dent, London, 1969)

T. Griffiths, *The Party* (Faber, London, 1974)

M.A. Hamilton, *J. Ramsay MacDonald* (Cape, London, 1929)

Arthur Henderson (Heinemann, London, 1938)

W. Hannington, *Unemployed Struggles 1919-36* (Reprint of 1936 edition, EP Publishing, Wakefield, 1973)

M. Harrison, *Trade Unions and the Labour Party Since 1945* (Allen & Unwin, London, 1960)

R. Harrison, 'The War Emergency Workers National Committee' in Briggs and Saville (eds.), *Essays in Labour History,* 2

T. Harrison, 'Who'll Win?' in *Political Quarterly,* January 1944

S. Haselar, *The Gaitskellites* (Macmillan, London, 1969)

E. Heffer, *The Class Struggle in Parliament* (Gollancz, London, 1973)

K. Hindall and P. Williams, 'Scarborough and Blackpool: An Analysis of Some Votes at the Labour Party Conferences of 1960 and 1961', *Political Quarterly,* July 1962

B. Hindess, *The Decline of Working Class Politics* (MacGibbon, London, 1971)

J. Hinton, *The First Shop Stewards Movement* (Allen & Unwin, London, 1973)

'The Clyde Worker's Committee and the Dilution Struggle' in Briggs and Saville (eds.), *Essays in Labour History,* 2

S. Holland, *The Socialist Challenge* (Quartet Books, London, 1975)

A. Howard, 'A Documentary Story', *New Statesman,* 30 June 1961 and R. West, *The Making of the Prime Minister* (Cape, London, 1965)

L. Hunter, *The Road to Brighton Pier* (Arthur Barker, London, 1959)

A. Hutt, *The Postwar History of the British Working Class* (Gollancz, London, 1937)

B. Jackson and D. Marsden, *Education and the Working Class* (Routledge, London, 1962)

R. Jackson, *Rebels and Whips* (Macmillan, London, 1968)

D. Jay, *The Socialist Case* (Faber, London, 1937)

P. Jenkin, 'Bevan's Fight with the BMA' in M. Sissons and P. French (eds.), *The Age of Austerity 1945-51* (Penguin, Harmondsworth, 1964)

The Battle of Downing Street (Charles Knight, London, 1970)

'The Wilson Years', *New Statesman,* 30 July 1971

'The Future of the Labour Party', *Political Quarterly,* October 1975

R. Jenkins, *Mr. Attlee: An Interim Biography* (Heinemann, London, 1948)

M. Kinnear, *The British Voter* (Batsford, London, 1968)

U. Kitzinger, *The Second Try* (Pergamon, Oxford, 1968)

H. Laski, *The Crisis and the Constitution* (Hogarth Press, London, 1932)

J. Lee, *Tomorrow is a New Day* (MacGibbon, London, 1963)

J. Lewis, *The Left Book Club: A Historical Record* (Gollancz, London, 1970)

R. Lyman, *The First Labour Government 1924* (Chapman & Hall, London, 1957)

A.W. McBriar, *Fabian Socialism and English Politics 1884-1918* (University Press, Cambridge, 1962)

J.R. MacDonald, *Syndicalism: A Critical Examination* (London, 1912)

L. Macfarlane, *The British Communist Party* (MacGibbon, London, 1966)

R. McKibbin: *The Evolution of the Labour Party 1910-24* (Oxford University Press, London, 1974)

'The Economic Policy of the Second Labour Government', *Past and Present,* August 1975

K. Martin, *Harold Laski 1893-1950: A Biographical Memoir* (Gollancz, London, 1953)

A. Marwick, *Britain in the Century of Total War* (Bodley Head, London, 1968)

R. Martin, *Communism and the British Trade Union Movement: A Study of the National Minority Movement* (Clarendon Press, Oxford, 1969)

K. Middlemass, *The Clydesiders* (Hutchinson, London, 1965)

R. Miliband, *Parliamentary Socialism* (Allen & Unwin, London, 1961)

L. Minkin, 'The British Labour Party and the Trade Unions: Crisis and

Compact', *Industrial and Labour Relations Review,* October 1974

K. Morgan, *Wales in British Politics 1868-1922,* 2nd edn. (University of Wales Press, Cardiff, 1970)

H. Morrison, *Socialisation and Transport* (Constable, London, 1933)
Autobiography (Odhams, London, 1960)

C.L. Mowat, 'Ramsay MacDonald and the Labour Party' in Briggs and Saville (eds.), *Essays in Labour History,* 2

T. Nairn, 'Hugh Gaitskell', *New Left Review,* 25, May-June 1964
'The Nature of the Labour Party' in P. Anderson (ed.), *Towards Socialism*
The Left Against Europe? (Penguin, Harmondsworth, 1973)

J. Naylor, *Labour's International Policy* (Weidenfeld, London, 1969)

The Next Five Years: An Essay in Political Agreement (Macmillan, London, 1935)

W. Norman, 'Signposts for the Sixties', *New Left Review,* 11, (September—October 1961)

Nuffield Election Studies

G. Ostergaard, 'Labour and the Development of the Public Corporation', *Manchester School,* 1954

F. Parkin, *Middle Class Radicalism* (University Press, Manchester, 1968)

H. Pelling, *The Origins of the Labour Party,* 2nd edn. (Clarendon Press, Oxford, 1965)
Popular Politics and Society in Late Victorian England (Macmillan, London, 1968)
A History of British Trade Unionism, 2nd edn. (Macmillan, London, 1972)

B. Pimlott, 'The Socialist League: Intellectuals and the Labour Left', *Journal of Contemporary History,* 1971

P. Poirier, *The Advent of the Labour Party* (Allen & Unwin, London, 1958)

R. Postgate, *The Life of George Lansbury* (Longmans, London, 1951)

J. Priestley, *English Journey* (Heinemann in association with Gollancz, London, 1934)

D.N. Pritt, *The Labour Government 1945-51* (Laurence & Wishart, London, 1963)

J.H.S. Reid, *The Origins of the British Labour Party* (University of Minnesota Press, 1955)

P. Renshaw, *The General Strike* (Eyre Methuen, London, 1975)

J. Rex, 'The Race Relations Catastrophe' in Tyrell Burgess (ed.), *Matters of Principle: Labour's Last Chance* (Penguin, Harmondsworth, 1968)

W. Richter, *Political Purpose in Trade Unions* (Allen & Unwin, London, 1973)

W. Rodgers (ed.), *Hugh Gaitskell* (Thames & Hudson, London, 1964)

A. Rogow and P. Shore, *The Labour Government and British Industry 1945-51* (Blackwell, Oxford, 1955)

R. Rose, 'The Relationship of Socialist Principles to Labour Foreign Policy' (Unpublished, Oxford D. Phil. Thesis, 1960)
Influencing Voters (Faber, London, 1967)

S. Rose, 'The Labour Party and German Rearmament: A View From Transport House', *Political Studies,* 1966

J. Saville, 'Trade Unions and Free Labour: The Background to the Taff Vale Decision' in A. Briggs and J. Saville (eds.), *Essays in Labour History* (Macmillan, London, 1960)
'Labour and Income Redistribution' in R. Miliband and J. Saville (eds.), *The Socialist Register,* 1965 (Merlin Press, London, 1965)
'The Ideology of Labourism' in R. Benewick and B. Parekh (eds.), *Knowledge and Belief in Politics* (Allen & Unwin, London, 1973)

A. Scargill, 'The New Unionism', *New Left Review,* 92 August–September 1975

P. Sedgwick, 'Varieties of Socialist Thought', *Political Quarterly,* 1969

E. Silver, *Victor Feather: TUC* (Gollancz, London, 1973)

R. Skidelsky, *Politicians and the Slump* (Macmillan, London, 1967)
'The British Labour Party: Sources of Resistance to Keynesianism' (Paper Presented to the Society for the Study of Labour History, November 1974)
Oswald Mosley (Macmillan, London, 1975)

D. Skinner and J. Langdon, *The Story of Clay Cross* (Spokesman Books, Nottingham, 1974)

Lord Snowden, *Autobiography,* 2 Volumes (Nicholson & Watson, London, 1934)

W.T. Stead, 'The Labour Party and the Books that Helped to Make It', *Review of Reviews* (33) June 1906

J.O. Stubbs, 'Lord Milner and the Patriotic Labour 1914-18', *English Historical Review,* October 1972

D. Taverne, *The Future of the Left* (Cape, London, 1974)

R.H. Tawney, 'The Choice Before the Labour Party', *Political Quarterly,* July–September 1932

H. Thomas, *John Strachey* (Eyre Methuen, London, 1973)

E.P. Thompson (ed.), *Out of Apathy* (Stevens, London, 1960)

P. Townsend and N. Bosanquet (eds.), *Labour and Inequality* (Fabian Society, London, 1972)

C. Tsuziki, *H.M. Hyndman and British Socialism* (Oxford University Press, London, 1961)

Unofficial Reform Committee South Wales Miners' Federation, *The Miners' Next Step* (1912)

S. and B. Webb, *Soviet Communism: A New Civilisation,* 2nd edn (Gollancz, London, 1937)

E. Wertheimer, *Portrait of the Labour Party* (G.P. Putnam & Sons, London, 1929)

R. Williams *et al., May Day Manifesto* (Penguin, Harmondsworth, 1968)

H. Wilson, *The New Britain* (Penguin, Harmondsworth, 1964)
Purpose in Power (Weidenfeld, London, 1966)
The Labour Government 1964-70: A Personal Record (Weidenfield, London, 1971)

Lord Windlesham, *Communication and Political Power* (Cape, London, 1966)

J. Winter, *Socialism and the Challenge of War* (Routledge, London, 1974)

N. Wood, *Communism and British Intellectuals* (Gollancz, London, 1959)

INDEX

London busmen (1937), 57;
gasmen (1950), dockers (1951),
164; London busmen (1958), 213;
seamen (1966), 253, 260-1; (1968),
262; Yorkshire Coal-field (1969),
267; postmen (1971), 287; miners
(1972), 287; miners (1974), 291
Industrial Organisation and Development Act, 161
Industrial Relations Act, 287
Industrial Reorganisation Corporation, 254
Integrationism, 112-18

Jay, Douglas, 191
Jenkins, Roy, 191, 251, 264, 279,
289; resigns as Deputy Leader,
290, 293
Johnson, Lyndon, 268
Jones, Jack, 246, 258, 293
Jowett, Fred, 12, 22

Keep Left, Keeping Left, 146-8, 169
Kendall, Dennis, 122
Kennedy, J.F., 268
Kenya, immigrants from, 270, 276
Key, Charles, 167
Keynes, John Maynard, 38
Keynesian economics, 11, 58-60,
119, 158-60, 191, 214, 236
Kitson, Alex, 247
Korea, Labour policy towards, 149,
172
Korean War, impact on wages policy,
164

Labour Governments: *1924*: 14, 17,
36; *1929*: 9, 38-40; diagnosis of
failure, 54-5; *1945-51*: relationship with PLP,138; revolts of
MPs, 139; relationships with
Conference and NEC, 140;
criticisms of these relationships,
142; and foreign policy, 144-9;
and National Health Service, 150-
2; and public ownership, 152-6;
and planning, 157-8; and private
industry, 160-2; and trade unions,
162-5; *1964-70*: and the economy,
251-6; and balance of payments,
252-3; use of deflation, 253; and
devaluation, 255; financial
pressures on, 255-6; foreign and
Commonwealth policies, 267-74;

1974: 292 *et seq.*
Labour Party, Advisory Committees,
17; Conference (1917), 11, 12;
(1907–), 13; (June 1918), 31;
(1919), 33; (1926, 1927), 36;
(1928), 37; (1931), 40; (1932),
65-6, 67, 73; (1933), 68, 70;
(1934), 69, 72, 75; (1935), 69,
76; (1936), 87; (1937), 87-8, 96,
99-100; (1939), 90, 92, 98-9, 101;
(1940), 104; (1942), 111, 114,
124; (1943), 124; (1944), 120,
125-6; (1948), 167; (1949), 167-8;
(1950), 171; after 1951 general,
182; (1952), 194; (1953), 198;
(1954), 188; (1955), 209; (1956),
210; (1957), 207, 212; (1958),
213-14, 216; (1959), 222; (1960),
224-5, 231; (1961), 227, 233;
(1962), 234-5; (1963), 235, 238,
260; (post-1964 changes),245-6;
(defeats for Government), 246;
(1965), 257; (record on incomes
policy), 258; (1966), 269; (1967),
259-60, 269, 272; (1968), 258-60,
271, 278; (1969), 258, 272, 279;
(1971), 288; (1972), 288; (1973),
288, 290; (1974), 293; (1975),
294-5; Constitution, 12, 14, 15,
31; (Conference decisions and the
PLP), 225-7; divisional Labour
Parties, formation of, 15;
Documents: *Statement on War
Aims*, 31; *Labour and The New
Social Order*, 31; *Labour and the
Nation*, 37-8, 54; *Socialism and
The Condition of the People*, 71;
For Socialism and Peace, 71-2, 96;
Labour's Immediate Programme,
95-6, 117; *The Old World and The
New Social Order*, 124; *The
Labour Party and the Future*, 124;
Labour Believes in Britain, 168;
Labour and the New Society, 171;
Facing the Facts, 194; *Challenge
to Britain*, 7; *Towards Equality*,
209-10; *Personal Freedom*, 210;
Homes of the Future, 210; *The
Future Labour Offers You*, 211;
Industry and Society, 211-12;
Learning to Live, 213; *Plan for
Progress*, 213-14; *Labour in The
Sixties*, 231; *Signposts for the
Sixties*, 232, 236; *Agenda for a*